Resilient and Sustainable Farming Systems in Europe

What exactly is resilience and how can it be enhanced? Farming systems in Europe are rapidly evolving while at the same time being under threat, as seen by the disappearance of dozens of farms every day. Farming systems must become more resilient in response to growing economic, environmental, institutional, and social challenges facing Europe's agriculture. Since the COVID-19 pandemic, the need for enhanced resilience has become even more apparent and continues to be an overarching guiding principle of EU policy-making. Resilience challenges and strategies are framed within four main processes affecting decision-making in agriculture: risk management, farm demographics, governance and agricultural practices. This empirical focus looks at very diverse contexts, with eleven case studies from Belgium, Bulgaria, France, Germany, Great Britain, Italy, Netherlands, Poland, Romania, Spain and Sweden. This study will help determine the future and sustainability of European farming systems. This title is available as Open Access on Cambridge Core.

MIRANDA P. M. MEUWISSEN is Professor of Risk Management and Resilience in Food Supply Chains in the Business Economics Group at Wageningen University & Research.

PETER H. FEINDT is Professor of Agricultural and Food Policy at the Thaer Institute for Agricultural and Horticultural Sciences, Humboldt-Universität zu Berlin.

ALBERTO GARRIDO is Professor of Agricultural and Natural Resource Economics and Vice-Rector of Quality and Efficiency at the Universidad Politécnica de Madrid.

ERIK MATHIJS is Professor of Agricultural and Resource Economics at KU Leuven.

BÁRBARA SORIANO is Assistant Professor in Agricultural Economics at the Universidad Politécnica de Madrid.

JULIE URQUHART is Associate Professor in Environmental Social Science at the Countryside & Community Research Institute, University of Gloucestershire.

ALISA SPIEGEL is a postdoc in the Business Economics Group at Wageningen University & Research.

Resilient and Sustainable Farming Systems in Europe

Exploring Diversity and Pathways

Edited by

MIRANDA P. M. MEUWISSEN
Wageningen University & Research

PETER H. FEINDT
Humboldt-Universität zu Berlin

ALBERTO GARRIDO
Universidad Politécnica de Madrid

ERIK MATHIJS
KU Leuven

BÁRBARA SORIANO
Universidad Politécnica de Madrid

JULIE URQUHART
University of Gloucestershire

ALISA SPIEGEL
Wageningen University & Research

CAMBRIDGE UNIVERSITY PRESS

CAMBRIDGE
UNIVERSITY PRESS

University Printing House, Cambridge CB2 8BS, United Kingdom

One Liberty Plaza, 20th Floor, New York, NY 10006, USA

477 Williamstown Road, Port Melbourne, VIC 3207, Australia

314–321, 3rd Floor, Plot 3, Splendor Forum, Jasola District Centre,
New Delhi – 110025, India

103 Penang Road, #05-06/07, Visioncrest Commercial, Singapore 238467

Cambridge University Press is part of the University of Cambridge.

It furthers the University's mission by disseminating knowledge in the pursuit of
education, learning, and research at the highest international levels of excellence.

www.cambridge.org
Information on this title: www.cambridge.org/9781009098281
DOI: 10.1017/9781009093569

© Miranda P. M. Meuwissen, Peter H. Feindt, Alberto Garrido, Erik Mathijs, Bárbara
Soriano, Julie Urquhart and Alisa Spiegel 2022

When citing this work, please include a reference to the DOI 10.1017/9781009093569

First published 2022

A catalogue record for this publication is available from the British Library.

ISBN 978-1-009-09828-1 Hardback

Contents

Figures

Tables

Contributors

Editors

MIRANDA P. M. MEUWISSEN is Professor of Risk Management and Resilience in Food Supply Chains at the Business Economics Group of Wageningen University & Research, the Netherlands. She coordinated the SURE-Farm project (Towards SUstainable and REsilient EU FARMing systems).

PETER H. FEINDT is Professor of Agricultural and Food Policy at the Thaer-Institute for Agricultural and Horticultural Sciences, Humboldt-Universität zu Berlin, Germany. His research addresses a broad range of questions in agricultural and food policy; in particular, its links to environmental policy, sustainability transitions, the bioeconomy and the resilience of farming systems.

ALBERTO GARRIDO is Professor of Agricultural and Natural Resource Economics and Vice-Rector of Quality and Efficiency at the Universidad Politécnica de Madrid. His research interests are risk management in agriculture, farming systems' resilience and agricultural insurance, water resources economics and policy, climate change and agriculture and agricultural policy.

ERIK MATHIJS is Professor of Agricultural and Resource Economics at KU Leuven. His research focuses on the practices, metrics and policies underpinning the transformation of the European agricultural and food system towards sustainability and resilience. He coordinated the FP7 project TRANSMANGO and the H2020 project SUFISA.

BÁRBARA SORIANO is an assistant professor at the agricultural economics, statistics and business administration group of Universidad Politécnica de Madrid. Her research focuses on agricultural risk management and resilience from a multi-stakeholder approach. She has expertise in empirical and quantitative methods in macroeconomic analysis of global food security.

JULIE URQUHART is an associate professor in environmental social science at the Countryside and Community Research Institute, University of Gloucestershire. She is an environmental social scientist with research interests in human–environment relationships, particularly relating to tree health, small-scale fisheries and farmer behaviour.

ALISA SPIEGEL is a postdoctoral researcher at the Business Economics Group of Wageningen University & Research, Netherlands. In her research, she focuses on risks and resilience in agriculture, risk management at farm and in farming systems, as well as decision-making under uncertainty.

Chapter Authors

FRANCESCO ACCATINO is a researcher at the French National Institute for Agriculture, Food, and Environment. His main current research focuses on building models and indicator systems for analyzing trade-offs and synergies between agricultural production, ecosystem services and environmental impacts. His main background is modelling of social-ecological systems.

FEDERICO ANTONIOLI is a research assistant in the Department of Economics and Management at the University of Parma, Italy. His research is focused on agricultural economics and policy, particularly on the impact of policies on agricultural incomes, price transmission analysis, and technical efficiency of EU-farms.

FRANZISKA APPEL is Research Associate at the Leibniz Institute of Agricultural Development in Transition Economies (IAMO) in Halle (Saale), Germany. She is an expert in participatory agent-based modelling and analysis of agrarian structural change and agricultural policies. At IAMO she coordinates the further development of the agent-based model AgriPoliS.

ALFONS BALMANN is Director at the Leibniz Institute of Agricultural Development in Transition Economies (IAMO) in Halle (Saale),

Germany and head of the department Structural Change. He is agricultural economist and works on agent-based modelling and analysis of structural change in agriculture and agricultural policies since thirty years.

KATARZYNA BAŃKOWSKA is an assistant professor at the Institute of Rural and Agricultural Development, Polish Academy of Sciences (IRWiR PAN). Her scientific interest involve: agri-environmental aspects of economic growth, farms' organization and economic efficiency, energy and climate policy, climate change and alternative energy sources, systems of biodiversity-friendly agricultural production.

ISABEL BARDAJÍ is Professor of Agricultural Economics and Policy at the Universidad Politécnica de Madrid and Director of CEIGRAM (Research Centre for the Management of Agricultural and Environmental Risks). She leads the Research Group of Agricultural Economics and Natural Resources Economics. She has more than thirty years of research experience focusing mostly on the analysis of Agricultural Policy and risk management.

ROBERT BERRY, University of Gloucestershire, is an experienced GIS specialist and geodata scientist with a strong record of applying geographical information systems (GIS) in a wide range of environmental and social science research areas.

DANIELE BERTOLOZZI-CAREDIO is a PhD student at Research Centre for the Management of Agricultural and Environmental Risk (CEIGRAM), Universidad Politécnica de Madrid. His research focuses on agricultural risk management and resilience of farming systems. He adopts mixed methodologies to carry on multidisciplinary investigation.

JO BIJTTEBIER is a senior researcher at the Social Sciences Unit of the Flanders Research Institute for Agriculture, Fisheries and Food (ILVO), Belgium. She builds her expertise on learning processes with stakeholders striving for sustainable agriculture, including topics as knowledge exchange, co-creation of innovation and systems thinking.

JASMINE E. BLACK is a research assistant at the Countryside & Community Research Institute, University of Gloucestershire. She blends social science with artistic practices in research on multi-level governance and bottom-up innovation for resilient socio-ecological landscape management. She has a PhD in soil carbon and is also a theatrical storyteller and illustrator.

YANNICK BUITENHUIS is a PhD candidate at the Public Administration and Policy Group of Wageningen University & Research, the Netherlands. His research focuses on expanding our understanding of how public policies, such as the EU's Common Agricultural Policy (CAP), influence the resilience and sustainability of farming systems. With his research, he aims to formulate suggestions for policy improvements that support complex system to deal with current and future resilience challenges.

JEROEN CANDEL is an associate professor at the Public Administration and Policy Group of Wageningen University & Research, the Netherlands. His research deals with the question of how governments can develop more effective and legitimate responses to deal with the pressing challenges that characterize modern-day food systems. Beside his research, he frequently advises Dutch and EU policymakers about possibilities for improved food governance.

ISABEAU COOPMANS is a PhD researcher at the Social Sciences Unit of Flanders Research Institute for Agriculture, Fisheries and Food (ILVO), Belgium; and at the Division of Bioeconomics, Department of Earth and Environmental Sciences, KU Leuven, Belgium. Her research aims to better understand resilience and continuity of farms and farming systems by using both quantitative and qualitative methods.

PAUL COURTNEY is Professor of Social Economy at the CCRI, University of Gloucestershire, UK. Paul's research coheres around Social Value, a lens through which he is currently exploring the relationship between health, well-being, inclusivity and socio-economic life in rural areas.

ROBERT FINGER is Professor of Agricultural Economics and Policy at ETH Zurich (Switzerland). He holds a PhD in Agricultural Economics from ETH Zurich.

CAMELIA GAVRILESCU is Senior Researcher and Associate Professor in Agri-Food Economics and Policies at the Institute of Agricultural Economics of the Romanian Academy. Her main areas of expertise include sustainable rural development, agricultural and rural development policies, farm economic and ecologic performance analysis, agri-food trade and competitiveness.

PIOTR GRADZIUK IS an associate professor at the Institute of Rural and Agricultural Development Polish Academy of Sciences (IRWiR PAN), Poland. He specializes and has a practical experience in analyses on efficiency of using renewable energy sources, patterns of socio-economic and institutional transformations in rural areas, as well as in efficiency and productivity of farms and farming systems.

HELENA HANSSON is a professor of Agricultural and Food Economics at Swedish University of Agricultural Sciences (SLU). Her work includes farm management, farmer decision-making and the economics of certain strategic choices, and production economic analyses related to the efficiency of farm production. She has worked extensively with inter-disciplinary approaches where behavioural models have been used to explain decision-making, or to explain economic behaviour and economic performance.

HUGO HERRERA received a MSc and a PhD System Dynamics from the University of Bergen, Norway. Hugo is passionate about system dynamics and applies it in a variety of contexts and projects from health care in the UK to food systems in Europe, to wildlife conservation in Africa.

AMR KHAFAGY is a research assistant at the Countryside and Community Research Institute at the University of Gloucestershire, UK. He is an economist with research interests in applied econometrics, agricultural productivity, finance and development, and cooperative economics.

BIRGIT KOPAINSKY is Professor in System Dynamics at The University of Bergen, Norway. In her research, Birgit explores the role that system dynamics analysis and modelling techniques play in facilitating transformation processes in social-ecological systems. Birgit works both in Europe and in several sub-Saharan African countries.

VITALIY KRUPIN is an assistant professor at the Institute of Rural and Agricultural Development, Polish Academy of Sciences (IRWiR PAN). Majoring in international economics and trade he is also involved in research concerning rural development, agricultural and environmental economics, bioenergy development and greenhouse gas emissions from agriculture.

FRANÇOIS LÉGER is Professor at AgroParisTech, Paris, France. His research and teaching activities focus on socio-ecological transition of agricultural and food systems, with particular attention to the interactions between social, economic, and ecological dimensions. His current work focuses on 'radical' forms of ecologizing systems, combining technical, organizational, commercial and social dimensions.

EEWOUD LIEVENS is a PhD candidate at the Division of Bioeconomics, Department of Earth and Environmental Sciences, KU Leuven, Belgium. His research focuses on institutional arrangements for the marketing of agricultural products, examining in particular how collective action and chain coordination are shaped by market and regulatory conditions.

GORDANA MANEVSKA-TASEVSKA is a researcher and policy analyst at the Policy Analysis Unit of the Department of Economics at the Swedish University of Agricultural Sciences (SLU). Her research field is the economic performance analysis of primary production in the agricultural sector, resilience analysis, acceptance of agro-ecological approaches, and its interplay with agricultural policy.

ANNA MARTIKAINEN is a PhD researcher at the Institute of Rural and Agricultural Development, Polish Academy of Sciences (IRWiR PAN). She acquired master degrees in spatial development and in psychology at the University of Warsaw. Her current research interests concern mostly agricultural policy, particularly its relation with sustainability of farming, and regional innovation policy.

DAMIAN MAYE is Professor of Agri-Food Studies at the Countryside and Community Research Institute, University of Gloucestershire, UK. His research focuses on the sustainability, resilience, ethics and governance of global, European and UK agri-food systems.

ANNEKE MEIER is a bachelor student of European Studies at the University of Osnabrück, Germany, and currently an intern at the Leibniz Institute of Agricultural Development in Transition Economies (IAMO) in Halle (Saale), Germany.

YANN DE MEY is Assistant Professor at the Business Economics Group of Wageningen University & Research on farm decision making under risk and uncertainty. He is an expert in econometric analysis and conducting survey-based research on risk management behaviour. He is currently focussing on the impact digitalization has on agricultural risk analysis.

DELPHINE NEUMEISTER is a project manager with a Master in Agricultural Economy and Development, specialized in network management and advisory approaches. She coordinated the Charter for Good Agricultural Practices in Cattle Production. She contributed to applied research and innovation projects on the CAP reforms, organic dairy farming and PDOs development in France.

PHILLIPA NICHOLAS-DAVIES is a principle investigator and lecturer at the Institute of Biological Environmental and Rural Sciences at Aberystwyth University, Wales, UK.

FRANZISKA OLLENDORF is a research associate at the Leibniz Institute of Agricultural Development in Transition Economies (IAMO), Halle, Germany. Her research focuses on CSR in global value chains, private food standards, the political economy of cocoa, and rural change and livelihood systems.

WIM PAAS is a PhD-candidate at the Plant Production Systems group and the Business Economics Group of Wageningen University & Research, the Netherlands. In his research, he studies the sustainability and resilience of agricultural systems through an interdisciplinary lens. He is keen on applying quantitative and qualitative research methods in complementary ways to adequately capture social, environmental and economic dimensions of system performance and dynamics.

MARIYA PENEVA is an associate professor in the Department of Natural Resource Economics, UNWE, Bulgaria in the field of Agricultural Economics, Policy and Rural Development. She is involved in projects working on the major issues of present interest, namely the interlinkages between agriculture, ecosystems, innovations and possible solutions for more resilient farming systems.

CHRISTÈLE PINEAU is a project leader in the Department of agricultural economics of the French Livestock Institute. She works at the Auvergne regional office in France. Her research focuses on understanding beef livestock systems and management of agricultural holdings. She studied best practices strategies of mountain farming and income improvement tools for livestock farmers.

CORENTIN PINSARD is a PhD researcher at the French National Institute for Agriculture, Food, and Environment. In his research, he models the resilience of agricultural systems to resource constraints through the analysis of nutrient fluxes on a regional scale. His main background is the modelling of mass and energy transport phenomena in physics.

P. MARIJN POORTVLIET is Associate Professor of Risk Communication at Wageningen University & Research, the Netherlands. He holds a PhD in Social & Organizational Psychology (University of Groningen). He is primarily interested in sustainability transitions by focusing on how individuals in social networks make decisions in the context of risk and uncertainty.

CHRISTINE PITSON is a PhD candidate at the Leibniz Institute of Agricultural Development in Transition Economies (IAMO) in Halle (Saale), Germany. She focuses on the economics of sustainable transitions. In the SURE-Farm project she employed mixed-method approaches to analyze the effects of labour availability and related policies on European agricultural regions.

PYTRIK REIDSMA is an associate professor at the Plant Production Group of Wageningen University & Research, the Netherlands. Her research focuses on sustainability and resilience of farming systems. She has expertise in integrated assessment, using quantitative and qualitative methods to assess impacts of various drivers on all dimensions of sustainable development at multiple scales (from field to global).

JENS ROMMEL is a researcher at the Department of Economics at the Swedish University of Agricultural Sciences (SLU). His primary research fields are experimental economics, behavioural economics, economic psychology, and agricultural economics. He studies consumers' and farmers' decision-making in the context of agriculture and the environment.

CAROLINA SAN MARTÍN is a postdoc researcher at the Research Centre for the Management of Agricultural and Environmental Risk (CEIGRAM), Universidad Politécnica de Madrid. Her main current research focuses on the study of farming systems resilience. Her background is related to the weed ecology and the integrated management of weeds.

SAVERIO SENNI is Associate Professor at the DAFNE Department of the University of Tuscia, Italy. His research is focused on rural development economics and policies, on multifunctional agriculture and on social farming.

SIMONE SEVERINI is Professor of Agricultural Economics and Policy at the University of Tuscia, Italy. He has more than twenty-five years of research experience addressing questions related to the analyses of farm income, risk management, farming system resilience and agricultural policy evaluation at the EU level.

THOMAS SLIJPER is a PhD candidate at the Business Economics Group and the Strategic Communication Group of Wageningen University & Research, the Netherlands. He studies how European farmers deal with several interrelated risks and under which conditions risk management decisions have the potential to contribute to farm resilience.

ALESSANDRO SORRENTINO is Full Professor of Agri-food System Economics and Coordinator of the Doctoral Program in Economics,

Management and Quantitative Methods at the University of Tuscia (Viterbo, Italy). He has published extensively in the field of agricultural markets and income policies, food value chain analysis and quality promotion.

KATRIEN TERMEER is Professor of Public Administration and Policy at Wageningen University & Research, the Netherlands. Her research addresses the governance of wicked problems in the interrelated fields of food, agriculture, climate, water and energy. She focuses on transformational change through accumulating small wins.

MONICA-MIHAELA TUDOR is Senior Researcher at the Institute of Agricultural Economics of the Romanian Academy. Her main fields of expertise are: socio-economic transformation of rural areas; rural entrepreneurship; farming systems analysis; research and support-action projects in the fields of rural development; development and monitoring of rural development strategies and regional plans; rural networking among farmers, public authorities and local actors.

MAURO VIGANI is Associate Professor in Agricultural Economics and Econometrics at the Countryside and Community Research Institute of the University of Gloucestershire, UK. He holds a PhD in Agricultural Economics from the University of Milan, Italy.

WILLEMIJN VROEGE did her PhD in the Agricultural Economics and Policy group at ETH Zurich (Switzerland) and has a strong interest in using (new) technologies to insure agricultural production, specifically in the context of climate change.

ERWIN WAUTERS is Senior Researcher at the Social Sciences Unit of the Flanders research institute for Agriculture, Fisheries and Food (ILVO), Belgium. He is an agricultural economist whose main aim is to understand how institutions, regulation, markets and social aspects determine farming systems and their performance, mainly in the livestock sectors.

KATARZYNA ZAWALIŃSKA is an associate professor at the Institute of Rural and Agricultural Development Polish Academy of Sciences (IRWiR PAN), Poland. Her research focuses on modelling the economic impact and evaluation of agricultural and rural development policies at the regional, national and EU level, using quantitative (CGE models, econometrics) and qualitative methods.

CINZIA ZINNANTI is an assistant research at the Department DAFNE of the University of Tuscia, Italy. Her research is focused on agricultural economics and risk analysis and management in agriculture.

Preface

This book showcases findings from the SURE-Farm research project which aimed to assess the resilience and sustainability of farming systems in Europe. The call for greater resilience responds to the accumulating economic, environmental, institutional, and social challenges facing Europe's agriculture. Since the COVID-19 pandemic, the need for enhanced resilience has become an overarching guiding principle of EU policymaking. But what exactly is resilience and how can it be enhanced? How can farming systems prepare for different and often simultaneous types of shocks and stresses, for unexpected and even unknown events?

The chapters in this book distinguish three resilience capacities: for some shocks and stresses *robustness* ('bouncing back') is adequate, but other circumstances require *adaptability* and *transformability* (deep learning and change). Putting these capacities at the centre, each chapter addresses key questions such as which characteristics of a system can enhance resilience, whether current governance systems enhance or constrain resilience, and which actors can actually influence and build resilience capacities.

The book is organised in three parts. The first part addresses resilience challenges and strategies for four main processes affecting decision-making in agriculture: risk management, farm demographics including the availability of labour, governance with a focus on EU and local policies, and agricultural practices. The second part portrays the empirical heart of the SURE-Farm project and presents eleven chapters referring to the eleven diverse case studies in the project. Each chapter provides a unique insight into the resilience challenges of Europe's diverse farming systems and thought-provoking ideas to respond to these. In the third part of the book, findings are synthesised into integrated assessments across case studies, principles to enhance the resilience of farming systems, lessons learned from co-creation processes, and a reflection on the SURE-Farm approach.

Promisingly, the chapters identify various pathways to enhance resilience. However, many of the suggestions require substantial change compared to current practices and policies. For instance, current resilience strategies are often geared too much towards increasing the profitability of farming systems and tend to neglect the coupling of agricultural production with local institutions, natural resources, and a facilitating infrastructure for innovation. Also, current policies are not sufficiently balanced in their support for robustness, adaptability, and transformability of Europe's farming systems.

Yet, there are reasons for optimism. First, the chapters express much spirit for change – and calls for more long-term vision and courage. Second, the systematic analysis of the multiple components contributing to resilience enables the development of a better understanding of processes of change in agri-food systems, the need to develop greater resilience in Europe's farming systems, and the priority areas to be addressed.

We wish you an inspiring read.

Acknowledgements

We are tremendously grateful to all members of the SURE-Farm consortium for their dedicated participation and collaboration throughout the duration of the SURE-Farm project. They conducted a broad range of research with multiple qualitative and quantitative methods in many different locations and contributed their analyses and interpretations. These diverse empirical engagements brought the SURE-Farm concept to life and enabled its further development.

We also sincerely thank the many participants in the interactive SURE-Farm methods, from the farmers and farming families to the wide set of stakeholders within and outside the farming systems. Bringing together multiple perspectives on historic trajectories and future scenarios is a necessary – and enjoyable and illuminating – part of understanding resilience.

We also express our gratitude to the scientific board of the SURE-Farm project. Their high-level reviews and constructive feedback contributed to the quality of project outcomes. Gratitude also goes to the co-creation group. Discussions through the online platform and during project meetings sharpened our thinking about practical implications.

Acknowledgements are also attributed to the external reviewers of the book outline and drafts of the chapters. Their fresh and critical look at our findings strengthened the coherence and conclusions of the chapters.

We also thank the European Commission for having financed the SURE-Farm project under the Horizon 2020 programme (grant 727520) and for the fruitful seminars and discussions on the resilience of European farming systems. We hope that these discussions will proceed and continue to inform the efforts of European policymakers to enhance the resilience of Europe's diverse farming systems.

We also record our thanks to the editorial team at Cambridge University Press for their expert guidance and recommendations.

1 | SURE-Farm Approach to Assess the Resilience of European Farming Systems

MIRANDA P. M. MEUWISSEN, PETER H. FEINDT, ALISA SPIEGEL, WIM PAAS, BÁRBARA SORIANO, ERIK MATHIJS, ALFONS BALMANN, JULIE URQUHART, BIRGIT KOPAINSKY, ALBERTO GARRIDO AND PYTRIK REIDSMA

Resilience is a latent property of a system.

The concept denotes a potential which is activated – and can be observed – only when a system is hit by stress or shocks.

It can thus be understood by learning from past trajectories and discussing future scenarios, and from assessing how actual shocks are dealt with.

(Meuwissen et al., 2021)

1.1 The Resilience Challenge for Europe's Farming Systems

Farming systems in Europe face accumulating economic, environmental, institutional, and social challenges. Examples include the impact of extreme weather events, reduced access to markets and value chains (e.g. due to trade wars, political boycotts or Brexit), less stable and less protective policy environments, increasing controversies about agricultural mainstream practices, and more recently the interruptions caused by the COVID-19 pandemic. These uncertainties exacerbate demographic issues such as a lack of successors to enable generational renewal at the farm level, and insufficient availability of qualified seasonal and permanent labour (Pitson et al., 2020). The compounding challenges raise concerns about the resilience of Europe's farming systems.

The ability of farming systems to cope with challenges can be conceptualized as resilience (Folke, 2016). Resilience theory emphasizes change, uncertainty, and the capacity of systems to adapt (Holling et al., 2002). Several resilience frameworks had already been developed and applied to systems at levels below or above the farming system, such as farms (e.g. Darnhofer, 2014), food supply chains (Stone and

Rahimifard, 2018) and socio-ecological systems (Walker et al., 2004). These frameworks provide useful insights into capacities and attributes that enhance or constrain resilience. However, it was still unclear how these and other attributes were to be assessed at the level of farming systems, where farmers compete and collaborate, interact with non-farm neighbours, contribute to variegated value chains and cooperate across sectors. How farming systems are expected to deliver their various functions differs across places and changes over time in response to inter alia changing consumer and societal preferences. Against this background we developed the SURE-Farm[1] approach. This approach consists of the SURE-Farm framework (Meuwissen et al., 2019) and the systematic consideration of regional contexts, the collaboration of multiple disciplines and the deployment of mixed methods. Each component of the approach is elaborated below.

1.2 The SURE-Farm Resilience Framework

In developing the SURE-Farm resilience framework (Meuwissen et al., 2019), we built on the social-ecological tradition of resilience thinking (Holling et al., 2002; Walker and Salt, 2006; Folke, 2016) and defined the resilience of a farming system as *its ability to ensure the provision of its desired functions in the face of often complex and accumulating economic, social, environmental and institutional shocks and stresses, through capacities of robustness, adaptability and transformability* (Meuwissen et al., 2019). In addition, we referred to insights from the Resilience Alliance (2010) that the resilience of a system is affected by its specific characteristics, i.e. the system's resilience attributes. This is brought together in the SURE-Farm resilience framework (Figure 1.1). The framework is designed to assess resilience to known and specific challenges such as extreme weather events (*specified resilience*) as well as a farming system's capacity to deal with the unknown, uncertain and surprise (*general resilience*). Due to the complex multifaceted nature of resilience, the framework suggests to follow five analytical steps with guiding questions: (1) characterization of the farming system – resilience of what, (2) identification of challenges – resilience to what, (3) analysis of system functions – resilience for what purpose, (4) evaluation of system responses – what resilience

---

[1] Towards SUstainable and REsilient EU-FARMing systems (SURE-Farm).

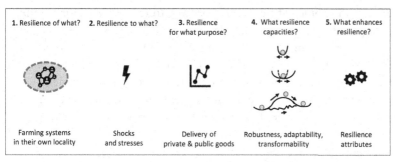

1. Resilience of what?	2. Resilience to what?	3. Resilience for what purpose?	4. What resilience capacities?	5. What enhances resilience?
Farming systems in their own locality	Shocks and stresses	Delivery of private & public goods	Robustness, adaptability, transformability	Resilience attributes

Figure 1.1 The five steps of the SURE-Farm resilience framework (Meuwissen et al., 2019).

capacities, and (5) examination of resilience attributes – what enhances resilience.

The first step of the framework (*resilience of what*) addresses the identification of farming systems in their own locality. A farming system consists of farmers producing (main) product(s) of interest, e.g. fruits and vegetables, and the regional context, e.g. the Mazovian region in Poland. Not all farms in a region are necessarily part of the same farming system, i.e. there may be several farming systems in one region which focus on different products. Besides farmers, further actors, including other members of the supply chain and local institutions, belong to the farming system. The other farming system actors are identified based on patterns of influence; farms and other farming system actors mutually influence each other. Because farming systems work in open agro-ecological systems and are linked to various social networks, value chains, economic processes and ecological systems, their activities can have multiple effects, e.g. through job and income creation, network effects, resource use, landscape impacts and emissions (see Step 3). These external effects and public goods also characterize the farming system. While the framework focuses on the farming system level, analyses include nested levels, such as the household, farm and farmer level, the farming system and higher levels which form the context of the farming system, such as national regulations; societal, economic and environmental macro-trends; or transnational flows of goods and services. This reflects the open character of farming systems.

The second step of the framework (*resilience to what*) identifies shocks and stresses that affect the farming system. We consider economic, environmental, social and institutional challenges that could impede the ability of the farming system to deliver the desired public and private goods. Stresses develop with gradual changes of the system's environment, such as the steady diffusion of pests and diseases, ageing of rural populations or changing consumer preferences. Looking back at historic trajectories, also shocks which were unknown, unexpected and unimagined at that moment can be assessed. For instance, the SURE-Farm approach was used to assess the impact of COVID-19 and to understand how and why systems were able to cope (Meuwissen et al., 2021).

The third step (*resilience for what purpose*) addresses the desired functions of the farming system. Farming systems' functions can be divided into the provision of private and public goods (Table 1.1). Private goods include the production of food and other bio-based resources, but also ensuring a reasonable livelihood and quality of life for people involved in farming. Public goods include maintaining natural resources and biodiversity in good condition, animal welfare

Table 1.1. *Typology of farming system functions in SURE-Farm (Meuwissen et al., 2019)*

	Short name
Private goods	
Deliver healthy and affordable food products	Food production
Deliver other bio-based resources for the processing sector	Bio-based resources
Ensure economic viability (viable farms help to strengthen the economy and contribute to balanced territorial development)	Economic viability
Improve quality of life in rural areas by providing employment and offering decent working conditions	Quality of life
Public goods	
Maintain natural resources in good condition (water, soil, air)	Natural resources
Protect biodiversity of habitats, genes and species	Biodiversity and habitat
Ensure that rural areas are attractive places for residence and tourism (countryside, social structures)	Attractiveness of the area
Ensure animal health and welfare	Animal health and welfare

and ensuring that rural areas are attractive places for residence and tourism. Farming systems generally provide multiple functions. Performance and importance of each function can be represented by one or more indicators.

In the fourth step (*what resilience capacities*) we distinguish three resilience capacities: robustness, adaptability and transformability. Robustness is the coping capacity of a farming system, i.e. its capacity to withstand stresses and (un)anticipated shocks. Adaptability is the capacity to change the composition of inputs, production, marketing and risk management in response to shocks and stresses but without changing the structures and feedback mechanisms of the farming system. Transformability is the capacity to significantly change the internal structure and feedback mechanisms of the farming system into a desired direction in response to either severe shocks or enduring stress that make business as usual impossible. The distinction between three resilience capacities (robustness, adaptability, transformability) ensures that the framework goes beyond narrow definitions that limit resilience to robustness. Furthermore, it highlights the importance of middle- and long-term analysis and strategies, as adaptation and especially transformation take time.

The fifth step of the framework (*what enhances resilience*) assesses the resilience-enhancing attributes defined as those system and enabling environment characteristics that contribute to resilience. We modified the list of Cabell and Oelofse (2012) as described by Paas et al. (2021a). Attributes are listed in Table 1.2. Most attributes relate to characteristics of the farming systems, such as 'reasonably profitable' (attribute 1) and 'optimally redundant farms' (attribute 7), while other attributes illustrate the role of the enabling environment. For instance, actors and institutions in the enabling environment can support the provision of functions as in attribute 8 ('supports rural life'), stimulate resilience capacities through 'diverse policies' (attribute 13) or invest resources, e.g. through 'reflective and shared learning' (attribute 20).

1.3 The Relevance of Regional Context

The resilience of farming systems must be understood in the regional context. Each farming system has co-evolved with a specific social-ecological environment. The activities of the different actors which constitute a farming system – e.g. farms, farmers' organizations, service

Table 1.2. *Resilience attributes in the SURE-Farm framework and short explanation of each attribute (based on Reidsma et al., 2020 and Paas et al., 2021a)[1]*

Resilience attributes[2]	Explanation
1. Reasonable profitability[a1]	Farmers and farm workers earn a livable wage while not depending heavily on subsidies.
2. Production coupled with local and natural capital[a2,b]	Soil fertility, water resources and existing nature are maintained well.
3. Functional diversity[c]	There is a high variety of inputs, outputs, income sources and markets.
4. Response diversity[c]	There is a high diversity of risk management strategies, e.g. different types of pest control, weather insurance, flexible payment arrangements.
5. Exposure to disturbance[d]	The amount of year-to-year economic, environmental, social or institutional disturbance is small in order to timely adapt to a changing environment.
6. Spatial and temporal heterogeneity of farm types[c,e]	There is a high diversity of farm types with regard to economic size, intensity, orientation and degree of specialization.
7. Redundancy between farms[e]	Farmers can stop without endangering continuation of the farming system and new farmers can enter the farming system easily.
8. Support of rural life[a3]	Rural life is supported by the presence of people from all generations, and also supported by enough facilities in the nearby area (e.g. supermarkets, hospital).
9. Social self-organization[a3,b]	Farmers are able to organize themselves into networks and institutions such as cooperatives, community associations, advisory networks and clusters with the processing industry.
10. Appropriate connectedness with actors outside the farming system[b]	Farmers and other actors in the farming system are able to reach out to policy makers, suppliers and markets that operate at the national and EU level.

Table 1.2. (*cont.*)

Resilience attributes[2]	Explanation
11. Legislation coupled with local and natural capital[a3]	Norms, legislation and regulatory frameworks are well adapted to the local conditions.
12. Infrastructure for innovation[a,d]	Existing infrastructure facilitates knowledge and adoption of cutting-edge technologies (e.g. digital).
13. Diverse policies[c]	Policies stimulate all three capacities of resilience, i.e. robustness, adaptability, transformability.
14. Ecological self-regulation[b]	Farms maintain plant cover and incorporate more perennials, provide habitat for predators, use ecosystem engineers and align production with local ecological parameters.
15. Redundancy of crops[e]	Planting multiple varieties per crop rather than one; keeping equipment for various crops.
16. Redundancy of nutrients and water[e]	Getting nutrients and water from multiple sources.
17. Redundancy of labour[e]	Labour comes from multiple sources.
18. Spatial and temporal heterogeneity (land use)[c,e]	Diverse land use on the farm and across the landscape; mosaic pattern of managed and unmanaged land; diverse cultivation practices; crop rotations.
19. Global autonomy and local interdependence[d]	Less reliance on commodity markets and reduced external inputs, more sales to local markets, reliance on local resources, existence of farmer cooperatives, close relationships between producers and consumers, shared resources such as equipment
20. Reflectivity and shared learning[d]	Extension and advisory services for farmers; collaboration between universities, research centres, and farmers; cooperation and knowledge sharing between farmers; record keeping; baseline knowledge about the state of the agroecosystem.

Table 1.2. (*cont.*)

Resilience attributes[2]	Explanation
21. Honoured legacy[b,a3]	Maintenance of old varieties and engagement of elders; incorporation of traditional cultivation techniques with modern knowledge.
22. Building up of human capital[a3]	Investment in infrastructure and institutions for the education of children and adults; support for social events in farming communities; programs for preservation of local knowledge.

[1] Attributes 1–13 were central in most of the SURE-Farm analyses; attributes 14–22 were used in the assessment of resilience in the future (Chapter 17).

[2] Superscripts indicate links with the general resilience attributes (Resilience Alliance, 2010), i.e. a: system reserves (a1: economic capital, a2: natural capital, a3: social capital); b: tightness of feedbacks; c: diversity; d: openness; e: modularity. General resilience attributes are reported in the annexes of the case study chapters (Chapters 6–16).

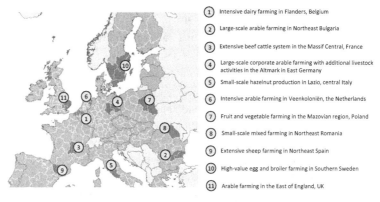

1. Intensive dairy farming in Flanders, Belgium
2. Large-scale arable farming in Northeast Bulgaria
3. Extensive beef cattle system in the Massif Central, France
4. Large-scale corporate arable farming with additional livestock activities in the Altmark in East Germany
5. Small-scale hazelnut production in Lazio, central Italy
6. Intensive arable farming in Veenkoloniën, the Netherlands
7. Fruit and vegetable farming in the Mazovian region, Poland
8. Small-scale mixed farming in Northeast Romania
9. Extensive sheep farming in Northeast Spain
10. High-value egg and broiler farming in Southern Sweden
11. Arable farming in the East of England, UK

Figure 1.2 The eleven farming systems included in the SURE-Farm assessments.

suppliers and supply chain actors – are enabled by regional environments and deliver the specific functions of the farming system, in particular agricultural products and public goods. The SURE-Farm approach was applied to eleven farming systems which represent different challenges, farm types, agro-ecological zones, products and public goods (Figure 1.2).

1.4 Involvement of Multiple Disciplines

Resilience is a multi-faceted concept and thus requires the involvement of multiple disciplines. We assessed adaptive cycle processes of risk management, farm demographics (including the availability of labour), governance with a focus on EU and local policies, and agricultural practices (Figure 1.3). These are the main processes informing the operational, tactical and strategic decisions on farms (Kay et al., 2016).

The concept of adaptive cycles originates in ecological systems thinking, where they represent different stages (growth, conservation, collapse, reorganization) through which systems might pass in response to changing environments and internal dynamics (Holling et al., 2002). Farming systems and their key processes differ from ecological systems in their production purpose and deliberate attempts to control their environment and to escape collapse. When applied to farming systems, the concept of adaptive cycles therefore serves not as a model but as a heuristic that guides the attention to system change (Meuwissen et al., 2019).

1.5 Mixed Methods

To obtain insights from the five steps of the framework, the SURE-Farm approach deploys mixed methods: qualitative methods, such as

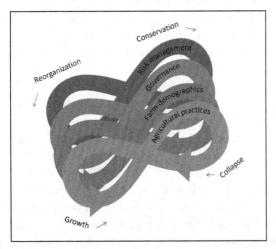

Figure 1.3 Resilience assessment requires knowledge from multiple disciplines.

interviews, participatory approaches and stakeholder workshops access experiential and contextual knowledge and provide holistic and nuanced insights; while quantitative methods, such as statistics and modelling, are used to identify underlying patterns and likely contributing factors, and focus more on specific challenges, functions and attributes. In total, we designed twenty-one different methods: fourteen qualitative methods and seven quantitative methods (Table 1.3). The methods address the level of farming systems, or the farm or household level (see first column for a specification per method). With regard to the qualitative methods, resource-intensive methods, such as the narrative interviews (method 4) and the co-design of policy options (method 10) were applied to fewer farming systems and had a lower number of total participants than some of the other qualitative methods. The highest number of participants was achieved with the farmer surveys, which included a total number of 996 farmers across farming systems.

Addressing the guiding questions of the framework requires an integration of very different perspectives and types of information. Methodologically, SURE-Farm therefore embraces a pragmatic eclecticism, i.e. a practical combination of methods rooted in different theoretical traditions, to arrive at a holistic and epistemologically robust assessment of the farming systems' state of resilience and resilience dynamics. Multiple methods are linked to each step of the SURE-Farm framework (Table 1.3). Some methods address all steps, such as the qualitative and quantitative system dynamics (methods 12 and 17, respectively) and the workshops on current resilience (method 7) and resilience in the future (method 11), while other methods focus on specific steps of the framework.

Farming system actors (Step 1) were identified based on patterns of influence, with mutual influence defining a farming system actor. In the narrative analysis, patterns of influence were assessed from the farmers' perspective. In the other methods, system actors were elicited through assessments in groups of stakeholders. With regard to the identification of challenges (Step 2), scenarios built on the Shared Socio-economic Pathways for European agriculture (Mitter et al., 2020). Other methods identified challenges by checking for structured predefined lists of challenges (e.g. in surveys and digital co-creation platforms), or they identified challenges inductively from open story-telling (narrative interviews) or semi-structured expert interviews (e.g. with members of farm households).

Table 1.3. *Methods employed in the SURE-Farm research* ... *of the framework covered*

		\multicolumn{5}{c}{Steps of the SURE-Farm framework covered[3]}
Method[1,2]	No. of FS (and total no. of participants)	1	2	3	4[4]	5[5]
Qualitative methods						
1. Scenarios linked to Eur-Agri-SSPs[6]	–					
2. Survey (F)	11 (996)		X	X	X[a]1	X[b]
3. Learning interviews (F)	11 (130)		X	X	X[b]1	X[b]
4. Narratives (F)	5 (46)	X	X		X[b]1	
5. Interviews with households (F, HH)	11 (169)		X	X	X[b]1	X[b]
6. Focus groups on risk management (FS)	11 (78)	X	X		X[a]2	
7. Workshops on current resilience (FS)[7]	11 (184)	X	X	X	X[a]3,[b]1,[b]2	X[a]
8. Assessment of policy instruments (FS)	11 (56)	X	X	X	X[a]2	
9. Bottom-up analysis of policy (FS)	5 (135)		X	X	X[b]1	X[b]
10. Co-design of policy options (FS)	7 (71)		X	X	X[b]1	X[b]
11. Workshops on resilience in future (FS)[7]	9 (130)	X	X	X	X[b]2,[b]3	X[b]
12. Qualitative system dynamics (FS)	5	X	X	X	X[b]1	X[b]
13. Digital co-creation platform (F, FS)	– (27)	X	X	X	X[a]2,[a]3,[b]1,[b]2	X[a]
14. Workshops on the enabling environment	11 (tbd)	X	X	X	X[b]1	X[b]
Quantitative methods						
15. Data analysis of ecosystem services (FS)	10			X		X[c]
16. Modelling of ecosystem services (FS)	11		X	X	X[c]1	X[b]
17. Quantitative system dynamics (FS)	2	X	X	X	X[b]1	X[b]
18. Statistical analysis of capacities (F)	Europe				X[c]1,[c]2	X[b]

11

Table 1.3. (cont.)

Method[1,2]	No. of FS (and total no. of participants)	1	2	3	4[4]	5[5]
					Steps of the SURE-Farm framework covered[3]	
19. Statistical analysis of functions (F)	1		X	X	X^{b2}	X^{b}
20. Simulation of structural change (FS)	2	X	X	X	$X^{b2,c1}$	X^{b}
21. Economic modelling of risk management (F)	1		X	X	X^{b1}	

[1] For qualitative methods, brackets indicate type of actors involved: farmers (F), other household members (HH) and multiple farming system actors (FS). For quantitative methods, brackets indicate level of analysis, i.e. at the level of farming systems (FS) or farms (F).

[2] Details of methods are described in 1: Mathijs et al. (2018); 2: Spiegel et al. (2021); 3: Urquhart et al. (2021); 4: Nicholas-Davies et al. (2021); 5: Coopmans et al. (2019); 6: Soriano et al. (2021); 7: Paas et al. (2021a); 8: Termeer et al. (2018); 9: Buitenhuis et al. (2020a); 9: Buitenhuis et al. (2019); 10: Buitenhuis et al. (2020b); 11: Paas et al. (2021b); 12: Herrera et al. (2018) and Reidsma et al. (2020); 13: Soriano et al. (2020); 14: Wauters et al. (2021); 15: Reidsma et al. (2019); 16/17: Accatino et al. (2020); 18: Slijper et al. (2021); 19: Paas et al. (2021c); 20: Pitson et al. (2019); 21: Zinnanti et al. (2019).

[3] The steps of the framework are 1: resilience of what, 2: resilience to what, 3: resilience for what purpose, 4: what resilience capacities, and 5: what enhances resilience. An 'X' indicates that the step was included in the method.

[4] Resilience capacities were assessed through a: *measurement of perceived capacities* with a1: current capacities and capacities to deal with expected challenges over the next five and twenty years; a2: contribution of instruments to the capacities; a3: the contribution of attributes to the capacities; b *inferring capacities* from b1: responses and strategies used by FS actors and the enabling environment to enhance resilience; b2: performance of functions, including whether critical thresholds are passed; b3: requirements for resilience attributes, strategies and enabling conditions to realize more sustainable and resilient systems in 2030; c: *statistical analysis and simulation* of c1: past and simulated robustness; c2: past adaptations and transformations.

[5] Performance of resilience attributes was assessed through a: *measurement of perceived performance of attributes*; b: *inferring performance of attributes* from responses and strategies used to deal with challenges; c: *calculated performance* (in method 15 specified to the attribute of diversity).

[6] Shared Socio-economic Pathways for European agriculture.

[7] Chapters refer to the participatory workshops on current resilience and resilience in the future as FoPIA-SURE-Farm 1 and FoPIA-SURE-Farm 2, respectively.

In the statistical analysis of functions, challenges were derived from, e.g., weather data. Some methods also built on information derived from other methods. For instance, the focus groups on risk management and the workshops on current resilience used challenges identified from the survey as a starting point, and the workshops on resilience in the future built on findings from the workshops on current resilience and used information from the scenarios. The importance of functions (Step 3) was identified through stakeholders weighing predefined private and public goods in surveys, workshops on current resilience and through a digital co-creation platform. The performance and trends of functions were assessed through scoring exercises to elicit stakeholder assessments in the workshops on current resilience, and from existing ecosystem and economic data, such as the analysis of ecosystem services and the statistical analysis of farm income.

Resilience capacities (Step 4) were assessed through the measurement of perceived current capacities and perceived capacities to deal with expected challenges over the next five and twenty years, and through perceived contributions from risk management and policy instruments to resilience capacities. In addition, insights into, among others, past responses and strategies used by farming system actors to enhance resilience and requirements for strategies and enabling conditions to realize more sustainable and resilient systems in 2030 were used to infer capacities. In the quantitative methods, we also used statistics and simulation to inform about capacities (e.g. quick farm income recovery rates indicate robustness). Similarly, performance of resilience attributes (Step 5) was assessed through measurement of their perceived performance, inferring performance from responses and strategies used to deal with challenges, and from calculations (see superscripts in Table 1.3).

1.6 Outline of the Book

Building on the systematic steps of the SURE-Farm framework, this book first presents findings on four key processes that affect the resilience of farming systems (Figure 1.3), i.e. risk management (Chapter 2), farm demographics (Chapter 3), governance (Chapter 4) and agricultural practices (Chapter 5). Findings are substantiated through a combination of methods and measurement approaches and build on results from multiple farming systems and their nested levels. For each process, the authors identify pathways to enhance resilience.

The empirical centrepiece of the book are the eleven case study chapters (Chapters 6–16). Each of these chapters provides a synthesis of the findings for one farming system based on the results from multiple methods and perspectives. The case study chapters provide in-depth insights into the challenges and resilience capacities and strategies of very different farming systems across Europe. Each of these chapters ends with an annex that summarizes the case study findings on each step of the framework and includes suggestions for future strategies.

In the final part of the book, insights from the systematic assessments are synthesized regarding the integrated assessments of farming systems (Chapter 17), roadmaps for the enabling environment (Chapter 18), lessons learned from the various co-creation methods (Chapter 19) and a synthesis of the findings and reflection on the SURE-Farm approach to assess the resilience of Europe's diverse farming systems (Chapter 20).

References

Accatino, F., Paas, W., Herrera, H., et al. (2020). Impacts of future scenarios on the resilience of farming systems across the EU assessed with quantitative and qualitative methods. Deliverable 5.5, SURE-Farm.

Buitenhuis, Y., Candel, J., Termeer, K., et al. (2019). Policy bottom-up analysis – All case study report. Deliverable 4.3, SURE-Farm.

Buitenhuis, Y., Candel, J., Feindt, P. H., & Termeer, K. (2020a). Does the Common Agricultural Policy enhance farming systems' resilience? Applying the Resilience Assessment Tool (ResAT) to a farming system case study in the Netherlands. *Journal of Rural Studies*, 80, 314–327. https://doi.org/10.1016/j.jrurstud.2020.10.004.

Buitenhuis, Y., Candel, J., Feindt, P. H., et al. (2020b). Improving the resilience-enabling capacity of the Common Agricultural Policy: Policy recommendations for more resilient EU farming systems. *EuroChoices*, 19(2), 63–71. https://doi-org.ezproxy.library.wur.nl/10.1111/1746-692X.12286.

Cabell, J. F., & Oelofse, M. (2012). An indicator framework for assessing agroecosystem resilience. *Ecology and Society*, 17(1), 18.

Coopmans, I., Dessein, J., Bijttebier, J., et al. (2019). Report on a qualitative analysis in 11 case-studies for understanding the process of farm demographic change across EU-farming systems and its influencing factors. Deliverable 3.2, SURE-Farm.

Darnhofer, I. (2014). Resilience and why it matters for farm management. *European Review of Agricultural Economics*, 41(3), 461–484.

Folke, C. (2016). Resilience (republished). *Ecology and Society*, 21(4), 44. https://doi.org/10.5751/ES-09088-210444.

Herrera, H., Kopainsky, B., Appel, F., et al. (2018). Impact assessment tool to assess the resilience of farming systems and their delivery of private and public goods. Deliverable 5.1, SURE-Farm.

Holling, C. S., Gunderson, L. H., & Peterson, G. D. (2002). Sustainability and panarchies. In: L. H. Gunderson & C. S. Holling (eds.), *Panarchy: Understanding transformations in human and natural systems*. Washington, DC: Island Press, 63–102.Kay, R. D., Edwards, W. M., & Duffy, P. A. (2016). *Farm management*. New York: McGraw-Hill Education.

Mathijs, E., Deckers, J., Kopainsky, B., Nitzko, S., & Spiller, A. (2018). Scenarios for EU farming. Deliverable 1.2, SURE-Farm.

Meuwissen, M. P. M., Feindt, P. H., Spiegel, A., et al. (2019). A framework to assess the resilience of farming systems. *Agricultural Systems*, 176, 102656. https://doi.org/10.1016/j.agsy.2019.102656.

Meuwissen, M. P. M., Feindt, P. H., Slijper, T., et al. (2021). Impact of Covid-19 on farming systems in Europe through the lens of resilience thinking. *Agricultural Systems*, forthcoming.

Mitter, H., Techen, A.-K., Sinabell, F., et al. (2020). Shared socio-economic Pathways for European agriculture and food systems: The Eur-Agri-SSPs. *Global Environmental Change*, 65, 102159.

Nicholas-Davies, P., Fowler, S., Midmore, P., et al. (2021). Evidence of adaptive capacities in farmers' narratives: accounts of robustness, adaptability and transformability in five different European farming systems. In preparation.

Paas, W., Coopmans, I., Severini, S., van Ittersum, M. K., Meuwissen, M. P. M., & Reidsma, P. (2021a). Participatory assessment of sustainability and resilience of three specialized farming systems. *Ecology and Society*, 26(2), 2. www.ecologyandsociety.org/vol26/iss2/art2/.

(2021b). Assessing sustainability and resilience of future farming systems with a participatory method: A case study on extensive sheep farming in Huesca, Spain. Under revision.

Paas, W, Meuwissen, M. P. M., Ittersum, M. K., & Reidsma, P. (2021c). Temporal variability of economic and environmental farm performance: a resilience perspective on potato producing regions in the Netherlands. In preparation.

Pitson, C., Appel, F., Dong, C., & Balmann, A. (2019). Report on the formulation and adaptation of an agent-based model to simulate generational renewal. Deliverable 3.4, SURE-Farm.

Pitson, C., Appel, F., & Balmann, A. (2020). Policy options for resilience-enhancing farm demographics. Policy brief SURE-Farm, https://www.surefarmproject.eu/wordpress/wp-content/uploads/2020/07/D3.9_Policy-brief-on-farm-demographics.pdf.

Reidsma, P., Spiegel, A., Paas, W., et al. (2019). Resilience assessment of current farming systems across the European Union. Deliverable 5.3, SURE-Farm.

Reidsma, P., Paas, W., Accatino, F., et al. (2020). Impacts of improved strategies and policy options on the resilience of farming systems across the EU. Deliverable 5.6, SURE-Farm.

Resilience Alliance (2010). Assessing resilience in social-ecological systems: Workbook for practitioners. Version 2.0. Online: http://www.resalliance.org/3871.php.

Slijper, T., de Mey, Y., Poortvliet, M. P., Meuwissen, M. P. M. (2021). Quantifying European farm resilience using FADN. In preparation.

Soriano, B., Bardaji, I., Bertolozzi, D., et al. (2020). Report on state and outlook for risk management in EU agriculture. Deliverable 2.6, SURE-Farm.

Soriano, B., Garrido, A., Bertolozzi, D., et al. (2021). Exploring how risk management contributes to farming systems' resilience. In preparation.

Spiegel, A., Slijper, T., de Mey, Y., et al. (2021). Resilience capacities as perceived by European farmers. Submitted.

Stone, J., & Rahimifard, S. (2018). Resilience in agri-food supply chains: A critical analysis of the literature and synthesis of a novel framework. *Supply Chain Management: An International Journal*, 23(3), 207–238. https://doi.org/10.1108/SCM-06-2017-0201.

Termeer, K., Candel, J., Feindt, P. H., & Buitenhuis, Y. (2018). Assessing how Policies enable or constrain the resilience of farming systems in the European Union: the Resilience Assessment Tool (ResAT). Deliverable 4.1, SURE-Farm.

Urquhart, J., Accatino, F., Antonioli, A., et al. (2021). Exploring the role of 'networks of influence' for risk management in European farming systems. In preparation.

Walker, B., & Salt, D. (2006). *Resilience thinking: Sustaining ecosystems and people in a changing world*. Washington, DC: Island Press.

Walker, B., Holling, C. S., Carpenter, S. R., & Kinzig, A. (2004). Resilience, adaptability and transformability in social–ecological systems. *Ecology and Society*, 9(2), 5.

Wauters, E., Mathijs, E., Coopmans, I., et al. (2021). Roadmaps for the implementation of principles for a resilience enabling environment. Deliverable 6.4, SURE-Farm.

Zinnanti, C., Schimmenti, E., Borsellino, V., Paolini, G., & Severini, S. (2019). Economic performance and risk of farming systems specialized in perennial crops: An analysis of Italian hazelnut production. *Agricultural Systems*, 176, 102645.

2 | The Importance of Improving and Enlarging the Scope of Risk Management to Enhance Resilience in European Agriculture

ROBERT FINGER, WILLEMIJN VROEGE,
ALISA SPIEGEL, YANN DE MEY,
THOMAS SLIJPER, P. MARIJN
POORTVLIET, JULIE URQUHART, MAURO
VIGANI, PHILLIPA NICHOLAS-DAVIES,
BÁRBARA SORIANO, ALBERTO GARRIDO,
SIMONE SEVERINI AND MIRANDA P. M.
MEUWISSEN

2.1 Introduction

Risk and risk management are essential elements of farming and affect the well-being of the farming population. Farm businesses face a wide range of risks, such as production risks (uncertain quantity and quality of production), market risks (volatile prices, changes in consumer demand), social risks (health issues, family breakdown, succession problems), financial risks (faulting on financial obligations) and institutional risks (shifts in the political and regulatory context). These risks and uncertainties reduce the well-being of risk-averse farmers and their incentives to produce, invest and innovate (e.g. Sunding and Zilberman 2001; Gardebroek 2006; Cerroni 2020; Iyer et al. 2020). Moreover, high uncertainty may also limit successful farm transition. Ultimately, the insufficient ability to address risks and uncertainty affects the resilience capacities (i.e. robustness, adaptability and transformability) of farm businesses and entire farming systems (e.g. Meuwissen et al. 2019; Slijper et al. 2020). Robustness relates to stability, aiming to absorb risks in order to maintain the status quo (Folke 2006). Adaptability represents a farm business's and farming system's ability to adjust processes in response to stresses and shocks, while transformability is the ability to radically change a business's and farming system mode of operation when needed (Darnhofer 2014; Meuwissen et al. 2019).

Agriculture has been traditionally one of the riskiest economic activities (e.g. due to its dependence on the variability of natural factors).

It is likely that exposure to risks will further intensify for European farm businesses and farming systems in the future. This will increase the demand for innovations in the field of risk management and for policy interventions (Chavas 2011). For example, climate change leads to increasing weather variability and a higher frequency and magnitude of extreme events such as heat waves, droughts and heavy rainfall that harm European agriculture (e.g. Trnka et al. 2014; Webber et al. 2018, 2020). Moreover, market risks such as volatile prices on liberalized markets and policy risks from changing agricultural and environmental policies are increasingly important for European farms (e.g. Tangermann 2011; Meraner and Finger 2019). For example, societal debates about agricultural policies and their effectiveness and efficiency in reaching desired (environmental, social and economic) goals may lead to policy regime shifts (e.g. Daugbjerg and Feindt 2017; Huber and Finger 2019; Pe'Er et al. 2019; Schaub et al. 2020). Moreover, farmers face previously unimaginable risks (i.e. so-called unknown unknowns), such as those experienced during the Covid-19 pandemic, the Russian Embargo or Brexit (Meuwissen et al. 2019, 2020; Vigani et al. 2021).

Farm businesses can respond to production, market and institutional risks by taking measures on or off the farm. Farmers' responses to risks are driven by past risk experience and perceived levels of risk (Meraner and Finger 2019). For example, farmers adjust production and marketing decisions in response to risk exposure or decide to allocate more resources (labour, money etc.) outside the farm (de Mey et al. 2016). Such risk management measures are often costly and have implications beyond the single farm and farm household. They can affect entire farming systems, including up- and downstream industries as well as the environment. For example, risk perceptions and risk preferences shape farm-level decisions on land use and the use of inputs that are critical to the environment, such as fertilizers, pesticides or water (Möhring et al. 2020a, b). Whether farmers reduce production risks by controlling yield losses (e.g. using hail nets or irrigation systems) or by using a financial insurance that may substitute or complement these measures has massive implications for the variability of the supply to regional markets (Behzadi et al. 2018). To cope with these risks at the level of agricultural and farming systems, the adaptive capacity and risk management options in European agriculture need to be improved at the system level, focusing on long-term, rather than short-term, viability of farming systems.

An enabling policy environment is crucial to support this process. Indeed, risk exposure and risk management are of great policy interest (see, e.g., Bardají et al. 2016; European Commission 2017; Meuwissen et al. 2018). As a response, the 2013 reform of the Common Agricultural Policy (CAP) emphasized the policy support for farmers' risk management and introduced new measures such as extended financial support for insurance schemes (e.g. Di Falco et al. 2014; Bardají et al. 2016; El Benni et al. 2016; European Commission 2017; Meuwissen et al. 2018; Popp et al. 2021).

The SURE-Farm (Towards SUstainable and REsilient EU FARMing systems) project (see Chapter 1), inter alia, aimed to inform policy responses to the new risk environment by (i) documenting the state of play of risk and risk management in European agriculture and (ii) synthesizing policy-relevant pathways for risk management at the level of farms and farming systems. We used a wide range of methodological approaches (surveys, interviews to assess farmers' learning processes, biographical narratives, focus groups, digital co-creation platforms and empirical simulations) that consider different scales (farm, household, farming system) and a broad scope of risk management solutions (financial risk management, joint learning and knowledge sharing). In this chapter, we discuss the link between risk management and resilience and contribute to expanding the scope of risk management, underlining the key role of a farming system perspective.

We show that a diversity of risk management solutions should be enabled by policy and industry. Strategies to cope with risk often extend (and even more often *should* extend) beyond the level of the individual farm. Cooperation, learning and sharing of risks play a vital role in European agriculture and should be further strengthened. Risks can affect both up- and downstream operators with significant consequences for the farm sector. Thus, coordinated policies which target actors beyond the individual farm and consider all stakeholders that are involved in risk management strategies are needed to ensure effective implementation. Moreover, policies need to take full advantage of the novel technological opportunities and improved data availability (e.g. based on satellite imagery) to develop a wider set of risk management strategies.

The remainder of this chapter is structured as follows. First, we identify risk management at the farm and farming system levels. Second, we investigate behaviour and perceptions in the context of risk and risk management in European agriculture. To this end, we identify the strategies of farmers and non-farm actors and consider a wide spectrum of risk management options. Third, we aim to sketch out exemplary pathways for improved risk management. We highlight the relevance of widening the focus beyond traditional financial risk management instruments and discuss the potential for novel insurance mechanisms, e.g. based on satellite data. Finally, we draw policy conclusions.

2.2 Farm-Level and Farming-System-Level Risk Management

Farmers have various tools at their disposal to reduce the impact of risk exposure, e.g. from extreme weather or market shocks. They can adopt risk management strategies on their farms (on-farm risk management strategies) and share risks with others (risk-sharing strategies). On-farm risk management strategies aim, e.g., at reducing the impact of risks (e.g. in terms of production or profit). This can include measures to prevent weather risks, such as the establishment of irrigation equipment. Production and income diversification are other important on-farm risk management strategies (e.g. Meraner et al. 2015). Farm businesses also adjust investment decisions in response to risk exposure. For example, increasing risks often make investments less attractive and lead to their postponement (e.g. Spiegel et al. 2020a). Farm businesses also build up reserves (e.g. knowledge, financial and social capital, fodder, or production capacities such as labour and machinery) to be better able to cope with and respond to shocks and stresses. Along these lines, farm businesses also respond to risks by adjusting their capital structure. For example, an increasing exposure to risks often leads to a reduction in the use of loans (e.g. de Mey et al. 2014). This holds for both family and non-family farms. For family farms, risk management usually also has implications for the farm household as the intermingling of business finances with household finances is common in most family farms (Wauters and de Mey 2019).

Yet, these strategies increase the costs of production because they require expenditures (e.g. for an irrigation system) and/or induce opportunity costs – e.g. a diverse production range precludes specialization to realize efficiency gains (Vigani and Kathage 2019). Moreover, some risks may be beyond the capacity to cope on-farm and consequently spread to the landscape/farming system level.

Extreme weather events such as droughts and heat waves can have severe impacts on farms and farming systems as these risks can affect several activities simultaneously.

We highlight here crucial aspects in the field of risk management, such as the importance of considering interdependencies between actors and instruments, the dynamics of decisions at the farm and farm household levels and the relevance of learning. Thus, agricultural risk management goes beyond the level of individual farms. It also spans across all dimensions of resilience, i.e. robustness, adaptability and transformability.

Risk-coping strategies often require interaction between farms and other actors. For example, farmers can reduce uncertainty by learning and sharing experiences with other farms. Farmers can also share risks with other farmers or transfer risks to markets to complement on-farm risk management strategies (Vroege and Finger 2020). Moreover, farms are increasingly connected to other actors along the value chain that look to ensure the procurement of agricultural commodities through contractual agreements – a phenomenon referred to as contract farming (Bellemare 2018). These kinds of contract serve, among other purposes, as a partial insurance mechanism against price risks (Bellemare et al. 2021). This example shows how some risk management strategies develop from interactions of the farm with other actors of the farming system. More generally, farmers can share price risks with up- and downstream partners using forward contracts or transfer price risks using futures (e.g. Assefa et al. 2017). Other instruments and mechanisms such as cooperatives and mutual funds, for example, further facilitate risk pooling (e.g. Severini et al. 2019). Moreover, agricultural insurance schemes pool production risks and play an increasing role in European agriculture (e.g. Meuwissen et al. 2018). The uptake of all these measures and the optimal portfolios of on-farm risk management and risk-sharing measures is farm-specific and depends on the characteristics of the farm and on the preferences of the farmers (e.g. de Mey et al. 2016; Meraner and Finger 2019). In the SURE-Farm project, we highlight the dynamic nature of these allocation problems. It is not only the sources of risk that are changing over time (e.g. due to changing market or climate conditions) but also farmers' risk perception and risk preferences (e.g. Bozzola and Finger 2021).

2.3 Insights into Risk Perception and Current Risk Management

The subjective perception of risk by farmers is crucial to explain observed behaviour and in particular to understand the adoption of risk management portfolios at the farm level. Three methodologies were employed in the SURE-Farm project to gain insights about the perception of risk and risk management by farmers: a farm survey, narrative interviews and learning interviews (see Chapter 1 for greater details on the methods adopted). The farm survey (n = 996) was conducted in eleven farming systems and aimed to capture perceptions of challenges and applied risk management strategies using different question formats, including open questions, multiple-choice questions and Likert-type scales (see also Spiegel et al. 2019, 2020b; Slijper et al. 2020). Semi-structured interviews (n = 130) sought to gain insights about influences on farmers' decision-making, as well as identify major learning strategies and their enabling and constraining factors. Biographical narratives were gathered in five farming systems (United Kingdom, Bulgaria, Belgium, Italy and Sweden) with early-, mid- and late-career farmers (Nicholas-Davies et al. 2020) to identify trigger points for change in risk management strategies.

In order to reveal the major challenges that European farmers expect in the future, in the survey (see also Chapter 1) we opted for a combination of closed and open questions. When assessing a predefined list of challenges (closed questions in the farm survey) based on their relevance for the future, farmers responded that they perceived institutional challenges (e.g. reduction of CAP direct payments and tighter regulations) and environmental challenges (e.g. extreme weather events and pest outbreak) as highly relevant in the future, with 39 per cent and 21 per cent of respondents, respectively, scoring them as the most challenging, while only 17 per cent of respondents perceived economic challenges (e.g. persistently low output prices and high input prices) as most challenging. In response to the open question in the farm survey, which asked respondents to name three major challenges they anticipate over the next twenty years, economic challenges, and in particular long-term pressures such as difficulty to improve profitability, were mentioned most frequently (Figure 2.1, left panel). From the open question we identified five categories, namely

Figure 2.1 Fifty most frequent words and word combinations in response to open questions on major perceived challenges and risk management strategies in the next twenty years. The size of each word reflects how frequently it was mentioned.

institutional, environmental, economic and social challenges and challenges related to access to technology and innovations. Examples of the latter category were 'lack of information about markets'; 'lack of information about climate'; 'keep on track with technologies'; 'influence of new research results in terms of production and its ecological aspects, e.g. insects, groundwater, fertilization'; 'introduce new technology'; or 'access to technology'. In sum, results of the farm survey indicate that European farmers expect to face multiple challenges in the future.

Biographical narrative interviews confirmed that challenges perceived by farmers range across a spectrum from purely internal factors arising from within the farming family, to factors arising from within the farming system, through combinations of factors to uniquely external pressures. Internal factors, such as intergenerational change, family breakdown, illness and death were more prominent in the narratives than external factors. The narratives revealed different approaches to risk alleviation, both within and across regional agricultural systems. For example, in the Northeast Bulgarian case, family relations were a fundamental part of the management of the very large corporate arable farm systems, and narrators emphasized that this legal structure provided a means to reduce personal financial risk. In other examples, family deaths and breakdowns in relationships (e.g. divorce, sibling disagreement) posed significant threats to the resilience of the family farm business and often resulted in enforced adaptation. In an example in the Flemish case study, small farm sizes and price volatility resulted in risk aversion and a disinclination by the farmer to invest in the business. Whilst this was a robustness response at that point in time, for the subsequent successor of the farm business it meant having to invest heavily to adapt the farm business in the early years of his farm management, thereby putting his business operation at greater risk. Factors that appear to be outside the control of the farm business (such as weather or price volatility) tended to be accommodated (robust response), rather than result in a considered, active change.

Addressing the manifold challenges perceived as relevant in the future requires adequate risk management portfolios. A combination of closed and open questions was used in the survey to reveal the most promising current and future risk management strategies (Spiegel et al. 2019). The closed question asked farmers to indicate which risk management strategies from a predefined list they had implemented in the past five years, while the open question asked farmers to list their three major risk management strategies they foresee as most relevant for the next twenty years (Spiegel et al. 2019; Slijper et al. 2020). Based on the responses to the closed question, we conclude that farms specializing in arable and perennial crops use more diverse risk management portfolios than livestock or mixed farms. For example, the risk-sharing strategies hedging and insurance were far less common in animal production compared to arable production. Yet, some risk management strategies were well adopted across all farm types. More specifically, cooperation between farms, such as membership of cooperatives and learning from others and their experiences, was an important risk management strategy. Results of the learning interviews add that a rather broad range of learning strategies were used by farmers to manage risk. Among on-farm risk management strategies, working harder to secure production in hard times and maintaining financial savings for hard times were found across all farm types. Our results further indicate that farmers elected highly specific risk management portfolios that were truly unique for each individual farmer in our sample. This finding underlines the importance of tailoring risk management efforts to the diversity of risks and challenges faced in the particular context of an individual farm (e.g. Meraner and Finger 2019; Vigani and Kathage 2019; Slijper et al. 2020). Understanding the adoption of different risk management strategies hence requires a holistic view on the diversity of risk management instruments available to farmers and how these interact in order to fully characterize how they allow managing multiple risks simultaneously, including the unknown (Spiegel et al. 2020b).

Responses to the open question in the survey are summarized in Figure 2.1 (right panel). In contrast to the existing literature, which mainly considers risk management in the context of short-term shocks for economic functions, farmers participating in the survey perceived risk management in a broader context. More specifically, their responses addressed also environmental and social functions of farms and targeted not only robustness, but also adaptive and transformative capacities. Likewise, examples from the biographical narratives of robustness in response to various challenges often appeared to relieve pressures in the short term and often forestalled opportunities for adaptation and transformation, as in the example of the Flemish farmer described earlier. Yet, sometimes this kind of long-term consideration was neglected by farmers. In an example from the Central Italian case, hazelnut farming was extremely profitable, and due to increased demand for land to establish hazelnut trees, the majority of new expansion was into more marginal land areas. Whilst this adaptation (expansion) ensured business resilience, it also came with the added risk of lower yield due to poorer growing conditions and greater prevalence of drought and heat waves (Zinnanti et al. 2019). The profits to be made clearly outweighed the risk in the short to medium term, but limited consideration was given to the potential long-term impacts of climate change on the sustainability of growing hazelnuts in these areas – perhaps a particularly pertinent issue given the long productive cycle of hazelnut trees. Results of the learning interviews provided further insights about the adoption of risk management strategies. More specifically, our analysis distinguishes between farmers who are 'proactive learners' and those who are 'reactive learners'. Proactive learners anticipate risk and adopt risk management strategies in anticipation of expected challenges; they are often identified as innovators or early adopters (Rogers 1995; Diederen et al. 2003). They experiment with new technologies and new approaches on their farm and are open to new ideas, seeking out new knowledge and engaging across social networks. Conversely, reactive learners are risk averse and deal with the consequences as and when they occur (van Winsen et al. 2016). They often perceive themselves as lacking self-efficacy, adopt a business-as-usual model and hesitate to try out new approaches or technologies. Their lack of flexibility and their reluctance to engage in social networks can constrain their ability to learn about potentially more resilient ways of working.

Adopting risk management strategies to respond to both shocks and stresses, as outlined in this chapter, often requires learning both how to deal with new challenges and how to adapt to changing circumstances. In the SURE-Farm project, and in particular in the learning interviews, we distinguished between cognitive, experiential and relational learning. Cognitive learning includes the acquisition of new skills or knowledge, and may take the form of training or learning about new technologies that can mitigate risks (precision farming, hail nets, etc.) or actively seeking out new information (e.g. market prices, technology, inputs, cultivars, breeds and land management techniques). An illustrative example of well-developed cognitive learning can be found, among others, in the Veenkoloniën, the Netherlands (see Chapter 12). Experiential learning is the experience gained over time through trial and error, including experimentation. It may also involve working outside of the agricultural sector (as in some cases in France and the United Kingdom), bringing back transferable skills from other industries, or working on farms overseas, observing and trying out different farming techniques in different countries. Experiential learning builds slowly over time and increases farmers' autonomy in decision-making and the ability to learn from past mistakes or successes. Relational learning was a key strategy in all case studies, with farmers indicating that they learn from their peers. This learning can take many forms, from talking to neighbouring farmers or farmer friends, engaging in farmer discussion groups, observing what other farmers are doing through field visits or interacting with farmers around the world through social media. In some case studies, such as the hazelnut production in Italy, shared learning occurred through involvement in cooperatives. As well as providing growers with stronger market power when dealing with wholesalers, the cooperatives also act as a forum for sharing information and experiences. Not all farmers in our interviews were open to learning from others, however. For instance, in the Spanish case study some farmers engaged in peer-to-peer learning, while others took a more individualistic approach to risk management. In this case, farmers who were involved in experimentation, social learning and sharing knowledge were more likely to innovate and improve their management systems. Individualistic farmers adopted more linear strategies such as cost reduction and intensification or transformed their business to a completely different activity.

2.4 Illustrative Opportunities towards Improved Risk Management

In this section, we aim to shed light on exemplary pathways of improved risk management. In particular, we highlight the relevance of widening the focus beyond traditional financial risk management instruments and demonstrate the potential for novel insurance mechanisms, e.g. based on satellite data, to cope with increasing production risk.

Several insights were identified from the biographical narratives, in particular. Structural issues, such as volatile prices, lack of available land and small farm size were highlighted as restricting the farmers' ability to adapt and evolve their farming businesses. Ensuring robustness was the dominant response to these challenges. Intergenerational transfer of farm businesses needs to be supported, e.g. in the form of vocational training and advisory support. Narrators considered this intergenerational transfer one of the greatest challenges facing a family farm business. Incremental change resulting in adaptation across time that was common in the narratives may be a better focus for policy support as it allows for experimentation and confidence building, perhaps resulting in more sustainable and resilient systems than radical transformation.

Our learning interviews identified reactive and proactive learner types that can strengthen resilience. Reactive learning-type farmers may facilitate farms to be robust in the short run, enabling their farm to recover from moderate shocks and stresses. However, they are less likely to be able to adapt though, persisting where possible in their tried and tested ways of working. In response to major shocks, they may be forced to undertake transformation or exit farming. However, proactive learners, while enabling robustness and transformability, are also able to adapt. These farmers are more entrepreneurial and are able to anticipate and prepare for future challenges, suggesting that they are more resilient towards a broader range of challenges. They can identify and respond to business opportunities, translating what they observe and learn from others into practice on their own farm. Farmers who align more with the reactive learner type may struggle with this process and find it difficult to overcome what they perceive as barriers beyond their control. This suggests there is a need for an advisor to fulfil this function for such farmers, to allow them to enhance their adaptive capacity.

To cope with increasing climatic risk exposure, existing risk management strategies have to be enriched with novel approaches. For example, agricultural insurance schemes are viable tools to manage weather risks, complementing other forms of risk management. Even though the current toolbox of insurance schemes offered to European farmers is rich (e.g. Meuwissen et al. 2018; Severini et al. 2019; Vroege and Finger 2020), the availability of insurance schemes to cover extreme weather risks, e.g. against droughts or heat waves, is currently limited. In this context, the SURE-Farm project investigated the potential of innovative insurance solutions such as weather index insurances. For example, we have shown that weather index insurance solutions based on different drought indices can be effective and efficient to cope with drought risk in crop production (Bucheli et al. 2021). We also found that these novel insurance solutions can complement traditional insurance arrangements for some farms because they specifically allow the establishment of efficient insurance mechanisms for previously uninsured crops (e.g. pastures and meadows) as well as under-insured risks such as droughts (Vroege et al. 2019). Ongoing technological developments such as remote sensing are expected to enable more effective, cheaper and more inclusive insurance mechanisms. The case study of crop production in Eastern Germany (Chapter 8) illustrates how drought insurance contracts that are based on satellite-retrieved soil moisture information could help farmers cope with drought risk (Vroege et al. 2021a,b). More generally, exploiting emerging opportunities of satellite data for crop insurance can reduce farmers' financial exposure to weather risks compared to a situation where no insurance option is available (Meuwissen et al. 2018; Vroege et al. 2021a,b).

2.5 Stakeholder Reflections and Insights in the Contribution of Risk Management to the Resilience Capacities at the Farming System Level

During the SURE-Farm project, we reflected with stakeholders (e.g. farming associations, insurance companies, policy makers) in the eleven case studies (see Chapter 1) on the ways that risk management may enhance the resilience capacities – i.e. robustness, adaptability and transformability – of their respective farming systems (Soriano et al. 2020). Stakeholders identified the following risk management strategies which they considered to be most relevant for the challenges threatening their farming systems: maintaining a strong financial base (financial savings and low debts), implementation of sanitary measures, diversification, risk-sharing strategies such as insurance, belonging to producer organizations, learning and information exchange, and diversifying the portfolio of suppliers. The stakeholders agreed that the selected risk management strategies may enhance all three resilience capacities, although robustness was perceived as the capacity most likely supported. Stakeholders saw a sound financial situation as the best alternative to be robust against shocks, since availability of funds usually helps to cope with unexpected losses. Low farm indebtedness increases the banks' confidence and credit scoring in credit/loan operations and farmers may find it easier to have access to financial resources to respond to challenges. This strategy also supports the adaptability and transformability capacities. Furthermore, stakeholders explained that farmers who build up financial savings have resources to support other adaptive/transformative on-farm strategies, such as production or income diversification. Also, the prevention of pests or diseases was emphasized by stakeholders as a key strategy to enhance robustness. Indeed, the stakeholders emphasized that the better the state of the natural resources, the higher the capacity of the system to face shocks. Insurances were also mentioned as a strategy that contributes to the robustness capacity to cope with weather shocks. Risk sharing strategies were seen by stakeholders as mainly contributing to adaptability and transformability. They explained that learning about challenges in agriculture gives farmers and other actors in the system the time to reflect on strategies for adaptation and/or transformation.

Stakeholders also reflected on ways how farmers and other actors implementing the risk management strategies in the farming system may enable the resilience capacities. A common perception was that the adoption of risk management strategies depends not only on farmers, but also on other actors in the farming system (Antón et al. 2011; Spiegel et al. 2020b). For example, according to stakeholders in the East German case study, when farmers diversify crops, other actors in the farming system also play relevant roles to implement this strategy. In this case these actors include: (i) local governments that provide funding programs and define the legal requirements; (ii) consultants who suggest new ideas, support strategy planning and monitoring; and (iii) financial institutions which provide funds, evaluate risks, provide counselling and monitoring. Furthermore, the stakeholders' insights suggest that every actor involved in risk management contributes to resilience capacities in a different manner. For example, the stakeholders explained that farmers, producer associations, cooperatives and financial institutions were the actors who contribute the most to robustness. They were seen as the main source of human capital, networks and financial resources of the farming systems. Value chain actors primarily were described as contributing to adaptability as they were triggering changes by advancing knowledge exchange, innovation and cooperation. Agricultural Knowledge Innovation Systems (AKIS) were reported to contribute to transformability by providing adequate information for investments, qualified technical assistance, multi-sector knowledge and long-term innovation. NGOs, consumers, media and banks may also enhance the transformative capacity of the systems as they are the main triggers of changes. NGOs, consumers and media question farming practices and pressure actors in the farming systems to move towards more sustainable processes (i.e. animal welfare or nutrients and water usage) or new practices that better meet the consumers' expectations. Banks support transformability if they facilitate funds for investments in innovation.

2.6 Conclusion

This chapter provides an overview of the risk and risk management practices in European agriculture and investigates opportunities for innovative and improved risk management strategies at the farm and farming system levels from a resilience perspective. Farmers need to deal with a diverse and volatile risk landscape that comprises short- and long-term risks. Consequently, risk management strategies differ across countries, farms, farm types and farming systems. The results of our analysis demonstrate the importance of tailoring risk management efforts to the diversity in the risks and challenges faced by a farm. Strategies to cope with risk often extend (and have to extend) beyond the level of the individual farm. Cooperation, learning and sharing of risks play a vital role in European agriculture and need to be strengthened. Risk management needs to go beyond instruments that focus on maintaining the status quo. For instance, setting up joint learning trajectories 'opens the door' for adaptability and transformability and thus for more resilient farming systems.

Coordinated actions and policies that target not only individual farms but consider all the stakeholders involved in the risk management strategies are needed to ensure their effective implementation. To this end, policies should define incentives specifically tailored to the different stakeholders in farming systems. For example, public collaterals that cover the increased credit risks of loans granted to small farmers for innovative projects could incentivize the banks' inclination to contribute to the adaptability and transformability of farming systems. Moreover, policies need to address long-term and diverse risk management strategies to account for the diversity of farming systems. Thus, policies need to enable long-term strategies, e.g. for dealing with intergenerational change, and need to address identified obstacles to change (e.g. cultural, legal, social welfare and policy). Finally, rapid technological progress and improved data availability enable the development of a wider set of risk management strategies. Pertinent examples are new insurance solutions which are based on satellite imagery and which will complement established approaches. Here policies should create an enabling environment in which a wide and diverse set of insurance solutions can be developed, e.g. by providing access to high-quality data.

Instead of a one-size-fits-all approach, more targeted and tailored policy mixes may be a sensible way to deal with the variegated and long-term risk landscape. At the same time, policy is often surpassed by new developments and needs to accommodate new realities. There are many unknowns out there, and policy mixes need to be designed in ways that are flexible and responsive to unforeseen events. Designing resilience-enhancing policies through improved risk management tools requires a holistic view on risk and risk management. More diverse risk management portfolios improve responses to risks, uncertainties and the unknown and help farmers to be better prepared for the future. To this end, we recommend agricultural policy makers to foster a more diverse risk management portfolio instead of focusing on optimizing a few risk management strategies which prolong a status quo situation that is not tenable in the long run.

Acknowledgements

We would like to thank two anonymous reviewers and Peter H. Feindt for helpful feedback on an earlier version of this chapter. This research was undertaken within the SURE-Farm (Towards SUstainable and REsilient EU FARMing systems) project, funded by the European Union (EU)'s Horizon 2020 research and innovation programme under Grant Agreement No 727520 (http://surefarmproject.eu). The content of this chapter does not reflect the official opinion of the European Union. The responsibility for the information and views expressed herein lies entirely with the authors.

References

Antón, J., Kimura, S., Martini, R. 2011. 'Risk management in agriculture in Canada'. OECD Food, Agriculture and Fisheries Papers 40.

Assefa, T. T., Meuwissen, M. P. M., Lansink, A. G. O. 2017. 'Price risk perceptions and management strategies in selected European food supply chains: An exploratory approach'. *NJAS – Wageningen Journal of Life Sciences* 80: 15–26.

Bardají, I., Garrido, A., Blanco, I., et al. 2016. 'Research for agri committee; state of play of risk management tools implemented by member states during the period 2014–2020: National and European frameworks'. Available at www.europarl.europa.eu/RegData/etudes/STUD/2016/573415/IPOL_STU(2016)573415_EN.pdf.

Behzadi, G., O'Sullivan, M. J., Olsen, T. L., Zhang, A. 2018. 'Agribusiness supply chain risk management: A review of quantitative decision models'. *Omega* 79: 21–42.

Bellemare, M. F. 2018. 'Contract farming: Opportunity cost and trade-offs'. *Agricultural Economics* 49: 279–288.

Bellemare, M. F., Lee, Y. N., Novak, L. 2021. 'Contract farming as partial insurance'. *World Development* 140: 105274.

Bozzola, M., Finger, R. 2021. 'Stability of risk attitude, agricultural policies and production shocks: Evidence from Italy'. *European Review of Agricultural Economics* 48(3): 477–501. https://doi.org/10.1093/erae/jbaa021.

Bucheli, J., Dalhaus, T., Finger, R. 2021. 'The optimal drought index for designing weather index insurance'. *European Review of Agricultural Economics* 48(3): 573–597. https://doi.org/10.1093/erae/jbaa014.

Cerroni, S. 2020. 'Eliciting farmers' subjective probabilities, risk, and uncertainty preferences using contextualized field experiments'. *Agricultural Economics* 51(5): 707–724.

Chavas, J. P. 2011. 'Agricultural policy in an uncertain world'. *European Review of Agricultural Economics* 38(3): 383–407.

Darnhofer, I. 2014. 'Resilience and why it matters for farm management'. *European Review of Agricultural Economics* 41(3): 461–484.

Daugbjerg, C., Feindt, P. H. 2017. 'Transforming public policies: Post-exceptionalism in food and agricultural policy'. *Journal of European Public Policy* 24(11): 1–20.

De Mey, Y., van Winsen, F., Wauters, E., Vancauteren, M., Lauwers, L., van Passel, S. 2014. 'Farm-level evidence on risk balancing behavior in the EU-15'. *Agricultural Finance Review* 74(1): 17–37.

De Mey, Y., Wauters, E., Schmid, D., Lips, M., Vancauteren, M., van Passel, S. 2016. 'Farm household risk balancing: Empirical evidence from Switzerland'. *European Review of Agricultural Economics* 43(4): 637–662.

Di Falco, S., Adinolfi, F., Bozzola, M., Capitanio, F. 2014. 'Crop insurance as a strategy for adapting to climate change'. *Journal of Agricultural Economics* 65(2): 485–504.

Diederen, P., van Meijl, H., Wolters, A., Bijak, K. 2003. 'Innovation adoption in agriculture: Innovators, early adopters and laggards'. *Cahiers d'Economie et de Sociologie Rurales, INRA Editions* 67: 29–50.

El Benni, N., Finger, R., Meuwissen, M. P. M. 2016. 'Potential effects of the income stabilisation tool (IST) in Swiss agriculture'. *European Review of Agricultural Economics* 43(3): 475–502.

European Commission. 2017. 'Risk management schemes in EU agriculture; dealing with risk and volatility'. Available at https://ec.europa.eu/agri culture/sites/agriculture/files/markets-and-prices/market-briefs/pdf/12_ en.pdf.

Folke, C. 2006. 'Resilience: The emergence of a perspective for social-ecological systems analyses'. *Global Environmental Change* 16(3): 253–267.

Gardebroek, C. 2006. 'Comparing risk attitudes of organic and non-organic farmers with a Bayesian random coefficient model'. *European Review of Agricultural Economics* 33(4): 485–510.

Huber, R., Finger, R. 2019. 'Popular initiatives increasingly stimulate agricultural policy in Switzerland'. *EuroChoices* 18(2): 38–39.

Iyer, P., Bozzola, M., Hirsch, S., Meraner, M., Finger, R. 2020. 'Measuring farmer risk preferences in Europe: A systematic review'. *Journal of Agricultural Economics* 71(1): 3–26.

Meraner, M., Finger, R. 2019. 'Risk perceptions, preferences and management strategies: Evidence from a case study using German livestock farmers'. *Journal of Risk Research* 22(1): 110–135.

Meraner, M., Heijman, W., Kuhlman, T., Finger, R. 2015. 'Determinants of farm diversification in the Netherlands'. *Land Use Policy* 42: 767–780.

Meuwissen, M. P. M., Mey, Y. D., van Asseldonk, M. 2018. 'Prospects for agricultural insurance in Europe'. *Agricultural Finance Review* 78(2): 174–182.

Meuwissen, M. P. M., Feindt, P. H., Spiegel, A., et al. 2019. 'A framework to assess the resilience of farming systems'. *Agricultural Systems* 176: 102656.

Meuwissen, M. P. M., Feindt, P. H., Midmore, M., et al. 2020. 'The struggle of farming systems in Europe: Looking for explanations through the lens of resilience'. *EuroChoices* 19(2): 4–11.

Möhring, N., Dalhaus, T., Enjolras, G., Finger, R. 2020a. 'Crop insurance and pesticide use in European agriculture'. *Agricultural Systems* 184: 102902.

Möhring, N., Ingold, K., Kudsk, P., et al. 2020b. 'Pathways for advancing pesticide policies'. *Nature Food* 1(9): 535–540.

Nicholas-Davies, P. K., Fowler, S., Midmore, P. 2020. 'Telling stories – Farmers offer new insights into farming resilience'. *EuroChoices* 19 (2): 12–17.

Pe'Er, G., Zinngrebe, Y., Moreira, F., et al. 2019. 'A greener path for the EU Common Agricultural Policy'. *Science* 365(6452): 449–451.

Popp, T. H., Feindt, P. H., Daedlow, K. 2021. 'Policy feedback and lock-in effects of new agricultural policy instruments: A qualitative comparative analysis of support for financial risk management tools in OECD countries'. *Land Use Policy* 103: 105313. https://doi.org/10.1016/j.landusepol.2021.105313.

Rogers, E. M. 1995. *Diffusion of Innovations*. New York: Free Press.

Schaub, S., Huber, R., Finger, R. 2020. 'Tracking societal concerns on pesticides – A Google Trends analysis'. *Environmental Research Letters* 15: 084049.

Severini, S., Di Tomasso, G, Finger, R. 2019. 'Effects of the Income Stabilization Tool on farm income level, variability and concentration in Italian agriculture'. *Agricultural and Food Economics* 7(1): 23.

Slijper, T., de Mey, Y., Poortvliet, P. M., Meuwissen, M. P. M. 2020. 'From risk behavior to perceived farm resilience: A Dutch case study'. *Ecology and Society* 25(4): 10. https://doi.org/10.5751/ES-11893-250410.

Soriano, B., Bardají, I., Bertolozzi-Caredio, D., et al. 2020. 'D2.6 Report on state and outlook for risk management in EU agriculture'. SURE-Farm project report – 727520. Available at www.surefarmproject.eu/word press/wp-content/uploads/2020/02/D2-6-Report-on-state-and-outlook-on-risk-magagment-in-EU.pdf.

Spiegel, A., Slijper, T., de Mey, Y., et al. 2019. 'D2.1 Report on famers' perceptions of risk and resilience capacities – A comparison across EU farmers'. SURE-Farm project report – 727520. Horizon 2020 Grant Agreement No. 727520. Available at www.surefarmproject.eu/word press/wp-content/uploads/2019/04/SURE-Farm-D.2.1-Report-on-farmers-perception-of-risk-and-resilience-capacities.pdf.

Spiegel, A., Britz, W., Djanibekov, U. Finger, R. 2020a. 'Stochastic-dynamic modelling of farm-level investments under uncertainty'. *Environmental Modelling and Software* 127: 104656.

Spiegel, A., Soriano, B., de Mey, Y., et al. 2020b. 'Risk management and its role in enhancing perceived resilience capacities of farms and farming systems in Europe'. *EuroChoices* 19(2): 45–53.

Sunding, D., Zilberman, D. 2001. 'The agricultural innovation process: Research and technology adoption in a changing agricultural sector'. *Handbooks in Economics* 18(1A): 207–262.

Tangermann, S. 2011. 'Risk management in agriculture and the future of the EU's Common Agricultural Policy'. International Centre for Trade and Sustainable Development, Issue Paper 34.

Trnka, M., Rötter, R. P., Ruiz-Ramos, M., et al. 2014. 'Adverse weather conditions for European wheat production will become more frequent with climate change'. *Nature Climate Change* 4(7): 637.

Van Winsen, F., de Mey, Y., Lauwers, L., van Passel, S., Vancauteren, M., Wauters, E. 2016. 'Determinants of risk behaviour: Effects of perceived risks and risk attitude on farmer's adoption of risk management strategies'. *Journal of Risk Research* 19(1): 56–78.

Vigani, M., Kathage, J. 2019. 'To risk or not to risk? Risk management and farm productivity'. *American Journal of Agricultural Economics* 101 (5): 1432–1454.

Vigani, M., Urquhart, J., Black, J. E., Berry, R., Dwyer, J., Rose, D. C. 2021. 'Post-Brexit policies for a resilient arable farming sector in England'. *EuroChoices* 20(1): 55–61. https://doi.org/10.1111/1746-692X.12255.

Vroege, W., Finger, R. 2020. 'Insuring weather risks in European agriculture'. *EuroChoices* 19(2): 54–62. https://doi.org/10.1111/1746-692X.12285.

Vroege, W., Dalhaus, T., Finger, R. 2019. 'Index insurances for grasslands – A review for Europe and North-America'. *Agricultural Systems* 168: 101–111.

Vroege, W., Bucheli, J., Dalhaus, T., Hirschi, M., Finger, R. 2021a. 'Insuring crops from space: The potential of satellite retrieved soil moisture to reduce farmers' drought risk exposure'. *European Review of Agricultural Economics* 48(2): 266–314. https://doi.org/10.1093/erae/jbab010.

Vroege, W., Vrieling, A., Finger, R. 2021b. 'Satellite support to insure farmers against extreme droughts'. *Nature Food* 2: 215–217.

Wauters, E., de Mey, Y. 2019. 'Farm-household financial interactions: A case-study from Flanders, Belgium'. *Agricultural Systems* 174: 63–72.

Webber, H., Ewert, F., Olesen, J. E., et al. 2018. 'Diverging importance of drought stress for maize and winter wheat in Europe'. *Nature Communications* 9(1): 4249.

Webber, H., Lischeid, G., Sommer, M., et al. 2020. 'No perfect storm for crop yield failure in Germany'. *Environmental Research Letters* 15(10): 104012.

Zinnanti, C., Schimmenti, E., Borsellino, V., Paolini, G., Severini, S. 2019. 'Economic performance and risk of farming systems specialized in perennial crops: An analysis of Italian hazelnut production'. *Agricultural Systems* 176: 102645.

3 | Demographic Dimensions of Resilient Farming Systems in the EU

ALFONS BALMANN, ERWIN WAUTERS,
FRANZISKA APPEL, JO BIJTTEBIER,
ISABEAU COOPMANS AND CHRISTINE
PITSON

3.1 Introduction

Since the beginning of the European Union (EU) and its predecessors with the Treaty of Rome in 1957, the agricultural sector's contribution to GDP and employment steadily declined compared to that of other sectors. This trend has taken place in both Old Member States, with a historical market economy, and New Member States, which have transitioned from a command to a market economy. In most Member States, the share of agricultural employment remains substantially higher than its share of GDP, causing relatively low average incomes in the sector. The comparatively low incomes drive structural change in agriculture and drive political measures intended to improve farmers' incomes.

In recent years, new demographic challenges have begun to affect the European agricultural sector. In the coming decade, the Baby Boomer generation and parts of Generation X will retire. Their cohorts are much larger than the Millennials and Generation Z, who are poised to take over the former generations' jobs. This means that a high share of farmers and the working population are approaching retirement age and that the farming sector will have to compete more intensively than before with other sectors and regions for the young generation entering the job market. The competition may intensify if rural areas face substantial outmigration due to urban areas offering substantially better income, career prospects, and better living conditions with more advanced infrastructure. The demographic changes overlap with an ongoing process of digitalisation in agriculture and society. While digitalisation may entail the substitution of labour input, it can be expected that digitalisation will increase the demand for skilled labour both on- and off-farm.

Aside from the specific demographic and economic challenges, EU agriculture is confronted with changing societal expectations of agriculture's private and public goods. Society no longer only expects that farms provide sufficient high-quality food but that it ensure high environmental standards, mitigate greenhouse gases, protect biodiversity and landscapes, increase animal welfare, etc. as expressed in the Farm to Fork Strategy (EC, 2020). These expectations have been accompanied by criticisms from citizens, NGOs, and the media about industrialised farming. This has caused many farmers to become concerned about their acceptance in society and their economic prospects. These concerns may further reduce the attractiveness for the younger generation to work in agriculture.

The economic, political, and social trends, as well as the farm demographic developments, raise the question to what extent the interplay of these trends affects the resilience of European farming systems? Secondary to that, in what ways can policy enhance resilience? To address these questions, this chapter is structured as follows. First, the concept of farm demographics and how demographics may interact with the resilience of farming systems will be illustrated. Next, we will present work from qualitative interviews focussing on farm demographics, specifically the process of generational renewal, at the farm level. After that, we will zoom out to focus on the effects of generational renewal at the regional level by presenting simulation results from two selected case studies. The chapter concludes with reflections on the presence of the three resilience capacities in the presented work and resilience-enhancing recommendations for policymakers.

3.2 Farm Demographics, Structural Change, and Resilience

3.2.1 Farm Demographics and Farm Structural Change

Demographics can be defined as the dynamics of populations, and how these dynamics change over time and space (MPIDR, 2021). The field of demographics encompasses the study of the size, structure, and distribution of a population, and spatial and temporal changes in response to birth, migration, ageing, and death, including, for example, gender and ethnicity. Demographics include quantifiable characteristics of a given population. Farm demographics as such can be described via quantifiable characteristics of a farmer population. From our perspective, a farmer population is made up of all people engaging in on-farm activities, the owner or manager of the farm, and farmworkers employed on a regular or non-regular basis, such as supporting family members and seasonal or permanent labour. The term farm demographics is thereby defined along two dimensions. First, from an institutional perspective, it represents the structure of the population of farms, for example, regarding legal forms and organisation. Second, from a human resource perspective, it represents the agricultural labour force structure considering characteristics like age, qualification, gender, and ethnicity.

In the literature, farmer populations' dynamics are approached mainly by analysing farm structural dimensions such as full- or part-time farming, size, intensity and specialisation (Chavas, 2001; Hansson and Ferguson, 2011). The insights derived from these works complement the analysis of farm demographics, as farm structural change and farm demographics are interwoven processes. Farm exit/entry choices are reflected in farm structural changes. For example, increased off-farm employment of farmers stimulates technologies that best fit part-time farming, including specialised production (Boehlje, 1992). Farmers who do not have the managerial skills to introduce cost-effective measures or find attractive opportunities off-farm might leave the sector, resulting in fewer and larger farms. The close link between farm structural change and farm demographics is further illustrated by Happe et al. (2009) (Figure 3.1).

Over the past several decades within the EU, there has been significant structural change in the agricultural sector. The most evident structural developments in European agriculture are reflected in the

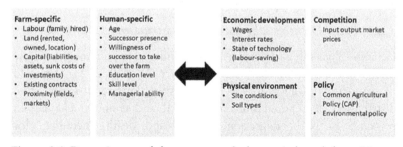

Figure 3.1 Determinants of farm structural change (adapted from Happe et al., 2009).

declining number of farms, farm size growth, and production special-isation over time (Neuenfeldt et al., 2019). As farm şize grows, farms tend to specialise into, for example, cereal cropping, granivores, or grazing livestock, moving away from labour-intensive permanent crops or mixed farming. In many regions, the total number of farms is decreasing while the age of the farm population increases. Analysis of Eurostat data by Zagata and Sutherland (2015) confirmed that the proportion of older farmers is growing while the numbers of younger farmers and the utilised agricultural area (UAA) they farm is decreas-ing EU-wide. Finding successors has become difficult for many family farms (Fennell, 1981; Wheeler et al., 2012); however, familial inter-generational transfer remains the main entry route into farming (Lobley et al., 2010). The EU support for generational renewal is rooted in the arguments that young farmers are more productive, that young farmers born and raised on farms possess knowledge inherent to the sector which needs to be retained (through succession), and that younger farmers have a different attitude towards risk and are more open to change (EIP-AGRI Focus Group, 2016).

3.2.2 Farm Demographics and Resilience

Besides structural adaptations in the agricultural sector, farm demo-graphics can also impact farming practices and processes to a large extent. Smooth and sufficient farm demographic change – including generational renewal, (new) entry and exit – might be a precondition for building resilient farming systems. Many European farming systems are developing towards fewer but larger farms, mainly to exploit economies of scale. Farm enlargement is often accompanied by automation and mechanisation processes, typically requiring sub-stantial investments and financial means. When farms prepare for such expansion, they often consider whether a successor is present at a farm, as this would further justify the investment. Thus, farm generational renewal in farming systems and adaptation or continuance (robust-ness) of farming systems are interwoven processes.

What does this mean for the agricultural sector of a region? From 2003 to 2018, the agricultural workforce within the EU 27 declined from ~13 million annual working units to ~9 million annual working units (Maucorps et al., 2019). This loss of 4 million working units or 30 per cent of the total agricultural workforce occurred within just fifteen years. That is an average annual decline of almost 2.5 per cent. Though this loss in the workforce is substantial, it did not result in a substantial decline in the UAA (Maucorps et al., 2019) or in a decline of the gross value added of the agricultural sector (Eurostat, 2018). Farm-level adjustments resulting in structural change on the sectoral level compensated for the loss in workforce. Arguably, despite the outflow of labour, the EU farming sector showed a substantial adaptive capacity. However, adjustments are not always smooth. This can be seen in the collapse of the former socialist European countries after 1990. These countries underwent a fundamental transition process where many employees lost their jobs and, in most countries, production was substantially reduced, which did not recover to pre-transition levels even after ten years (Rozelle and Swinnen, 2004). Moreover, substantial amounts of agricultural land have been abandoned (Alcantara et al., 2013).

While much of the literature, including the studies presented in this chapter, focuses on farm succession, the role of hired labour must also be considered when discussing farm demographics. Across the EU, farms using only family labour cultivate just about half of the agricultural land (Eurostat, 2015), meaning the rest of the land is cultivated in part or fully by hired labour. This share is particularly high in the New Member States, where the former command economies established various forms of large-scale agriculture. As structural change continues to increase farm sizes, hired labour will play an even more prominent role in future European farming systems. Many agricultural regions with a former command economy are already feeling pressure from their dependence on hired labour and the increasing difficulties to secure labour due to rural areas being unattractive and farms' inability to offer competitive wages (Pitson et al., 2019). As hired labour's role across agriculture grows and shortages continue or intensify, European farming systems' resilience will be challenged.

Farm demographics are inherently linked with the resilience of farming systems, both as a determinant of farming system resilience and its manifestation. Changes in the dynamics of farmer populations come from growth, equilibrium, collapse, and reorientation stages of adaptive cycles and the farmer population's response to changing environments and internal dynamics. Farm demographics are affected by several overlapping cycles at various scales. On family farms, the cycle of generational renewal by succession has been widely studied, as well as a variety of factors that influence this continuous process (see, e.g., Lobley et al., 2010; Darnhofer et al., 2016; Conway et al., 2017; Joosse and Grubbström, 2017). Besides affecting individual farms, and entrepreneurial and employment opportunities in the agricultural sector, succession or farm continuance also affects rural landscapes. Cultural and environmental aspects of farming practices have significant implications for rural areas' attractiveness and demographic stability (Copus et al., 2006).

Farm demographics are influenced by the adaptive cycles of agricultural production, both from within and outside the sector. Cochrane's (1958) model of the technology treadmill describes how farmers must either adopt new technology (growth) or suffer from decreasing incomes that might lead to a market exit. Such exits occur through bankruptcy (collapse) or involuntary or consciously planned professional reorientation (push factor). A conscious reorientation is more likely when wages outside of agriculture grow (pull factor), and farm employees have transferable skills. At the farming system level, technological progress tends to reduce total labour input per unit of output and increase the capital-to-labour ratio. This results in higher financial capital demands and more effective use of labour, requiring specialised technical and managerial skills. This type of development can enable growth of production and per capita income. However, the accumulation of push and pull factors combined with demands for highly specialised skills may result in a structural deficit of farm successors and skilled farm labour. This type of deficit could trigger reorientation or even collapse of regional farming systems. Such a reorientation can include seasonal and permanent migration of farm labour and farmers. This was seen after 1990 when farmers from western Germany, the Netherlands, and Denmark established new operations in eastern Germany and other former socialist countries. The seasonality of agricultural production is also tied to farm demographic processes; particularly, the peak labour requirements drive the (seasonal) movements of the labour force.

Farm demographic processes are affected by policies. They do so directly through agricultural policies, such as early retirement or new entrant schemes. However, governance mechanisms can also indirectly affect farm demographics, for example, through regulations on international labour migration (Hess et al., 2011) and differing national taxation rules on intergenerational asset transfers.

Previous discussions in the literature show a need for a deeper understanding of what enhances the resilience of farming systems concerning farm demographic processes. For example, although the predominant focus of past research lies on the importance of attracting the next-generation farmers and facilitating succession processes (Suess-Reyes and Fuetsch, 2016; Chiswell and Lobley, 2018; Leonard et al., 2017), it is however still not clear whether or not Europe is facing an acute succession crisis (Fischer and Burton, 2014; Chiswell and Lobley, 2015; Zagata and Sutherland, 2015; Coopmans et al., 2020). This uncertainty raises several questions. Apart from the question about the general availability of successors and hired labour, the following sections address two particular questions. The first addresses the underlying processes shaping the quality of farm succession and its implications for the resilience of farms (Section 3.3). The second raises the question to which extent the availability of potential farm successors affects the resilience of farming systems (Section 3.4).

3.3 Lessons from a Qualitative Inquiry on Generational Renewal in European Farming Systems

A deep understanding of generational renewal processes and their links to resilience is necessary to have before prescribing resilience-enhancing measures of farm demographics. In order to achieve this deeper understanding, a large-scale qualitative investigation into generational renewal was conducted within the SURE-Farm project.

The study was based on empirical data gathered from farms in eleven EU regions. The farms in the study varied extensively regarding their current position in the generational renewal process. For example, farms where no demographic changes had recently taken place or were foreseen to take place in the near future and farms that were in the middle of an intense reorganisation of labour in terms of increasing in size or in the midst of the take-over. On each farm, researchers interviewed multiple relevant farm stakeholders to collect different perspectives on farm demographic change. As a result, the final sample of informants were farm owners/managers, their spouses, co-workers, (possible) successors and offspring who decided not to take over the farm. In total, a sample of 86 farms across 11 EU regions was obtained, involving 155 interviews with 169 respondents (see Coopmans et al., 2019; and Chapter 1 for more details). The analyses

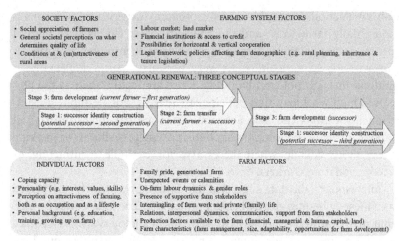

Figure 3.2 Understanding farm generational renewal through three conceptual stages and factors influencing them at four different levels: the individual, farm, farming system, and society.

of these interviews revealed that a complex intermingling of various aspects determine the farm demographic processes, including entry, exit, and other decisions taken by farm-level decision-makers. The most important aspects observed to affect generational renewal in European agriculture are summarised in Figure 3.2 and discussed hereafter.

To start with, we found that there are many perceptions about farming, both as an occupational choice and as a lifestyle choice. Some of these perceptions primarily act as push factors out of agriculture, others as pull factors into agriculture, yet most of them can work in both directions, depending on the person, region, and sectoral context.

Across all regions and farms consulted, the combination of high workload and expected low remuneration was among the most recurring themes explaining why entering the agricultural sector was considered unattractive by many respondents or why farmers felt discouraged or frustrated by their passion for their craft. Other often-mentioned aspects that make farming (as an occupation) unattractive were related to stress associated with farm management, fast-changing regulations, increasingly complex administrative work, and increasing political and societal pressures to change production practices. On the other hand, respondents often mentioned aspects that make farming attractive, which positively influences farm entry decisions and farmer job satisfaction. Examples are the autonomy experienced when managing daily farm work and the ability to work closely with natural processes and living species. Such perceptions determining motivations for working in agriculture are very personal, hence challenging to address through policies. However, there are factors such as the perceived high workload that policies can address. For example, government institutions can help accommodate seasonal spikes in external labour demand by simplifying bureaucratic procedures or making them more flexible where necessary, for example, contracting or accommodating workers.

Interestingly, the data suggested that farming was widely interpreted as a lifestyle besides clearly being a profession. The interviews revealed that many farmers found it hard to establish a good work-life balance due to, amongst others, intensive physical labour requirements, long working hours, and lack of leisure time, all of which is perceived to negatively affect their quality of life. We found that the extent to which a farmer could address and cope with such challenges sometimes influenced the next generations' perceived attractiveness of farming. Therefore, this coping capacity indirectly impacted the farm generational renewal process. The farming lifestyle also implies a rural life, which seemed in some of the study regions to be associated with a pleasant environment to work, raise children, and be preferred over urban life. In sharp contrast to this, respondents from certain other study regions allocated the lack of young people entering the agricultural sector to the countryside's unattractiveness. Here, frequently mentioned factors associated with abandoned rural regions and discouragement of the young generation to enter into farming were, amongst others, rural outmigration, insufficient basic facilities, isolation from community life, and lack of access to markets. In these regions, policymakers aiming to attract more young people into farming might focus on making rural life more attractive rather than only focussing on making the farming profession itself more attractive or (further) increasing direct payments to farmers.

A second key finding was that generational renewal through farm transfer or succession, which is a complex process affected by many dynamics and influencing factors, can be better understood by distinguishing the process in three stages. Such a conceptualisation facilitates the evaluation of generational renewal processes and how they can be supported by policies to increase farming system resilience.

During the first stage, potential entrants gradually view themselves as successors to a particular farm, thereby constructing a farmer/successor identity, or they do not. From the interviewees' testimonies, it is clear that direct financial aid available to farmers, such as the young farmer payment, have very little or even no impact at all on the formation of a willingness, ambition, or any other type of intrinsic motivation to go into agriculture. This contradicts some studies in the literature (May et al., 2019). Factors that have much more influential power during this stage are characteristics inherently present at the farm or individual level. For example, being born and raised on a farm was often mentioned by our respondents, either as a push factor out of agriculture or as a fact that contributed to the established self-identification as a farmer. What often distinguished farm successors from their siblings exiting the agricultural sector was that the latter emphasised the negative aspects of the farming life they were confronted with during childhood (e.g., not being able to go on vacation with the family). In contrast, the succeeding siblings paid more attention to the positive aspects (such as working and building the family life on the parental farm).

Moreover, it was observed that being a farmer was for successors an important part of their identity. Some other potential successors seemed to be 'balancing' between the extent to which a farmer's self-identity was present and the extent to which the potential hardship of being a farmer was perceived as being manageable. On family farms, which constituted the largest share of the sampled farms, typically all family members were involved with the daily farm work in one way or another. The overlap between the farm and private life was often observed to create a shared dedication to the perseverance of the farm, creating emotional drivers for entry. At the same time, the combination of work and family can be the source of conflicts and lead to farm exit. On corporate farms, the interference with private life tended to be lower. This, for instance, reduces the chance of someone choosing to continue the farm out of emotions and regardless of the farm's current profitability and future opportunities for development.

Furthermore, the production factors land, labour, and capital determine farm characteristics like farm size, scope, specialisation, and adaptability. Since these farm characteristics, in turn, affect how attractive a farm is to a potential future successor or employee, they indirectly influence farm demographics through the first stage (i.e., when someone is forming an opinion on how attractive working in agriculture is and consequently whether farming is a possible option for future occupation or not).

During the second stage, the farm is (gradually) transferred to the next generation. Farm transfer or farm succession typically entails multiple practical, symbolical, juridical, and accounting actions. It is this stage that currently receives the most attention through policy, education, and advisory services. The data illustrated that lack of access to and/or quality of the production factors land, labour, capital, and management could hamper the generational renewal process extensively during this stage. Indeed, farm succession requires cognitive capital to manage the often-complicated legal steps that need to be carried out correctly to materialise farm transfer. The absence of such qualifications may result in discontinuance.

Similarly, on many farms there is typically a period of transition wherein both the transferor and successor work together on the farm, hence the need to gain two full-time wages out of the farm. The absence of such ability to organise the farm in such a way that this output is created, due to, for example, financial or managerial deficits, once again may result in discontinuance. Because of these reasons, policymakers aiming to support farm transfers should evaluate whether access to the production factors is sufficient. If not, they should assess how the access can be optimised and address the relevant policy measures or domains to address the identified bottlenecks. Next to policymakers, other farming system actors, such as agricultural extension services, may play a central role in supporting the farm transfer process in all its complexity.

Besides the production factors, relationships and communications between the most important farm stakeholders influence the smoothness of the farm succession process. Good interpersonal skills act as an enabler, whereas bad relationships and poor interpersonal skills may prevent (smooth) farm transfer and increase the need for specific advice and support. On some farms in the sample, the successor and transferor could not reach a compromise in their conflicting opinions about future farm development, which delayed or sometimes even negated farm succession. This illustrates that the intention to take over a farm, which is a required outcome of the first stage to initiate entry into farming, does not always materialise into farm succession. Similarly, relationships between farmers and various acquaintances like landowners, especially in non-family farm transfer, were observed to serve as an important provider of opportunities for farm transfer.

When challenges relating to these production factors and interpersonal dynamics are overcome, a farm can successfully be transferred from the older to the younger generation. The latter is known in the literature for bringing innovations into farm businesses. Our empirical data provided additional examples wherein alternative practices improving farm performance were brought in by the incoming generation preceding, during, or just after farm take-over. Interestingly, young potential successors going through stage one (successor identity construction) were observed to often spend a period away from the family farm, for example, by an internship or other (non-)agricultural career experiences abroad. Sometimes, such experiences pulled them away from agriculture because they realised other careers are financially more beneficial. In other cases, farming remained their preferred career path, but potential successors encountered barriers to innovate and therefore decided not to continue the farm. This illustrates the central role of innovation and technology in generating resilient farm demographic developments in the future.

The family farm succession model is known for overcoming typical entry barriers occurring in this second stage, like the need for a considerable starting capital for necessary investments or to acquire a farm. Inheritance of farmland and farm infrastructure and temporarily shared ownership between different family members facilitate entry into the sector. Likewise, the (often unpaid) family labour can enable the successor to overcome financial pressures, especially shortly after take-over, when debts are usually high due to investments that are often made during the farm transfer process. If farm demographics in the future moves away from the traditional family farming model, for example, as a result of more frequent occurrence of non-family farm transfer, policymakers should think of other solutions to offer entrants specific opportunities in addition to those that have made it possible for family successors to continue the farm.

During the third stage, the farmer makes strategic decisions about farm development, which typically affect the (long-term) demographic structure and need for labour on the farm. Such decisions often influenced the next generation's decision-making process about whether or not to enter agriculture. The experienced imbalance between what farmers invest into their farm development (input prices and labour efforts) and what they get out of it (job satisfaction and farm profit-ability) seemed to put considerable pressure on the farmers' overall well-being. When facing challenges, farm survival could largely depend on the farmer's ability and their surrounding network to cope with the challenges at hand successfully. In this regard, support from family members, often in the form of long unpaid working hours and psycho-social support, was sometimes stated as crucial for farm continuity. This illustrates how current farm demographics can impact future farm (non-)entry and (non-)exit decisions. It was observed that these nega-tive aspects of farming could be overcome by one's personality or compensated by one's ambition to be a farmer. However, the weight of these factors adversely impacting well-being seemed high on all farms in the sample, which implies that shifting focus from supporting farmers in terms of income stability towards protecting farmers' well-being and mental health may better contribute to resilience-enhancing farm demographics. Besides, some interviewed farmers seemed to struggle with a perceived low appreciation towards farmers from the wider society, and some of the non-entrants even mentioned that low social appreciation was another reason discouraging them from becoming farmers.

Some of the interviewees – not necessarily young individuals – were settled farmers with a genuine entrepreneurial profile. They continu-ously kept looking for new opportunities to implement innovative activities on their farm. It seemed their motivation to enter or to stay in the farming sector was strongly driven by their high interest in agricultural-related topics and their eagerness to keep learning more. Altogether, these findings illustrate that a lack of a farming back-ground is not necessarily a barrier to entry, as other respondents sometimes assumed. More generally, creating a social network to be able to rely on during difficult times was observed to shape opportun-ities for future farm succession. Policy can respond to this observation by stimulating the organisation of training on knowledge and skills development and events that connect farmers with potential successors.

Risk management and resilience appear to be very important in the third stage. Certain events such as extreme losses, physical or mental health issues, intra-family conflicts, changing regulations that invoke a need for adaptation or transformation, trends such as technological development, and supply chain organisational changes can cause a farm to enter the farm transfer/succession stage in an unanticipated way and at an unforeseen moment. This puts farm continuity at risk because, often, this process' outcome is non-entry and exit rather than succession and entry. Even when the outcome is farm transfer and entry, it is often under less-than-ideal circumstances, putting the farm's future at risk. Nonetheless, unexpected events can, very occasionally, have a positive impact on farm transfer/succession. This can be the case, for instance, in situations where the generation wants to enter the farm transfer stage, whereas the old generation is not ready for this.

Some of the interviews indicated that management and hired labour on corporate farms are affected by similar processes of generational renewal. In every new generation of a family or turnover of employees (especially managers) on a corporate farm, similar decisions need to be made. Such examples are whether to continue and how to adapt the organisation of the farm to changing needs and abilities.

3.4 Adaptive Capacities of Structural Change in Selected Regions

On the farm level, demographic trends can affect the process of generational renewal in several ways. Family farms may lack a farm successor, corporate farms may have difficulties securing a new manager or managing the generational change within the group of main shareholders, and farms relying on hired labour may face labour market shortages and increasing salary levels. These factors can cause farms to exit as well as to restructure, for example, by reducing labour-intensive production activities. In certain cases, farms may collaborate with other neighbouring farms and establish partnerships that may allow for a mixed-age structure. These farm-level adjustments accumulate on the system, regional or sectoral level and result in structural change. However, farm-level adjustments are interdependent. Farms can usually only increase the amount of land they farm if other farms reduce their land bank or exit farming.

To study the consequences of a lack of potential farm successors, simulation analyses with the spatial and dynamic agent-based model AgriPoliS (Happe et al., 2006; Pitson et al., 2019) have been carried out within the SURE-Farm project. AgriPoliS simulates structural change of selected farming regions over periods of fifteen to twenty-five years. Within AgriPoliS, farms make decisions every period (year)

Table 3.1. *Scenarios of alternative availabilities of farm successors*

| | Share of farms with potential successor | | | |
| | Altmark | | Flanders | |
Scenario Name	Family farms	Corporate farms	Family farms	Corporate farms
100%	100%	100%	100%	–
50%	50%	80%	50%	–
25%	25%	50%	25%	–

Source: based on Pitson et al. (2020)

on investments, production, hiring labour, land rentals, and farm exit. Farms interact via the land rental market. If a farm exits or loses its rental contracts, other, usually neighbouring, farms can rent the newly available land.

Here, we present analyses of two case study regions of the SURE-Farm project, the Altmark region in eastern Germany and Flanders in the north of Belgium. The study regions are described in more detail in Chapters 6 and 8. The Altmark region's farm structure was greatly affected by its socialist history and is still dominated by large (often corporate) farms. Flanders is a typical family farming region in the western part of the EU. Since one major concern of EU policy is that farms have no successor, several scenarios with alternative probabilities of a potential successor's availability are defined. These scenarios are presented in Table 3.1. Farms without a successor exit at the time of generational change. If a successor is available, the farm continues if it is expected to be profitable.

The scenarios have a substantial effect on the speed of structural change. With a lower availability of potential successors, the annual exit rate of farms increases from about 2 per cent p.a. to 3 per cent p.a. (Flanders) or 3.5 per cent p.a. (Altmark). However, irrespective of the scenario, most farms exit due to low profitability, not because of lacking a successor. Nevertheless, with fewer potential successors and reduced competition, other farms' survival probability increases. The land which the exiting farms release is rented mainly by larger farms. Figure 3.3 shows that in Altmark when there are fewer potential successors, more land would be farmed by farms larger than 1,000 ha. In the same situation in Flanders, more land would be farmed by

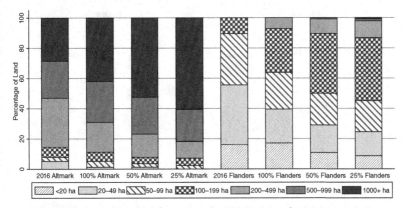

Figure 3.3 Shares of land by farm size class in 2016 and 2040.

farms larger than 100 ha. In addition to increases in the farms' acreage, the land-use intensity increases in terms of livestock density. The surviving farms benefit from exploiting returns to scale. Their land growth allows them to invest in more efficient livestock facilities.

To illustrate the economic effects of a lack of farm successors, Figure 3.4 shows the evolution of the components of agricultural gross value-added (GVA) per hectare for each scenario and region. On the regional level, the GVA is hardly affected by a lack in successors. Irrespective of the farms' performance and profitability, even when most farms do not have a successor and exit at the age of retirement, the GVA does not decline. In Flanders we find in the long run a slightly higher GVA when there are fewer successors. Moreover, there are slight shifts from profits (i.e. farm income from owned production factors) towards payments for land rentals and hired labour wages.

A lack of farm successors will cause farm closures. From an economic point of view, the effects on the sectoral level can be compensated by the remaining farms' adjustments. That means that the farming system shows the capacity to adapt on the regional level even if many farms collapse. This also means that structural change is not just the exit of farms but also the exploitation of new opportunities and particularly efficiency potentials by the surviving farms.

The adaptability on the regional level is, however, based on certain preconditions. The farms that grow in size and intensity need to finance their investments and hire additional labour. If loans and hired labour are not available or if these factors are too expensive, farms' capacity

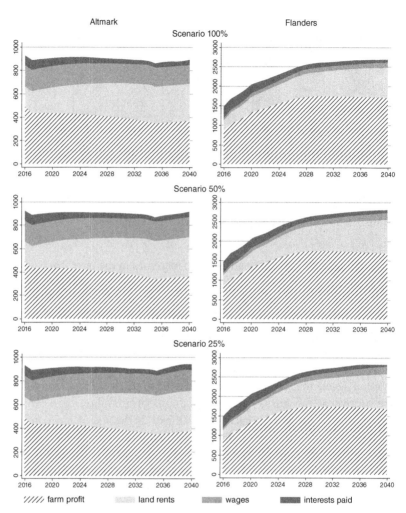

Figure 3.4 Evolution of Gross Value Added based on farm profits, rent, wages, and interest (in €/ha).

to adapt would be constrained. Similar effects would result if agricultural output prices are (expected to be) low.

Moreover, resilience capacities, such as sectoral adjustments through structural change, can be inhibited by institutional frictions that aim to discriminate against large farms (e.g., through capping direct payments) or investments into new production capacities for livestock, would be inhibited due to bureaucratic burdens. In such cases, market mechanisms may facilitate adaptations. Reduced economic land rents may be translated into lower land prices and/or extensification towards less labour- and capital-intensive production systems. These adjustments, however, do not occur immediately and take time.

3.5 Conclusions

From a farming systems perspective, structural change has to be considered as a resilience capacity. In general, structural change in response to economic growth, technological progress, or demographic changes, which is often expressed by farm exits and other farms' growth, means adaptation on the system level. Conscious farm exits need to be understood as transformation, another resilience capacity (Appel and Balmann, 2019). In principle, this means that a lack of a successor can be understood as a transformation on the farm level if the older generation plans and prepares the exit. At the same time, involuntary farm exits because of bankruptcy or insolvency may be seen as a sign of limited resilience on the farm level. On the farming system level, such involuntary exits may result in adaptations. As demonstrated in the AgriPoliS simulations, farm-level resilience is often lower than regional-level resilience. This scale difference between the micro and the macro levels must be understood as an emergent property of the farming system or the sector (Klasen et al., 2016).

Contrary to the role of these emergent properties, the current EU Common Agricultural Policy (CAP) seeks to target farm demographic change by a unique focus on the farm level and the farms' robustness. Thus, policies such as the young farmer payment fail to support the farming systems' capacity to adapt or transform (Vigani et al., 2020). Instead, these policies only support farms' robustness in the critical phase of farm succession and preserve the status quo. This problem also exists for the CAP direct payments (Balmann et al., 2006). Direct payments inhibit structural change by providing a financial buffer for farms, thus enhancing their robustness. At the same time, these payments may bear certain risks. Incentivising the continuation of uncompetitive farms often prevent necessary adaptations in time and are postponing or even provoking a collapse. Second, the exit of uncompetitive farms provides opportunities for farms competing for scarce factors such as land. In the end, farm-level support may constrain the resilience capacities on the system level.

If policymakers decide to continue to target increasing the amount of generational renewal, there are several factors they should take into account which would increase the policies' effectiveness. First, policies regarding the continuation, exit, and structure of farming should be based on territorial, that is, spatial, considerations. Because it is usually not clear what a desired or even sufficient level of intergenerational transfer is, a starting point could be the definition of a resilient delivery of system functions (public and private goods) in a particular region. Defining a sufficient level of public and private goods may inform desired levels of intergenerational renewal and structural change.

The main policy approach to stimulate generational renewal has been to support young farmers. In particular, the EU executive proposed that a minimum of 2 per cent of direct payments allocated to each EU country (Pillar 1) should be set aside for young farmers, complemented by financial support under rural development objectives and measures facilitating access to land and land transfers. However, these measures typically reach young farmers after they have already decided to enter farming and do not target the crucial stage – the farmers' identity formation. Indeed, if enabling more intergenerational renewal is the policy objective, policymakers should be aware that many exit and non-entry decisions have been made before the farm transfer stage. When there was no possible successor present or the designated potential successor has eventually decided not to continue the farm, measures to facilitate the farm transfer are ineffective. Policy measures that increase the attractiveness of farming, both as a career and as a lifestyle (including by increasing the attractiveness of rural areas) are likely to have a more considerable influence than measures that enable the transfer/succession process itself.

Policies and strategies that can increase the mobility of production factors land, labour and capital will improve the smoothness of farm demographic change processes. Whereas in some countries, land mobility is the limiting factor, in other regions, labour mobility is more challenging, which leads to a need for locally adapted policies.

Furthermore, non-agricultural policies such as fiscal, inheritance, and corporate law policies precisely limit production factor mobility. These policies are often specific to the region/country and often the result of a policy mix. Therefore, policymakers should take a more systemic view on a broad combination of policies rather than relying on one single policy instrument.

Overall, however, policymakers need to be realistic regarding policies' ability to impact the level of generational renewal. The analysis suggests that the relatively low number of young farmers is part of a typical farm structural change process. Moreover, generational renewal is the result of decisions being made at all individual farms, which are often personal and influenced by a very specific mix of personal, interpersonal and familial, and structural and economic characteristics. The ability to influence such processes with one or more policy instruments is relatively limited.

There is a bias of studies and policies on farm demographic change in general and generational renewal in particular towards the family farm model. Generational renewal and farm demographics should be seen much broader. Particularly in the New Member States of the EU but also other regions of the EU, the agricultural sector heavily depends on the availability of hired permanent and seasonal labour. The Covid-19 pandemic in 2020 demonstrated the dependence of EU agriculture and food processing on labour mobility and migration. Accordingly, hired labour and migration need to be addressed by agricultural policies which aim to enhance the resilience of the EU agricultural and food systems. In general, our data shows there is enough evidence to at least question whether the family farming model has positive or negative impacts on farm continuity, farm demographic change, and resilience. Whereas the family farm model could overcome some typical entry barriers such as the need for a substantial starting capital and labour demands, it could also be a nuisance, for example, when interpersonal relations within farm families falter or even create barriers for other forms of generational renewal such as new entrants or share-farming. As such, the bias towards the family farm model could be seen as a normative model rather than rooted in evidence. The different forms of generational renewal beyond intra-family succession should receive more consideration.

Finally, many agricultural and non-agricultural policies at the regional and national level affect the achievement of the goals and pathways towards agricultural resilience. Apart from policies that address generational renewal, regulations on permits, leases, land market mobility, migration, development of rural infrastructure and the resulting attractiveness of rural areas, and rural planning policy have a substantial impact on farming. Together with issues such as administrative requirements, fiscal policy, and inheritance policy, regional and national governments have powerful possibilities to drive the level and direction of generational renewal and farm demographic change, regardless of European regulations and policies. National policymakers often underestimate their possible influence and overestimate the influence of the CAP.

By understanding how the farm demographic trends affect resilience, policies can be better directed towards enhancing resilience. As emphasised in this chapter, policies need to be explored at a regional level. For example, in areas where poor infrastructure drives away potential successors, infrastructure-improvement policies could target the farm system's resilience capacities more effectively than agricultural policies: robustness may be improved by retaining successors; adaptation or transformation may facilitate new opportunities. Policies that support furthering education and training will likely enhance the systems' adaptive and transformative capacities, as farmers will likely look to integrate the obtained knowledge on-farm. At the same time, such opportunities offer farmers the chance to exchange knowledge and grow their networks – thus further targeting systems' robustness and adaptive, and transformative capacities. National and regional governments have the possibility to implement policies with a potentially profound impact on farming system resilience. How these policies should look depends on the normative assumptions on acceptable farming and production activities, speed of structural change, and a desired level of intergenerational renewal.

References

Alcantara, C., Kuemmerle, T., Baumann, M., et al. 2013. 'Mapping the extent of abandoned farmland in Central and Eastern Europe using MODIS time series satellite data'. *Environmental Research Letters* 8 (3): 035035. https://doi:10.1088/1748-9326/8/3/035035

Appel, F. and Balmann, A. 2019. 'Human behaviour versus optimising agents and the resilience of farms – Insights from agent-based participatory experiments with FarmAgriPoliS'. *Ecological Complexity* 40: 1007–1031.

Balmann, A., Dautzenberg, K., Happe, K. and Kellermann K. 2006. 'On the dynamics of structural change in agriculture: Internal frictions, policy threats and vertical integration'. *Outlook on Agriculture* 35(2): 115–121.

Boehlje, M. 1992. 'Alternative models of structural change in agriculture and related industries'. *Agribusiness* 8(3): 219–231.

Chavas, J. P. 2001. 'Structural change in agricultural production: Economics, technology and policy'. *Handbook of Agricultural Economics* 1: 263–285.

Chiswell, H. M. and Lobley, M. 2018. 'It's definitely a good time to be a farmer: Understanding the changing dynamics of successor creation in late modern society'. *Rural Sociology* 83(3): 630–653. https://doi.org/10.1111/ruso.12205

2015. 'A recruitment crisis in agriculture? A reply to Heike Fischer and Rob JF Burton's *Understanding Farm Succession as Socially Constructed Endogenous Cycles*'. *Sociologia Ruralis* 55(2): 150–154.

Cochrane, W. W. 1958. 'The agricultural treadmill'. In: *Farm Prices, Myth and Reality*. University of Minnesota Press, Minneapolis, pp. 85–107.

Conway, S. F., McDonagh, J., Farrell, M. and Kinsella, A. 2017. 'Uncovering obstacles: The exercise of symbolic power in the complex arena of intergenerational family farm transfer'. *Journal of Rural Studies* 54: 60–75.

Coopmans, I., Dessein, J., Bijttebier, J. et al. 2019. 'Report on a qualitative analysis in 11 case-studies for understanding the process of farm demographic change across EU-farming systems and its influencing factors'. Sustainable and Resilient Farming systems (SURE-Farm) project report (D3.2). www.surefarmproject.eu/wordpress/wp-content/uploads/2019/07/D3.2-Report-on-a-a-qualitative-analysis-in-11-case-studies-for-understanding-the-process-of-farm-demographic-change-across-EU-farming-systems-and-its-influencing-factors.pdf

Coopmans, I., Dessein, J., Accatino, F., et al. 2020. 'Policy directions to support generational renewal in European farming systems'. *EuroChoices* 19(2): 30–36.

Copus, A. K., Hall, C., Barnes, A., et al. 2006. 'Study on employment in rural areas'. https://core.ac.uk/download/pdf/74032988.pdf

Darnhofer, I., Lamine, C., Strauss, A. and Navarrete, M. 2016. 'The resilience of family farms: Towards a relational approach'. *Journal of Rural Studies* 44: 111–122.

EC (European Commission). 2020. 'A Farm to Fork Strategy for a fair, healthy and environmentally-friendly food system'. https://eur-lex .europa.eu/legal-content/EN/TXT/HTML/?uri= CELEX:52020DC0381&from=EN

EIP-AGRI Focus Group. 2016. 'New entrants into farming: Lessons to foster innovation and entrepreneurship'. Final report. https://ec.europa.eu/eip/ agriculture/sites/default/files/eip-agri_fg_new_entrants_final_report_ 2016_en.pdf

Eurostat. 2015. 'Farm structure statistics'. Eurostat Statistics Explained. https://ec.europa.eu/eurostat/statistics-explained/index.php/Farm_struc ture_statistics

    2018. 'Agricultural output, price indices and income'. Statistics Explained. https://ec.europa.eu/eurostat/statistics-explained/pdfscache/1192.pdf

Fennell, R. 1981. 'Farm succession in the European Community'. *Sociologia Ruralis* 21(1): 19–42.

Fischer, H. and Burton, R. J. F. 2014. 'Understanding farm succession as socially constructed endogenous cycles'. *Sociologia Ruralis* 54(4): 417–438. https://doi.org/10.1111/soru.12055

Hansson, H. and Ferguson, R. 2011. 'Factors influencing the strategic decision to further develop dairy production – A study of farmers in central Sweden'. *Livestock Science* 135(2–3): 110–123.

Happe, K., Kellermann, K. and Balmann, A. 2006. 'Agent-based analysis of agricultural policies: An illustration of the agricultural policy simulator AgriPoliS, its adaptation and behavior'. *Ecology and Society* 11(1): 49. www.ecologyandsociety.org/vol11/iss1/art49/

Happe, K., Schnicke, H., Sahrbacher, C. and Kellermann, K. 2009. 'Will they stay or will they go? Simulating the dynamics of single-holder farms in a dualistic farm structure in Slovakia'. *Canadian Journal of Agricultural Economics/Revue canadienne d'agroeconomie* 57(4): 497–511.

Hess, S., von Cramon-Taubadel, S., Zschache, U., Theuvsen, L. and Kleinschmit, D. 2011. 'Explaining the puzzling persistence of restrictions on seasonal farm labour in Germany'. *European Review of Agricultural Economics* 39(4): 707–728.

Joosse, S. and Grubbström, A. 2017. 'Continuity in farming – Not just family business'. *Journal of Rural Studies* 50: 198–208. https://doi.org/ 10.1016/j.jrurstud.2016.11.018

Klasen, S., Meyer, K. M., Dislich, C., et al. 2016. 'Economic and ecological trade-offs of agricultural specialisation at different spatial scales'. *Ecological Economics* 122: 111–120. https://doi.org/10.1016/j .ecolecon.2016.01.001

Leonard, B., Kinsella, A., O'Donoghue, C., Farrell, M. and Mahon, M. 2017. 'Policy drivers of farm succession and inheritance'. *Land Use Policy* 61: 147–159. https://doi.org/10.1016/j.landusepol.2016.09.006

Lobley, M., Baker, J. R. and Whitehead, I. 2010. 'Farm succession and retirement: Some international comparisons'. *Journal of Agriculture, Food Systems, and Community Development* 1(1): 49–64.

Maucorps, A., Münch, A., Brkanovic, S., et al. 2019. 'The EU farming employment: Current challenges and future prospects'. Research for Agri Committee of the European Parliament. www.europarl.europa .eu/RegData/etudes/STUD/2019/629209/IPOL_STU(2019)629209_ EN.pdf

May, D., Arancibia, S., Behrendt, K. and Adams, J. 2019. 'Preventing young farmers from leaving the farm: Investigating the effectiveness of the young farmer payment using a behavioural approach'. *Land Use Policy* 82: 317–327.

MPIDR (Max Planck Institute for Demographic Research). 2021. 'Glossary of demographic terms'. www.demogr.mpg.de/en/about_us_6113/what_ is_demography_6674/glossary_of_demographic_terms_6982/

Neuenfeldt, S., Gocht, A., Heckelei, T. and Ciaian, P. 2019. 'Explaining farm structural change in the European agriculture: A novel analytical frame-work'. *European Review of Agricultural Economics* 46(5): 713–768. https://doi.org/10.1093/erae/jby037

Pitson, C., Appel, A., Dong, C. and Balmann, A. 2019. 'Open-access paper on the formulation and adaptation of an agent-based model to simulate generational renewal'. SURE-Farm Deliverable, D3.4. www .surefarmproject.eu/wordpress/wp-content/uploads/2019/05/D3.4- Paper-on-adapting-an-ABM-to-simulate-generational-renewal.pdf

Pitson, C., Bijttebier, J., Appel, A. and Balmann, A. 2020. 'How much farm succession is needed to ensure resilience of farming systems?' *EuroChoices* 19(2): 37–44. https://doi.org/10.1111/1746-692X.12283

Rozelle, S. and Swinnen, J. F. M. 2004. 'Success and failure of reform: Insights from the transition of agriculture'. *Journal of Economic Literature* 42(2): 404–456.

Suess-Reyes, J. and Fuetsch, E. 2016. 'The future of family farming: A literature review on innovative, sustainable and succession-oriented strategies'. *Journal of Rural Studies* 47: 117–140.

Vigani, M., Urquhart, J., Pitson, C., et al. 2020. 'Impact of the young farmers payments on structural change'. SURE-Farm Deliverable, D3.8. www .surefarmproject.eu/wordpress/wp-content/uploads/2020/06/D3.8- Impact-of-the-Young-Farmers-payment-on-structural-change.pdf

Wheeler, S., Bjornlund, H., Zuo, A. and Edwards, J. 2012. 'Handing down the farm? The increasing uncertainty of irrigated farm succession in Australia'. *Journal of Rural Studies* 28(3): 266–275.

Zagata, L. and Sutherland, L. A. 2015. 'Deconstructing the "young farmer problem in Europe": Towards a research agenda'. *Journal of Rural Studies* 38: 39–51.

4 | Policies and Farming System Resilience
A Bottom-Up Analysis

YANNICK BUITENHUIS, JEROEN CANDEL,
KATRIEN TERMEER, ISABEL BARDAJÍ,
ISABEAU COOPMANS, EEWOUD LIEVENS,
ANNA MARTIKAINEN, ERIK MATHIJS,
JULIE URQUHART, ERWIN WAUTERS
AND PETER H. FEINDT

4.1 Introduction

The interest in the concept of resilience is growing in both academic and practitioner circles concerned with food systems and policymaking (e.g. Fan *et al.* 2014; Civita 2015). The mere fact that, at the time of writing, the impact of COVID-19 alone initiated a surge in research on how to enhance the resilience of food systems worldwide only confirms this growing interest. It is because of such shocks, but also worldwide competition, volatile markets, geo-political tensions and ongoing stresses like climate change and environmental issues, that the European Commission (EC) is increasingly realising the importance of having resilient EU agricultural and food systems in all circumstances. Hence, when presenting its legislative proposals for the Common Agricultural Policy (CAP) post-2020, the EC already explicitly emphasised that the CAP should contribute to 'ensuring a more resilient agricultural sector in Europe' (EC 2018). Moreover, the Farm-to-Fork Strategy, as part of the EU's Green Deal, is introduced with the aim to strengthen EU food systems' resilience (EC 2020). Whereas shocks and stresses affect food systems at large, enhancing resilience includes supporting local farms and farming systems to manage and respond to the different shocks and stresses while maintaining their essential functions, like producing food, providing employment and income, and preserving rural areas, ecosystem services and biodiversity (Meuwissen *et al.* 2019 and Chapter 1). The increasing attention on resilience reflects a need among policymakers to find ways to better support complex systems and their critical functions in times of rapid and unpredictable economic, social, environmental and political change.

The concept of resilience has received attention in the Policy Sciences, primarily by scholars who focused on how to design policies that are capable to deal with uncertainties, i.e. the resilience of policies themselves (e.g. Swanson *et al.* 2009; Howlett 2019). However, public policy research to date has barely analysed the (potential) effects of policies on the resilience of complex systems (Feindt *et al.* 2020). In contrast, the system resilience literature was more interested in understanding how public policies can reinforce the resilience of complex systems, such as bio-based production systems (Ge *et al.* 2016), energy systems (Gatto & Drago 2020) and urban infrastructures (Béné *et al.* 2016). This body of literature has provided valuable insights into the policy variables that can affect the resilience of complex systems, mostly by following a top-down approach to analysing (potential) policy impacts and the degree of goal attainment over time. However, less knowledge is available on how public policies influence the resilience of farming systems 'in practice' (i.e. within the implementing environment and its contextual factors, Berman 1978). The effects of agricultural policies are mostly studied at the farm level. Effects at the level of farming systems, where multiple policies interact, leading to synergies or trade-offs that might also affect system resilience, have received less attention. Contextual routines and private incentives might affect the resilience effects of policies, too. Moreover, whereas a policy might be designed with the intention to support the resilience of farming systems, its actual effects might be experienced differently on the ground, depending on the farming systems' characteristics, local context and the expectations of the targeted actors. Comprehending how actors in farming systems experience policies and their resilience effects is indispensable for understanding the relationship between policies and resilience. This can also help policymakers draw lessons and adjust policy design and delivery.

Against this background, this chapter seeks to address whether and how policies enable or constrain the resilience of farming systems through the perspectives of actors at the farming-system level. We set out a bottom-up approach for policy analysis, in which we analyse how actors within and surrounding a farming system experience the resilience effects of the CAP and relevant adjacent policies (e.g. regulation of plant protection products, legislation on manure and fertilisers, support for weather risk insurance, environmental policies or land tenure legislation). Our analysis draws on in-depth interviews with a broad array of relevant actors in five European farming systems. The interviews provided us with a wider picture on the enabling or constraining effects of policies on the resilience of farming systems from the respondents' perspectives. Subsequently, the findings of the interviews were reviewed in regional focus groups and, eventually, compared. The chapter proceeds with elaborating the theoretical perspective that guides our analysis (Section 4.2). This is followed by an explanation of the research methods (Section 4.3). Subsequently, the main findings of the bottom-up analyses of the CAP and relevant adjacent policies in the five European farming systems are presented (Section 4.4). The chapter ends with reflections on the key findings that have emerged from the bottom-up analysis (Section 4.5).

4.2 Theoretical Framework

4.2.1 Public Policy and Resilience Capacities

Resilience is understood as the capacity of farming systems – i.e. regional networks of comparable farm types and other non-farm actors within an agroecological context (Chapter 1) – to absorb or respond to shocks and stressors, while maintaining their essential functions (Chapter 1). Following this book's approach, we distinguish between three resilience capacities of farming systems: robustness, adaptability and transformability (Chapter 1). As farming systems are open systems, not only internal features (Chapters 1–3 and 5) but also external influences, such as public policies, affect the systems' capacity to maintain the desired functions in the face of adverse developments.

Both the resilience and policy sciences literature have acknowledged the potential of public policies to affect a system's resilience in several ways. Various academics have made efforts to identify specific policy characteristics that may improve the resilience of complex systems, e.g. through enabling polycentricity, accommodating self-organisation and knowledge networks or by encouraging learning and experimentation (van den Brink *et al.* 2013; Béné *et al.* 2016; Karpouzoglou *et al.* 2016). These studies, however, generally do not distinguish between the robustness, adaptability and transformability of farming systems. Supporting each of these resilience capacities requires different types of policies, each with different priorities and goals, instruments and budget requirements. In a previous study (Buitenhuis *et al.* 2020), we have argued that **robustness-enabling policies** are characterised by a short-term focus on recovery of existing functions of the system, protecting the status quo, providing buffer resources and government-supported modes of risk management. (Chapter 2 discusses different forms of risk management in more detail.) **Adaptability-enabling policies** are characterised by a focus on the medium term (one to five years) and flexibility that allows for tailor-made responses, they enable variety between and within farming systems, and support social learning. Policies may enable **transformability** through a long-term focus, dismantling incentives that support the status quo, and supporting in-depth learning and niche innovations.

Even when policymakers design *specific* policies in such a way that they may support the different resilience capacities, systems are affected by a broad *range* of policies which possibly produce divergent effects. This collection of policies forms a complex policy mix in which many policy goals and instruments interact (Howlett & Rayner 2007; Howlett 2019). Farming systems in the EU are affected by the CAP which pursues numerous goals, uses a diverse set of instruments, and operates at the European, national and regional levels, making it a complex policy mix in its own right. At the same time, the CAP is only one of many policies affecting EU farming systems, the interactions between which remain unclear, adding extra instruments to the mix. Various academics have discussed that one risk associated with overly complex policy mixes is that they likely contain inconsistent instruments with ambiguous means–ends relations that lead to trade-offs and reduced effectiveness (Howlett & Rayner 2007; Howlett 2018). Specifically, certain policy instruments can support one resilience capacity, while at the same time constraining others (Ashkenazy *et al.* 2017). For example, whereas subsidies related to existing production methods may enhance robustness, they may also constrain adaptability or transformability by reducing recipients' motivation to diversify practices or to explore niche innovations.

Following a top-down policy analysis approach, previous SURE-Farm research analysed the operational logic of the CAP and its national implementations from a resilience perspective. Whereas the CAP and its national implementation aim to support farmers, to ensure food security, and to contribute to sustainable agriculture and rural development in Europe, they were not necessarily designed with

Table 4.1. *How CAP instruments affect the resilience capacities of farming systems*

Robustness	Adaptability	Transformability
• Direct payments (basic payment scheme, greening payments, and young farmer payments); • Market safety net instruments; • Crisis reserves; • Support for insurance schemes.	• Agri-environmental programmes in the RDPs; • Investment support linked to sustainable farming practices; • LEADER programme in RDPs; • Options to tailor national and/or regional implementation of the CAP (e.g. modulation between Pillar I and II; optional direct payment measures; and options for designing RDPs).	• Support for organic farming; • The European Innovation Partnerships 'Agricultural Productivity and Sustainability' (EIP-AGRI); • Support for new rural value chains to encourage niche innovations.

Source: Feindt *et al.* 2018; SURE-Farm 2020

resilience intentions. However, the resilience concept proved useful to examine the CAP's capability of supporting complex farming systems. The top-down analysis revealed that different CAP instruments unequally affect different resilience capacities of EU farming systems (Feindt *et al.* 2018; SURE-Farm 2020). Despite some differences in the national CAP implementations, a comparison across EU farming systems revealed regular connections between certain instruments and resilience capacities (Table 4.1).

The top-down analysis showed that the CAP is strongly focused on supporting robustness. Most of the CAP financial resources are used for income support measures that provide buffer resources and allow farmers to continue their current business model. At the same time, the CAP offers less resources for instruments that enable adaptability. Only some measures in the Rural Development Programs (RDPs) encourage social learning, cooperation and innovations. Finally, the top-down analysis found that the CAP constrains transformability because business-as-usual remains strongly supported. Only the CAP's support for organic farming, new rural value chains or the EIP-AGRI were found to be designed to support changes in the operational logic of farms or value chains. Generally, the CAP provides little support or direction for long-term change through, e.g., in-depth learning or by encouraging radical innovations. While the top-down analysis provided a systematic examination of the extent to which the CAP's policy output is expected to enable or constrain the three resilience capacities, our previous findings were not necessarily congruent with the experiences of actors who deal with the CAP as part of their everyday practices. A bottom-up analysis of how actors involved in farming systems experience the policies and their effects, therefore, offers complementary insights into how the CAP and adjacent policies enable or constrain farming systems' robustness, adaptability, and transformability in practice.

4.2.2 A Bottom-Up Approach to Analysing Policy Effects on Farming Systems' Resilience

Bottom-up approaches to policy analysis differ from top-down approaches in that they move the analytical focus away from policy outputs and goal attainment to the specific contexts in which a policy is implemented. As such, they share an interest in local actors' perspectives on policy delivery and impacts (Nilsen *et al.* 2013). Bottom-up approaches have, for instance, often been used in policy implementation research, where they have demonstrated that putting public policies into practice and attaining intended outcomes is far from straightforward (Berman 1978; Matland 1995). For example, the EU aims to improve regional economic development and collaboration through its Cohesion Policy, which follows principles that are identical across the Member States. However, Dąbrowski (2013) used a bottom-up approach to show that the Cohesion Policy's implementation and effectiveness vary across regions due to differences in, e.g., traditions of decentralisation and collaborative policymaking, or the administrative capacity and resources of sub-national authorities. So, whereas European policymakers can influence the policy output, they can hardly control how the local-level context will affect the policy, leading to variation in policy effects (Berman 1978). Given that policies and their effects seem to differ depending on the context in which they are implemented, we studied the effects of the CAP and adjacent policies on resilience in view of the farming systems' setting, key functions and main challenges, i.e. shocks, stresses and opportunities (see Chapter 1).

Bottom-up approaches to policy analysis usually start with collecting the perspectives of actors who interact at the local level of the implementing environment or are related to a specific policy problem for different reasons (Sabatier 1986). First, actors closest to the farming system provide valuable insights into the effects of policies on the system through their practical experiences (Huttunen 2015). Actors within and surrounding farming systems deal with the policies in practice almost daily and, therefore, have important insights into the policies' effects and implications at the farming-system level. For example, Huttunen *et al.* (2014) analysed the perspectives of stakeholders in Finnish biogas production, revealing that cross-sectoral policies related to biogas production were incoherent and led to opposing influences in triggering the adoption of innovative biogas technologies. Furthermore, how actors experience and respond to policies is partly a retrospective and interactive process. Actors' identities, experiences, knowledge, attitudes and interactions shape their perceptions of the policies' effects (Termeer *et al.* 2007; de Lauwere *et al.* 2016). Bottom-up approaches make it possible to consider the interactions and exchange of information about policies between actors related to the system.

Whether and how actors within and surrounding farming systems experience and respond to policies also influences the policies' effects on resilience. As argued by Hemerijck (2003), successful policy implementation also entails that a policy is deemed acceptable by the affected groups to receive sufficient support and be effective. For example, Huttunen (2015) found that agri-environmental policy measures hardly received support, as farmers perceived them as incoherent with their farming practices, experiences and daily lives, resulting in poor uptake and functioning of the measures. Similarly, Bouma *et al.* (2020) found that the decision of Dutch farmers whether to adopt more nature-inclusive farming measures partly depended on the level of rules, regulations and obligations that come with these measures and whether the farmers considered them acceptable. Policy research on bureaucratic rules and procedures further confirms that when actors experience rules, regulations and procedures as complex or burdensome, they are more likely to experience negative emotions, such as confusion, frustration and anger that reduce acceptance and support of the policy (Hattke *et al.* 2019).

In order to effectively analyse actors' experiences regarding the CAP and adjacent policies' effects on farming systems' resilience, we draw on the theoretical insights presented earlier and develop our bottom-up approach to focus on specific topics. Starting from the challenges that the actors within and surrounding the farming systems perceive as most urgent, we analyse how actors experience the effects of policies on the farming systems' resilience capacities. We do so by examining which instruments of the CAP or adjacent policies are considered most influential – supporting or hindering – in dealing with the previously identified challenges, as perceived by the actors. Subsequently, we analyse if the intended effects of the most influential CAP instruments or adjacent policies corresponded with how the actors within and surrounding the farming systems experienced the policy effects. We argue that differences between intended and experienced effects might indicate that the policies interact with one another or with contextual factors at the farming-system level. If actors suggested changes to the CAP or adjacent policies to better fit the context of their local farming system, these suggestions were analysed as well, because they potentially reveal causes behind problems and possible solutions that can go unnoticed by conducting a top-down analysis. We end our bottom-up analysis by investigating how actors involved in the farming systems access information and learn about the most influential policy instruments to consider the influence of interactive processes on how actors experience policy effects.

4.3 Research Methods and Data

To comprehend the resilience effects of complex policy mixes through the perspectives of actors within and surrounding farming systems, we conducted bottom-up analyses of the CAP and relevant adjacent policies in five European farming systems. Since the CAP affects all EU farming systems, we decided to analyse its resilience-effects for different types of farming systems across the EU. The selected farming systems are: dairy farming in Flanders (Belgium), intensive arable farming in De Veenkoloniën (the Netherlands), private family fruit and vegetable farming in Mazovia and Podlasie (Poland), extensive sheep farming in Aragón (Spain) and large-scale arable farming in the East of England (United Kingdom). The farming systems differ considering their challenges, farming types, production of private goods, agro-ecological context and affected public goods (Chapters 6, 9, 12, 13, 16), ensuring variety between systems and allowing us to explore variations in policy influences.

Across the farming systems, we conducted ninety-eight semi-structured interviews with a broad range of farming system actors between January and April 2019.[1] In addition, we organised regional focus groups in each of the five farming system regions between August and October 2019, allowing respondents to review our interpretation of the data. Interview respondents included farmers and family members, (regional) policy practitioners, farm accountants, advisors, representatives of farmers' organisations, environmental NGOs, agro-industry and farmers' co-operatives. The interviews were designed to collect data about the enabling or constraining effects of the CAP and adjacent policies on the resilience of farming systems from the respondents' perspectives. In order to ensure comparability, each interview broadly covered the following themes: (1) farming systems' setting and main challenges (e.g. Can you describe the farming system? What challenges do you identify?) (Table 4.2); (2) policies and their effects (e.g. Which policies are most influential on the farming system? How do you experience the effects of these policies on the functioning of the farming system to deal with the identified challenges?); (3) information and learning (e.g. How do you acquire knowledge about the CAP and other policies? With whom do you have contact and communicate with about the most influential policies?).

After the interview rounds, we coded the interviews starting from a preset code book (deductive coding) that allowed inclusion of concepts and themes relating to the specific farming systems' context that emerged from the data (inductive coding). Our code book followed the interview themes and related guiding interview questions. For each theme, codes were set up by the researchers that followed from desk research (i.e. exploring research articles, policy documents, statistics)

---

[1] Number of respondents per farming system case: Belgium = 20 (13 farmers; 7 stakeholders); the Netherlands = 22 (7 farmers; 15 stakeholders); Poland = 20 (9 farmers; 11 stakeholders); Spain = 21 (16 farmers; 5 stakeholders); UK = 15 (8 farmers; 7 stakeholders).

Table 4.2. *The main challenges of the farming systems as identified by respondents*

Farming system	Main challenges
Dairy farming in Flanders (BE)	**Economic:** Input and output price volatility; access to land **Social:** Lack of farm successors or new entrants; low societal appreciation for agriculture; low horizontal collaborations between farmers due to competition; farmers' health and well-being **Environmental:** Increasing environmental regulations and requirements **Institutional:** Policies and legislation are perceived as inconsistent, inflexible and unpredictable; increasing administrative burdens
Intensive arable farming in De Veenkoloniën region (NL)	**Economic:** Increasing input and maintenance prices; increasing competition for land and increasing land prices; costly farm succession **Social:** Lack of new entrants; low societal appreciation for agriculture **Environmental:** Soil health; concerns about pests and plant diseases; more extreme weather events (climate change); water supply, holding and drainage **Institutional:** Inconsistent and unpredictable policies and legislation
Private family fruit and vegetable farming in Mazovian region and Lubelskie region (PL)	**Economic:** Low profitability and price fluctuations; increasing input and maintenance prices; increasing (international) competition; high insurance costs **Social:** Lack of seasonal labour due to (rural) outmigration; lack of farm successors and new entrants; low horizontal and vertical collaboration due to distrust between actors **Environmental:** More extreme weather events (climate change); water supply and drainage; soil depletion; concerns about pests and plant diseases **Institutional:** Inconsistent and unpredictable policies and legislation that lack a long-term vision

Table 4.2. (*cont.*)

Farming system	Main challenges
Extensive sheep farming in Aragón (ES)	**Economic:** Decreasing incomes and lowering prices; increasing (international) competition; increasing competition for land and increasing land prices **Social:** Lack of farm successors, new entrants and labour due to (rural) outmigration **Environmental:** More extreme weather events (climate change); water supply and drainage; wild fauna attacks; overgrazing due to intensification **Institutional:** Inconsistent and unpredictable policies and legislation
Large-scale arable farming in East of England (UK)	**Economic:** Price volatility; increasing (international) competition **Social:** Lack of (seasonal) labour; lack of farm successors and new entrants **Environmental:** Soil health; concerns about pests and plant diseases; more extreme weather events (climate change); water supply **Institutional:** Uncertainty due to Brexit, including changes in agricultural and trade policies; inconsistent and unpredictable policies and legislation; lack of access to advice and service

and data of previous SURE-Farm research. The codes were provided with a comprehensive definition, making clear the criteria for inclusion. The coding served to identify and critically analyse text fragments that contained references to policies in general, specific policy instruments and policy effects. Use of the code book and coding decisions were discussed within the research team on several occasions. The researchers interpreted and organised the respondents' policy-related experiences and connected them by determining how the policies affect farming systems' resilience in relation to the three capacities, i.e. robustness, adaptability and transformability. We used the specific policy indicators for resilience-enabling policies identified by Buitenhuis *et al.* (2020) (Section 4.2.1) to guide this step. The researchers thus engaged in a process of 'double hermeneutics', in which they interpret the answers and statements shared by respondents that aim to make sense of their own experience (Smith *et al.* 2009). Finally, we conducted a cross-case comparison of how the interviewed actors experienced the effects of policies on the farming systems' robustness, adaptability and transformability.

4.4 Results

We now present the key results of the comparative bottom-up analysis of the five farming systems. For our comparison, we especially focused on examining similarities and differences regarding the resilience enabling or constraining effects of the most influential instruments of the CAP and adjacent policies, as perceived by the respondents. We structured the respondents' experiences with the policy effects according to their congruence with the capacities of robustness, adaptability and transformability.

4.4.1 Robustness

Many respondents indicated that policies are mainly designed to offer farmers income support and funding opportunities to ensure that their farming system remains productive and to maintain a certain income stability in case of shocks or fluctuations. The CAP's direct payment scheme was especially considered by many respondents an influential policy instrument for supporting the robustness of farming systems, particularly in the Flemish, Dutch, Spanish and UK cases. The direct payments scheme, which consists of basic payments, greening payments and young farmer payments, is perceived as offering a guaranteed income for farmers, while the payments are recognised as hardly requiring any major changes to the established practices within the farming system. In the Polish case, the direct payments were regarded less influential because the fruit and vegetable farmers in this farming system own relatively little land. Therefore, the area-based payments do not make a significant contribution to their income, while profits per hectare are generally higher for fruit and vegetable farmers compared to arable or grassland-based farming systems. Moreover, direct payments per hectare are historically lower in Central and Eastern European Member States compared to Western European Member States. Respondents across the five farming systems suggested that the direct payments were a financial compensation for increasing costs and requirements imposed on agricultural practices, allowing existing (small-scale) farms to continue their businesses. Moreover, the payments were also perceived by multiple actors within and surrounding the farming systems as payments to buffer for financial losses due to market-related shocks. A decline in direct payments could thus be regarded as a threat to farmers' ability to deal with financial shocks. However, for many farmers the received income support exceeds the increasing costs, whilst the payments are also paid in times without shocks. In this view, income support then exceeds the minimum level required for enabling robustness, possibly leading to dependence on income support that can undermine longer-term resilience.

Respondents of all five farming system cases, however, also experienced different negative effects of the CAP's income support measures on the robustness of their farming system. For example, the post-2013 CAP reform introduced decoupled direct payments linked to the area farmed and convergence mechanisms that adjusted these payments towards a uniform rate per hectare within each Member State or region, instead of being calculated on the basis of historic entitlements. Whereas the introduction of these direct payments was intended to decouple payments from the quantity produced, actors in the Spanish case indicated that the decoupled payments made it difficult to maintain the extensive sheep farming system. In addition, Spain opted for applying the direct payments and its internal convergence at the level of regions based on land use, creating large regional differences in the value of the entitlements to the detriment of extensive grazing systems. Spanish extensive sheep farmers have limited access to land that is eligible for CAP payments, making it hard for them to maintain a profitable farming business. As one Spanish farmer said: 'Of 800 hectares of rented land, only 300 hectares are eligible for CAP payments ... So, people [farmers] who usually pasture in the mountains, do not have eligible pastures to receive CAP payments. So, they have to search for land in other areas'.

In addition, the CAP's decoupled direct payments seriously affect farmers' access to land in almost all farming systems. For instance, Spanish respondents mentioned that they experienced high competition for land in their farming system as land eligible for CAP payments was scarce. The direct payments therefore contributed to increasing land prices, specifically of CAP-eligible land. The Spanish farmers experienced this as a constraint to their long-term planning, as they were uncertain if they were still able to obtain or lease CAP-eligible land to remain profitable for subsequent years. Similarly, Dutch respondents identified increasing land prices as a major challenge to their farming system. They felt that the decoupled direct payments indirectly increased the already relatively high prices of agricultural land in the Netherlands, and the payments did not outweigh the land price increase. The increasing land prices affect the functioning of the Dutch farming system by constraining farmers to upscale their businesses and, in the long run, to realise farm succession. Likewise, Polish respondents argued that farmers' access to land was constrained as they experienced that the direct payments incentivised non-active farmers to continue to own agricultural land just to receive payments. Whereas the CAP's decoupled direct payments were felt to have less impact on land prices than the tax regimes in the UK farming system, UK respondents felt that the payments constrained access to land. However, the respondents largely spoke in terms of turnover of land and people, actually showing the decoupled direct payments' contribution to protecting the status quo. Low availability and high competition for land were also experienced by several Flemish respondents. However, they perceived Flemish land tenure legislations to have a stronger impact on access to land than direct payments.

Lastly, Dutch and Polish respondents indicated that more extreme weather events caused by climate change were a prominent challenge for their farming systems. The availability of insurance schemes that cover weather-related risks were, therefore, mainly discussed in the Dutch and Polish cases. Different weather insurance schemes are available for Dutch and Polish farmers to protect against financial losses incurred by adverse weather events. In the Netherlands, private hail insurance is marketed, and public-private weather insurances are offered whereby the Dutch government provides a subsidy rate on the insurance premium, using payments under the RDP. In Poland, a nationally designed and funded insurance scheme is preferred by the government and Polish farmers are obligated to insure at least 50 per cent of their agricultural land to receive direct payments (Meuwissen *et al.* 2018; Popp & Nowack 2020). Whereas the insurance systems differ between the Netherlands and Poland, the insurances offered were largely not regarded as appropriate risk management tools as the effectiveness of the insurance schemes was called into question, especially by farmers. Taking out weather insurance was considered an individual choice as part of a farmer's strategy to deal with weather-induced risks. The general experience of the interviewed Dutch and Polish farmers was that the benefits of the insurance did not outweigh its costs, resulting in the decision not to subscribe to these insurances. In addition, Polish farmers generally seemed to be reluctant to enter insurance contracts for their crops (Wąs & Kobus 2018). Our interviews showed that unfavourable attitudes of the Polish farmers towards insurances were based on past experiences and contributed to the experience of weather insurance as an ineffective risk management tool. As stated by Polish farmers:

We do not insure for another time because insurance costs and insurers are dishonest. This is one more reason. I do not insure. I have not insured for many years.

We've insured for 15 years, maybe more. We have not been insuring for some time, there once was hail and we did not receive compensation.

Insurances can be regarded as relevant for contributing to farming systems' robustness against short-term shocks; however, it seems that creating an insurance-accepting environment requires extra effort (Popp & Nowack 2020). Moreover, government-supported insurance schemes are only one way of risk management. Chapter 2 discusses the separate processes of risk management in more detail, elaborating on the larger contribution of risk management towards farming systems' resilience.

4.4.2 Adaptability

The national implementations of the CAP's Pillar II in the form of RDPs and associated agri-environmental schemes were considered by many actors across the five case studies to have the potential to enable the adaptability of their respective farming system. Respondents referred to the possibility to apply for RDP project funding for innovations in production methods, collaborations or developments that increase the sustainability of the agricultural sector and rural areas. The agri-environmental schemes are seen to encourage a mid-term focus among farmers and other actors. Nevertheless, we found that the same respondents, especially in the Flemish, Dutch, Polish and UK cases, were also very critical of their RDP and agri-environmental programmes. A common reason provided by the respondents (both farmers and non-farmers) was that the RDPs' application procedures were perceived as complex and bureaucratic and participation often required significant investments of capital and time. In addition, actors' past experiences with RDP funding applications, such as refusals, pay-out delays and the lack of flexibility to adjust the measures to fit local contexts, form barriers to apply for RDP funding. For example, in the Flemish case, respondents perceived the RDP to have the capacity to support adaptability within the dairy farming system. However, the perceived administrative complexity related to the application and allocation discouraged actors to apply. Similarly, the Polish RDP were regarded as an important source of funding, but the application and allocation were perceived as bureaucratic, and the required multiyear business plan was regarded as hindering flexibility to deal with changing circumstances within the fruit and vegetable farming system. For similar reasons, respondents in the British and Dutch case studies had reservations about applying for RDP funding and questioned the functioning of the RDP. As one Dutch respondent said: 'In principle, the measures [RDP programmes] are not suitable for innovation. Because they take way too long. It goes too slow. This means that someone who has a good idea has to wait for two years before he or she can get the money'.

So, the adaptability-enabling potential of RDPs is constrained by bureaucratic procedures, which were often perceived as unnecessary. Whereas bureaucracy was not regarded as negative if it contributes to the functionality of the policy, the effective delivery of policies, such as the RDPs, can be obstructed if actors perceive the rules, regulations or administrative procedures as overly burdensome and redundant.

The CAP's direct payments were considered to have *constraining* effects on the adaptability of farming systems. In almost all farming system cases, except for the Spanish farming system, respondents witnessed that offering income support also has the effect of stifling competition and change. Especially in the Dutch and English cases, respondents argued that the guaranteed source of income provided through the CAP's direct payments allowed otherwise less profitable or dysfunctional farming business models to continue. The direct payments were therefore seen as discouraging adaptation of inferior business models or the search for innovative or alternative business opportunities. These findings resonate with the dominant orientation on competition in the Dutch and English cases. Similarly, whereas direct payments were regarded less important in the Polish case, respondents did indicate that the direct payments hindered adaptability because the payments constrained competition. In the Flemish case, several respondents had similar opinions about how the direct payments might constrain adaptability. However, some respondents argued that the direct payments provided extra financial means for investing in adapting farming practices.

Respondents in the Dutch, Spanish and English cases recommended changes in the system of direct payments to reduce their adaptability-constraining effects. For instance, many respondents from the Dutch and English farming systems suggested that they would favour a shift in the allocation of direct payments from area-based to performance-based. This would imply that farmers and landowners would receive payments for maintaining and providing public goods and services or for adopting farming practices that address environmental issues. Interestingly, such a shift in payments has been proposed to become part of the British agricultural policy after Brexit. The Eco-schemes proposed by the European Commission for the CAP post-2020 could play a similar role. Several Spanish respondents perceived advantages in coupling the direct payments to livestock instead of land, with conditionalities based on demographic, quality or production criteria. Such coupled payments would support sheep farmers to continue their extensive farming practices and offer incentives for providing ecosystem services.

Finally, Chapter 2 already examined the larger role that learning plays across the resilience capacities. Nevertheless, we researched the specific aspect of social learning within the farming systems and especially whether policies support this type of social learning. We found that actors across all farming systems agreed that actively engaging in social learning processes was essential to learn about policies and their implications, but also about, e.g., new innovative farming techniques, agri-environmental practices or business strategies. The respondents

commonly mentioned several ways, both public and privately supported, for attaining and exchanging knowledge, for instance,
attending information and training sessions, being an active member
of a farmers' association or farming cooperative, participating in networking events, and making use of advisory services. Whereas actors
across farming systems generally believed that access to information or
advisory services was widely available, several respondents in the
Flemish, Polish and English cases favoured more comprehensive and
independent advisory services with knowledge of the farming
system's context.

However, most social learning seems to take place within the
respondents' professional network. For instance, farmers mentioned
conversations with trusted peers, such as (financial) advisers, suppliers
or employees of farmers' associations to gain and exchange information. Also non-farming actors (e.g. policymakers, advisors, suppliers)
acknowledged the importance of their professional network.
Governmental actors said they interacted internally or across governmental levels, while advisers and suppliers brought up their access to
research departments. Less commonly mentioned by farmers were
interactions with civil servants, scientists or other farmers.
Interestingly, the non-farming actors regularly mentioned that they
learn about policy effects in practice, for instance, by participating in
the previously mentioned social learning events or as 'sparring partner'
to farmers. These findings suggest that interactions to share information and experiences about policies occur largely in networks within or
closely related to the farming systems. These closed networks should be
regarded as a context condition for policy interventions which might
complicate the introduction of new actors, knowledge or perspectives
from outside the farming system, potentially constraining in-depth
learning within the farming system.

4.4.3 Transformability

A recurrent experience among most of the respondents in all farming
systems was that the CAP and other policies hardly allowed them to
focus on the long term. A prominent reason provided by actors within
and surrounding the Flemish, Dutch, Polish and UK farming systems
was that policies were experienced as changing too often, thereby
constraining a certain stability and predictability that was seen as

necessary to engage in more long-term planning and investments. As stated by a UK farmer:

There are so many things happening, particularly at the moment, but all the time really, and so many bits of legislation that impact the farmer, that I wouldn't even come close to having a complete view. But there are all kinds of different directives coming in ... So, I would say I would be some way off having a good grasp of that.

Several respondents indicated that the inability to develop a longer-term focus within the farming system had negative consequences. For instance, in the Flemish case, actors indicated that the unpredictable policy environment discouraged potential new entrants to start a farming business. Dutch farmers explained, e.g., that policies that were experienced as constantly changing limited their ability to deal with more long-term challenges, such as soil depletion. While transform-ability can be enabled by small but immediate in-depth changes, many farming system actors seemed to experience these changes as constrain-ing a long-term focus.

The CAP was perceived as a policy that predominately supports robustness. Therefore, policy initiatives to dismantle incentives to maintain the status quo were hardly identified. However, respondents in all five cases perceived several policy instruments to have detrimental effects on their farming systems' status quo. An often-mentioned example – mainly by farmers – were the changing regulations relating to plant protection products. Although reducing the use of plant protection products was considered as a necessary move away from the status quo by some (e.g. environmental NGOs), the arable and fruit and vegetable farmers in our case studies experienced these policy changes largely as hindering their ability to deal with pests and plant diseases. Plant protection products were perceived as being withdrawn too quickly without providing alternatives, which raised concerns whether farmers could maintain and increase the quality and quantity of their crops. Similarly, legislation on manure and fertilisers are introduced to reduce nitrate pollution and improve surface and ground water quality, forcing changes to current farming practices to improve the environment in the long term. However, several Dutch respondents argued that legislation on fertiliser use was constraining farmers' abil-ity to deal with long-term loss of soil quality, while intensive farming practices continue to put pressure on the region's soils. Furthermore, while dairy farmers in the Flemish case perceived the legislation as necessary for improving environmental quality and reducing misconduct, they felt forced to implement income-reducing measures (e.g. fertiliser-free buffer strips) or invest in new infrastructure (e.g. manure storage facilities). These findings suggest that the manure and fertiliser regulations often conflict with the farmers' daily practices and their idea of 'good farming'. While the regulations incentivised limited change, they were not successful in winning farmers' support for broader change. Overall, changes to the status quo were hardly experienced as enabling transformability. Farming system actors rather perceived them as demanding, constraining or threatening their regular farming activities and business profitability. However, it is precisely these associations with change – being demanding and challenging regular routines – that would indicate that change was transformative.

4.5 Reflections and Conclusion

Whilst the interest in the potential of public policies for improving the resilience of farming and food systems is growing among academics and policymakers, systematic understanding of how public policies affect the resilience of these systems is still limited. This chapter therefore addressed the question of whether and how farming system actors in five case studies experience the effects of the CAP and relevant adjacent policies on the resilience of their respective farming systems.

First, we found that actors generally perceived the CAP and adjacent policies as affecting the resilience capacities of their respective farming system in uneven ways. Broadly speaking, the actors experienced these policies as mostly supportive for the robustness of their farming systems. They expected the CAP's area-based direct payments to provide income support as a financial buffer against shocks. However, the actors also felt that the CAP did not effectively support the adaptability of their farming systems. Many measures in the RDPs, while recognised as aiming to enable adaptability, were seen as ineffective or even constraining due to bureaucracy. The transformability of farming systems was seen as constrained by the CAP since a long-term focus was not supported. At the same time, interventions that require change (e.g. environmental regulations) were perceived as threatening resilience. These results confirm the previous top-down research that found that the CAP's support for the three resilience capacities is largely skewed towards robustness (Feindt *et al.* 2018). To enable the resilience of Europe's farming systems in a more comprehensive way, the CAP and its national implementations would need to rebalance the budget and ensure that the overall policy design does not discourage or hinder adaptability and transformability. In contrast, the EC's proposals for the CAP post-2020 continue their focus on income transfer, which enhances robustness for unprofitable farming systems but discourages adaptation or transformation.

Second, our comparison revealed that the perceived resilience effects of public policies depend systematically on specific farming system characteristics. The findings make clear that the CAP's support for robustness was mostly attributed to the area-based direct payments which were seen as providing buffer resources. Consequently, robustness is strongly supported for land-intensive farming systems (arable farming and grasslands), but not for those who require relatively little land (e.g. poultry production, horticulture or perennials). Moreover, the robustness-enhancing effect is mediated through access to land and land ownership, as the Spanish case with its declining extensive sheep grazing system demonstrates. This case also shows that decoupled direct payments do not support the continuation of extensive grazing systems where cheaper methods are available to meet the eligibility requirements. In a broader perspective, the long-term resilience of arable farming and horticultural systems would be better served if the CAP and adjacent policies enabled adaptation to climate change and other environmental challenges (Table 4.2). Whereas the RDPs could serve this purpose, EU legislators and Member States need to identify and reduce bottlenecks and barriers within the RDPs that stand in the way of effective implementation. Altogether, to determine the effectiveness as well as the desirability of certain policy instruments, it is essential to consider how the policy mechanisms and their effects are influenced by each farming system and its enabling or constraining environment. Enabling the EU's farming systems to become more resilient would therefore require a mix of instruments that can be tailored to fit their divergent resilience needs. In this respect, the Member States should use the proposed national strategic plans to implement the CAP with flexible and context-tailored policy designs that strengthen all resilience capacities of their farming systems. For instance, Member States could design their Eco-schemes as a performance-based payment scheme that incentivises and remunerates farmers for implementing (sets of) agri-environmental or climate measures. If national governments define clear guidelines that reflect ambitious national and EU objectives regarding, e.g., climate change, natural resource quality or protection of biodiversity, suitable Eco-scheme measures can be collaboratively identified by regional public and private actors that fit both with the regional context and the overarching objectives and enhance farming systems' long-term resilience.

Finally, the qualitative nature of our bottom-up approach requires that we critically reflect on how actors seem to understand resilience and appropriate the concept. For instance, we found that farming system actors seemed to prefer a robustness-oriented approach for enabling resilience, which partly resonates with established narratives that often justify the CAP's income support and the special policy treatment for agriculture as an exceptional sector (Daugbjerg & Feindt 2017). In contrast, policy instruments that steer towards adjustments or even change are often met with scepticism about their implementation or resilience-enabling effects (e.g. the RDPs or environmental regulations). Such bias towards robustness possibly exposes actors' limited engagement with the idea of adaptability and transformability as being integral to resilience and might very well explain which policy effects are perceived as resilience-enabling and which not. However, further research would be needed to analyse how this bias might vary across different farming methods within the systems (e.g. conventional versus organic farming, agroforestry). Actors' reluctance to embrace adaptation or transformation might further be understood by reflecting on the presence of lock-in mechanisms within farming systems that reinforce established practices. Moreover, we found that actors within our farming system cases had relatively closed networks, mostly consisting of other farming system actors, which might partly explain the relatively similar policy experiences and views on the resilience concept. Clearly, whereas distinguishing between robustness, adaptability and transformability allowed us to systematically analyse actors' experiences with policy effects, it should not be taken for granted that actors understand resilience in a similar way. Actors might only partially adopt or mix elements of the resilience capacities to understand the resilience of farming systems, or they might assume that resilience capacities are generally closely bound together (Chapter 2). Hence, we see the need for further research that explores the resilience-related perspectives owned by actors. Such a follow-up research could entail a frame analysis that focuses on identifying and studying the processes in and through which specific actors perceive and give meaning to resilience and which corresponding policies are preferred for enabling resilience and for what reasons.

References

Ashkenazy, A., Chebach, T. C., Knickel, K., Peter, S., Horowitz, B. & Offenbach, R. 2017. 'Operationalising resilience in farms and rural regions – Findings from fourteen case studies'. *Journal of Rural Studies* 59: 211–221.

Béné, C., Mehta, L., McGranahan, G., Cannon, T., Gupte, J. & Tanner, T. 2016. 'Resilience as a policy narrative: potentials and limits in the context of urban planning'. *Climate and Development* 29(1): 1–18.

Berman, P. 1978. 'The study of macro- and micro-implementation'. *Public Policy* 26(2): 157–184.

Bouma, J., Koetse, M. & Bandsma, J. 2020. 'Natuurinclusieve landbouw: wat beweegt boeren? Het effect van financiële prikkels en gedragsfactoren op de investeringsbereidheid van agrariërs'. PBL (Planbureau voor de Leefomgeving), The Hague.

Brink, van den, M. A., Meijerink, S. V., Termeer, C. J. A. M. & Gupta, J. 2013. 'Climate-proof planning for flood-prone areas: assessing the adaptive capacity of planning institutions in the Netherlands'. *Regional Environmental Change* 14(3): 981–955.

Buitenhuis, Y., Candel, J. J. L., Termeer, K. J. A. M. & Feindt, P. H. 2020. 'Does the Common Agricultural Policy enhance farming systems' resilience? Applying the Resilience Assessment Tool (ResAT) to a farming system case study in the Netherlands'. *Journal of Rural Studies* 80: 314–327.

Civita, N. M. 2015. 'Resilience: The food policy imperative for a volatile future'. *Environmental Law Reporter* 45(7): 10663.

Dąbrowski, M. 2013. 'EU Cohesion Policy, horizontal partnership and the patterns of sub-national governance: Insights from Central and Eastern Europe'. *European Urban and Regional Studies* 21(4): 364–383.

Daugbjerg, C. & Feindt, P. H. 2017. 'Post-exceptionalism in public policy: Transforming food and agricultural policy'. *Journal of European Public Policy* 24(11): 1565–1584.

EC (European Commission). 2018. 'EU budget: The Common Agricultural Policy beyond 2020'. Press release, 1 June 2018. https://ec.europa.eu/com mission/presscorner/detail/en/IP_18_3985. Accessed 11 March 2020.

2020. 'Reinforcing Europe's resilience: Halting biodiversity loss and building a healthy and sustainable food system'. Press release, 20 May 2020.

https://ec.europa.eu/commission/presscorner/detail/en/ip_20_884. Accessed 2 February 2021.

Fan, S., Pandya-Lorch, R. & Yosef, S. (eds.). 2014. *Resilience for food and nutrition security*. Washington, DC: IFPRI (International Food Policy Research Institute).

Feindt, P. H., Termeer, K., Candel, J., *et al.* 2018. 'D4.2: Assessing how policies enable or constrain the resilience of farming systems in the European Union: Case study results'. Sustainable and Resilient EU Farming Systems (SURE-Farm) project report. https://surefarmproject.eu/wordpress/wp-content/uploads/2019/05/SURE-Farm-D-4.2-Resilience-Assessment-Case-Studies-RP1.pdf

Feindt, P. H., Proestou, M. & Daedlow, K. 2020. 'Resilience and policy design in the emerging bioeconomy – The RPD framework and the changing role of energy crop systems in Germany'. *Journal of Environmental Policy & Planning* 22(5): 636–652.

Gatto, A. & Drago, C. 2020. 'A taxonomy of energy resilience'. *Energy Policy* 136: 111007.

Ge, L., Anten, N. P. R., van Dixhoorn, I., *et al.* 2016. 'Why we need resilience thinking to meet societal challenges in bio-based production systems'. *Current Opinion in Environmental Sustainability* 23: 17–27.

Hattke, F., Hensel, D. & Kalucza, J. 2019. 'Emotional responses to bureaucratic red tape'. *Public Administration Review* 80(1): 53–63.

Hemerijck, A. 2003. 'Vier kernvragen van beleid'. *Beleid en Maatschappij* 30(1): 3–19.

Howlett, M. 2018. 'The criteria for effective policy design: character and context in policy instrument choice'. *Journal of Asian Public Policy* 11 (3): 245–266.

    2019. *Designing public policies: Principles and instruments*, 2nd ed. Abingdon/New York: Routledge.

Howlett, M. & Rayner, J. 2007. 'Design principles for policy mixes: cohesion and coherence in "New Governance Arrangements"'. *Policy and Society* 26(4): 1–18.

Huttunen, S. 2015. 'Farming practices and experienced policy coherence in agri-environmental policies: the case of land clearing in Finland'. *Journal of Environmental Policy & Planning* 17(5): 573–592.

Huttunen, S., Kivimaa, P. & Virkamäki, V. 2014. 'The need for policy coherence to trigger a transition to biogas production'. *Environmental Innovations and Societal Transitions* 12: 14–30.

Karpouzoglou, T., Dewulf, A. & Clark, J. 2016. 'Advancing adaptive governance of social-ecological systems through theoretical multiplicity'. *Environmental Science & Policy* 57: 1–9.

Lauwere, de, C., Bock, B., Broekhuizen, van, R., *et al.* 2016. 'Agrarische ondernemers over de mestwetgeving: beleving van het mestbeleid: draagvlak, knelpunten en oplossingen'. Wageningen Economic Research Rapport No. 2016-103. Wageningen Economic Research.

Matland, R. E. 1995. 'Synthesizing the implementation literature: the Ambiguity-Conflict Model of policy implementation'. *Journal of Public Administration Research and Theory* 5(2): 145–174.

Meuwissen, M. P. M., Mey, de, Y. & Asseldonk, van, M. 2018. 'Prospects for agricultural insurance in Europe'. *Agricultural Finance Review* 78 (2): 174–182.

Meuwissen, M. P. M., Feindt, P. H., Spiegel, A., *et al.* 2019. 'A framework to assess the resilience of farming systems'. *Agricultural Systems* 176: 102656.

Nilsen, P., Ståhl, C., Roback, K. & Cairney, P. 2013. 'Never the twain shall meet? – A comparison of implementation science and policy implementation research'. *Implementation Science* 8: 63.

Popp, T. R. & Nowack. W. 2020. 'Resilience through the financialisation of risks? The case of a dairy system in Northwest Germany'. *Sustainability* 12(15): 6262.

Sabatier, P. A. 1986. 'Top-down and bottom-up approaches to implementation research: a critical analysis and suggested synthesis'. *Journal of Public Policy* 6(1): 21–48.

Smith, J. A., Flowers, P. & Larkin, A. 2009. *Interpretative phenomenological analysis: Theory, method and research.* London: Sage.

SURE-Farm. 2020. 'Policy brief with a critical analysis of how current policies constrain/enable resilient European agriculture and suggestions for improvements, including recommendations for the CAP post-2020 reform'. August 2020. www.surefarmproject.eu/wordpress/wp-content/uploads/2020/08/D4.6_Policy-Brief-on-the-CAP-post-2020.pdf

Swanson, D., Barg, S., Tyler, S., *et al.* 2009. 'Seven guidelines for policy-making in an uncertain world'. In D. Swanson & S. Bhadwal (eds.). *Creating adaptive policies: A guide for policy-making in an uncertain world*, pp. 12–24. Newbury Park: Sage.

Termeer, C. J. A. M., Breeman, G., Geerling-Eiff, F. A., Berkmortel, van den, N., Schaick, G. J. & Hubeek, F. B. 2007. 'Omgaan met mest; betekenisgeving aan landbouw, milieu en mestregelgeving'. LEI Rapport 3.07.07. LEI (Landbouw Economisch Instituut), Den Haag.

Wąs, A. & Kobus, P. 2018. 'Factors determining the crop insurance level in Poland taking into account the level of farm subsidising'. In M. Wigier & A. Kowalski (eds.). *The Common Agricultural Policy of the European Union – the present and the future EU Member States point of view*, 125–146. DOI: 10.30858/pw/9788376587431.11

5 Constrained Sustainability and Resilience of Agricultural Practices from Multiple Lock-In Factors and Possible Pathways to Tackle Them

An Assessment of Three European Farming Systems

JASMINE E. BLACK, PAUL COURTNEY, DAMIAN MAYE, JULIE URQUHART, MAURO VIGANI, WIM PAAS, SAVERIO SENNI, DANIELE BERTOLOZZI-CAREDIO AND PYTRIK REIDSMA

5.1 Introduction

Following the Second World War, agricultural production for food security was prioritised, and the use of chemicals in agriculture started to override previous agricultural practices dominated by crop rotation, diversification and traditional knowledge (Drinkwater & Snapp, 2007; Savary, 2014; Tilman et al., 2001). As an unintended consequence, nitrogen, phosphorus and pesticides have caused water-body pollution, decreased biodiversity and contributed to climate change (Geiger et al., 2010; Hoang & Alauddin, 2010). The focus is now geared towards the need for more environmentally sustainable practices, to sustain and regenerate natural resources and the health benefits for the resilience of nature and people (Black et al., 2021, UNU-IAS & IGES, 2018). Whilst other factors such as economics are of importance for resilience, the environment is also intrinsic to it through resources such as healthy soil. Despite European policies aimed at enhancing environmental sustainability, such as agri-environment schemes, farmers have struggled to put more environmentally sustainable practices in place.

Since the rise of chemical and industrial agriculture, a spectrum of farming systems and related practices have emerged, from which Therond et al. (2017) have usefully created a contextual framework. It distinguishes three biotechnical categories: 'chemical input-based', 'biological-input based' and 'biodiversity input-based'. The first includes only a few crops or a monoculture to which external chemical inputs are usually applied. Farmers try to make input use as efficient as possible, whilst adding other elements to the land only through regulatory bodies imposing this upon them. This often leads to low environmental sustainability, although efficient use may limit environmental impacts (Jägermeyr et al., 2015; Mueller et al., 2012). The second system also uses monocultures, or short crop rotations, and enforced landscape elements; however, as much as possible it incorporates biologically based inputs such as manure. The final 'biodiversity-based' system has a diversified crop sequence, voluntary landscape elements for wildlife, integration of livestock for fertiliser and aims to reduce external inputs (Therond et al., 2017). This system is often considered to have greater environmental sustainability, although in many conventional systems inputs need to be sufficient to avoid degradation (Aarts, 2016; Rosset & Altieri, 1997). Encompassing these farm types, Therond et al. describe the socio-economic systems that may surround them. 'Global commodity-based systems' aim to increase production and efficiency using standardised processes, leading to global competition, with power usually centred within global corporations. 'Circular economies' aim to reduce waste with closed resource loops, therefore giving farmers more control and autonomy. 'Alternative food systems' aim to create locally specialised values-based products using short supply chains. Again, this gives farmers more autonomy, whilst supporting biodiversity. 'Integrated landscape approaches' span local–regional scales and require cooperation between landowners, who work together to develop diverse, multi-functional landscapes spanning the food–non-food–natural resource nexus. There is variability within these categories, meaning that different farming systems may be at different positions within, for example, 'chemical input-based', as we explore through our case studies in the chapter.

The environment underlies resource availability, the processing of societal waste (such as CO_2 and water purification) and therefore a suitable climate to grow in, which in turn affects the economy and societal issues. Systems with low environmental sustainability lack or undermine resilience in the long term, and could be vulnerable to collapse (Meuwissen et al., 2019). This is especially the case when anthropogenic inputs put pressure on resilience (Rist et al., 2014) and environmental feedback signals are subdued through long-distance producer–consumer connections (Rist et al., 2014; Sundkvist et al., 2005). It is therefore important to improve the resilience of farming systems to ensure the provision of both public and private goods in the face of multi-faceted and increasingly complex pressures, through their robustness, adaptability and transformability (Meuwissen et al., 2019).

In order to improve farming system resilience across Europe, the predominant chemical-based agriculture within the global commodity system needs to readdress its reliance on both chemicals and global trade (Willett et al., 2019). Whilst global trade is important for businesses, diverse diets and inter-country relationships, an overreliance on it can be economically crippling when other countries are able to produce and sell for less money, pushing profits down. Better utilising and regenerating local resources whilst creating stronger links to local and regional socio-economic systems will establish greater balance and diversity in the system, enhancing sustainability and resilience (Duru et al., 2015; Willett et al., 2019). In 2020, the EU released its 'Farm to Fork Strategy', the first to encompass the whole food system (European Union, 2020). In order to achieve its goals, the inadequacies of previous agri-environment schemes and the barriers to adopting more environmentally sustainable production will need to be addressed (Arnott et al., 2019).

The three systems described in Therond et al. (2017) each constitute 'socio-technical regimes' and these regimes have structural rules that guide, in this case, farmers' perceptions and actions, otherwise known as social and cultural lock-ins (Burton and Farstad, 2020). The chemical-based system, for example, has created a 'lock-in', which means it is perceived as unworthwhile by farmers to change current practices that may be more environmentally sustainable (Plumecocq et al., 2018). A range of studies on lock-in have shown that it is complex and occurs across multiple farming sectors. For example, institutional lock-in through policies and selective agronomic advice incentivising yield; cultural lock-in through historic social events related to agricultural products and social lock-in through the need for family farm continuity (Beudou et al., 2017; Glover, 2014; Vanloqueren & Baret, 2008; Weis, 2008). Burton and Farstad (2020) stress that lock-in does not mean agricultural systems are unchanging, but that change is geared towards creating stability for the current system, as opposed to challenging it.

5.2 Aim of This Chapter

While other chapters focus more upon economic and production factors and their contribution to resilience, this chapter focuses on environmental sustainability and its inherent importance to resilience. Using Therond *et al.*'s farming system classification framework and the theory of lock-in in agricultural systems, we assess the environmental sustainability and therefore resilience of three case studies within Europe. We demonstrate how the challenges they face lock them in to their current systems, despite EU policies geared towards agri-environment schemes. With multi-stakeholder input, we then show how tackling these lock-in factors can create more sustainable and resilient systems.

5.3 Research Methods

We use three case studies (CS), namely (i) extensive ovine breeding in Huesca (Spain), (ii) hazelnut production in Lazio (Italy) and (iii) arable farming in the East of England (UK).[1] These three CS cover livestock, perennial and arable farming sectors, which are experiencing a heterogeneous range of challenges to resilience. In each CS, researchers in their respective countries identified the baseline information about the current farming systems through interviews and grey literature. Using this baseline information to assess against Therond et al.'s (2017) framework on farming system model diversities, we classify the current CS farming systems in order to understand the environmental sustainability and resilience of each.

The information used to outline the challenges and potential future systems to tackle these comes from workshops held as part of the SURE-Farm project across the three CS (Paas et al., 2019, 2020; Reidsma et al., 2020a). These workshops consisted of different types of stakeholders (researchers, farmers, policy makers and NGOs) of the farming system in the CS regions. The workshops identified multi-stakeholder perspectives and knowledge on the current challenges faced in each CS as well as creating strategies for alternative systems with improved sustainability and resilience (Reidsma et al., 2020a).

---

[1] The reader is referred to Chapters 9, 11 and 16, which specifically describe in detail the case studies of Spain, Italy and the UK, respectively.

From the challenges, the authors of this chapter have identified how they create lock-in conditions across multiple factors (e.g. social, institutional, economic and cultural) for farmers and other actors in each CS. For example, social trends towards eating less lamb have impacted the Spanish CS, lowering profits and pushing some farmers towards stabled intensive methods or an abandonment of farming, and, therefore, also having potential unintended environmental consequences. The future scenarios included what the multi-stakeholder's thought could be possible in a scenario where challenges (and therefore lock-in conditions) were actively tackled.

5.4 Placing Current Systems within a Biotechnical and Socio-economic Framework

Here, each CS is summarised and placed within Therond et al.'s spectrum of possible biotechnical and socio-economic systems (see Figure 5.1).

Extensive ovine breeding in Huesca, Spain – biological input-based, global commodity system:
The Spanish CS consists of extensive ovine breeding oriented to lamb production and is located in the Province of Huesca, Aragón. Most of the agricultural practices take place in the mountain foothills and on the lower plains, with traditional environmentally sustainable transhumance practices, when herds do not exceed the natural resources (Navarro, 1992). Grazing preserves the grasslands, which may otherwise undergo encroachment from shrubs and trees, lowering biodiversity (Bernués et al., 2005; Peco et al., 2017). Livestock are largely fed on grasslands; however, some straw feed is bought in externally, more so in lowland areas where less land is available. The ovine sector was a strong economic contributor to the region; however, its importance has declined heavily in the last twenty years, moving to intensive stabled or semi-stabled rearing (Fau, 2016). Whilst the main markets have traditionally been local (regional and national), changing preferences towards meats with a milder taste, which are easier to cook and cheaper (Mandolesi et al., 2020) mean that the products are increasingly supplied into the globalised market system, particularly to Islamic countries (Alcalde et al., 2013; MAPA, 2019). To cope with the decreasing popularity of sheep meat, new sales initiatives have been established such as the Protected Geographical Indication (PGI) label,

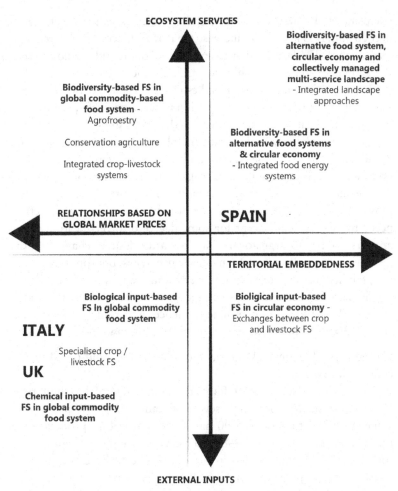

Figure 5.1 Position of the three European CS agricultural systems on Therond et al.'s biotechnical and socio-economic framework
(adapted from Therond et al., 2017).

'Ternasco de Aragon'. This label can include both outdoor, extensively reared lamb and stabled lamb (Sans et al., 1999), and is used by ~30 per cent of the farms in the CS region (Spiegel et al., 2019). Typically, family-based small (<100 sheep), medium (100–499 sheep) and large (>500 sheep) farms of equal representation exist (Aragon.es, 2019). Performance of economic, social and environmental system functions is perceived to be low by stakeholders in the CS

(Reidsma et al., 2020b). This perception indicates that more change is needed at the CS in order to increase the performance of the system and its resilience. The farms' reliance on financial public aids could enhance the system's robustness (while constraining the other capacities), but the excessive dependence on subsidies poses a challenge for robustness in the future. Further, the intensification process includes specialization and industrialization, which can strengthen robustness but somewhat constrain adaptability and transformability (see also Hoekstra et al., 2018). Innovations in the pasture and flock management and feeding systems, as well as new farmers' organizations to improve sales and knowledge exchange, may promote the system's adaptability. However, these processes are rather recent, and their overall effect needs to be assessed. Except for some degree of diversification, there appears to be no transformability towards desired change in the farming system. In general, the resilience relies on robustness and adaptability that, in turn, appear weak and relate largely to the economic performance and less so to the social or environmental, which creates a bias and may undermine resilience. According to Meuwissen et al.'s (2019) framework, resilience is therefore low.

Hazelnut production in Viterbo, Italy – chemical input-based global commodity system:

In Viterbo province, central Italy, the cultivation of hazelnut trees (*Corylus avellana*) goes back several decades. In 2018 production reached 46,200 tons on 23,000 ha (ISTAT). Hazelnut production in the area values on average 70–80 million €/year, and is a major income source. Specialization started in the 1960s due to hazelnuts being a convenient cropping system here. Previously, hazelnuts used to be cultivated alongside other species (e.g. olives, vines, chestnuts). In the last decades, increased demand from the confectionary industry has led to price growth, specialisation and expansion (Bijttebier et al., 2018). The landscape has gone through a profound change, with large parts of the farming system now dominated by hazelnut monocultures. Farm sizes are predominantly small (<10 ha) and based mostly on family labour (Bijttebier et al., 2018). Chemicals such as pesticides are widely used, with organic production limited as it is less profitable (Coppola et al., 2020). Farmers maintain that chemical use is not particularly high in this farming system. Despite this, local opposition (e.g. civil society and environmental groups), have voiced concerns to municipal authorities. This has had limited success, with restrictions only on some chemicals close to residential areas, partly because legal chemicals cannot be prohibited by municipalities. Although chemicals are used, some hazelnut farmers use a Designation of Origin (PDO) label. However, as most farms send hazelnuts to large multinational corporations for processing, most do not use the PDO label with which local processing is required. Food production and economic viability is perceived to be good, while the level of maintenance of natural resources is perceived to be low to moderate according to farming system stakeholders (Reidsma et al., 2020b). As in the previous CS, a level of robustness is seen through the ability of the farming system to withstand changes described over the last several decades, whilst adaptability has further been demonstrated through intensifying hazelnut production. Transformability of this farming system has not been evidenced. However, whilst the current economic resilience may be good, environmental resilience is low and may therefore undermine longer-term overall resilience (economic, environmental and social) through resource depletion, such as underground water. A long-term view of economic resilience is usually considered by farmers with perennial crops such as trees, as they are productive for thirty years or more. Therefore, environmental resilience is an important consideration, especially when these crops are less 'flexible' in making changes because of their life span and initially high set-up costs for such systems. The economic resilience also depends upon the changing pressure of global markets and is uncertain. This uncertainty stems from the disconnect between farmers and multinational corporations, who dictate prices makes future economic resilience a challenge.

Arable production in East Anglia, UK – chemical input-based global commodity system:
The case study of the UK is in the East of England where intensive arable agriculture using chemicals and short crop rotations prevail on fertile soils, which results in high production capacity (Bijttebier et al., 2018). This region is responsible for one third of the country's cereal production, consisting mainly of wheat and barley. The farms are mostly large-scale family or corporate; in the last ten years the size of the farms grew considerably whilst their numbers decreased by more than 40 per cent, yet farmland surface area remained the same (Bijttebier et al., 2018). Product prices are influenced by globalised food systems (Reidsma et al., 2020a; Vigani et al., 2020). A small number of farmers use livestock for manure, reduced ploughing and

grow cover crops. This is because environmental awareness of agricultural impacts and public goods develops alongside increased chemical regulations. Performance levels of economic, environmental and social system functions – which indicate system sustainability – are perceived by stakeholders to be moderate, suggesting that improvement is indeed required (Reidsma et al., 2020b). A level of robustness is apparent from the ability of the farming system to withstand pressures of product prices from the global market without collapse; however, the amalgamation of farms (increased farm size) suggests that some have collapsed. Robustness is therefore variable across farms, but likely low. It is evident from some of the remaining farms that they have been able to adapt to resource and regulatory pressures by, for example, incorporating cover crops and livestock. These are incremental changes, however, and again transformation of the system is not apparent in this CS. As stakeholders allude to, greater resilience needs to be developed across the environmental, social and economic functions of the farming systems.

5.4.1 Analysis

Two of the CS (Italy and the UK) reside in the bottom-left corner of the framework, highlighting intensive practices and the global market influence on them. Spain, however, sits in the top right corner (biodiversity-based, territorially embedded food system), but is being pulled towards the bottom left (biologically based, global commodity food system) by current pressures, hence it is near the intersection of these two different systems. Despite Italy and the UK being in the same category, there are nuances between them which set them apart within the category itself. In the UK, whilst there are some farmers starting to use biologically based inputs, the overall system is dominated by chemical inputs. Italy differs in that whilst chemicals are used, the levels of use are not high and the perennial crops mean that there is more biological input, e.g. leaf litter, aiding carbon sequestration as well as nutrient input (Fireman, 2019). The CS in Spain is based on largely local and biological inputs and contributes to biodiversity through extensive grazing; however, recent trends are pulling local sales towards international markets and their resulting influence, such as using more intensive methods like stabling. It is therefore apparent that all three systems require substantial changes to tackle their challenges and move towards greater environmental sustainability; out of the bottom-left corner to the top-right corner of Figure 5.1. The challenges are outlined next, from which we illustrate how they are 'locked-in' to their current practices.

5.5 Challenges and Lock-Ins to Current Agricultural Systems

The three CS each have a range of challenges associated with low environmental sustainability. In Table 5.1, these challenges and their associated lock-in factors are presented. In the following section, these challenges and potential solutions are discussed.

Economic lock-ins are particularly complex, evidenced by apparent contradictions between the CS countries in the table (i.e. both low and high profitability can cause poor environmental sustainability, affecting resilience) and are therefore worthy of greater explanation here. In Spain the decreasing lamb consumption within the region and nationally – where most of the product is sold – is a key lock-in factor as it decreases profits and economic viability. With the Spanish CS region now moving into the global market for income, it has had to intensify production through stabling sheep, due to increasing competition both nationally and internationally, therefore reducing environmental sustainability and resilience. Similarly, the UK CS farmers are economically restricted through the global market, again creating competition that drives arable crop prices down, resulting in intensification of crop production. Both these CS are therefore constrained by low profitability, restricting their ability to undertake environmentally sustainable production options. In Italy, economic stability is currently provided by selling high-quality hazelnuts into the global market, as potential competition from other production regions, such as Turkey, has not yet caused an economic problem. However, interestingly, in opposition to the Spanish and UK CS, where low profits are constricting environmental efforts, the economic stability prevents farmers from considering more environmentally sustainable practices such as no chemical use/organic methods. This is because the quality of produce needed to sell into the global markets is associated with low pests and diseases – for which chemicals are used. These chemicals may bioaccumulate in the environment over time and cause problems to the surrounding ecosystem and health of the local population. Such economic lock-ins are, however, only part of the picture, as Table 5.1 demonstrates.

Table 5.1. *Challenges and lock-ins to the three CS systems*

		Economic	Social	Cultural	Institutional
Spain	Challenge	Decreasing demand for lamb meat; increasing feeding costs	Out-migration of people from rural areas due to poor perception of lifestyle quality; land abandonment	New consumers' preferences alongside social media causes the perception of meat to be distorted	Lack of government support to continue pastoral farming; poor access to pastures and information on the benefits of rural living
	Lock-in	Low profit creates an inability to invest in sustainable methods	Lack of labour and new farmers to progress the farming system and implement on-farm changes	Compounds economic lock-in through lack of sales and low profit margins	Using fewer pastures increases intensive practices, whilst poor support for continuation is compounded by economic and social challenges, creating lower capacity to progress sustainable practices
Italy	Challenge	International markets provide profit and favour intensive production, as opposed to local markets	Increasing need for high hazelnut quality; out-migration of people from rural areas	Growing opposition within civil society to the hazelnut monocultures and to the spread of new plantations in the area	Instability from CAP changes; poor knowledge exchange support to change practices; local R&D hazelnut-focused Local Action Group (LAG) supports current practices

Lock-in	Economies of scale, profits and favourable land values prevent the search for alternatives	Strong interdependencies between different FS actors creates difficulty in changing practices	Local annual cultural events create a feeling of identity with hazelnuts among the population	Instability and low knowledge make it difficult to change practices; R&D focused on single crop rather than diversity; LAG promotes system stability
UK Challenge	Global price competition; lack of economic support to change practices; risk of post-Brexit subsidy loss	Out-migration of people from rural areas	Farmers' perception of fields looking 'neat'; fear of failure in alternative practices; growing public environmental awareness	Lack of advice on sustainable practices or innovation; lack of support through transitions; uncertainty of Brexit; short-term tenancies; landowners hold power in management decisions
Lock-in	Decreasing prices and profit margins cause further intensification	Lack of labour and new farmers to progress the farming system	Prevents transition to alternative practices; inadvertent public pressure could prevent integrating livestock	Prevents farmers from transitioning to or learning about more sustainable and resilient farming practices

All challenges are compounded by the lack of overarching government support regarding financial aid in transitioning practices, providing independent and coherent advice, accessing knowledge exchange and encouraging future generations to farm. This is despite EU and national government agri-environment schemes, which have failed to give such holistic support (Arnott et al., 2019). In addition to these challenges, the environment externally influences the CS through increased droughts, wild fauna attacks and pathogens (Reidsma et al., 2020a).

As the individual lock-ins compound each other, it is apparent that they collectively hold, or pull, the CS to the lower-left corner of Therond et al.'s diagram (specialised crops or livestock in a global commodity food system). Therefore, they need to be addressed collectively, which necessitates substantial changes and thus positive transformation to the upper-right corner of Therond et al.'s diagram (biodiversity-based, circular landscape-scale food systems).

There are some signs of the lock-ins beginning to be broken open in each CS, however, which are described in the following section. Strategies to better develop and add to these break through mechanisms, as discussed in multi-stakeholder workshops, are also discussed below.

5.5.1 Towards More Environmentally Sustainable Systems

Future systems, which were envisioned in stakeholder workshops, in order to tackle these challenges are equally unique, but also have some common themes. In Spain and Italy, where public environmental awareness is perceived to give strong feedback signals to farming systems, valorising environmentally sustainable products and practices for local markets and consumers through awareness raising and advertising is likely to be central to any strategy. Indeed, Kneafsey et al. (2013) set out the importance of short supply chains in Europe towards greater social and environmental impacts and the need for them to be better supported by public policy. In Spain, particular attention is needed to address the poor public understanding of ecosystem diversity and value of extensive sheep farming. Alongside access to land and wild fauna attacks, this has added to farmers in the CS region feeling that the main viable option is to become more intensive in production and take on global market opportunities. Stakeholders envision that increasing the publics' knowledge and understanding of the intricacies of the system will help provide support to farmers, making their local and regional markets more robust and adaptable, whilst diversifying markets. Such a strategy begins to break a developing lock-in: the movement towards a reliance on global markets (and therefore the pull towards the lower left corner of Therond et al.'s diagram). This will need investment and support from government in educating, creating routes to market and training. The PGI label given to some lamb meat may also help to improve consumers' perceptions of it. Along with the new CAP reform post-2020, there is also room for delivering tailored support for the environmental benefits provided by extensive sheep farms, mainly within the framing of the Eco-schemes.

In Italy, stakeholders suggest that local processing of hazelnuts and diversifying of monocultures will be an important element for a shift towards greater environmental sustainability. Likewise, local processing and direct selling could then increase employment and incomes while shorter supply chains will also positively impact the environment. Stakeholders also think that this may attract younger generations, who have a greater propensity to organic farming. Such actions are likely to have a positive impact upon the robustness and adaptability elements of resilience through diversifying away from one market avenue and having more participatory actors directly involved with the running of the system. As in Spain, this would begin to break some of the economical lock-in to the lower left of Therond et al.'s diagram. However, investment will be needed to develop local markets, processing facilities and potentially training depending upon skill levels. Governments therefore need to encourage hazelnut companies to invest some of their own profits into this, or provide funding itself. Van Ittersum et al. (2007) and a recent European survey (Kantar, 2020) showed that European consumers have an awareness of PGI (20 per cent of respondents) and PDO (14 per cent of respondents) labels and place importance when buying produce upon high-quality (81 per cent of respondents) locally produced foods (87 per cent of respondents), including organic (56 per cent of respondents), of which awareness has generally increased since 2017. This appreciation of labels and organic could potentially help create more market opportunities in these regions (Kneafsey et al., 2008). Due to consumers placing importance on these types of production, care and transparency will be needed in building consumer trust, as current agricultural practices that are permitted within these labels include indoor rearing and chemical use. Public mistrust and confusion could be alleviated by redefining the production practices to align with environmentally sustainable methods, such as organic and lamb feed sourced only from local hay, for example.

In the UK, workshop stakeholders agreed that greater institutional support is needed through government payments such as public money for public goods (Bateman & Balmford, 2018; Food Farming and Countryside Commission, 2019). This may be realised through the new Environment Land Management Scheme (ELMS). ELMS has, to date, indicated three levels of agricultural management: farm-scale, farm clusters and a wider landscape scale across England. Bringing together farmers and landowners in groups, whilst working with existing groups, aims to manage the landscape more holistically. However, at the time of writing, this is subject to being jeopardised by international free trade agreements allowing imports of cheaper produce grown to lower environmental sustainability standards (DEFRA, 2020; Vigani et al., 2020). These changes to agricultural policy, which are currently under planning, indicate that ways to address lock-ins are being considered. However, careful consideration and comparison to other policies such as trade, which may slow or reverse positive progress, is required. Stakeholders further discussed that a 'volatility payment' may also be needed to support farmers through a transition period where yields may suffer due to changing soil conditions (Vigani et al., 2020). Farmers who are already tackling lock-ins to chemical use through green manures and cover crops, for example, could be better supported and connected for knowledge transfer, therefore spreading these practices. Improving knowledge exchange and transition support could further aid change through implementing practices which actively encourage biodiversity and regeneration of natural resources. Given the unique context of tenure in UK agriculture, stakeholders considered that well mediated, transparent three-way conversations between tenants, land owners and government may be needed to address challenges of land owners making unsustainable management decisions (Vigani et al., 2020).

Alongside these socio-economic changes, stakeholders have voiced the need for technology to be better developed. In Spain, this takes the form of geo-location and surveillance of sheep and wild fauna, and in Italy through processing plants, efficient irrigation and auto-propelled harvesting machines (Reidsma et al., 2020a). Brauman et al. (2013) have demonstrated how gains in agricultural efficiency, whilst reducing waste and changing diets, can benefit the environment. Such practices can enhance resilience through ensuring a more robust (plentiful or regenerative) supply of natural resources. In Italy, there is already a rather high technological level, which contributes to its competition on the global markets. However, the prospect of further developing such technologies is thought to be attractive to the younger generation, who are able to improve technical and organizational innovation in the sector. In the UK, farming stakeholders envision having a greater ability to feed into technological innovation through partnerships with researchers and industry. For instance, farmer-led innovation is gaining traction, and their participation in new technology can lead to further innovation and more effective use of equipment or practices (Ingram, 2010; Reed et al., 2017). Engaging farmers with advisory services and building trust can lead to greater learning and a willingness to undertake more environmental practices (Mills et al., 2017). Such technology could also aid environmental sustainability, through water conservation and a more efficient use of fertilisers (Brauman et al., 2013; Smith et al., 2014; Tilman et al., 2011). Farmer-led technology allows for greater resilience through empowering the end-user to create connections with a range of stakeholders and plan what technology would increase their farm robustness and adaptability across environmental, social and economic fora. However, while infrastructure for innovation is needed for transformability, strategies implemented in the past (e.g. mechanization in Italy) were often seen as constraining transformability (Reidsma et al., 2020b). The type of technology is important, and path dependency needs to be avoided. Well-considered technological innovation could tackle economic and social lock-ins, where farmers need not be reliant on tech companies, and younger generations are attracted by positive opportunities to innovate.

In all three CS, stakeholders discussed the need for better facilitating cooperation amongst farmers and other actors to help foster knowledge exchange and sense of community (Reidsma et al., 2020a). Such cooperation could engender greater resilience through increasing the knowledge of stakeholders and strengthening their networks for communication, thereby providing robustness across multiple actors and the ability to adapt by transferring knowledge. In Spain, increasing cooperation between farmers is opening up opportunities to align the traditional extensive sheep farming supply with the changing consumer preferences, by creating new high-quality lamb meat products and emphasising their value to ecology. Fostering cooperation can help tackle the institutional lock-in of poor knowledge exchange. As ideas and knowledge grow, such networks may also develop the capacity to transform the system if actors feel this is needed. In the UK, the creation of more farmer groups will help effectively reach isolated farmers and create a supportive base for knowledge exchange on alternative sustainable practices – whilst also tackling social lock-in issues, such as maintaining 'neat' fields. The base of existing groups and 'demonstration farms' which help farmers to address agricultural issues such as declining soil conditions can be built on and improved. In Italy stakeholders suggest that challenging farmer learning, knowledge exchange and financial aid through agri-environment schemes is likely to be important, which in turn has implications for the design and delivery of such schemes.

On a national and European scale, the strategies outlined by the stakeholders of each CS – if implemented well – could positively contribute towards the EU's 'Farm to Fork Strategy' and international Sustainable Development Goals. However, each strategy separately will not help substantially tackle the overall lock-in: the lock-ins feed into each other and therefore an individual strategy to address one will eventually be constrained by another. For example, fostering greater cooperation can break institutional lock-in by empowering farmers with knowledge to produce in more sustainable ways, but support is then needed economically to allow for the creation of new local market avenues. Separately, they can only make small, incremental changes to the system, which aids robustness and adaptability to an extent, but does not allow for holistic transformation to a desired system which would engender greater overall resilience. The CS farming systems are either dependent on global market prices and external inputs, and therefore positioned at the bottom-left of the framework of Therond et al., or pulled towards that direction (the system in Spain). Transformation towards the upper-left requires government support to improve agricultural practices (including cover crops, crop diversity, biodiversity and wider landscape management), develop local markets and processing, improve the understanding and perception of the public about good agricultural practices, invest in appropriate technology and facilitate cooperation among farmers and other actors. Therefore, government support must not put agricultural policy and support in a separate silo, as agricultural practices are also dependent upon trade policies, research and development priorities and public health policies (Willett et al., 2019). A vicious cycle can only be changed to a virtuous cycle when all these strategies are addressed, and when policies that limit their implementation, such as trade policies, are addressed.

5.6 Conclusions

This assessment of three European CS in diverse farming sectors has highlighted that exposure to global market prices, reliance on external inputs and pathways of intensification (productivism) have created low environmental sustainability and resilience across all of them. Many of the challenges therefore cross all three sectors and agricultural systems, including low profitability, failing governmental support, climate change and public pressure for more environmental practices. Together, these cause a lock-in, and single strategies are not enough for a transformation towards more desirable, sustainable systems.

An enabling environment for each CS, and for wider European farming systems, is needed to move towards greater environmental sustainability and resilience in their agricultural practices. Government support needs to tackle the multi-faceted and compounding sets of factors that create lock-in, which will require a strategic and systematic plan through policy and multi-stakeholder input and collaboration. At present, institutional arrangements introduce measures to improve environmental sustainability but do so without challenging or contradicting the rules that underpin the system (i.e. change *within* the socio-technical regime). A greater appreciation of lock-in is therefore essential in agricultural policy, because overcoming structural rules that constrain environmentally sustainable agricultural practices in farming systems is difficult.

Before sustainable practices can be realised on the ground, the social and cultural context of farming systems needs to be understood and institutional and structural barriers need to be overcome. Whilst farmers are locked-in to ever-decreasing profit margins in the global market, decreasing natural resources and complex environmental issues, policy needs to be agile enough to support them through various sustainability transitions. Such policy support would be with a view to long-term saving both financially and environmentally as soil health, water availability and biodiversity re-establish. Such an overall strategy for transformation of the farming systems would also create a more supportive social and cultural basis for transitioning farmers, whilst attracting new entrants to farming.

References

Aarts, F. H. M. (2016). *Boeren in Peel en Kempen, omstreeks 1800*. BoekenGilde, Enschede. http://peelenkempen.nl/wp-content/uploads/2018/11/Boeren-in-Peel-en-Kempen-omstreeks-1800-HFM-Aarts.pdf

Alcalde, M. J., Ripoll, G. & Panea, B. (2013). Consumer attitudes towards meat consumption in Spain with special reference to quality marks and kid meat. In M. Klopčič, A. Kuipers & J. F. Hocquette (Eds.), *Consumer attitudes to food quality products*. EAAP – European Federation of Animal Science (133rd ed., pp. 97–107). Wageningen Academic Publishers, Wageningen. https://doi.org/10.3920/978-90-8686-762-2_7

Aragon.es (2019). Instituto Aragonés de Estadística (IAEST), Gobierno de Aragón. www.aragon.es/-/agricultura-ganaderia-selvicultura-y-pesca-1#anchor4

Arnott, D., Chadwick, D., Harris, I., Koj, A. & Jones, D. L. (2019). What can management option uptake tell us about ecosystem services delivery through agri-environment schemes? *Land Use Policy*, 81, 194–208. https://doi.org/10.1016/j.landusepol.2018.10.039

Bateman, I. J. & Balmford, B. (2018). Public funding for public goods: A post-Brexit perspective on principles for agricultural policy. *Land Use Policy*, 79, 293–300. https://doi.org/10.1016/j.landusepol.2018.08.022

Bernués, A., Riedel, J. L., Asensio, M. A., et al. (2005). An integrated approach to studying the role of grazing livestock systems in the conservation of rangelands in a protected natural park (Sierra de Guara, Spain). *Livestock Production Science*, 96(1), 75–85. https://doi.org/10.1016/j.livprodsci.2005.05.023

Beudou, J., Martin, G. & Ryschawy, J. (2017). Cultural and territorial vitality services play a key role in livestock agroecological transition in France. *Agronomy for Sustainable Development*, 37(4), 1–11. https://doi.org/10.1007/s13593-017-0436-8

Bijttebier, J., Coopmans, I., Appel, F., Unay Gailhard, I. & Wauters, E. (2018). Report on current farm demographics and trends. SURE-Farm D3.1.

Black, J. E. , Short, C.J. and Phelps, J. (2021) Chapter 9: Water with Integrated Local Delivery (WILD) for Transformative Change in Socio-Ecological Management. In: Fostering Transformative Change for Sustainability in the Context of Socio-Ecological Production Landscapes and Seascapes (SEPLS). Springer, Singapore, pp. 155–173.

Brauman, K. A., Siebert, S. & Foley, J. A. (2013). Improvements in crop water productivity increase water sustainability and food security – A global analysis. *Environmental Research Letters*, 8(2), 24030. https://doi.org/10.1088/1748-9326/8/2/024030

Burton, R. J. F. & Farstad, M. (2020). Cultural lock-in and mitigating greenhouse gas emissions: The case of dairy/beef farmers in Norway. *Sociologia Ruralis*, 60(1), 20–39. https://doi.org/10.1111/soru.12277

Coppola, G., Costantini, M., Orsi, L., et al. (2020). A comparative cost-benefit analysis of conventional and organic hazelnuts production systems in center Italy. *Agriculture (Switzerland)*, 10(9), 1–16. https://doi.org/10.3390/agriculture10090409

DEFRA. (2020). Environmental Land Management Policy discussion document. https://consult.defra.gov.uk/elm/elmpolicyconsultation/supporting_documents/ELMPolicyDiscussionDocument230620.pdf

Drinkwater, L. E. & Snapp, S. S. (2007). Nutrients in agroecosystems: Rethinking the management paradigm. *Advances in Agronomy*, 92, 163–186. https://doi.org/10.1016/S0065-2113(04)92003-2

Duru, M., Therond, O. & Fares, M. (2015). Designing agroecological transitions: A review. *Agronomy for Sustainable Development*, 35(4), 1237–1257. https://doi.org/10.1007/s13593-015-0318-x

European Union. (2020). Farm to fork strategy. https://ec.europa.eu/food/farm2fork_en#:~:text=The Farm to Fork Strategy aims to accelerate our transition,neutral or positive environmental impact&text=ensure food security%2C nutrition and,%2C safe%2C nutritious%2C sustainable food

Fau, L. R. (2016). El ovino y el caprine en Aragón, evoluciòn en los ultimos 20 años (Sheep and goats in Aragón, trends in the last 20 years). http://bibliotecavirtual.aragon.es/

Fireman, N. (2019). Oberlin's Experimental Hazelnut Orchard: Exploring Woody Agriculture's Potential for Climate Change Mitigation and Food System Resilience [Oberlin College]. Honors Papers. https://digitalcommons.oberlin.edu/honors/122

Food Farming and Countryside Commission. (2019). Our future in the land. www.thersa.org/globalassets/reports/rsa-ffcc-our-future-in-the-land.pdf

Geiger, F., Bengtsson, J., Berendse, F., et al. (2010). Persistent negative effects of pesticides on biodiversity and biological control potential on European farmland. *Basic and Applied Ecology*, 11(2), 97–105. https://doi.org/10.1016/j.baae.2009.12.001

Glover, J. L. (2014). Gender, power and succession in family farm business. *International Journal of Gender and Entrepreneurship*, 6(3), 276–295. https://doi.org/10.1108/IJGE-01-2012-0006

Hoang, V. N. & Alauddin, M. (2010). Assessing the eco-environmental performance of agricultural production in OECD countries: The use of nitrogen flows and balance. *Nutrient Cycling in Agroecosystems*, 87(3), 353–368. https://doi.org/10.1007/s10705–010-9343-y

Hoekstra, A. Y., Bredenhoff-Bijlsma, R. & Krol, M. S. (2018). The control versus resilience rationale for managing systems under uncertainty. *Environmental Research Letters*, 13(10), 103002. https://doi.org/10.1088/1748-9326/aadf95

Ingram, J. (2010). Technical and social dimensions of farmer learning: An analysis of the emergence of reduced tillage systems in England. *Journal of Sustainable Agriculture*, 34(2), 183–201. https://doi.org/10.1080/10440040903482589

Jägermeyr, J., Gerten, D., Heinke, J., Schaphoff, S., Kummu, M. & Lucht, W. (2015). Water savings potentials of irrigation systems: Global simulation of processes and linkages. *Hydrology and Earth System Sciences*, 19(7), 3073–3091. https://doi.org/10.5194/hess-19-3073-2015

Kantar. (2020). Europeans, agriculture and the CAP – Special Eurobarometer 504. https://ec.europa.eu/commfrontoffice/publicopinion/index.cfm/Survey/getSurveyDetail/instruments/special/search/agriculture/surveyKy/2229

Kneafsey, M. R., Cox, R., Holloway, L., Dowler, E., Venn, L. & Tuomainen, H. (2008). *Reconnecting consumers, producers and food: Exploring alternatives*. Berg, Oxford.

Kneafsey, M., Venn, L., Schmutz, U., et al. (2013). Short food supply chains and local food systems in the EU. A state of play of their socio-economic characteristics. Publications Office of the European Union.

Mandolesi, S., Naspetti, S., Arsenos, G., et al. (2020). Motivations and barriers for sheep and goat meat consumption in Europe: A means–end chain study. *Animals*, 10(6). https://doi.org/10.3390/ani10061105

MAPA. (2019). Consumo alimentario anual en los hogares españoles (Statistics on Food Consumption in Spain). www.mapa.gob.es/es/alimentacion/temas/consumo-tendencias/panel-de-consumo-alimentario/series-anuales/default.aspx

Meuwissen, M. P. M., Feindt, P. H., Spiegel, A., et al. (2019). A framework to assess the resilience of farming systems. *Agricultural Systems*, 176(June), 102656. https://doi.org/10.1016/j.agsy.2019.102656

Mills, J., Gaskell, P., Ingram, J., Dwyer, J., Reed, M. & Short, C. (2017). Engaging farmers in environmental management through a better understanding of behaviour. *Agriculture and Human Values*, 34(2), 283–299. https://doi.org/10.1007/s10460-016-9705-4

Mueller, N. D., Gerber, J. S., Johnston, M., Ray, D. K., Ramankutty, N. & Foley, J. A. (2012). Closing yield gaps through nutrient and water management. *Nature*, 490(7419), 254–257. https://doi.org/10.1038/nature11420

Navarro, V. P. (1992). La producción agraria en Aragón (1850–1935). *Revista de Historia Economica – Journal of Iberian and Latin American Economic History*, 10(3), 399–429. https://dialnet.unirioja.es/ejemplar/9600

Paas, W., Accatino, F., Antonioli, F., et al. (2019). D5.2 Participatory impact assessment of sustainability and resilience of EU farming systems. Sustainable and resilient EU farming systems (SURE-Farm) project report.

Paas, W., Accatino, F., Appel, F., et al. (2020). D5.5 Impacts of future scenarios on the resilience of farming systems across the EU assessed with quantitative and qualitative methods. Sustainable and resilient EU farming systems (SURE-Farm) project report. www.surefarmproject.eu/wordpress/wp-content/uploads/2020/06/D5.5.-Future-scenarios-on-the-FS-resilience.pdf

Peco, B., Navarro, E., Carmona, C. P., Medina, N. G. & Marques, M. J. (2017). Effects of grazing abandonment on soil multifunctionality: The role of plant functional traits. *Agriculture, Ecosystems & Environment*, 249, 215–225. https://doi.org/10.1016/j.agee.2017.08.013

Plumecocq, G., Debril, T., Duru, M., Magrini, M.-B., Sarthou, J. P. & Therond, O. (2018). The plurality of values in sustainable agriculture models: Diverse lock-in and coevolution patterns. *Ecology and Society*, 23(1). https://doi.org/10.5751/ES-09881-230121

Reed, M., Ingram, J., Mills, J. & Macmillan, T. (2017). Taking farmers on a journey: Experiences evaluating learning in Farmer Field Labs in UK. In IFSA Conference, Harper Adams, June 2016 (Unpublished).

Reidsma, P., Paas, W., Accatino, F., et al. (2020a). D5.6 Impacts of improved strategies and policy options on the resilience of farming systems across the EU. Sustainable and resilient EU farming systems (SURE-Farm) project report, EU Horizon 2020 Grant Agreement No 727520.

Reidsma, P., Meuwissen, M., Accatino, F., et al. (2020b). How do stakeholders perceive the sustainability and resilience of EU farming systems? *EuroChoices*, 19(2), 18–27. https://doi.org/10.1111/1746-692X.12280

Rist, L., Felton, A., Nyström, M., et al. (2014). Applying resilience thinking to production ecosystems. *Ecosphere*, 5(6), art73. https://doi.org/10.1890/ES13-00330.1

Rosset, P. M. & Altieri, M. A. (1997). Agroecology versus input substitution: A fundamental contradiction of sustainable agriculture. *Society and Natural Resources*, 10(3), 283–295. https://doi.org/10.1080/08941929709381027

Sans, P., de Fontguyon, G. & Wilson, N. (1999). Protected product specificity and supply chain performance: The case of three PGI lambs (Issue 241751). https://econpapers.repec.org/RePEc:ags:eaae67:241751

Savary, S. (2014). The roots of crop health: Cropping practices and disease management. *Food Security*, 6(6), 819–831. https://doi.org/10.1007/s12571-014-0399-4

Smith, P., Bustamante, M., Ahammad, H. & Al., E. (2014). Climate change 2014: Mitigation of climate change contribution of Working Group III to the Fifth Assessment Report of the Intergovernmental Panel on Climate Change. In O. Edenhofer, R. Pichs-Madruga, Y. Sokona & E. Al. (Eds.), *Agriculture, forestry and other land use (AFOLU)* (pp. 829–836). Cambridge University Press, Cambridge and New York.

Spiegel, A., Slijper, T., de Mey, Y., et al. (2019). Report on farmers' perceptions of risk and resilience capacities – A comparison across EU farmers. SURE-Farm D2.1. www.surefarmproject.eu/wordpress/wp-content/uploads/2019/04/SURE-Farm-D.2.1-Report-on-farmers-perception-of-risk-and-resilience-capacities.pdf

Sundkvist, Å., Milestad, R. & Jansson, A. (2005). On the importance of tightening feedback loops for sustainable development of food systems. *Food Policy*, 30(2), 224–239. https://doi.org/10.1016/j.foodpol.2005.02.003

Therond, O., Duru, M., Roger-Estrade, J. & Richard, G. (2017). A new analytical framework of farming system and agriculture model diversities: A review. *Agronomy for Sustainable Development*, 37(3), 21. https://doi.org/10.1007/s13593-017-0429-7

Tilman, D., Fargione, J., Wolff, B., et al. (2001). Forecasting agriculturally driven global environmental change. *Science*, 292(5515), 281–284. https://doi.org/10.1126/science.1057544

Tilman, D., Balzer, C., Hill, J. & Befort, B. L. (2011). Global food demand and the sustainable intensification of agriculture. *Proceedings of the National Academy of Sciences of the United States of America*, 108 (50), 20260–20264. https://doi.org/10.1073/pnas.1116437108

UNU-IAS & IGES. (2018). Sustainable use of biodiversity in Socio-ecological Production Landscapes and Seascapes (SEPLS) and its contribution to effective area-based conservation. In *Satoyama Initiative Thematic Review* (vol. 4). United Nations University Institute for the Advanced Study of Sustainability.

Van Ittersum, K., Meulenberg, M. T. G., Trijp, V. H. C. M. & Candel, M. J. J. M. (2007). 'Consumers' appreciation of regional certification labels: A Pan-European study. *Journal of Agricultural Economics*, 58(1), 1–23.

Vanloqueren, G. & Baret, P. V. (2008). Why are ecological, low-input, multi-resistant wheat cultivars slow to develop commercially? A Belgian agricultural 'lock-in' case study. *Ecological Economics*, 66 (2–3), 436–446. https://doi.org/10.1016/j.ecolecon.2007.10.007

Vigani, M., Urquhart, J., Black, J. E., Berry, R., Dwyer, J. & Rose, D. C. (2020). Post-Brexit policies for a resilient arable farming sector in England. *EuroChoices*, 20(1), 55–61. https://doi.org/10.1111/1746-692X.12255

Weis, T. (2008). The global food economy: The battle for the future of farming. *Journal of Agrarian Change*, 8(4), 618–623. https://doi.org/10.1111/j.1471-0366.2008.00182.x

Willett, W., Rockström, J., Loken, B., et al. (2019). Food in the Anthropocene: The EAT–Lancet Commission on healthy diets from sustainable food systems. *The Lancet*, 393(10170), 447–492. https://doi.org/10.1016/S0140-6736(18)31788-4

6 Resilience of Dairy Farming in Flanders

Past, Current and Future

ISABEAU COOPMANS, ERWIN WAUTERS,
JO BIJTTEBIER AND ERIK MATHIJS

6.1 Introduction

6.1.1 Agriculture in Flanders

Flanders is a mostly flatland region occupying a size of about 13,500 km² in the Northern, Dutch-speaking part of Belgium. Due to its fertile soils combined with a temperate climate, the agricultural sector in Flanders has a rich history and has generally been perceived as an important societal pillar for at least more than one and a half centuries. As in most European regions, the structural evolutions during the last decade include a shrinking population of farms (from 28,331 in 2010 to 23,225 in 2017), increasing average farm sizes, mechanisation and automation of agricultural activities and an increasing share of older farmers over younger farmers. Due to a very high population density, competition for agricultural land is very high in Flanders, resulting in high land prices (Danckaert et al. 2018a).

6.1.2 Dairy Farming in Flanders

In 2017, dairy farming accounted for about 13 per cent of the total final production value of Flemish agriculture. As Figure 6.1 shows, dairy farms are spread over the whole of Flanders, but tend to show some regional concentration, whereby the provinces of Antwerp, East Flanders and West Flanders contain regions with a relatively high amount of intensive dairy farms. Over the last decades, the Flemish dairy sector has gone through major structural changes (Danckaert et al. 2018b). The number of farms holding dairy herds has shown some fluctuations between 2012 and 2017, but on the whole, remained at around 6,000 farms (Departement Landbouw en Visserij 2020). About half of these are specialised dairy

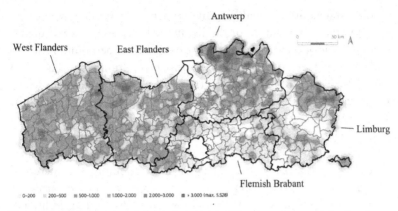

Figure 6.1 Importance of dairy farming in Flanders per municipality (euro standard output per hectare) in 2017.
Source: Departement Landbouw en Visserij, VLM-Mestbank en Informatie Vlaanderen

farms, and especially this group has remained stable since 2012 (Danckaert et al. 2018b). Therefore, the proportion of specialised dairy farms in relation to the total number of dairy farms is increasing. The average number of dairy cows on these specialised dairy farms has increased sharply: from fifty dairy cows in 2007 to eighty-five in 2017. Scale enlargement, combined with increased productivity, has led to a remarkable increase in milk production in Flanders, as will be elaborated in Section 6.3. In 2019, on all Flemish dairy farms included, 339,087 dairy cows produced almost 3 billion litres of milk. Farm sizes are substantially increasing, yet family farming remains the predominant business management model in this agricultural sector. Very rarely is all the cultivated land also in the property of the farmer or farming family. Legally speaking, most farms are sole proprietorship. On these farms, a Flemish dairy farm manager was aged 51 on average in 2016, and 18 per cent of them had a designated successor. Interestingly, recently more and more partnerships are being founded (currently 14 per cent), parallel to the risks associated with increasing farm sizes in terms of economic performances (expressed by EU SO typology) (Danckaert et al. 2018b).

6.1.3 Outlook for This Chapter

The underlying causes of these structural changes are discussed in what follows, as well as the role of different actors in the Flemish dairy farming system and its enabling environment. Government has played a major role as regulation of the EU market has disappeared (quota, production levies, etc.) over the last decades and liberalisation of free trade is increasing. The extra litres of milk resulting from this quota abolishment need to be processed further down the chain and eventually marketed. Besides causes, the impact of structural changes will be discussed. A great deal of the produce is traded, especially within Europe (Danckaert et al. 2018b). Export-oriented production makes the farming system susceptible to events in neighbouring countries and, by extension, in the rest of the world. In addition, the increased intensification of production also has a number of consequences for the public functions of the farming system, which pose additional challenges. Some strengths and weaknesses of the farming system are highlighted, which have an impact on its current and future resilience capacities. The remainder of this chapter discusses these aspects based on various research activities from the SURE-Farm project. All findings presented hereafter are also summarised in Annex 6.1. The methods used for data gathering and data interpretations are carefully explained in Chapter 1. These included: (1) an online survey assessing farmers' perceived risks and resilience capacities (Spiegel et al. 2019); (2) both desk research (policy document analysis) (Lievens and Mathijs 2018) and bottom-up research (in-depth interviews) (Coopmans et al. 2019c) about policy impacts on the resilience of the farming system; (3) interviews with farmers and farm household members exploring factors that affect generational renewal in agriculture (Coopmans et al. 2019b); (4) interviews investigating sources and informants impacting operational, tactical and strategic decision-making by farmers (Urquhart et al. 2019); (5) biographical narratives with farmers to understand farm developmental trajectories (Fowler et al. 2019); (6) agent-based modelling of farm structural change (Pitson et al. 2020); and (7) a workshop examining broad stakeholder perceptions on the current resilience of the system (Paas et al. 2019). Hence, this chapter is based on both qualitative and quantitative data, all aimed at better understanding different building blocks of resilience.

6.2 The Dynamics and Growth in the Sector Are Both a Sign of and a Challenge for Resilience

The Flemish dairy farming sector has experienced quite some dynamics in recent years. A combination of factors has induced structural investments that lead to an overall growth and structural change. Amongst the most important factors are the quota abolishment in 2015, a relatively favourable long-term market outlook, low profitability in the beef sector pushing these farmers into milk production, and technological development. Total milk production in Flanders increased by 21 per cent between 2015 and 2019 (BCZ 2020a). In the same period, the total number of cows increased by 7 per cent and average production per farm increased by 33 per cent. In 2015, some farms grew to over 1,000 cows for the first time. There is evidence of spatial structural change whereby dairy farming is losing relative importance in some areas, but gaining relative importance in other areas, as was also illustrated in Figure 6.1. This development is both a sign of and a challenge for the future resilience of the farming system, as we argue next.

The growth of and structural change within the sector are signs that the sector as a whole, and many individual farms within it, possess a substantial degree of resilience, both in terms of robustness and adaptability/transformability. Since 2010, the growth in the sector has been continuous and structural change has been accelerating. Yet, the dairy farming system has been subjected to a number of challenges in this period, such as at least two periods with very low prices, the Russian import ban, drought, more stringent environmental regulation and growing societal pressure on milk production from an environmental, animal welfare and health point of view. Some of these challenges have to some extent triggered the structural developments; however, the latter also took place in spite of many of these challenges. Dairy farmers have been able to profit from an enabling environment that supported the system's robustness against these challenges relatively well. Pillar 1 payments, a strong agricultural knowledge and innovation system (AKIS), a milk-processing sector that attempts to support its farmers, and governments that provided additional support during crises contributed to this. Furthermore, investment subsidies, banks and a strong and diverse AKIS also provided support for structural investments by many dairy farmers. Although instruments for investments into adapted or transformed modes of farming are available, and have to some extent been used by a small share of dairy farms, the main investments have been in business-as-usual modes of farming. Nonetheless, agent-based model simulations suggest that this enabling environment is also keeping inefficient farms in the sector, and as such hinders further structural change and prevents remaining farms to exploit economies of scale (Pitson et al. 2020; Chapter 3).

At the same time, this growth in total production and in dairy cows is a challenge for the future of the dairy sector that potentially threatens its system functions. Through the growth in total production and cow numbers, its' environmental footprint might increase, thereby leading to further societal pressure and, possibly, political restrictions. For instance, whereas productivity gains resulted in a decrease of the total sector's greenhouse gas emissions, its share in nitrate pollution is increasing. The sector reacts in two main ways, aiming to increase the robustness of the sector against these challenges. One is technological developments that improve the eco-efficiency of milk production, the other is attempting to counter this pressure by communication activities that highlight improvements in environmental performance and the possible place of dairy products in a healthy and sustainable diet.

Another threat that arises from this increase in milk production is the increased vulnerability to market disturbance. Flanders' degree of self-sufficiency increases and is above 100 per cent. Hence, for the milk price, the sector is dependent on the global market, export possibilities and the capacity of the processors to add value. This leads to a vulnerable situation, as, for example, the price decrease during the COVID-19 crisis has shown.

6.3 Social Capital as a Robustness-Increasing Asset of the Farming System

Social self-organisation has the potential to contribute to resilience (Cabell and Oelofse 2012; Meuwissen et al. 2019), particularly when connections are expanded to include supply chain actors. Due to milk's high perishability, the incentive to vertically coordinate is particularly high in the dairy sector. In addition, the sector's ability to cope with market changes strongly depends on the dairy processing industry's ability to switch between different products (fresh milk, cheese, butter, skimmed milk powder, ice-cream, etc.), while also the sector's adaptation strongly depends on dairies' abilities to innovate and add value.

The Flemish dairy sector has a strong history in collaboration. First, about two-thirds of all milk is processed by dairy cooperatives. Second, several initiatives bringing together dairy farmers and processors have been established. In 1999, the Flemish dairy sector established a

Complete Dairy Quality Assurance (DQA) Scheme to incorporate all food safety, environmental and animal welfare regulations. The scheme is based on farmers' self-monitoring and involves the three Belgian farmers' organisations and the Belgian association of the dairy industry (IKM 2020). In 2019, an interbranch organisation (MilkBE) has been established by the same actors. MilkBE currently focuses on milk contaminants and botulism (BCZ 2020b).

In the Flemish dairy sector, self-organisation mainly contributed to increased robustness and less to adaptability and transformability. Expanding the base for self-organisation to supply chain actors, such as dairies, increased the ability to cope with shocks, because it entailed more storage capacity available for processed milk, and more flexibility and modularity for milk processing activities. This is particularly the case for cooperative dairies as it is their aim to support their members. Supply chain actors can also assist farmers in implementing innovations aimed at adapting their farming. However, self-organisation in which supply chain actors are involved results in lower incentives to transformative change. Dairies have high asset specificity and strongly depend on their local supply base. Hence, it is in their interest to stabilise or even increase milk volumes (to capture economies of scale), which makes them oppose adaptations or transformations aimed at reducing milk production or marketing dairy products in different ways. Furthermore, collaboration implies coordination costs, which increase with increasing heterogeneity in farmers' attitudes and practices. Our results showed that some farmers felt that their influence on the course of cooperatives had decreased in the last twenty years. The increasing sizes and commercialisation of these organisations made these farmers feel left out (Coopmans et al. 2019a).

6.4 Public and Private Functions of the Farming System: Search for Balance

Results from the stakeholder workshop showed that the most important functions attributed to the dairy farming system are income generation for farmers and the delivery of high-quality food products for consumers. Not surprisingly, farmers rated economic viability as more important, while industry and other stakeholders gave higher rates to food production and maintaining natural resources. In contrast to the perceived importance of different system functions, their performances were rated similarly by both farmers and industry stakeholders, whereby they unanimously perceived the provision and maintenance of public goods (e.g. biodiversity) as better compared to that of private goods (e.g. food products) (Coopmans et al. 2019a). However, official statistics do not fully confirm this, as, for instance, nitrate pollution from dairy farming is increasing. In the same line, farmers perceived environmental challenges as less constraining compared to economic and institutional challenges (Fowler et al. 2019).

These results are also reflected in coping strategies of the farming system over the last decades. Increasing production efficiency and scale enlargement are mainly strategies to deal with decreasing margins, and have resulted in increased milk production, per cow, per farm and at the level of the farming system. Having to cope with environmental issues is mainly the result of measures imposed by regional and European regulations. However, despite increasingly strict regulations on manure application, the quality of surface and groundwater in Flanders remains inadequate. Expectations regarding emissions from the Flemish agricultural sector in 2020 show that additional measures will be needed to achieve the 2050 objectives. These objectives indicate a reduction of greenhouse gas emissions from the agricultural sector (both energetic and non-energetic) to 3.5 Mton CO_2eq by 2050 (7.5 Mton CO_2eq in 2017). Besides that, by 2050, agricultural practices should allow a continuous rise of soil carbon content or remain stable at a high level (Vlaamse Overheid 2018). At the European level, the 'farm to fork strategy' and 'biodiversity strategy' will force the sector into taking additional measures to meet ambitions regarding biodiversity and environmental impact in general. However, our results showed that farmers believe that they already put sufficient effort into maintaining natural resources and protecting biodiversity. They occasionally argue that sectors other than agriculture should also contribute towards a climate-neutral society, instead of agriculture always being looked upon as the 'predominant polluting industry'. Farmers feel that their efforts are undervalued, with sometimes a negative impact on their motivation to continue farming (Fowler et al. 2019; Urquhart et al. 2019).

Nevertheless, the trend of increasing environmental awareness and societal concerns on animal welfare will likely continue. The dairy processing industry adapts its product portfolio by including more and more plant-based alternatives for milk. A recent report from think tank RethinkX predicted the disruption of dairy farming systems in the following decade due to the emergence of lab-grown proteins (Tubb and Seba 2019). It is highly questionable whether it will go that fast, but it does not seem impossible that the industry and/or technological development will force adaptation and/or transformation of the current farming system. Or will regional and European policies provide sufficient incentives or actions so as to enable the farming system to respond to the ever-increasing pressure on current production methods? The reaction of milk production and dairy processing (supported by many stakeholders from agricultural government department, banks and input suppliers) has mainly been to try to counteract these trends by communicating about environmental improvements that have been realised and about the possible health benefits of dairy products.

6.5 Resilience: More than Robustness – What Can Policies Do?

Past and current strategies to deal with shocks and stresses contributed to the robustness of the Flemish dairy farming system. Both strategies implemented by the actors in the farming system and by actors in the enabling environment contributed mainly to robustness. This is not surprising as this is in line with the long existing goal of providing high-quality food at low prices, so it is important to maintain milk production both in quantitative and in qualitative terms.

Robustness is an important capacity as a short-term answer to disturbances and shocks, while adaptation to change happens on an intermediate time span, and transformations of the system are mainly observed over longer time scales (Chapter 4 of this book). Because of this, robustness is easier to assess, compared to responses that imply gradual changes in the farming system, ultimately resulting in adaptation or transformation. However, in the project, we do acknowledge the importance of adaptive and transformative capacity as contributing to the resilience of farming systems. Also, other stakeholders from the Flemish dairy sector are of the opinion that maintaining status quo is not always the best contributor to a better resilience. However, there is no full consensus on whether the emphasis of policies that enhance robustness is disproportional. Some agree that this emphasis is illustrated by the share of the CAP budget that flows to the dairy farmers under the form of pillar 1 payments. Taking up one quarter of the total Flemish direct payments budget in 2016, dairy farming is supported considerably more compared to horticulture and pig farming, yet arable and beef cattle farming are more known for being dependent on direct payments. However, some underline that the robustness-oriented character of the agricultural policy has been mitigated during the last few decades by a systematic shift of budget shares from pillar 1 to pillar 2 combined with a drastic decrease in the amount of market management measures (which are notorious for extending economic problems rather than providing a constructive solution) in order to comply with the European ambition to encourage farmers to engage in market-oriented production (Flemish Government 2013).

Nevertheless, it is important to consider what resilience capacities are aspired to with certain policies. Sometimes a focus on robustness can have a negative impact on adaptation and/or transformation, because the support for status-quo modes of production outcompetes adapted modes of production. Striving for uniformity in production, for example, makes it easier to support farmers, both technically and policy-wise. Less diversity between producers is also more efficient for the processing industry as well as for input suppliers. Nevertheless, heterogeneity between farms is considered a characteristic of resilience, as it has a positive impact on functional and response diversity. Another example is the intervention during the recent COVID-19 crisis. Short-term interventions (in this case private storage aid) are still important for crisis management. Some stakeholders ask for more emphasis on adaptability- and transformability-facilitating policies. A sector-wide dialogue can support a shared long-term vision for agricultural production in Flanders and the role of dairy production in the provision of public and private functions. This might result in tailored actions to make the Flemish dairy sector more resilient to future challenges.

It might be valuable to focus on strategies and policies that contribute to all resilience capacities. SURE-Farm policy research has revealed that policy goals are to a large extent aiming to support both robustness and long-term adaptability of the dairy-farming system, while aspects related to transformability are seldom implemented in policy goals (Lievens and Mathijs 2018). Remarkably, although robustness and adaptability characteristics are clearly present in policy ambitions, the corresponding policy measures do not always succeed in realising the anticipated effects. One of the observations that led to this finding was that farmers are either not aware of the variety of support measures at their disposal, or they are confronted with multiple obstacles like administrative complexities that hinder or even withdraw receipt (Coopmans et al. 2019c). By way of contrast, where transformability-related ambitions are lacking in policy objectives, there are policy instruments in place, such as specific subsidised trainings and a budget exclusively destined for innovative projects, which offers strong potential to improve transformability in the sector. The main lesson learnt herein is twofold. First, policymakers should better evaluate and monitor the feasibility of the measures in force to achieve the proposed and foreseen results. Second, policymakers should be aware of the opportunity to broaden and enrich the scope and use of existing measures, particularly with transformability-enabling elements.

6.6 Conclusion

The main findings of the SURE-Farm research in the Belgian case study are visually summarised in Annex 6.1. The Flemish dairy farming system has been showing signs of robustness and adaptive capacity, mainly materialised in large structural changes of the sector. This robustness has been supported by strong social organisation of the farming system, both at the level of the AKIS and a long history of collaboration among supply chain actors.

However, putting much effort in robustness might slow down the adaptive and transformative capacity of the farming system. Some specific long-term stresses, however, warrant mainly adaptation and/ or transformation in the long run. In this respect, policymakers should also be aware of the limitations of robustness-enabling instruments. Resilience was explicitly taken up in the central themes formulated by the Flemish government to guide the implementation of Rural Development Programme-related measures, which indicates that policymakers acknowledge, at least implicitly, that resilience is more than protecting the status quo through direct financial support and market management – measures that are often related to robustness.

Resilience capacities can be supported by a wide range of resilience attributes, which might be the subject of future policies. Some attributes stimulate particularly one capacity. Others stimulate mainly all capacities. Attributes influence each other. Further study is needed to identify the relationship between resilience attributes and all capacities of the dairy farming system in Flanders. This might be a prerequisite to further tailor support from the enabling environment.

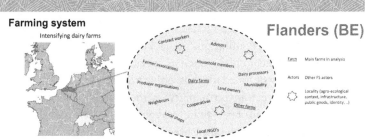

Farming system
Intensifying dairy farms

Flanders (BE)

Farm   Main farms in analysis

Actors   Other FS actors

   Locality (agro-ecological context, infrastructure, public goods, identity, ...)

Challenges

Institutional
- Changing regulations
- Low availability & high price of land

Environmental
- Extreme adverse weather events

Economic
- Volatile milk prices, including possible price drops
- Changing consumer demand to less animal-based food

Social
- Societal acceptability

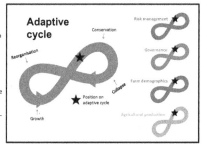

Adaptive cycle

Essential functions' performances

Private goods
- Income generation: low for those employed in agriculture, good for those employed in food industry
- High-quality dairy production: good
- Dairy farmers' quality of life & wellbeing: low

Public goods
- Maintaining natural resources in good condition, animal welfare: potential pitfall in (nearby) future

Resilience capacities

Robustness has been relatively high, yet mainly through enabling environment support

High focus on protecting status quo; low interest in support and perceived need for transformability

Low to moderate adaptability and transformability; support exists but is much less used. However, low interest in and need for transformations makes analysis of transformability difficult

Resilience attributes

Diversity low	Although dairy farms are diverse in terms of sizes and functions, high specialization and intensification levels induce low functional diversity at sector level. Lack of policy support instruments dismantling status quo.
Modularity moderate	High capacity to absorb shocks but low flexibility of farming system. High asset specificity. High dependence on value creation by processors.
System reserves low	High soil levels of Nitrogen, but low soil organic carbon. Low profitability, low financial buffer and low succession rate.
Tightness of feedbacks moderate	Already high degree of horizontal cooperation, but room for improvement in both horizontal and vertical cooperation
Openness moderate	End of quota has increased susceptibility to world market events.

Future strategies

Risk management	Governance	Farm demographics	Agricultural production
• Hedging • Market information • Financial buffer • Technological optimization • Better vertical cooperation and coordination	• More stable policies with long-term vision • Accommodate flexibility and variety • Stimulate and regulate vertical and horizontal cooperation	• Govern land availability • Tackle succession at an early stage • Labour flexibility schemes • (Inter)personal advice and coaching • Alternative financing and organisational models	• Precision dairy farming • Improve eco-efficiency • Insurance against weather events and diseases • Increase agronomic awareness and knowledge about alternative production systems

This project has received funds from the European Union's Horizon 2020 research and innovation programme under Grant Agreement No 727520

ILVO
Flanders research institute for agriculture, fisheries and food

SURE Farm

Annex 6.1 Factsheet synthesising resilience of the current farming system in Flanders (Belgium).

References

BCZ. 2020a. *Jaarverslag 2020 – Werkingsjaar 2019*. Leuven.
  2020b. MilkBE. https://bcz-cbl.be/nl/over-bcz/milkbe/.
Cabell, J. F. and M. Oelofse. 2012. An indicator framework for assessing agroecosystem resilience. *Ecology and Society* 17(1), 18–30.
Coopmans, I., J. Bijttebier, J. Becking and E. Wauters. 2019a. FoPIA-Surefarm case-study report Belgium. SURE-Farm project Deliverable Supplementary Materials A.
Coopmans, I., J. Dessein, J. Bijttebier, et al. 2019b. Report on a qualitative analysis in 11 case-studies for understanding the process of farm demographic change across EU-farming systems and its influencing factors. Sustainable and resilient EU farming systems (SURE-Farm) project report (D3.2).
Coopmans, I., E. Lievens, E. Mathijs and E. Wauters. 2019c. Report on policy bottom-up analysis – Belgian case-study: The dairy farming system in Flanders. Five case study reports with the results of the assessments in the five regional case study areas. Sustainable and resilient EU farming systems (SURE-Farm) project report (D4.3).
Danckaert, S., E. Demuynck, E. de Regt, et al. 2018a. Land- en Tuinbouw. Pages 59–137 *in: Uitdagingen voor de Vlaamse land- en tuinbouw. Landbouwrapport 2018*. Editors: J. Platteau, G. Lambrechts, K. Roels and T. Van Bogaert. Departement Landbouw en Visserij, Brussel.
  2018b. Melkvee. Pages 335–380 *in: Uitdagingen voor de Vlaamse land- en tuinbouw. Landbouwrapport 2018*. Departement Landbouw en Visserij, Brussel.
Departement Landbouw en Visserij. 2020. Landbouwcijfers – sectoroverzichten: sectorbarometer melkvee. https://lv.vlaanderen.be/nl/voorlichting-info/publicaties-cijfers/landbouwcijfers.
Flemish Government. 2013. *Vlaamse implementatie van de GLB2020-hervorming voor het onderdeel directe steun. Conceptnota aan de leden van de Vlaamse Regering*.
Fowler, S., P. Midmore, P. Nicholas-Davis, et al. 2019. Report on analysis of biographical narratives exploring short- and long-term adaptive behaviour of farmers under various challenges. Sustainable and resilient EU farming systems (SURE-Farm) project report (D2.2).
IKM. 2020. IKM, Integrale Kwaliteitszorg Melk, een kwaliteitsborgingssysteem. http://ikm.be/voorstelling/index_nl.html.
Lievens, E. and E. Mathijs. 2018. Assessing how policies enable or constrain the resilience of the intensive dairy farming system in Flanders, Belgium. Sustainable and resilient EU farming systems (SURE-Farm) project report.

Meuwissen, M. P. M., P. H. Feindt, A. Spiegel, et al. 2019. A framework to
    assess the resilience of farming systems. *Agricultural Systems* 176,
    102656.

Paas, W., F. Accatino, F. Antonioli, et al. 2019. Participatory impact assess-
    ment of sustainability and resilience of EU farming systems. Sustainable
    and resilient EU farming systems (SURE-Farm) project report (D5.2).

Pitson, C., F. Appel, F. Heinrich and J. Bijttebier. 2020. Report on future
    farm demographics and structural change in selected regions of the EU.
    Sustainable and resilient EU farming systems (SURE-Farm) project
    report (D3.5).

Spiegel, A., T. Slijper, Y. D. E. Mey, et al. 2019. Report on farmers' percep-
    tions of risk and resilience capacities – A comparison across EU farmers.
    Sustainable and resilient EU farming systems (SURE-Farm) project
    report (D2.1).

Tubb, C. and T. Seba. 2019. Rethinking Food and Agriculture 2020–2030:
    The second domestication of plants and animals, the disruption of the
    cow, and the collapse of industrial livestock farming. RethinkX.

Urquhart, J., F. Accatino, F. Appel, F. Antonoili and R. Berry. 2019. Report
    on farmers' learning capacity and networks of influence in 11 European
    case studies. Sustainable and resilient EU farming systems (SURE-Farm)
    project report (D2.3).

Vlaamse Overheid. 2018. Vlaams Klimaatbeleidsplan 2021–2030. https://
    omgeving.vlaanderen.be/sites/default/files/atoms/files/
    VoorontwerpVlaamsKlimaatbeleidsplan2021–2030_VR20180720.pdf.

7 | Resilience-Enhancing Strategies to Meet Future Challenges

The Case of Arable Farming in Northeast Bulgaria

MARIYA PENEVA

7.1 Introduction

This chapter focuses on the results and analyses concerning the resilience of the specialized arable farming system in the Northeast region of Bulgaria. The analysed farming system consists mainly of large-scale grain producers (both corporate and family farms) and other actors, who affect and are affected by the grain farmers. The research is based on the SURE-Farm methodology as presented in Chapter 1. The analysis in this chapter is organized in three main parts: first the case study is presented describing the historical context, actors involved and system functions. Next, the challenges are presented, followed by the sections discussing resilience capacities and future strategies for enhancing farming system resilience. Conclusions are made in the last section. The Annex 7.1 presents the overview of the case study findings.

7.2 The Case Study

Crop production is important and has a long tradition in Bulgaria. The share of crop production in utilized agricultural land increases constantly and reached 60 per cent in 2020 (MAFF, 2020). This development results from specialization and concentration in the agricultural sector, induced by many factors, policy being the major one, according to the stakeholders. Simultaneously, specific production structures have developed, whose effectiveness increases with expansion of farm size and level of mechanization. Farms specialized in crop production achieved the highest economic capabilities with productivity close to the EU average (Koteva, 2019). Thus, their role has increased, thereby also strengthening the international competitiveness of the sector.

Northeast Bulgaria, known as 'the granary of the country' is considered of high importance for crop production. The share of total crops produced in the case study region is between 45 per cent and 60 per cent of the national output and consists of mainly wheat, barley, maize and sunflower. The case study region produces 1/3 of the total gross value added in agriculture in the country (MAFF, 2020). The arable farming capacity in the region results from the natural conditions, i.e. fertile soils; varied landscape, including river valleys and lowlands; and a continental type of climate, and it is defined by the historical developments and transformations.

To understand the current status and processes in arable farming in Northeast Bulgaria, we have to consider the decisions taken in the country during the communist time and the transformations afterwards. The collectivization during the communist time interrupted the private ownership and the inheritance of land as well as the family nature of agricultural businesses, entrepreneurship and market-oriented business behaviour (Nicholas-Davis et al., 2020). In the 1990s, the reverse process occurred, including liquidation of collective farms from the communist regime, restoration of land ownership to the owners from the pre-socialist period or their heirs and privatization of all assets in the food chains. Thus, the land reform and continuously changing legal base for land ownership and stewardship led to land fragmentation. According to the most recent data approximately 88 per cent of utilized agricultural land is owned by 1.8 million holders (MAFF, 2020), which complicates the relationship between landowners and farmers and also puts significant administrative burden and financial costs on the latter (Nicholas-Davis et al., 2020). The resulting dualistic structure of agricultural production consists of economically viable and competitive, large-scale farms specialized in arable farming and economically non-viable farm structures, including small farms specialized in labour-intensive production (Koteva, 2019). There are also many other challenges and opportunities which have recently affected the farming system.

Crop production has always been considered to be the dominant farming system in Northeast Bulgaria. Even changes during and after the communist time have not changed the main specialization of the system, except for its actors and structures.

In this region, the changes after the collapse of communism (1989–1990) resulted in the emergence and development of a completely new structure of farming enterprises, and the transformation has continued since the introduction of the CAP in Bulgaria (2007).

Figure 7.1 Northeast Bulgaria landscape during the spring and autumn.
Photos by Mariya Peneva.

Land consolidation and constantly increasing farm size have been accelerated by the introduction of direct payments (Koteva and Ivanov, 2020). The stakeholders characterized the processes as rapid and the increase in farm size as large. Farm sizes increased due to land purchase and renting. Large-scale farms own on average 40–50 per cent of the land they cultivate. The main farm type in the case study area gradually developed into its current form in the past twenty years, consisting of large-scale (above 1,000 ha of arable land) mechanized farms, specialized in the production of grains, maize and sunflower. The studied farming system includes also actors who are influenced by and who influence these farms, namely: other farm types such as livestock farms, farms with perennials, vegetable growers, beekeepers, smaller arable farms, land owners and farmers' households.

The identity of the farming system is characterized further by its ability to provide essential functions, including both private and public goods. This is one of the factors enhancing the resilience of the arable system in Northeast Bulgaria and answers the question for what purpose resilience is studied (Meuwissen et al., 2019). The results from farm survey, FoPIA-SureFarm (Reidsma et al., 2020) and quantitative assessment of the current state of the ecosystem services (Accatino et al., 2020) show that stakeholders prioritized the delivery of private over public goods. Also, the evaluation demonstrates that the grain farming system in Northeast Bulgaria performs better in the provision of private goods than in the provision of public goods. The food production and economic viability functions are considered as the most important functions which were perceived to perform at good and medium levels. The farmers value and take pride in the high levels of productivity achieved. This also illustrates the understanding that viable farms help strengthen the economy and contribute to the regional development, which is often present as justification for policy and other interventions. The provision of public goods scored well in regard to habitat quality. However, the performance in biodiversity function provision is perceived to be low and still needs improvement. The public functions in the social domain, namely quality of life (encompassing sources of incomes and employment conditions in the workplace) and attractiveness of the area (referring to the participants' perception of the region as a place of living), are considered as important for the case study and from the stakeholders' perspective they perform moderately.

In the course of the assessment, it was revealed that the stakeholders are more inclined to discuss and consider functions that are associated with their businesses more directly and which are relevant to the economic domain, such as productivity and net farm income. The study identified an inconsistency between the understanding of farming system development and assigning high importance to the environment as a precondition. Environment performance is underestimated despite stakeholders being aware of the negative consequences of increased specialization and established monoculture production structure for natural resources (e.g. soil fertility) maintenance and preservation. Another important issue which was revealed during the study was the fact that to some extent the large-scale grain producers contribute negatively to the implementation of the functions from the social domain. This is illustrated by the high level of inequality between the different types of farmers in regard to access to production factors. The grain producers are more powerful and their growth affected negatively the other producers by unfair competition for land and human resources. It led to substantial increase in farms' expenditures to lease/ hire them. After the introduction of subsidies for agriculture in 2007, the sector has become more attractive for business, which has increased the competition additionally.

7.3 The Challenges

The arable farming system in Northeast Bulgaria faces many different challenges, which are recognized by the stakeholders across the different methods applied. There is consensus on the most important challenges from the economic, environmental, institutional and social domains. In regard to each domain, the main challenges for the farming system that emerged through the analysis of the stakeholders' opinions are: lack of stability in farmers' income, climate changes, legislation changes and negative demographic changes in rural areas (depopulation and ageing). It should be pointed out that usually the challenges are interpreted as changes which have brought negative consequences for the stakeholders and which have led to lower profitability/effectiveness of their activity. More generally, the challenges were perceived to have negative impacts on the production output of the grain farms, and stakeholders questioned the future of the arable farming system in the region as a whole. The research acknowledges that many of the challenges forced farming system actors to undertake specific actions, which in the long-term perspective increased its resilience, as discussed in the next section.

The economic challenges identified to influence resilience of the system are mainly associated with price fluctuations and the level of subsidies. Price volatility of inputs and outputs are important factors for the economic viability of farms. In this regard the marketing and financial management of the farms predefine the farmers' ability to sustain the system. That is why there is a need for improvements in order to allow farmers to better respond to the globalization of value chains and unequal distribution of power across the agri-food chain. Grains and oilseeds are world trade commodities and the capacity of the country's production is limited compared to the international players from the region. The most influential are Russia and Ukraine, which as regional price-makers also impact the studied arable system despite the fact that it is dominated by large-scale and competitive production structures. Thus the knowledge about market trends and data is a factor for economic success. The farmers should find trustworthy sources of information, assess their importance and learn and gain knowledge on how to manage and properly estimate that information. Better understanding of world markets and gaining knowledge to predict their future developments is part of dealing with the economic challenge. Yet, the market effects differ across the different stages of farm development and are influenced by the farmers' ability to accumulate financial resources. Furthermore, the current economic performance and profitability of the farm business correlate with the farmers' risk perceptions and acceptance of insurance (which are at a very low level at present), especially against climate risks. Part of the suggested response is to invest in better irrigation systems but it is an economic challenge to mobilize resources at the system level since it is often not affordable by single farmers, and even to the large-scale ones.

Last but not least, the stakeholders considered the changing needs and expectations of the society as a factor influencing economic viability of the farming system. Ultimately there is a need to invest in more sustainable production methods, which stimulate farmers to invest in new technologies, new machineries and new varieties and to bear the costs of their adaptation to the local conditions. Other economic shocks with short-term impacts which were mentioned by stakeholders include political trends, like the Russian embargo, and more general political risks originating from global conflicts between groups of countries.

According to the stakeholders, the most important issues after the economic ones are the environmental challenges. There is a specific focus on climate change which is the most topical, alongside natural resources preservation with an emphasis on soil and plant diseases. Extreme weather events are of the greatest concern, as for the arable farming system in Northeast Bulgaria droughts are the most cited as well as rain if occurring in the decisive moments of the production process. Farmers realize their dependence on natural and climate conditions and challenge themselves to apply good agricultural and environmental practices. They include crop rotation and technologies which preserve and increase soil fertility in order to ensure long-term preservation of the production capacity of the land. The agronomic conditions predetermine the productivity levels and require strict combination of resources, e.g. ensuring machineries in proportion to the land for timely execution of operations. On the other side the increased requirements as a result of the greening of the agricultural policy are perceived as shocks for those farmers who have not considered the mentioned agri-environmental practices before they became a compulsory condition for receiving subsidies. Monoculture-intensive farming is considered to be damaging for natural resources, which compels farmers to look for and introduce these practices, which is in turn related to the values and knowledge of the system actors. It should be mentioned that parts of the region are designated nitrate vulnerable zones, which imposes restrictions for all type of farms and specializations. The restrictions aim at preventing underground water and air contamination and require new approaches to farming practices and natural resources management.

Never-ending changes in the legislation and policy regulations (including requirements and restrictions) affect farmers' long-term decisions. The most important issue related to this challenge, which holds back farmers, is the constitution and control of land relationships. These relationships are very complicated both by the existing structure of fragmented land ownership and by the unstable legislation. Both impede longstanding commitments between landholders and landlords. Negative effects relate to the land market, as the level of land prices (including rents/leases) increased enormously, and to production expenditures of farmers. One of the side effects mentioned by the stakeholders is that the established relations affect the territorial allocation of the farmed plots as well. Tenants look for solutions to merge scattered parcels and to consolidate farmed land each year and these negotiations between them are not always fair and efficient. The next negative effect for the farming system is the decreased numbers of initiated changes, including investments in productions where the biological lifecycle of crops/animals is longer than a year. For example, changing the production to, e.g., perennials requires investments and it demands persistent actions for several years to start cropping. The short-term contracts for land rent prevent these long-term decisions. The challenge originates from the overall lack of a holistic approach and the absence of a long-term national strategy that outlines a sustainable vision for the future development of the sector which adjusts the CAP implementation according to the national priorities and specifics. In conjunction with these issues is the issue of bureaucracy. On the one hand, it is part of the low level of coordination between government departments and governmental levels in terms of administrative burdens to the beneficiaries of both subsidy schemes and measures implemented under the Rural Development Program. On the other hand, it is partially predetermined by the skills and capacities of public officials. As a result, the governance process is not effective and the trust in institutions decreases.

The challenges associated with the negative demographic changes in the rural areas are depopulation of rural areas, which is inevitably interconnected with the ageing population, and the lack of generational renewal in the labour force. Both of which lead to lack of skilled labour force for field work and for managerial staff in the crop farming system. These challenges are regarded as equally important as climate change. The outcomes, such as lack of entrepreneurship, decreased amount of successors, resistance to changes and falling ambition for novelties and innovations, caused shortages in the performance and outcomes of agricultural activities. Stakeholders acknowledged that despite the high level of mechanization and intensification of the processes in the arable farming, farmers struggle to secure workers for timely operations during the periods with high pressures and for the implementation of new technologies. The question is related to the quantity as well as the quality of the labour force. The process is controversial and it is admitted that the intensification and mechanization led to loss of jobs and forced depopulation of the region. Therefore, grain farmers should be an active part of rural revitalization. The specific aspect of the challenges from the social domain, which requires their efforts, is to increase the attractiveness (1) of the rural areas (for highly educated potential entrants offering them less personal risks and higher average wages, providing social benefits for workers living a long distance from the farm, and adequate public services) and (2) of the sector (development of joint programs with schools and universities to revive the vocational and agricultural education and training and acquisition of relevant skills). Part of this domain is the need to respond to society's expectations and consumers' preferences as well.

Other long-term social challenges are more specifically related to farming activities. These include the interaction and cooperation with neighbouring farmers during the production process and social self-organization within the crop farming system. The former is mostly related to the lack of physical borders when working with biological organisms, which exposes the grain farmers to the risk of actions undertaken by the neighbouring farmers, e.g. use of controversial seeds and inputs, spread of diseases, pests, etc. The latter is related to the resistance of the actors in the system to cooperate and collaborate on improving the system's capacity to respond to the challenges and to realize the effects of scale. It is rather an exception than a common action but it happens, usually during the policy decision-making process. Farmer collaboration gives them better positions to defend their interests and to champion their cause as an agricultural producers' community.

The field work studied in detail past and current challenges. But future challenges were also discussed. According to the stakeholders' perceptions, the main challenges in the next years will continue to be: extreme weather events, labour force availability, the speed of innovation implementation, market competition, policy arrangements and bureaucracy. Each of these challenges could not be studied independently. Their effects interrelate and accelerate the need for changes in the system to preserve its future functioning.

7.4 The Coping Efforts for Current Resilience of Crop Production in Northeast Bulgaria

The crop production in Northeast Bulgaria still copes with the mentioned challenges and proves its ability to be resilient in the years after the transformation of the political and economic systems in the country at the end of the last century. Actually, the past processes forced the overall agricultural system, including crop production in the case study region, to transform into its current state. But the current system's capacity towards transformability is not proved by the study. The existing and developing alternatives based on innovations in technology and varieties are sporadic and still unacceptable for the mainstream. The crop production has its traditions in the region and incremental changes or radical transformation could not happen without radical change in beliefs and values of wide range of actors. From this point of view, the unexpected severe shock or continuous stresses in a long-term period would induce the transformation in the studied farming system. At present, the general resilience of the system is assessed to be medium to low. Indeed, the arable farming system in the region showed a relatively high capacity to keep the status quo and proved to be at a relatively low level of transformation. This results also from the current policy configurations, which foster robustness and neglect transformability.

Robustness is represented by persistence in keeping up the same activities and lack of intentions for change in the long term because farming at the current size and specialization is mainstreamed as a profitable business. It is also supported by farmers' commitment and attachment to the sector, its traditions in land cultivation, the high share of labour of the farmer and their family, the annual area-based direct payments (corresponding to the short-term focus of policy instruments and providing buffer resources) and lack of need for change in the recent years. The study revealed that the major driving factor for the discontinuation of this status quo is the continuous presence of shocks and pressures caused by climate change, lack of available labour and policy reforms.

However, many changes have been implemented at the farm level in regard to optimization of the production costs and preservation of the food production levels, enhancing the economic viability and increasing the quality of life and attractiveness of the area, which indicates the capacity of the overall system to adapt. This adaptability is conceptualized by Meuwissen et al. (2019) as the capacity of the farming system to change and adjust its internal elements and processes in response to shocks and stresses but without changing its structures and feedback mechanisms. Therefore, it is proved that adaptability of the studied system is evolving. First, small adjustments of the on-farm production have been introduced from conventional to innovative, experimenting with new technologies and varieties (even diversification). They aim at better economic performance, but are also a response to the climatic challenges. The need for adaptation in order to meet future challenges and to continue the business is clear, and the improvement in access to the main production factor through owning the land gives the actors security to continue adaptation of farming. The process of business growth through increasing the farm size within the system goes along with buying new land (it is also the way to overcome instability of regulations of land relationships) and identifying new market opportunities, both of which require more adaptations than robustness. Scarce labour accelerates the adaptability of the grain farming system influencing its mid- and long-term resilience, and farmers initiate investments in and engagement with human capital. The research admits the importance of education and training (even abroad) combined with open-mindedness to new ideas and technologies as factors of adaptability (and even transformability) and exploring new opportunities for business development. Adaptability also receives stronger support through policy goals rather than through actual policy instruments. Every change in CAP stimulates farmers to adjust their practices to the new regulations. This is especially valid for grain production dependent on subsidies, in which case the adaptability is not intentionally pursued but externally induced. Recently, the adaptability in the arable system has been enhanced through policies aiming at innovations and agri-environmental measures available to crop farmers.

The transformability is the capacity of the system to change significantly its internal structure, to develop new elements, processes and feedback mechanisms (changes in the functions) in response to either severe shocks, or enduring stress that make business as usual impossible (Meuwissen et al., 2019). Transformability in studied arable farming system is least supported, according to the results, because there is no long-term view for change which can take the farming system to a different equilibrium state. Growth has been observed in the agricultural production process in the last decades. This growth is determined by the soil fertility and limited capacity to increase land productivity by additional investments (e.g. fertilisers). The current crop farming system in Northeast Bulgaria has reached the limit where innovations in varieties, technologies, etc. improve economic performance of the farm through optimization of costs. The soil fertility improvement and yield growth are bounded and a transformation of the system may offer better prospects with regard to diversification and cooperation within the value chain. This statement is proved by the quantitative study of ecosystem services. The model showed that the indicator of food crop production in the studied system is lower compared to the average for the EU (Accatino et al., 2020) but has the capacity to utilize different diversification opportunities. Transformability is also facilitated at the household level within the system through the participation of the next generation in the current farm business. Young people are less connected to the tradition and more influenced by the technological innovations and trends. Otherwise, the demographic processes are tend to collapse, which would disrupt the smooth succession process as well as intensify the concerns for labour availability in quality and quantity. The transformation is observed in two directions at the moment. First, the farmers start to diversify their production to nonconventional crops driven by the new perspective sought after by their children. Examples include lavender cultivation and set up of processing facilities for oil extraction. Second, transformations occur when the current intensive crop farming system is changed to more environment-friendly management practices, including transformation to organic production. This process involves using new techniques (strep-till and no-till) which support the building up of organic matter in the soil. This is expected to ultimately result in a more sustainable farming system with improved soil fertility and water holding capacity. The latter is the system's response to climate change (drought) and economic challenge to restore and maintain the irrigation systems in the case study region.

7.5 Strategies for the Future Resilience of the Crop Farming System in Northeast Bulgaria

The research of the different resilience capacities of arable farming acknowledges that it is not realistic to expect that a single strategy could improve the resilience of a complex system as the one in Northeast Bulgaria. The future system would combine elements from different alternatives which stakeholders consider as possible adaptations/transformations. Hence, the combination of several strategies would improve the system's resilience with regard to the identified critical thresholds of resilience indicators (productivity, farm income, nutrient balance), attributes (coupled with local and natural capital, exposed to disturbances, socially self-organized) and challenges (price fluctuations and changes in climate, legislation and labour force).

During the discussions, a general consensus was achieved on the essential strategies in the preservation of the system's resilience in response to any challenges and changes (future but also current), namely implementation of new production technologies, technical modernization and soil quality preservation. These strategies all entail behaviour towards adaptation or transformation, which eventually would improve the productivity and facilitate higher net farm income, reduce the dependency on external factors and utilize the main learning strategies adopted by the actors. The innovation strategies and implementation of labour-substituting technologies in particular also facilitate the reduction of the negative consequences from the lack of skilled labour. Another underestimated possible strategy is production diversification (any kind including territorial diversity of plots), which preserves farms from the risk of income instability. In the case study region, the farming system is poorly diversified to on- and off-farm activities, as stated by the stakeholders. In this regard, experimentation is an important strategy for all the respondents, focusing on adaptation of new technologies and crop varieties to the local conditions and trying out different crops on different plots across the farm.

For Bulgarian farmers, a key challenge was to learn how to act as entrepreneurs in a market economy after decades of a centrally planned economy. In this regard strategies to reduce market risks are still needed and some suggestions to be applied include using market instruments (insurance contracts, futures), participation in trade platforms and organization and dissemination of market bulletins.

Future strategies are also proposed in the institutional domain implying more stable policies with long-term vision and better cooperation with actors inside and outside the farming system. An emphasis is put on the interlinkages with research institutions and universities, the expectation for improvement in knowledge networks, and opportunities to exchange ideas and information. As the innovations are perceived as vital for the future resilience of the farming system, the mentioned strategies are expected to make farmers more open-minded to different viewpoints and improve their attitude towards participating in trainings, seminars and exhibitions. But we have to be aware that the mentioned processes may be controversial since many farmers feel more familiar with the newest technologies and innovations than researchers and lecturers. The point is that due to underfinance of science and education in the agriculture field, farmers have better opportunities as long as they decide to invest and ensure funding.

The key strategies for the future system's resilience will be the stimulation of succession and improved attractiveness of the sector. The realization of any mentioned strategy depends on human capital. Moreover, the process of first-generation change in the grain production system is observed at the moment, keeping in mind historical developments and the fact that the tradition of farm inheritance was broken for many years. In regard to these strategies, policy support is important. The experience and results from the implementation of young farmer support schemes show its capacity to enable farming accession and to accelerate succession, which positively impacts farm demographics. The strategies increase the influence of the farmers' children as they grow up and contribute to the decision-making on the farm. They also influence the strategies related to the use of information sources due to increased use of the internet and social media.

Another important part are the strategies for improvement in societal appreciation, which significantly influences the cooperation, the succession and the willingness of locals to work for and together with the farmers. These strategies include participation in open farm days (increased transparency and trust) and actively engaging with the local community by organizing fairs and public events.

7.6 Conclusions

The studied grain farming system in Northeast Bulgaria is very important in the context of the regional and national development of agricultural and rural areas. The system demonstrated capacities to achieve effectiveness in economic terms due to large-scale production structures and specialization. However, there are shocks and pressures challenging the future system's performance and stimulating implementation of strategies targeting improvements in its resilience. The actions related to the environmental and social domain are considered crucial to trigger the system's adaptability and transformability in the future. The policy is important to support the performance and success of the strategies formulated by different actors, to smooth adaptations and transformations to new realities and to enable the overall resilience of the studied arable system.

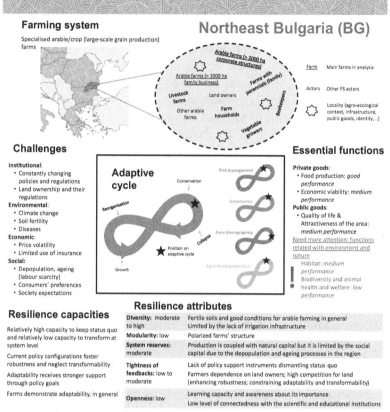

Farming system

Specialised arable/crop (large-scale grain production) farms

Northeast Bulgaria (BG)

Farm — Main farms in analysis

Actors — Other FS actors

Locality (agro-ecological context, infrastructure, public goods, identity, ..)

Arable farms (> 2000 ha corporate structures)
Arable farms (> 1000 ha family business)
Livestock farms
Land owners
Farms with perennials (family)
Other arable farms
Farm households
Beekeepers
Vegetable growers

Challenges

Institutional:
• Constantly changing policies and regulations
• Land ownership and their regulations

Environmental:
• Climate change
• Soil fertility
• Diseases

Economic:
• Price volatility
• Limited use of insurance

Social:
• Depopulation, ageing (labour scarcity)
• Consumers' preferences
• Society expectations

Adaptive cycle

Risk management
Conservation
Reorganisation
Governance
Farm demographics
Collapse
★ Position on adaptive cycle
Growth
Agricultural production

Essential functions

Private goods:
• Food production: *good performance*
• Economic viability: *medium performance*

Public goods:
• Quality of life & Attractiveness of the area: *medium performance*
Need more attention: functions related with environment and nature
Habitat: *medium performance*
Biodiversity and animal health and welfare: *low performance*

Resilience capacities

Relatively high capacity to keep status quo and relatively low capacity to transform at system level

Current policy configurations foster robustness and neglect transformability

Adaptability receives stronger support through policy goals

Farms demonstrate adaptability, in general

Resilience attributes

Diversity: moderate to high	Fertile soils and good conditions for arable farming in general
	Limited by the lack of irrigation infrastructure
Modularity: low	Polarized farms' structure
System reserves: moderate	Production is coupled with natural capital but it is limited by the social capital due to the depopulation and ageing processes in the region
Tightness of feedbacks: low to moderate	Lack of policy support instruments dismantling status quo
	Farmers dependence on land owners; high competition for land (enhancing robustness; constraining adaptability and transformability)
Openness: low	Learning capacity and awareness about its importance
	Low level of connectedness with the scientific and educational institutions

Future strategies

Risk management	Governance	Farm demographics	Agricultural production
• Optimization of production costs and securing proper assets	• More stable policies with long-term vision	• Stimulating succession	• New technologies and varieties
• Exchange of information about farming and risks through networking and trainings	• Improve societal appreciation	• Reflexivity, open-minded, self-criticism, appreciate farm workers	• Adaptation of innovations to the local conditions
• Reduction of market risks	• Infrastructure improvements to attract young generation to live in rural areas	• Better cooperation with research institutions and universities	• Improved soil management
			• Diversification: crops, territorial diversity of plots and non-farm activities

This project has received funds from the European Union's Horizon 2020 research and innovation programme under Grant Agreement No 727520

SURE Farm

Annex 7.1 Factsheet synthesizing resilience of the current farming system in Northeast Bulgaria.

References

Accatino, F., W. H. Paas, H. Herrera, et al. 2020. 'D5.5 Impacts of future scenarios on the resilience of farming systems across the EU assessed with quantitative and qualitative methods'. Sustainable and resilient EU farming systems (SURE-Farm) project report. www.surefarmproject.eu/wordpress/wp-content/uploads/2020/06/D5.5.-Future-scenarios-on-the-FS-resilience.pdf

Koteva, N. 2019. 'Changes of the organizational and economic structure of Bulgarian agriculture'. *Bulgarian Journal of Agricultural Economics and Management*, 64(2), 3–22

Koteva, N. and B. Ivanov. 2020. 'Analysis of farms support under direct payments'. *Bulgarian Journal of Agricultural Economics and Management*, 65(3), 3–22

MAFF. 2020. 'Agrarian report 2019'. Ministry of Agriculture, Food and Forestry, Bulgaria

Meuwissen, M., P. Feindt, A. Spiegel, et al. 2019. 'A framework to assess the resilience of farming systems'. *Agricultural Systems*, 176, 102656

Nicholas-Davis, P., S. Fowler and P. Midmore. 2020. 'Telling stories – Farmers offer new insights into farming resilience'. *EuroChoices*, 19 (2), 12–17

Reidsma, P., M. Meuwissen, F. Accatino, et al. 2020. 'How do stakeholders perceive the sustainability and resilience of EU farming systems?'. *EuroChoices*, 19(2), 18–27

8 | Historical Legacies and Current Challenges for the Future Resilience of the Farming System in the Altmark

FRANZISKA APPEL, ANNEKE MEIER
AND FRANZISKA OLLENDORF

8.1 Introduction

Throughout Europe, farming systems experience multiple challenges which put pressure on the performance of their essential functions and long-term resilience (see Chapter 1 and Meuwissen et al. 2019 for the introduction to the resilience concept). This chapter provides insights into the main factors that shape the resilience of the farming system in the Altmark, the German case study within the SURE-Farm project. The farming system in the Altmark represents a structure typical of Eastern German farming systems due to its specific historical trajectory. Until the point of research, little was known about how historical circumstances and current dynamics shape the farming system's resilience attributes and capacities. The chapter aims to shed some light on these processes by providing selected findings of the SURE-Farm project supplemented by further literature focussing on the region. The findings are based on a set of qualitative research tools applied during the SURE-Farm project, such as key informant interviews (*Demographic* and *Learning Interviews*), focus group discussions (*Risk Management Focus Group*), and participatory impact assessments (*FoPIA I and II*). Table 8.1 provides an overview of the research tools and participants. After the system went through a transformation from the socialist to a market economy in the past three decades, currently adaptability appears to be the strongest resilience capacity. The chapter closes by presenting future strategies, suggested by workshop participants and interviewees, to enhance the resilience of the farming system.

8.2 Structural Features of the Farming System

The Altmark is located in the German Federal State of Saxony-Anhalt and captures important features of the large-scale agricultural

Table 8.1. *Overview of applied methods in the Altmark case study*

Method	Date	Participants' institutional affiliation	Reference
Farm Demographic Interviews	05–11/2018	12 farmers	Coopmans et al. (2019)
Framework for Participatory Impact Assessment I (FoPIA I)	01/2019	5 farmers, 3 politicians, 1 NGO, 1 researcher, 2 consultants	Paas et al. (2019)
Framework for Participatory Impact Assessment II (FoPIA II)	02/2020	5 farmers, 1 consultant, 1 NGO, 3 politicians, 1 machinery ring, 2 public agricultural support institutes	Accatino et al. (2020)
Learning Interviews	05–11/2018	12 farmers	Urquhart et al. (2019)
Risk Management Focus Group	06/2019	3 farmers, 1 consultant, 1 bank, 1 assurance company	Soriano et al. (2020)

Source: own compilation

structures of Eastern German agriculture. The region has a relatively high proportion of grassland in agricultural land, at nearly 27 per cent. The soil quality is rather poor, and the arable farming yield levels are relatively low. The majority of the land is cultivated by farms with more than 200 ha. Farm types are heterogeneous, but mixed and arable farms are most prevalent. In terms of numbers of farms, individual full and part-time farms as well as partnership farms dominate the Altmark. Despite most of the farms being family farms, they are often ten times the size of family farms found in Western Germany and rely on hired labour. Although farms categorised as legal persons (mainly limited companies and producer cooperatives) only account for ~10 per cent of the farms, they farm 45 per cent of the agricultural land. The family and cooperative farms have a high share of loan capital and rented land, and therefore a relatively low capital base. The main commodities produced are cereals, oil seeds, potatoes, and sugar beets as well as meat and milk, which are marketed as standard via wholesalers, large dairies, and slaughterhouses. Livestock production is dominated by large stocks. Fattening pigs are mainly kept in herds of more than a thousand animals and dairy cows in herds of 100 to more than 500. Around 40 per cent of the dairy cows and 53 per cent of the specialised dairy farms in Saxony-Anhalt are located in the Altmark, although the region contains only 23 per cent of the agricultural land of Saxony-Anhalt (in 2007) (StaLa-Statistisches Landesamt Sachsen-Anhalt 2008, 2014), emphasising the relative importance of livestock production. The production of biogas is also an important activity of many farms in the region (Regionale Planungsgemeinschaft Altmark 2012).

8.3 Historical Circumstances That Have Shaped the Farming System

The farming system in the Altmark is still shaped by structures created with the agricultural policy measures of the former Democratic Republic of Germany (GDR) and by spatial and social marginalisation processes resulting from the societal transformation in the aftermath of Germany's reunification. In the 1950s and 1960s, private family farms were transformed into state-managed agricultural production cooperatives (Landwirtschaftliche Produktionsgenossenschaft, LPG). The collectivisation process established very large farms of pooled land as well as large herd sizes. During this time, the region saw a specialisation in arable farming and in livestock production. Agriculture in the late GDR was characterised by low productivity due to lack of modernisation and investment in the final years of the by-then almost bankrupt GDR. At the same time, 11 per cent of the workforce was employed in agriculture in 1989, compared to just 3.5 per cent in Western Germany. In the Altmark, even every fourth to fifth employee worked in the agricultural sector (Bernien 1995).

After German reunification, farmers had the opportunity to reclaim their land, but only a small number decided to become independent entrepreneurs. Due to their lack of capital and knowledge on how to individually manage a farm, many farmers pooled their returned land

and other resources to re-establish cooperative farms. In addition, a number of local farmers and many external investors established limited liability companies. The farming system managed to successfully adapt to the sudden integration into the Common Agricultural Policy of the European Union. Both cooperative and corporate farms adjusted quickly to the new political and economic conditions. They achieved a remarkably rapid increase in productivity mainly due to mechanisation, the reduction of workforce, and an increased application of chemical inputs. In other sectors, the transformation in the Altmark was not as efficient. In many villages and entire regions, the LPG was the only employer and often responsible for communal and social roles like running nurseries or fire departments (Weiß and Corthier 2016). The privatisation of the LPGs left a large void in both the employment and the municipal service structure. Lower wage levels compared to urban areas, few opportunities for career advancement, poor infrastructure, and lack of employment opportunities contributed to a large population exodus post-reunification. Particularly well-educated young women turned their backs on rural areas (Weiß and Corthier 2016). This outmigration and the general demographic change led to a decline of 13 per cent in the Altmark's population since reunification. Today it is one of the least densely populated regions in Germany. This, in turn, makes attracting young people one of the most challenging tasks for the region (Michaelis 2009). The ageing and declining population also affects the farming system since farms find it difficult to attract and retain a skilled staff (*Learning Interviews*).

8.4 Characteristics and Associated Challenges of the Farming System

8.4.1 Agro-ecological Factors

The Altmark region does not offer the best environmental conditions for agriculture: poor soils (sandy or clay rich) and low average annual rainfall limit agricultural productivity. Historically, weather challenges such as floods and droughts have been recurrent. However, in recent years, the farming system in the Altmark has been repeatedly affected by an increasing occurrence of extreme weather events such as frost, drought, heavy rain and floods. After extremely dry summers in 2018 and 2019, all participants in the stakeholder workshop *FoPIA*

II were concerned about the future climatic conditions for agriculture in the Altmark. The application of pesticides and other chemical inputs has negative impacts on the biodiversity and natural habitats in the region. Another problem is that many water channels and extraction rights for irrigation water date back to the pre-reunification period. The outdated extraction rights mean that access to water is unequally distributed and some farms have insufficient access (Bijttebier et al. 2018; Unay-Gailhard et al. 2018). Not only the quantity, but also the quality of water is expected to become a problem because of a structural shift in dairy production. While the number of smaller dairy farms in the Altmark is continuously decreasing, especially during periods with low milk prices, medium and large-scale dairy farms are becoming the dominant form of dairy production in the region. Some interviewees of the *Farm Demographic Interview* stated the concern that this might lead to an increase of water pollution in the region.

8.4.2 Agro-economical Characteristics

Although growth could be seen in other economic sectors such as the food industry, energy production, and wood processing (Schmidt 2010), agriculture is still relatively important in the Altmark. It accounts for 5 per cent of gross value added in the Altmark region, compared to 0.9 per cent for Germany as a whole in 2018 (Statistikportal 2019). However, the weak capital base per hectare, the high share of rented land in large farms, the low proportion of high-quality arable land, and the reliance on hired labour, which is often not available constrain agricultural productivity and make the farming system vulnerable. In the *FoPIA II* workshop, as in all previous stakeholder discussions, there was a broad consensus that market prices for agricultural products would remain low whilst costs increase. In this context, creating value-added opportunities was mentioned several times as a response, but no strategic approaches were suggested. Most farms focus on primary production; meaning there is not a clear avenue for increasing value-added through product differentiation. Direct marketing was regarded as a difficult undertaking in the Altmark because of the weak demand in the region. Generally, participants in the *FoPIA II* workshop saw an urgent need to adapt the farming system to increase the market power of farmers. Several external economic factors that influence the resilience of agriculture in the Altmark were discussed by the participants in the *FoPIA I* workshop. For instance, the 2008 financial crisis led to strongly fluctuating market prices of agricultural products which, according to participating farmers, had negative impacts on their business. Another example was the introduction of minimum wages in Germany in 2015. The minimum wage improved farm workers' livelihoods but put more pressure on the farms' financial profitability. In the *Farm Demographic Interviews* farmers mentioned competition with foreign producers as an economic challenge. Simultaneously, rising land prices further challenge the system.

8.4.3 Institutional Embedding

In the *Risk Management Focus Group* as well as the *Learning* and *Farm Demographic Interviews*, farmers mentioned policy makers not paying enough attention to farmers' needs, continuously changing political regulations, and increasing bureaucratic requirements as challenges for the resilience of the farming system. Similarly, in the *FoPIA II* workshop, the effect of policies and regulations was generally seen as ambivalent, particularly when they change frequently. Some group members invoked the ideals of a free market and self-regulation and saw overregulation as a risk for system efficiency. Others did not share this view and highlighted the protective and supportive roles of policies and regulations. The impact of the political framework on the farming system was further assessed by applying the *ReSAT* tool (see Chapter 4). Direct payments from the Common Agricultural Policy (CAP) of the European Union provide buffer resources to stabilise farm incomes and thereby support the status quo of the farming system. Therefore, the current policy constellation strongly enhances the robustness of the farming system. The European Agricultural Fund for Rural Development (EAFRD) programming of the state Saxony-Anhalt within the 2nd pillar of the CAP focusses on objectives which address challenges for the medium to long term such as protection of agricultural resources. But it suffers from a limited budget, as Germany transferred only 4.5 per cent of the 1st pillar budget into the 2nd pillar (European regulations would have allowed a 15 per cent transfer). A key problem, however, seems to be that these voluntary measures were taken up by fewer addressees than expected. Participants in all research activities during the SURE-Farm study in the Altmark highlighted the poor infrastructure in the region as a key challenge for the farming system. The low levels of internet coverage, access to financial services, availability of medical and care services, cultural offerings, and commuting possibilities reduce the attractiveness of living in the Altmark. In the *FoPIA II* workshop, these issues were assessed as already being beyond their critical thresholds. As a response, some farmers fulfil municipal tasks which are no longer sufficiently provided by the municipality (Weiß and Corthier 2016).

8.4.4 Social Environment

Participants in the different SURE-Farm research activities repeatedly highlighted that a bad image of agriculture has contributed to the unattractiveness of the sector. Many participating farmers stated that the media had played a central role in transmitting a negative picture of conventional farming to the broader society. Moreover, participants saw little contribution from society to the farming system's resilience in the form of, for example, supporting rural life or improving natural capital. In addition to economic challenges and the low level of rural development, the negative reputation of agriculture was seen as a major factor for the limited availability of workers and farm successors.

8.5 Impact of the Challenges on Essential System Functions

Each farming system fulfils a number of essential functions which can be divided into the provision of public and private goods (Chapter 1; Meuwissen et al. 2019). Stakeholders' perceptions of the importance and performance of the farming system functions in the Altmark were assessed in the *FoPIA I* workshop. The functions which were regarded as most essential concern both private and public goods (see Annex 8.1). While farmers scored the importance of the function 'economic viability' as highest, non-farmer participants such as politicians and NGO representatives attributed most importance to the function 'food production'. While the importance of these two functions was scored highest, the actual performance was assessed as low to medium for the function 'economic viability' and as moderate to good for the function 'food production'. Regarding public goods, the function 'maintaining natural resources in good condition' was perceived as most important by all stakeholder groups and its performance was assessed as moderate to good. One main finding is that while the function 'quality of life' was perceived as important, its performance scored lowest and therefore requires particular attention.

All of these essential system functions are directly shaped by several of these challenges, showing a high degree of complexity of the factors that affect resilience (for a detailed discussion, see Mathijs et al. 2021). Most notably, the experiences of extreme weather events in 2018 and 2019 exposed the vulnerability of agriculture and its most essential functions such as the 'production of food' and the 'conservation of natural resources'. Once the function of 'food production' is affected by extreme weather events, this spills over to the function of 'economic viability' of farms. Both functions are affected by issues of continuously changing policies and regulations, which were seen as making long-term planning for improved risk management and innovations more difficult for farm owners and managers. Furthermore, the functions 'food production' and 'economic viability' of farms are also affected by the shortage of labour supply due to the unattractiveness of the region. Finally, the various negative effects of the low level of rural development and infrastructure provision in the Altmark directly affect the system functions 'quality of life' and 'attractiveness of rural areas'.

8.6 Resilience Capacities and Attributes of the Farming System

The SURE-Farm methodological framework (Chapter 1; Meuwissen et al. 2019) conceptualises resilience attributes and capacities. Understood as the 'individual and collective competences and the enabling (or constraining) environment' (Meuwissen et al. 2019), resilience attributes provide conditions for the resilience of a farming system and its capacities. In the present case study, during different research activities, participants assessed resilience attributes in the Altmark as generally low to moderate. The manifestation of the attributes is directly shaped by the systems' characteristics and challenges described in the previous sections. In the *FoPIA I* workshop, the participants assessed the 'functional diversity' of the farming system to be low. This is mainly due to the poor soils which limit the diversity in arable farming. Mixed farms with a diverse production system show a higher degree of functional diversity. The diversity of the systemic responses to shocks and stresses was estimated by participants as moderate to good. While mixed farms were generally seen to have a greater set of responses, for all farm types diversification into other on-farm activities such as biogas or tourism was regarded as feasible. The *Learning Interviews* revealed a moderate to good level of 'openness' of the farming system. Learning was seen as potentially contributing to resilience by learning from others, acquiring information, implementing best practices from colleagues or cooperating with other farmers (experimenting, sharing inputs). Interviewees reported that learning strategies (e.g. experimentation, learning from others, acquiring new information, and reflexivity) enabled them to adopt better risk management strategies and thereby improve resilience. Regarding agricultural practices, 'system reserves' were seen to be at a low level. In several workshops, participating farmers described their low equity base as a main challenge for their farms (see Section 4.2). In addition, given the described societal and institutional characteristics, human capital is low (labour and succession). Yet, agricultural practices were strengthened by a moderate to good level of 'natural capital' and coupling good farming practices with it. However, there is a risk of deterioration of the natural capital due to climate change, and the loss of water quality and biodiversity. Regarding farm demographics, levels of diversity and modularity are low. Farmers reported difficulties in attracting the young generation and women (reducing diversity), and skilled labour in general (limiting modularity). Governance measures were perceived as not being responsive enough to system challenges and were ranked low to moderate in *FoPIA I*, indicating a low level of the resilience attribute 'tightness of feedback'. In contrast, the 'tightness of feedback' was assessed as good among farmers but the perceived low level of institutional support or institutionalisation of exchange activities was a major finding of *FoPIA II*.

The resilience framework suggests three capacities which a given farming system needs to develop or strengthen in order to achieve resilience: robustness, adaptability, and transformability. In the *FoPIA I* stakeholder workshop, participants were asked to assess these three capacities for the farming system in the Altmark. All three resilience capacities were estimated by workshop participants to be generally low to moderate in the Altmark. At the time of research, adaptability was perceived as the strongest among them, mainly because of the farms' ability to increase their efficiency, a good level of self-organisation of farmers, and the potential to diversify their activities. After the farming system went through a transformation from a socialist to a market economy after the German reunification, the analyses of the SURE-Farm research activities provide little evidence on whether the current system is able to apply its past capacity to transform to the current challenges.

8.7 Future Strategies to Enhance Resilience of the Farming System

Future strategies were discussed with farming system stakeholders in the *Risk Management* and *FoPIA II* workshops. The characteristics and challenges, and the farming systems' functions and attributes presented here provide a sound base for reflecting on appropriate strategies to enhance the resilience of the farming system in the Altmark. Strategies target all four interwoven processes of the adaptive cycle: risk management, governance, farm demographics, and agricultural production (see Chapter 1; Meuwissen et al. 2019). Concerning *risk management*, the low economic capital of farms as well as farmers' perceptions to be at or even beyond a threshold (*FoPIA II*) demonstrate a clear need to increase the financial security of farms. During the *Risk Management* focus group, participants expressed the necessity to improve the information flow within the system, particularly with regard to information on funding opportunities, best practices, and research findings, as well as the handling of regulatory measures. Farmers stated a need to be more appropriately supported by the government (financially and knowledge-wise) during the adaptation and mitigation of climate change effects. In order to better respond to the risk of an acute labour shortage, participants suggested farmers should increase their investment in training and education of potential workers. Regarding *governance* processes, the challenges arising from what were seen as continuously changing policies and regulations were often mentioned. Future strategies should therefore consider the medium- and long-term planning needs of farming system stakeholders. Similarly, high bureaucratic barriers were deemed to reduce farmers' ability to adapt or even transform. Participants suggested to take addressees' experiences with legislation and bureaucracy more into consideration when developing public policy. *FoPIA II* participants saw public support of societal appreciation of agriculture as another important governmental strategy which would improve the resilience of the farming system. The joint implementation of projects which aim to educate the public about agriculture was seen as a strategy to enhance the attractiveness of agriculture as an employer.

As the findings reveal, *farm demographics* are under particular pressure in the Altmark. The low level of rural development, negative demographic change, and high investment needs are the main obstacles for this process. Consequently, resilience-enhancing strategies have to address these factors. While several infrastructure projects are ongoing, the progress is slow and participants in the various focus groups have not yet experienced any positive effects of these projects. The increase in the Federal State's efforts for a dedicated encompassing development strategy, targeting infrastructure deficits (mobility, communication, social services) in the rural areas of the Altmark would have a positive effect on most of the resilience attributes and can therefore be seen as a key strategy to enhance the resilience of the system. Measures which improve the stimulation of succession (e.g. through improved access to finance) or which enhance the attractiveness of agricultural jobs (e.g. through higher wages, a more positive social reputation) were seen as feasible. In addition, the transfer of farm land of closed or closing farms to existing or new farms will also gain more importance in the future since likely more farms will exit.

One key strategy concerning *agricultural production* which was brought up by participants in the *Risk Management* focus group was improved integration of research findings in production activities. In order to do so, research findings would have to be more easily accessible and new channels of information flow would need to be established either by the research organisations, farmers' groups, or with public support. Farms' adaptation of new technologies is a strategy which responds to several challenges by, for instance, adapting to climate change, improving soil management, and increasing farm efficiency. Machinery rings reduce costs for farmers and foster cooperation between and self-organisation among farmers. In the *FoPIA II* workshop the participants stated that if water in the Altmark were to become scarcer, not only more efficient irrigation systems would be needed but also the production would have to be adjusted to the new climate conditions. An increased functional diversity of farms would foster resilience at the farm level and then at the farming system level. As there is currently an increase in demand for organic and local products in Germany, a potential transformation to organic farming was discussed as one alternative system in *FoPIA II*. While the main changes would occur at the farm level and mainly affect production methods and plant and animal varieties used, a number of changes in both upstream and downstream segments would also be required since the inputs would change and new marketing channels would need to be established. However, most of the participating conventional farmers showed a rather sceptical attitude towards a transition to organic farming.

8.8 Conclusion

The profitability of farms is low, the natural capital soil is relatively well conserved but biodiversity and habitats are decreasing. Maintaining sufficient water qualities and quantities are possible future challenges arising from climate change and intensification of dairy production. The availability of labour and successors is limited due to low profitability, negative societal reputation of the sector, and general demographic trends. The structural marginalisation of the Altmark, regarding lack of social and cultural opportunities, internet, and transport connections to the next metropolitan areas, further adds to the low standard of living in the region and reduces the attractiveness of farming there as well. Overall, the farming system of the Altmark was assessed as adaptable and also robust in particular processes, but also as experiencing a lock-in due to low wages and insufficient infrastructure. Consequently, transformability of the farming system was considered to be low. Strategies to enhance the resilience of the farming system should address all four processes in the adaptive cycle – risk management, governance, demographics, and production practices – with particular emphasis on rural development and fostering exchange between all farming system stakeholders in order to develop joint strategic approaches, and to improve spreading of information and best practices.

Farming system

- Large-scale mixed and arable corporate farms have highest share in agricultural area but majority are family farms
- Main commodities: cereals, oil seeds, potatoes, sugar beets, meat and milk
- No major difference in resilience perceptions between farm and farming system levels.

Altmark (GER)

Farm — Main farms in analysis

Actors — Other FS actors

☆ — Locality (agro-ecological context, infrastructure, public goods, identity,...)

Input suppliers/traders — Consultants
Producers associations — Contractors
Mixed farms — Arable farms
Financial Institutions — Local government
Farm Household — Employees (staff, hired)

Challenges

Environmental:
- Climate change (increase extreme weather events);
- Poor soils

Economic:
- Price volatility, low margins, low equity base, low wages;
- Rising land prices

Institutional:
- Constantly changing policies and regulations;
- High bureaucratic barriers

Social:
- Rural development (infra-structure, attractiveness of the region, demographic change);
- Societal expectations;
- Labour and farm succession

Adaptive cycle

Risk management
Conservation
Reorganisation
Growth
Position on adaptive cycle
Collapse
Farm demographics
Agricultural production

Essential functions

Private goods:
- Ensuring sufficient farm income: *Low to medium performance*
- Delivering high-quality food products: *medium to good performance*

Public goods:
- Maintaining natural resources in good condition: *medium to good performance*

Needs more attention
! Quality of life: *lowest performance among all functions*

Resilience capacities

- Overall low to moderate resilience capacities;
- Adaptability as main resilience capacity, farmers already went through a huge transformation process (reunion of Germany) but difficulties to apply these experiences to current challenges
- Policies rather foster robustness and partly adaptability, no focus on transformability

Resilience attributes

Diversity: moderate
- Soil type limits diversity of farm activities;
- Diversification into other on-farm activities (biogas, tourism)

Modularity: moderate
- Moderate heterogeneity of farm types

System reserves: low to moderate
- Production is moderately coupled with local and natural capital;
- Low profitability of farms, successors need high investments

Tightness of feedbacks: low to moderate
- Lack of policy support instruments dismantling status quo;
- Good level of self-organised horizontal cooperation but lack of institutionalisation of exchange platforms

Openness: moderate
- Learning capacity and awareness about its importance;
- Low level of infrastructure for innovation

Future strategies

Risk management	Governance	Farm demographics	Agricultural production
• Increase of financial security • Improve information flow • Invest in training and education of potential workers • Improve alignment of production with market demand • Financial support for climate change adaptation/mitigation	• Increase continuity and transparency of regulations • Decrease the rigidity of legislation and bureaucracy • Support societal appreciation (facilitate cooperation among FS stakeholders and between farmers and schools) • More attention to gender issues	• Increase relevance of taking over or farm land of closed/passive farms • Foster rural development through expansion of infrastructure • Stimulate succession via improved access to finance • Improve attractiveness of agricultural jobs	• Increase integration of research on crops and breeding • New technologies >> improve access through machinery sharing rings • Improve soil management • Improve irrigation schemes and access to water extraction rights • Increase diversification

This project has received funds from the European Union's Horizon 2020 research and innovation programme under Grant Agreement No 727520

IAMO
Leibniz Institut für Agrarentwicklung in Transformationsökonomien

SURE Farm

Annex 8.1 Factsheet synthesising resilience of the current farming system in the Altmark (Germany).

Source: own compilation

References

Accatino, F.; Paas, W.; Herrera, H.; Appel, F.; Pinsard, C.; Shi, Y. et al. (2020): Impacts of future scenarios on the resilience of farming systems across the EU assessed with quantitative and qualitative methods. SURE-Farm Deliverable 5.5. Paris: INRAE. Available at www.surefarmproject .eu/wordpress/wp-content/uploads/2020/06/D5.5.-Future-scenarios-on-the-FS-resilience.pdf, last accessed on 17 March 2021.

Bernien, M. (1995): Umbruch der Arbeit in der Landwirtschaft der neuen Bundesländer. In R. Schmidt, B. Lutz (Eds.): *Chancen und Risiken der industriellen Restrukturierung in Ostdeutschland.* Wiesbaden: VS Verlag für Sozialwissenschaften (KSPW: Transformationsprozesse), pp. 356–374.

Bijttebier, J.; Coopmans, I.; Appel, F.; Gailhard, I.; Wauters, E. (2018): Report on current farm demographics and trends. SURE-Farm Deliverable 3.1. Melle: OCILVO. Available at www.surefarmproject.eu/wordpress/wp-content/uploads/2019/05/D3.1-Report-on-current-farm-demographics-and-trends-RP1.pdf, last accessed on 17 March 2021.

Coopmans, I.; Dessein, J.; Bijttebier, J.; Antonioli, F.; Appel, F.; Berry, R. et al. (2019): Report on a qualitative analysis in 11 case-studies for understanding the process of farm demographic change across EU-farming systems and its influencing factors. SURE-Farm Deliverable D3.2. Melle/Halle: OCILVO/IAMO. Available at www.surefarmproject.eu/wordpress/wp-content/uploads/2019/07/D3.2-Report-on-a-a-qualitative-analysis-in-11-case-studies-for-understanding-the-process-of-farm-demographic-change-across-EU-farming-systems-and-its-influencing-factors.pdf, last accessed on 17 March 2021.

Mathijs, E.; Bijttebier, J; Accatino, F.; Feindt, P.; Gavrilescu, C.; Manevska-Tasevska, G. et al. (2021): Report on combinations of conditions for successful and unsuccessful fostering of resilience in agricultural sectors. SURE-Farm Deliverable 6.2. Melle: OCILVO. Available at www .surefarmproject.eu/wordpress/wp-content/uploads/2019/07/D3.2-Report-on-a-a-qualitative-analysis-in-11-case-studies-for-understanding-the-pro cess-of-farm-demographic-change-across-EU-farming-systems-and-its-influ encing-factors.pdf, last accessed on 17 March 2021.

Meuwissen, M.; Feindt, P.; Spiegel, A.; Termeer, C.; Mathijs, E.; de Mey, Y. et al. (2019): Framework to assess the resilience of farming systems. In: Agricultural Systems 176.

Michaelis, D. (2009): Die Altmark – eine Kulturlandschaft im Spannungsfeld von Schrumpfung, Chancen und Visionen. In R. Friedel, E. A. Spindler (Eds.): *Nachhaltige Entwicklung ländlicher Räume. Chancenverbesserung durch Innovation und Traditionspflege.* 1. Aufl. Wiesbaden: VS Verlag für Sozialwissenschaften, pp. 398–404.

Paas, W.; Accatino, F.; Antonioli, F.; Appel, F.; Bardaji, I.; Coopmans, I. et al. (2019): Participatory impact assessment of sustainability and resilience of EU farming systems. SURE-Farm Deliverable D.5.2. Wageningen: WU. Available at www.surefarmproject.eu/wordpress/ wp-content/uploads/2019/06/D5.2-FoPIA-SURE-Farm-Cross-country-report.pdf, last accessed on 17 March 2021.

Pitson, C.; Appel, F.; Dong, C.; Balmann; A. (2019): Open-access paper on the formulation and adaption of an agent-based model to simulate . generational renewal. SURE-Farm Deliverable D3.4. Halle (Saale): IAMO. Available at www.surefarmproject.eu/wordpress/wp-content/ uploads/2019/05/D3.4-Paper-on-adapting-an-ABM-to-simulate-gener ational-renewal.pdf, last accessed on 17 March 2021.

Regionale Planungsgemeinschaft Altmark (2012): Wieder erfolgreich im Bundeswettbewerb: Die Altmark ist Bioenergie-Region. Available at http://altmark.eu/bioenergie-region, last accessed on 17 March 2021.

Schmidt, U. (2010): Gleichwertigkeit der Lebensbedingungen im ländlichen Raum – das Beispiel Altmark. In M. Rosenfeld (Ed.): *Gleichwertigkeit der Lebensverhältnisse zwischen Politik und Marktmechanismus. Empirische Befunde aus den Ländern Sachsen, Sachsen-Anhalt und Thüringen.* Hannover: Akad. für Raumforschung und Landesplanung. Arbeitsmaterial der ARL, Nr. 351, pp. 220–236.

Soriano, B.; Bardaji, I.; Bertolozzi, D.; San Martin, C.; Spiegel, A.; Slijper, T. et al. (2020): Report on state and outlook for risk management in EU agriculture. SURE-Farm Deliverable D2.6. Madrid: UPM. Available at www.surefarmproject.eu/wordpress/wp-content/uploads/2020/02/D2-6-Report-on-state-and-outlook-on-risk-magagment-in-EU.pdf, last accessed on 17 March 2021.

StaLa-Statistisches Landesamt Sachsen-Anhalt (2008): Agrarstrukturerhebung Teil 3: Betriebswirtschaftliche Ausrichtung, Standarddeckungsbeiträge, sozialökonomische Verhältnisse der landwirtschaftlichen Betriebe. Halle (Saale). Available at www.stala.sachsen-anhalt.de/download/stat_ber ichte/6C404_4j_2007.pdf, last accessed on 17 March 2021.

(2014): Ausgewählte Merkmale der landwirtschaftlichen Betriebe nach Kreisen 2013. Halle (Saale). Available at www.stala.sachsen-anhalt.de/ Internet/Home/Daten_und_Fakten/4/41/411/41121/Ausgewaehlte-Merkmale-nach-Kreisen-2013-.html, last accessed on 17 March 2021.

Statistikportal (2019): Volkswirtschaftliche Gesamtrechnungen der Länder. Bruttoinlandsprodukt, Bruttowertschöpfung in den kreisfreien Städten und Landkreisen der Bundesrepublik Deutschland 1992 und 1994 bis 2018 (2). Available at www.statistikportal.de/de/vgrdl/ergebnisse-kreise

bene/bruttoinlandsprodukt-bruttowertschoepfung-kreise#alle-ergeb
nisse, last accessed on 27 November 2020.

Unay-Gailhard, I.; Balmann, A.; Appel, F. (2018): Dimensions of SURE-
Farm farm typology for farm resilience assessments. SURE-Farm
Deliverable D1.3. Halle (Saale): IAMO. Available at www
.surefarmproject.eu/wordpress/wp-content/uploads/2019/05/D1.3-
Farm-Typology-RP1.pdf, last accessed on 17 March 2021.

Urquhart, J.; Accatino, F.; Appel, F.; Antonioli, F.; Berry, R.; Bertolozzi, D.
et al. (2019): Report on farmers' learning capacity and networks of
influence in 11 European case studies. SURE-Farm Deliverable D2.3.
Gloucestershire: UoG. Available at www.surefarmproject.eu/wordpress/
wp-content/uploads/2019/07/D2.3-Report-on-farmers-learning-cap
acity-and-networks-of-influence.pdf, last accessed on 17 March 2021.

Weiß, W.; Corthier, J. (2016): Beitrag der Landwirtschaft zur Sicherung der
Daseinsvorsorge in ländlichen Räumen. In M. Herbst, F. Dünkel, B.
Stahl (Eds.): *Daseinsvorsorge und Gemeinwesen im ländlichen Raum.*
Wiesbaden: Springer, pp. 127–149.

9 Opportunities to Improve the Resilience of Extensive Sheep Farming in Huesca (Spain)

BÁRBARA SORIANO, ALBERTO GARRIDO, CAROLINA SAN MARTÍN, DANIELE BERTOLOZZI-CAREDIO AND ISABEL BARDAJÍ

9.1 The Extensive Sheep Sector in Huesca

The extensive sheep farming system (FS) is located in Huesca, in the region of Aragón, North-eastern Spain. The region has a long history of ovine production (Navarro, 1992), although the number of farms and sheep have more than halved in the last twenty years. Nowadays, the province has around 521,500 head of sheep and 930 farms (Gobierno de Aragón, 2020; MAPA, 2020b) dedicated to lamb meat production (Figure 9.1). Farms are mainly medium-size (200–1,000 sheep) family businesses, diversified with almond orchards, olive trees, cereal crops and vineyards (Pardos et al., 2008; Gobierno de Aragón, 2020). The territory comprises a mountainous geomorphology in the North and a flat area in the South. This geographical characterization harbours different types of sheep farming: (i) specialized farms where animal feeding is mainly based on pasture lands to the North and (ii) mixed animal and crop farms where animals feeding is based on stubble fields to the South.

The FS embraces farmers and the actors who mutually influence one another (Meuwissen et al., 2019). In the centre of the extensive sheep farming system in Huesca are the farmers and farm households closely connected with the technical services providers (veterinarians), the cooperatives and farmers' associations. Crop farmers (as stubble fields' providers), local public administration, universities and research institutes, and distributors (slaughterhouses) are also closely linked to the farmers.

The following sections explain the main conclusions that can be drawn from the multiple research activities conducted in Huesca: farmers' surveys, farmers and stakeholders' in-depth interviews,

156

Figure 9.1 Sheep in farms in Huesca.
Source: Universidad Politécnica de Madrid

workshops and focus groups (see Chapter 1 for a detailed outline of the methods used). The conclusions build on the perceptions of the actors in the FS, supported by official statistics and a literature review.

9.1.1 What Are the Functions Provided by the Extensive Sheep Farming System?

According to actors' perceptions, the main functions provided by extensive sheep farming are guaranteeing sufficient farm incomes (gross margin), delivering high-quality food at affordable prices (number of sheep) and generating employment in rural areas (number of farms) (Annex 9.1). The provision of these functions exhibits a downward trend in recent years (Becking et al., 2019; Reidsma et al., 2019). In terms of farm income, the actors in the FS explained that gross margins have been decreasing since the beginning of the century, reaching almost negative values (tipping point) in current times. According to MAPA (2020b), the gross margins in Aragón was 47 €/head in 2017. The number of animals decreased by 43.7 per cent in the period 2005–2019 in Huesca (Gobierno de Aragón, 2020; MAPA, 2020b). The decrease has been less pronounced since 2010 (by 17.5 per cent) as the remaining farms acquired the herds of the exiting farmers. In fact, the number of sheep per farm increased by 50.2 per cent in the period 1995–2015 (Gobierno de Aragón, 2016). Finally, the number of farms decreased around 65 per cent in the period 2005–2019 in Huesca (Gobierno de Aragón, 2016, 2020).

The actors in the FS perceived that the FS also provides a range of public goods (Annex 9.1). Primarily, the extensive sheep sector maintains and preserves the natural resources. It contributes to maintaining the biodiversity of the region and the soil quality, and preventing forest fires by keeping the area clean from weeds and scrub (Casasús et al., 2007; Rodríguez-Ortega et al., 2014; Peco et al., 2017; Kok et al., 2020). Additionally, the extensive sheep sector follows practices that enhance animal welfare. The animal welfare in extensive production systems is challenged by some authors in the literature. Koidou et al. (2019) explained that animal welfare conditions can deteriorate due to variations in forage availability and nutritive value as well as the lack of infrastructure in grasslands. Munoz et al. (2018) found that the main welfare issues in ewe extensive production are under- and over-feeding, ewe mortality, lameness, ecto-parasites (flystrike) and mastitis. Finally extensive farming contributes to the attractiveness of rural areas, as this specilization requires farmers, families and workers to live close to the farms, to keep rural areas alive and in good condition (Kristensen et al., 2016).

It has become evident that there is a lack of indicators to measure the provision of the mentioned public goods. Indicators to measure the effect of the sector on the biodiversity are difficult to implement (Kok et al., 2020). There are no indicators to measure the contribution of extensive farming to fire prevention. Research and indicators normally focus on grazing effects on the reduction of wood biomass, the land use and cover change (Ruiz-Mirazo et al., 2011; Mancilla-Leytón and Martín Vicente, 2012; Oliveira et al., 2017; Castro et al., 2020). Indicators to measure animal welfare are not always reliable (Llonch et al., 2015) or are perceived differently by stakeholders (Doughty et al., 2017).

9.1.2 What Challenges Threaten the Farming System's Functions?

The extensive sheep farming in Huesca faces interconnected economic, institutional, social and environmental challenges that threaten the provision of private and public goods. Most of the challenges

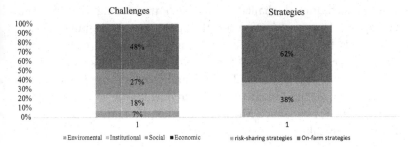

Figure 9.2 Perceived challenges and strategies to deal with them.
Source: Fifty farmers' surveys conducted in the CS. The percentages show the number of times the challenge nature (economic, social, institutional or environmental) on the left side and the strategy type (on-farm or risk-sharing strategy) on the right side have been mentioned over the total challenges and strategies mentioned, respectively (Soriano et al., 2020)

correspond to long-term pressures, but shocks related to stochastic variables (production, market price, disease outbreak, wild fauna attacks, droughts etc.) also impact on the FS's functions (Annex 9.1).

Most of the challenges identified by the actors in the FS are related to the low profitability of the sector (economic dimension) (Figure 9.2), which is explained by the decreasing incomes. Lamb meat consumption decreased by 40 per cent in the period 2006–2017 (MAPA, 2018) leading to stagnated and low lamb prices (MAPA, 2020a). The decreasing consumption is in turn explained by changing consumers' preferences (Martin-Collado et al., 2019) and the bad image of the livestock industry (animal welfare, greenhouse gas emissions, etc.). Downward pressures on market prices are also explained by the increased competence of imports and lower producers' bargaining power in the value chain (Corcoran, 2003). On the other hand, the increasing feeding and labour costs and land prices reduce the farms' profitability.

Social challenges mainly relate to the intense process of depopulation in the region that began in the middle of the last century (Bosque and Navarro, 2002). Depopulation has been accompanied by an ageing population and a reduced investment in public services (schools, medical centres, etc.), which in turn discouraged family succession and the availability of skilled workers (Bertolozzi-Caredio et al., 2020). Moreover, there is no interest in working in the extensive sheep sector because of its low profitability and labour intensity that hinders the balance between work and personal life.

Some institutional challenges are also threatening the FS. The decoupling from production of the Common Agricultural Policy (CAP) aids have resulted in a reduction in the farms' income since 2004, as the sector is greatly dependent on aids (De Rancourt et al., 2006; Bernués and Olaizola, 2012). Finally, farmers are facing environmental challenges, such as more frequent and severe droughts (Turner, 2005; Hernández-Mora et al., 2012), wolf attacks and animal diseases outbreaks.

9.2 Why Has the Extensive Sector Showed a Low Resilience Capacity in the Past?

The assessment of the resilience of the FS revealed three main reasons explaining the low resilience capacity of the extensive sheep farming sector in Huesca, which are detailed in the following sections.

9.2.1 Mismatches between the Challenges and Implemented Strategies

Farmers and other actors in the FS in Huesca have been implementing several strategies to face the challenges threatening the system (Soriano et al., 2020). Most of the implemented strategies are on-farm strategies (Figure 9.2), although farmers in the FS also pursued risk-sharing strategies involving other actors in the FS, such as participating in farmers' organizations and/or cooperatives and taking out insurances (liability and animal diseases).

Among the on-farm strategies, three groups of strategies can be differentiated: (i) strategies to ensure a sound financial situation, such as keeping savings, keeping debt levels low and adding extra income from off-farm jobs; (ii) strategies to improve production efficiency such as increasing herd prolificacy (improved genetics), improving herd management (e.g. use of chips, to invest in feeding systems and handling facilities, virtual or drone shepherds, and GPS), maintaining herd health (preventive measures, e.g. vaccines) and learning from other farmers' experiences (mainly through cooperatives); and (iii) strategies to reduce labour costs. Most of the farmers in the region decided to invest extra time and involve their family in farm management, instead of hiring external workers (Annex 9.1).

The low performance of the FS functions (Section 9.1.1) suggests that the implemented strategies have turned out to be efficient but not sufficient to deal with the challenges threatening the sector. Most of the strategies are on-farm actions oriented to cope with the profitability from the supply side (reducing costs and increasing efficiency) while lower attention has been paid to the demand side to deal with the lowering of lamb meat consumption. Although cooperatives have already carried out campaigns to increase public awareness about the positive contribution of extensive farming to the environment and developed new prepared products to better meet consumers' needs, e.g. the *Hornear y listo* ('Bake and go') campaign,[1] the effort has not been enough. Involvement of other actors in the farming system is needed to reverse the downward trend of lamb meat consumption. For example, public administration and financial institutions could develop new finance products to support research on consumers' behaviour and new lamb products and implement new communication channels and marketing campaigns. Distributors in the value chain could open the sector to new markets and consumer niches to sell the products at competitive and fair prices.

Finally, greater support from the public sector could have helped to better deal with one of the greatest challenges of the sector that is the depopulation and low attractiveness of the rural areas. There is room to better tailor the rural development programme in the region as well as design legislation (sanitary /urban) that promotes businesses linked to farms (restaurants, direct sales, product elaboration) and avoids the current limitations it generates on the sector.

9.2.2 Misalignments between Agricultural Policies and the Farming System's Capacities and Functions

In interviews conducted to assess the role of policy in enabling resilience in the farming sector (see Chapter 1 for details about the method), the actors in the FS assessed the impact of the CAP on the resilience capacities of extensive sheep farming (Feindt et al., 2019). The results revealed that the CAP instruments and goals are mainly tailored to support the robustness and adaptability capacities and to a lower extent the transformability capacity. Indeed, the CAP's basic payments scheme seems to constrain farmers' robustness. Farmers have seen their aids reduced since basic payments were decoupled from production (De Rancourt et al., 2006). The historical payments scheme has created

---

[1] www.alimarket.es/alimentacion/noticia/256772/pastores-se-adentra-en-el–hornear-y-listo–de-cordero

distortions amongst the aids perceived by established and new entrants and unequal aids distribution. Additional related policies also seem to constrain the robustness capacity of the FS. Environmental legislation (wildlife and natural parks protection), sanitary (animal health and slaughter practices) and urban legislation resulted in farmers and other actors in the FS incurring increased production costs and having to comply with ever more complex procedures that hinder the FS's robustness capacity. For example, many slaughterhouses in the region were not able to meet sanitary legislation (transposition of the regulation (EC) No 853/2004 of The European Parliament) and were forced to close, followed by butcheries and other local retailers. As a consequence, farmers lost distribution channels to sell their products and bargaining power.

The limited CAP support to the extensive sheep farming resilience may be explained by the fact that the aids so far have been mainly tailored to support farmers' income instead of strengthening other relevant and specific functions of the FS, i.e. environmental protection and biodiversity contribution through pasture management (Casasús et al., 2007; Ruiz-Mirazo and Robles, 2012) and contribution to keep the rural areas alive (Kristensen et al., 2016). This is in line with Meuwissen et al. (2020), who found that many enhancing resilience strategies focused on the delivery of private goods.

9.2.3 *Weakened Resilience Attributes*

The resilience attributes are specific system characteristics which make socio-ecologic systems more resilient. Among the seventeen resilience attributes identified by Cabell and Oelofse (2012), some examples of the resilience attributes found in extensive sheep faming are resource availability (profits, human capital, natural resources, infrastructures), co-operation (intra and inter systems) and diversity of responses and policies.

We found that the scarcity of the mentioned resilience attributes in the extensive sheep sector also explains the low level of the resilience of extensive sheep farming. For example, as a result of the sector's low profitability, there is little economic leverage for undertaking investments, but also the workforce in the region is very limited, hampering the potential to grow. The lack of resources has resulted in farmers and other actors having low confidence in the sector and, thus, they are reluctant to invest. In addition, the cooperation between actors has been weak and indecisive, hampering the success of many strategies to overcome the challenges faced. It has been also identified that there is a lack of diversity of policies in the system that resulted in a limited response of the policies to the singularities of the sector. For example there is no support in place to help farmers deliver environmental objectives. On the other hand, we found that there are resilience attributes that have positively contributed to the sector's resilience. For instance, farmers, their commitment, in-depth knowledge of the sector and love for animals improved the robustness of the farming system as farmers invest their time, savings and experience to keep farms running. Finally, the strength of commercial relationships with third countries helps the capacity of the system to adapt to the decreasing national lamb consumption.

9.3 It Is Time for Extensive Sheep Farming to Transition

9.3.1 Alternative Resilient Scenarios

The actors in the FS sketched two alternative systems in which functions and resilience attributes could be improved. The first alternative system is a sustainable intensive system characterized by increasing the herd-stabling and animal-handling mechanization. There are several boundary conditions to implement this alternative system, such as bringing existing technologies closer to farmers, reinforcing training in handling (prolificacy and improved breeds), feeding and animal health issues in stables as well as investing in infrastructure and machinery, and diversifying activities to crop production to feed the herd. Additional conditions are strengthening market orientation (new trade channels and market niches) and reviewing sanitary legislation to regulate the new stabling. This alternative scenario would fit better in the southernmost and flat areas where pastures are scarcer and crop diversification is easier to implement. Moving towards this alternative scenario would improve the provision of private goods, i.e. increased meat production and improved labour conditions. It could also enhance some of the FS's resilience attributes such as investing in innovating infrastructure (through mechanization), improved profitability through cost reduction and enhancing the attractiveness of the sector, thus ensuring maintenance of rural livelihoods. But it could also constrain attributes such as 'production coupled with the local and natural capital' as feeding the herd will be coupled with pasture to a lower extent. This alternative scenario could lead to a deeper unbalance between the provision of private and public goods.

The second alternative system is the high-tech extensive system mainly characterized by an improved management of pastures and stubble lands as the basis to feed the herds. To put this alternative scenario in place, innovation in herd geo-location, weather information and wild fauna surveillance are key aspects. New communication and network tools are also needed to boost farmers' collaboration to improve the coordination in pasture management. In addition, public support is essential to reach this system for three reasons. First, public aid is needed to support the provision of public goods; second, a legal framework is the basis to regulate and protect the access to pasture land and stubble fields for grazing purposes; and third, revised sanitary legislation is requested to increase the number of actors in the region (e.g. slaughterhouses, butcheries, retail companies, restaurants) and boost short supply chains and regional consumption. This alternative system would be more suitable in the northernmost and mountainous locations, where there are more pasturelands and the geographical features make other sectors less appropriate, reducing the pressure of land competition.

Putting this alternative scenario in motion would improve the provision of private goods. Although the production is not expected to increase, reduced feeding costs and increased support for environmental enhancement would increase the farms' gross margins. Simultaneously, better performance of public functions would be accomplished as it is based on pasture and stubble field management. Additionally resilience attributes to those identified in the sustainable intensive system could be improved in this alternative system, such as 'self-organization' as cooperation is needed to manage pasture lands and herds; 'production coupled with the local and natural capital' as herd feeding will be coupled with pasture land availability; and 'diverse policies' as new policy instruments and regulations will be tailored to support the provision of the public goods provided by the sector.

9.3.2 Suggestions for Business and Policy-Enabling Actions

The actors in the FS identified many opportunities that could turn the extensive sheep farming into a more resilient FS. For example, there is room for rural banks to reinforce their knowledge about the sector and farmers' profile. Banks are called to design improved long-term financing products (including grace payments, payments linked to cash flows and longer terms). Insurance companies are asked to improve grasslands insurance based on satellite data, to invest in improving data collection and modeling to better cover farmers' risk exposures and develop widespread insurance coverage for new diseases. Cooperatives have the opportunity to reinforce public awareness about the public goods provided by extensive sheep farming, improve the labelling to better inform consumers (IT technologies, like blockchain) and increase transparency to reinforce farmers' trust.

Farmers need to balance their effort between on-farm activities and market activities such as being more pro-active in communication and awareness campaigns. Greater cooperation among farmers could help enhance resilience. Cooperation should span herd management to price sale negotiation. Finally, knowledge is a key variable to ensure the functioning of the farming system. Shepherding requires an in-depth knowledge of the region, pastures, habitats, weather and herd management. This knowledge is being lost and farmers are crucial to avoid losing it. Farmers should commit to keep, enrich and transfer shepherding knowledge and have an open attitude to learn from others' innovative techniques.

Finally, policy recommendations of the CAP post 2020 emerged to support the FS resilience capacities, mainly focused on strengthening cooperation, redefining basic payments tailored to extensive farming needs, fostering innovation, enabling access to new entrants, support-ing knowledge exchange, training and awareness about extensive live-stock farming, valuing the extensive livestock farming, increasing pasture availability, revitalizing rural communities and supporting commercialization (Buitenhuis et al., 2020).

The definition of eco-schemes devoted to grazing is one of the main policy recommendations proposed by the actors in the FS to support the provision of public goods of the FS. As explained, it previously requires a clear definition of the extensive farming system and its environmental, health and rural development contribution, to foster innovation for better pasture management and animal handling and to develop proced-ures to monitor the exploitation of grazing land. Aids should be strictly limited to effective extensive farming instead of land. The removal of historical rights is also a key priority among the actors in the FS.

Actors in the FS also proposed concrete policy recommendations to foster new entrants' access such as more in-depth research about the reasons behind the reluctance to enter the sector, relaxing the require-ments of new entrants to be eligible for aids, easing the access to training programmes, defining measures to avoid the high rate of abandonment (improved business plans, ongoing advice, internships in farms) and sharing good practices.

Regarding cooperation, the actors in the FS proposed new measures to boost collaboration in production processes allowing farmers to improve their profitability and reduce their workload. Currently, the effort is mainly focused on cooperation in commercialization instead of production issues. Innovation on collaborative apps is requested to boost farmers' contacts and knowledge exchange. Furthermore, this measure needs to consider cooperation not only among farmers' but also among different actors in the FS.

It was discussed with the actors in the FS that the policy proposals mainly foster resilience by enhancing robustness and adaptability and to a lower extent transformability. The robustness-enhancing policy recommendations are improving the coupled and basic payments schemes, supporting the commercialization of extensive farming products, valuing extensive farming and its positive contribution to the environment, health and rural areas. The adaptability-capacity-enhancing recommendations are fostering innovation, supporting knowledge exchange and training, strengthening cooperation, increasing the pasture areas and enabling access to new entrants. Finally, the recommendation referred to revitalizing rural communities clearly emerges as one of the main actions to strengthen the transformability capacity of the FS.

9.4 Final Remarks: Lessons Learnt from the Past to Foster Future Resilience

Through the active participation of farmers and other actors in extensive sheep farming we have been able to assess the resilience of the FS by identifying the major challenges faced by the sector, the strategies to deal with them and their impact on the provision of the FS functions. As a result, it can be concluded that the extensive sheep FS in Huesca has shown a low resilience capacity to deal with the multiple challenges it is facing.

There are encouraging opportunities for the FS to improve its resilience in which not only farmers but also farmers' associations, cooperatives, actors in the value chain, financial institutions, NGOs, research centres and public administration are called to be a part.

Instead of focusing just on farmers' income, policies should support the wide variety of the functions provided by the sector by adding the provision of public goods. In this way, policies should open the scope to broaden the support to adaptability and transformability capacities. Furthermore, there is no unique way to improve FS resilience and hence policies should be flexible enough to support equally the diverse resilience-enabling patterns and hence promote diversity into the farms but also diversity among farms.

Research about indicators to measure the provision of public goods, innovation to foster herd and pasture management and strengthened collaboration between actors in the FS have to accompany policy initiatives.

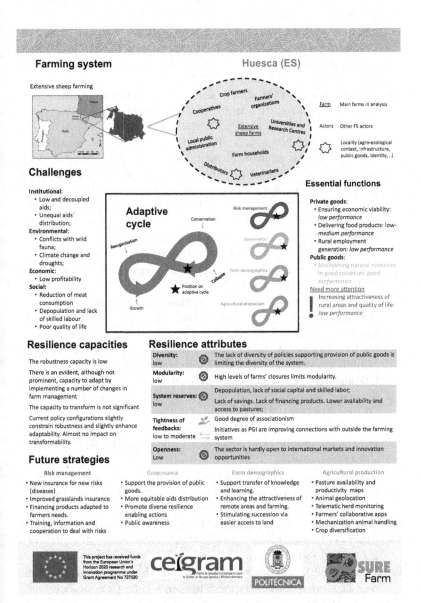

Annex 9.1 Factsheet synthesising resilience of the current farming system in Huesca (Spain).

References

Becking, J., Soriano, B. and Bardaji, I. (2019) 'FoPIA-SURE-Farm case-study report Spain', in Paas, W. *et al.*, 'D5.2 Participatory impact assessment of sustainability and resilience of EU farming systems', Sustainable and resilient EU farming systems (SURE-Farm) project report.

Bernués, A. and Olaizola, A. (2012) 'La ganadería en los Pirineos: Evolución, condicionantes y oportunidades', in Lasagabaster, I. (ed.) *Los Pirineos: geografía, turismo, agricultura, cooperación transfronteriza y derecho.* Universidad del País Vasco, pp. 29–67.

Bertolozzi-Caredio, D. *et al.* (2020) 'Key steps and dynamics of family farm succession in marginal extensive livestock farming', *Journal of Rural Studies*, 76, pp. 131–141. doi: 10.1016/j.jrurstud.2020.04.030.

Bosque, M. A. and Navarro, V. P. (2002) 'El proceso de desertización demográfica de la montaña pirenaica en el largo plazo: Aragón', *Ager: Revista de estudios sobre despoblación y desarrollo rural = Journal of Depopulation and Rural Development Studies*, (2), pp. 101–138.

Buitenhuis, Y. *et al.* (2020) 'Improving the resilience-enabling capacity of the Common Agricultural Policy: Policy recommendations for more resilient EU farming systems', *EuroChoices*, 19(2), pp. 63–71.

Cabell, J. F. and Oelofse, M. (2012) 'An indicator framework for assessing agroecosystem resilience', *Ecology and Society*, 17(1), art18. doi: 10.5751/ES-04666-170118.

Casasús, I. *et al.* (2007) 'Vegetation dynamics in Mediterranean forest pastures as affected by beef cattle grazing', *Agriculture, Ecosystems and Environment*, 121(4), pp. 365–370. doi: 10.1016/j.agee.2006.11.012.

Castro, M., Ameray, A. and Castro, J. P. (2020) 'A new approach to quantify grazing pressure under Mediterranean pastoral systems using GIS and remote sensing', *International Journal of Remote Sensing*. Bragança, Portugal: Taylor and Francis Ltd., pp. 5371–5387. doi: 10.1080/01431161.2020.1731930.

Corcoran, K. (2003) 'Marketing red meat in the European Union: Extending the options', Final report of project FAIR (SME) FA-S2-CT98–9093 (CRAFT programme).

De Rancourt, M. *et al.* (2006) 'Mediterranean sheep and goats production: An uncertain future', *Small Ruminant Research*, 62(3), pp. 167–179. doi: 10.1016/j.smallrumres.2005.08.012.

Doughty, A. K. *et al.* (2017) 'Stakeholder perceptions of welfare issues and indicators for extensively managed sheep in Australia', *Animals*, 7(4). doi: 10.3390/ani7040028.

Feindt, P. *et al.* (2019) 'Assessing how policies enable or constrain the resilience of farming systems in the European Union: Case study results',

SURE-Farm Deliverable (7527520). Available at https://surefarmproject .eu/wordpress/wp-content/uploads/2019/05/SURE-Farm-D-4.2-Resilience-Assessment-Case-Studies-RP1.pdf.

Gobierno de Aragón (2016) 'El ovino y el caprino en Aragón'. Evolución en los últimos 20 años (1996–2016).

(2020) *Datos estadísticos sobre ganadería en Aragón: efectivos ganaderos, distribución de ganadería, movimiento comercial pecuario, producciones ganaderas.*

Hernández-Mora, N. *et al.* (2012) *La sequía 2005–2008 en la cuenca del Ebro: vulnerabilidad, impactos y medidas de gestión.* UPM-CEIGRAM-Madrid.

Koidou, M. *et al.* (2019) 'Temporal variations of herbage production and nutritive value of three grasslands at different elevation zones regarding grazing needs and welfare of ruminants', *Archives Animal Breeding*, 62 (1), pp. 215–226. doi: 10.5194/aab-62-215-2019.

Kok, A. *et al.* (2020) 'European biodiversity assessments in livestock science: A review of research characteristics and indicators', *Ecological Indicators*, 112, 105902. doi: 10.1016/j.ecolind.2019.105902.

Kristensen, S. B. P. *et al.* (2016) 'Patterns and drivers of farm-level land use change in selected European rural landscapes', *Land Use Policy*, 57, pp. 786–799. doi: 10.1016/j.landusepol.2015.07.014.

Llonch, P. *et al.* (2015) 'A systematic review of animal based indicators of sheep welfare on farm, at market and during transport, and qualitative appraisal of their validity and feasibility for use in UK abattoirs', *Veterinary Journal*, 206(3), pp. 289–297. doi: 10.1016/j.tvjl.2015.10.019.

Mancilla-Leytón, J. M. and Martín Vicente, A. (2012) 'Biological fire prevention method: Evaluating the effects of goat grazing on the fire-prone Mediterranean scrub', *Forest Systems*. Spain: Instituto Nacional de Investigación y Tecnología Agraria y Alimentaria, pp. 199–204. doi: 10.5424/fs/2012212-02289.

MAPA (2018) *El sector ovino y caprino en cifras. Principales indicadores económicos.*

(2020a) *Datos de las Denominaciones de Origen Protegidas DOPs, Indicaciones Geográficas Protegidas IGPs y Especialidades Tradicionales Garantizadas ETGs de Productos Agroalimentarios.*

(2020b) *Encuestas de efectivos de ganado ovino y caprino.*

(2020c) *Estudios de costes y rentas de explotaciones ganaderas (ECRAN).*

Martin-Collado, D. *et al.* (2019) 'Sheep dairy and meat products: From urban consumers' perspective to industry innovations', *Options Méditerranéennes*, 123, pp. 277–281.

Meuwissen, M. P. M. *et al.* (2020) 'The struggle of farming systems in Europe: Looking for explanations through the lens of resilience', *EuroChoices*, 19(2), pp. 4–11.

Munoz, C. *et al.* (2018) 'Using longitudinal assessment on extensively managed ewes to quantify welfare compromise and risks', *Animals*, 8(1). doi: 10.3390/ani8010008.

Navarro, V. P. (1992) 'La Produccion Agraria En Aragon (1850–1935)', *Revista de historia Económica / Journal of Iberian and Latin American Economic History*, 10(3), pp. 399–429. doi: 10.1017/S021261090000358X.

Oliveira, S. *et al.* (2017) 'Assessing the social context of wildfire-affected areas. The case of mainland Portugal', *Applied Geography*. Lisbon, Portugal: Elsevier SCI LTD, pp. 104–117. doi: 10.1016/j.apgeog.2017.09.004.

Pardos, L., Maza, M.T., Fantova, E. and Sepulveda, U. (2008) 'The diversity of sheep production systems in Aragon (Spain): Characterisation and typification of meat sheep farms', *Spanish Journal of Agricultural Research*, 6(4), pp. 497–507.

Peco, B. *et al.* (2017) 'Effects of grazing abandonment on soil multifunctionality: The role of plant functional traits', *Agriculture, Ecosystems and Environment*, 249, pp. 215–225. doi: 10.1016/j.agee.2017.08.013.

Reidsma, P. *et al.* (2019) 'Resilience assessment of current farming systems across the European Union', SURE-Farm Deliverable (727520). Available at https://surefarmproject.eu/wordpress/wp-content/uploads/2019/12/D5.3-Resilience-assessment-of-current-farming-systems-across-the-European-Union.pdf.

Rodríguez-Ortega, T. *et al.* (2014) 'Applying the ecosystem services framework to pasture-based livestock farming systems in Europe', *Animal*, 8 (8), pp. 1361–1372. doi: 10.1017/S1751731114000421.

Ruiz-Mirazo, J. and Robles, A. B. (2012) 'Impact of targeted sheep grazing on herbage and holm oak saplings in a silvopastoral wildfire prevention system in south-eastern Spain', *Agroforestry Systems*. Granada, Spain: Springer, pp. 477–491. doi: 10.1007/s10457-012-9510-z.

Ruiz-Mirazo, J., Robles, A. B. and Gonzalez-Rebollar, J. L. (2011) 'Two-year evaluation of fuelbreaks grazed by livestock in the wildfire prevention program in Andalusia (Spain)', *Agriculture Ecosystems & Environment*. Granada, Spain: Elsevier Science BV, pp. 13–22. doi: 10.1016/j.agee.2011.02.002.

Soriano, B. *et al.* (2020) 'D2.6 Report on state and outlook for risk management in EU agriculture', SURE-Farm Deliverable (727520). Available at www.surefarmproject.eu/wordpress/wp-content/uploads/2020/02/D2-6-Report-on-state-and-outlook-on-risk-magagment-in-EU.pdf

Turner, N. (2005) 'Sustainable production of crops and pastures under drought in a Mediterranean environment', *Annals of Applied Biology*, 144(2), pp. 139–147.

10 | Thinking Outside the Box in the Bourbonnais

Transforming the Value Chain and Conserving the Landscape

FRANCESCO ACCATINO, CHRISTÈLE
PINEAU, CORENTIN PINSARD,
DELPHINE NEUMEISTER
AND FRANÇOIS LÉGER

10.1 Introduction

Bocage Bourbonnais is a small natural region in the centre of France appreciated for its traditional and beautiful landscapes. The landscape, referred to as *bocage* in French, is dominated by meadows bordered by quickset hedges. The region is situated on the northern border of the highland region of Massif Central in the Charolais basin and corresponds broadly to the department of Allier. Most of the economy is devoted to agriculture and the agri-food industry. According to the agricultural census, 45 per cent of the 5,523 farms were devoted to beef production (Ministère de l'Agriculture et de l'Alimentation, 2010), with *Charolais* being the most present cow breed (Figure 10.1). The farmers serve primarily two markets: they either export weaners, mostly to the Po valley in Italy, or they fatten and finish heifers and cull cows for French consumers. The hedges were traditionally planted to delimit pastures and to protect cattle from wind, but they also provide ecosystem services (Montgomery et al., 2020). They sequester carbon, protect against soil erosion, and provide shelter that supports biodiversity. Meadows and beef cattle farming can be mutually beneficial. Grasslands provide the primary source of cattle feed and are maintained by the grazing cattle, which reduce the need for industrial nitrogen fertilizers (Lüscher et al., 2014). Cattle farming provides ecosystem services and other public functions, as has been reviewed by Dumont et al. (2019).

In this chapter, we describe our analysis of the Bourbonnais farming system and suggest strategies for enhancing its resilience. We

Figure 10.1 *Charolais* cows in the grassland landscape of the Bocage Bourbonnais.
Source: Delphine Neumeister

considered not only the viability of the farms but also, and importantly, the coupling of cattle farming with the aesthetic and cultural value of the landscape. Agro-environmental policies implemented over the past thirty years have been designed to perpetuate grass-based livestock farming to preserve the characteristic *bocage* of the region (see La Région Auvergne-Rhône-Alpes, 2020, pp. 94–96). More specifically, we analysed the perspective of local stakeholders about several factors: the functions provided by the farming system, the challenges presented by the current system, and the strategies that had been proposed or adopted to deal with the challenges (see the definition of challenges and functions in Chapter 1). We considered farms, their surrounding landscape, and withal participants in the farming systems. The analysis was based on interactions with local stakeholders over two years, from the second half of 2018 to the first half of 2020, and was done within the framework of the SURE-Farm project.

These activities consisted of workshops, focus groups, and interviews. We hosted one workshop with twenty-six participants, namely farmers, public administration agents, as well as members of the agricultural chamber, non-governmental organizations (NGOs), cooperatives, agricultural schools, and research institutes. We held two focus groups with a total of thirteen participants, which included experts, bankers, public administration agents, farmers, and insurance agents. We held twenty-three interviews with farmers and three with non-farmers. The information in this chapter is based on statements by local stakeholders and not on data or measured indicators, therefore findings about functions, challenges, and possible strategy reflect the actors' point of view. Quotes from interviews are reported in italics.

10.2 Beef Production in a Beautiful Landscape: Where Is the Trade-Off?

We organized a participatory workshop for stakeholders in the Bourbonnais farming system in February 2019, called FoPIA-SURE-Farm 1 (see Accatino and Neumeister, 2019). The stakeholders assessed the importance and performance of the functions provided by the farming system. They scored the performance of each function from 1 (poor) to 5 (strong). They also evaluated the relative importance of each function by assigning it a percentage. Results are reported in Figure 10.2. Participants also discussed and proposed indicators for measuring the performance of each function.

10.2.1 High-Performing Functions

10.2.1.1 Food Production and Natural Resources

Considering the functions in Figure 10.2, 'Food production' was the most important, which was expected because the region's economy is devoted to the agri-food industry. The high value for performance of this function was based on indicators proposed by stakeholders concerned with both food quantity (assessed as 'Total quantity of beef produced') and quality (assessed as 'Taste quality and regularity of beef' and 'Percentage of beef produced under label'). The two functions 'Natural resources' and 'Biodiversity and habitat' were also deemed high performing and relatively important, demonstrating the value

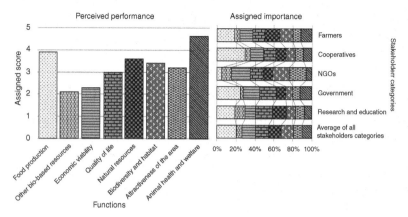

Figure 10.2 Perceived performance of functions (left panel) and importance assigned by different groups of stakeholders (right panel) during a participatory workshop in the Bourbonnais farming system held in February 2019. Patterns in the right panel correspond to the function with the same patterns in the left panel.
Source: Data from Accatino and Neumeister (2019)

stakeholders place on the landscape. 'Animal health and welfare' was also perceived to perform very well and confirmed in interviews, revealing the high importance stakeholders place on the health and wellness of their animals. There was a discrepancy between the high-performance rating for this function and its low-importance rating; however, this was explained by the fact that stakeholders do not consider animal welfare a 'function', but rather a normal and intrinsic element of beef production. The high performance of food production and environment-related functions agrees with an analysis of France done by Ryschawy et al. (2017).

10.2.1.2 Quality of Beef: A Long Tradition in the Bourbonnais Area
Many farms in the Bourbonnais farming system currently produce beef under label, mostly *Label Rouge,* a sign of quality assurance in France. Many members of the Bourbonnais farming system wish to continue and enhance traditional practices of beef production. The first *Label Rouge* farm in the Bourbonnais was certified in 1974, and since then many more have subscribed. Production under label follows specific

rules, such as type of feed, grazing period, and minimum slaughter age. In 1992, SICABA, the main slaughterhouse in the area, was certified to slaughter organic cattle.

10.2.2 Functions Assessed as Performing Poorly

Two functions, 'Economic viability' and 'Quality of life', were assessed as relatively important but performing poorly. It was apparent from our interactions with farmers in the Bourbonnais region that they often struggle economically. From an interview: '...*we do not choose the price of what we buy and we do not choose the price of the cattle we sell. We lose 200 to 250 euros per animal. It's a huge loss, it's huge...*' This quote reflects the view of many of the farmers. Debts are another source of concern, hampering both initiative and willingness to invest ('...*we cannot afford to make it wrong...*').

The farmers identified factors that reduce their work satisfaction. Cattle breeding can require a seven-day work week, with several working hours each day. It can be difficult to find suitable employees to assist, either because there are few qualified workers available or because the farmers lack the cash to pay salaries. Some of the interviewees commented on the risk of injury associated with the profession as an additional concern, and they also considered the bureaucracy and administrative work associated with the work to be a heavy burden, which is accompanied by the worry of costly mistakes.

The function 'Other bio-based products' was assessed as both performing poorly and not important. Given that the region is centred on beef production, it is reasonable that non-food-related bio-based products are of minor importance. However, some of the stakeholders pointed out that agroforestry and timber production through development of hedges is becoming more common. The function 'Attractiveness of the area' performed moderately well but was unimportant; it was not a priority among stakeholders.

10.2.3 Challenges

In addition to these difficulties mentioned, the Bourbonnais farming system faces other serious challenges (Reidsma et al., 2019). These are summarized in the factsheet in the Annex 10.1 (see also explanations in

Chapter 1). Droughts constitute a growing and serious threat; in recent decades, there have been more and more severe droughts. Drought reduces the productivity of permanent grasslands and other forms of forage. Summer droughts are particularly detrimental to the well-being of the cattle, which struggle in the heat.

Other challenges faced by the Bourbonnais farmers are associated with social dynamics, both internal and external. A major challenge is the demographic makeup of the region, with many farmers approaching retirement age and difficulty to find successors. The high level of debt associated with starting a farming venture as a newcomer or expanding an existing enterprise detracts from the appeal of the profession, particularly for the farmers' children. This difficulty in finding younger farmers to continue the work threatens the vitality of this rural area and may lead to de-population and abandonment of the land.

10.3 Coping with Challenges: Maintaining the Status Quo versus Adapting

The strategies suggested by the Bourbonnais farmers and other participants in the farming system to address the challenges they face involve two approaches: to maintain the *status quo* (i.e., to enhance robustness) or to alter the system's configuration to anticipate disturbances or mitigate their effects (i.e., by enhancing adaptability.)

Droughts illustrate the tension that exists between these two strategies. Farmers respond to droughts by buying insurance, buying external feed, reducing their herd size, or acquiring as much feed and straw as they can, whether by growing it or storing it. However, this increases expenses and may alter the landscape: as the farmers grow more crops or temporary grassland than they would otherwise, they decrease the area of meadows, use more nitrogen fertilizer, and may not maintain the hedges. The transformation of grassland into arable fields is seen as a threat to grassland ecosystems in Europe (Habel et al., 2013), and this form of adaptation to droughts threatens the balance between beef production and landscape quality that is the historic and cultural identity of the Bourbonnais. The players here are not only the farmers – there are conservation associations devoted to the maintenance of the hedges and landscape conservation and valorisation. Adapting to droughts without putting pressure on the natural capital would require making the landscape more drought-tolerant. A possible form of adaptation comes from agroforestry practices (Mosquera-Losada et al., 2018). One example pointed out by some farmers in our study is that trees provide shade for cattle during heat waves and maintain grass growth in late spring, making it possible to start distributing harvested fodder later.

Diversification either in production or market outlets was mentioned as a strategy for coping with climate uncertainty and price volatility (Dumont et al., 2020). It was suggested as a buffer against uncertainty in order *'to have always a form of production to rely on'*. Another type of diversification is in the type of livestock raised, and some farmers do invest in other livestock, such as poultry and pigs, which they raise alongside cattle.

Historically, agriculture in the Bourbonnais region has been a family enterprise. Individual farms were often involved in cooperatives for the supply and marketing of products and in collective genetic improvement schemes. According to the *Recensement Général de l'Agriculture* 2015 (see Ministère de l'Agriculture et de l'Alimentation, 1988–2018), there are considerably fewer corporate farms in the Bourbonnais region than there are in other French livestock or mixed crop-livestock farming regions. However, involvement in cooperative organizations is increasing in the Bourbonnais. The development of associations and cooperatives improves adaptability to the different challenges and provides the farmers with resources to address their problems. According to interviews, collective action leads to sharing tools and equipment, making larger investments in machinery, and collectively organizing the sale of products, which strengthens the farmers' position with buyers. It also meets a social need for mutual assistance in the event of an accident or temporary difficulty, and an opportunity to exchange information and ideas.

10.4 Pressure from the Society: A Source of Stress and a Trigger for Transformation

Society has high expectations for farmers (Mathijs, 2015), as is becoming increasingly apparent in public discourse. Many of the farmers feel that a lack of trust is amplified by the media, especially social media. Beef producers feel particularly under public scrutiny because of the rise of the vegan movement. They also see a potential conflict between the growing demand for improved animal husbandry practices and the likelihood of increased prices; they are unsure that even the potentially improved quality of the meat would compensate for this. The farmers do not believe that the public understands their work ('...*the French people are not sufficiently aware of the work of farmers*...') and think a better understanding of their life and work would be mutually beneficial. We also note that, while the concern about vegan or animal rights movements was often expressed, the farmers never mentioned having the sense that they were likely to experience any direct confrontation from these groups.

The concerns about the effects of social distrust are tempered by two factors. First, the export market to Italy is a major, reliable market and relatively impervious to the social pressures from the French. This market, then, can be considered as a factor in the resilience of the regional farming system to societal challenges. Second, the recent increase in direct selling and short value chains demonstrate that there is a local or a niche market that values the practices of the Bourbonnais farmers and is willing to pay a fair price.

Several participants considered it necessary to change their practices to satisfy consumers: '...*we are going to adapt, it will not be the other way around*...'. Suggested changes included the introduction of environmentally friendly practices, such as optimizing fertilization, reducing or stopping ploughing, and reducing the use of pesticides. The need for improving conditions in slaughterhouses and subscribing to a quality label was also recognized. Some farmers are already making these changes. One of the farmers we interviewed is growing and selling vegetables for human consumption, such as lentils, and buying animal feed from an organic source as much as possible. Some of the farmers are transitioning to organic farming. These ideological and economic considerations should enable farmers to sell their products at a better price and fulfil social expectations. The presence of SICABA, the local organic-certified slaughterhouse, provides an extra opportunity for the farmers to adapt to organic farming.

The COVID-19 pandemic, with the associated lockdown measures in 2020, has raised public awareness of the importance of agriculture in sustaining the population during difficult times. A press release from the French ministry of Agriculture and Nutrition (Ministère de l'Agriculture et de l'Alimentation, 2020) acknowledged the fundamental role of all players in the food supply chain during this crisis and expressed gratitude for the food industry and appreciation for the minimal disruption in supply during the pandemic (Meuwissen et al., 2021). The ministry also asked for action within the value chain to counteract falling meat prices. The Bourbonnais region is likely to benefit from this positive image, especially from the opportunity to satisfy its consumers' desire for food production practices that are respectful of nature and the environment.

10.5 Transformation Strategies for Maintaining Tradition and the Natural Landscape

We suggest that the Bourbonnais farming system must do more than adapt to changing circumstances: a transformation of the system is necessary. The challenges and problems identified in this study have created for farmers a difficult life, which does not encourage potential recruits to replace retiring farmers. According to the description of resilience used here, transformation of a system should always maintain its core identity. For the Bourbonnais region, such identity is beef production in a natural and traditional landscape. Some potentially useful adaptative strategies, particularly those that might mitigate economic problems, should be considered with caution as they conflict with functions of the system, for example, by threatening permanent grassland or the natural environment.

In a July 2019 focus group, three strategies for promoting transformability were identified. Farmers are the most important actors in this transformation, as farming practices are the link between the landscape and agriculture. While some farmers have adopted innovations acquired from other farmers or advisers, others are resistant to change, either because they are preoccupied with their overwhelming problems or are strongly attached to tradition. Innovation should be fostered with appropriate training, information, and financing, and cooperatives or agriculture advisors are important in this regard. The second strategy involves a coordinated action of all actors of the farming system – retailers, advisors, feed suppliers, cooperatives – to improve the farmers' position in the value chain, allowing them to gain more bargaining power with better prices at the farm gate. Unfortunately, the participants to the focus group also recognized that the farming system is still a long way from such coordinated action. A third strategy is to promote some policy measures aimed at facilitating the inclusion of farmers in the public market, for example in school canteens.

10.6 Conclusions

The future of beef production in Europe may require continuous integration of environmental, economic, and social issues (Hocquette et al., 2018). The Bourbonnais farming system is a case in point, and we consider it a good candidate for reconciling the objectives of food production and natural resource conservation. However, challenges are also present. As argued by Darnhofer et al. (2010), monetary resources such as bank loans and insurance schemes can provide some short-term solutions, but do not strengthen the long-term resilience of the farming system. We believe that improving the resilience of the Bourbonnais farming system will require building new social links, improving policies, and education. Farmers are the cornerstone for correcting problems and implementing transformation, but they cannot act alone. The Bourbonnais farming system, as well as other SURE-Farm case studies, requires a resilience-enabling environment that helps the farmers to shift their perspective from short-term economic survival to a wider view in which environmental and social issues can also be addressed (Reidsma et al., 2020).

The comparison of the Bourbonnais region with other SURE-Farm case studies reveals that the balance that exists between food production and landscape quality in the area is unique and needs to be considered as an opportunity to enhance resilience. However, the responsibility for landscape conservation cannot be left entirely to farmers, who often lack time and economic resources. Landscape maintenance is and should be promoted by policymakers, especially at the territorial level, and with input from local conservation associations. Droughts hinder landscape conservation efforts, and mitigating their consequences requires concerted research. At present, decision-making is done by different administrative units linked to municipalities. An administrative unit exclusively dedicated to the maintenance of the *bocage* landscape, composed of those with a strong connection to it, could be a highly effective management tool.

The farmers in the Bourbonnais would benefit from agents who act as intermediaries between them and the other members of the value chain. While farmers of the Bourbonnais have a good dialogue with local consumers, as shown by the recent increase in direct on-farm selling, a wider dialogue should be facilitated between the farmers and consumers who are not local, but who have specific concerns. This dialogue should be built around the topics of concern, for example, animal welfare, and involve groups of stakeholders and consumers (Miele et al., 2011). This communication effort should expand to reach more people, and eventually be facilitated with communication campaigns that reach the general public. In France, this is happening with the help of producers and inter-professional organizations (Pact for Societal commitment [*Pacte d'engagement sociétal*], Interbev, 2020). These campaigns focus on reducing environmental impacts, enhancing animal welfare, assuring a good remuneration to farmers and others involved, and education on meat in a healthy diet.

The value chain for the French non-local market and for the export market seems to, at present, constrain the resilience of the Bourbonnais farming system; we believe that its unbalanced structure lowers the farmers' profit margins. Addressing this requires understanding the mechanisms within the value chains that lead to low profitability for farmers and to promote remedial policy tools. The appropriate arena for this action is outside the farming system, and it should be handled by entities such as inter-professional organizations and government.

Some participants proposed, in a workshop, the value of promoting a good image of the region. Sustainable and responsible tourism offers a novel approach to transformation, and this beautiful region has much to offer: stunning landscapes, historical sites (medieval cities and thermal springs), areas for trekking and horseback riding, and the famous wine 'Saint Pourçain'. There has been little concerted effort to develop tourism in the area, but agri-tourism might provide farmers with not only a new source of income but also the opportunity to enhance understanding of their profession (Accatino et al., 2020). This path to transformation may contradict some of our findings, as low importance was assigned to 'attractiveness of the area' by stakeholders (Figure 10.1); however, the path to transformation comes from thinking outside the box and from gaining confidence in the asset of this territory.

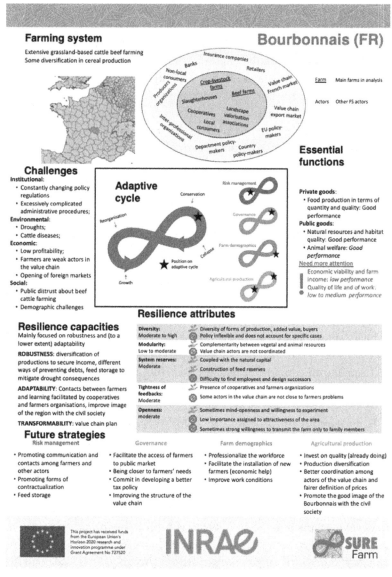

Annex 10.1 Factsheet synthesising resilience of the current farming system in the Bocage Bourbonnais (France).

References

Accatino, F. and Neumeister, D. (2019) In: Paas, W., Accatino, F., Antonioli, F., et al., 'D5.2 Participatory impact assessment of sustainability and resilience of EU farming systems', Sustainable and resilient EU farming systems (SURE-Farm) project report, EU Horizon 2020 Grant Agreement No 727570.

Accatino, F., Pineau, C. and Neumeister, D. (2020) In: Accatino, F., Paas, W., Herrero, H., et al., 'D5.5 Impacts of future scenarios on the resilience of farming systems across the EU assessed with quantitative and qualitative methods', Sustainable and resilient EU farming systems (SURE-Farm) project report, EU Horizon 2020 Grant Agreement No 727570.

Darnhofer, I., Fairweather, J. and Moller, H. (2010) 'Assessing a farm's sustainability: Insights from resilience-thinking', *International Journal of Agricultural Sustainability*, 8, pp. 186–198.

Dumont, B., Ryschawy, J., Duru, M., et al. (2019) 'Review: Associations among goods, impacts and ecosystem services provided by livestock farming', *animal*, 18, pp. 1773–1784.

Dumont, B., Puillet, L., Martin, G., et al. (2020) 'Incorporating diversity into animal production systems can increase their performance and strengthen their resilience', *Frontiers in Sustainable Food Systems*, 4, p. 109.

Habel, J. C., Dengler, J., Janiskova, M., Török, P., Wellstein, C. and Wiezik, M. (2013) 'European grassland ecosystems: Threatened hotspots of biodiversity', *Biodiversity Conservation*, 22, pp. 2131–2138.

Hocquette, J.-F., Ellies-Oury, M.-P., Lherm, M., Pineau, C., Deblitz, C. and Farmer, L. (2018) 'Current situation and future prospects for beef production in Europe – A review', *Asian-Australasian Journal of Animal Sciences*, 7, pp. 1017–1035.

Interbev – French Meat and Livestock Industry (2020) 'Sustainability report', available at www.interbev.fr/wp-content/uploads/2021/01/rapport-rso-english-v2021-planches-1.pdf (accessed 3 March 2020).

La Région Auvergne-Rhône-Alpes (2020) 'Programme de Développement Rural Auvergne 2014–2020', available at www.europe-en-auvergnerhonealpes.eu/sites/default/files/base-documentaire/PDR_AUVERGNE_FEADER_AdopteCE_29-10-2020.pdf (accessed 3 March 2020).

Lüscher, A., Mueller-Harvey, I., Soussana, J. F., Rees, R. M. and Peyraud, J. L. (2014) 'Potential of legume-based grassland-livestock systems in Europe: A review', *Grass and Forage Science*, 69, pp. 206–228.

Mathijs, E. (2015) 'Exploring future patterns of meat consumption', *Meat Science*, 109, pp. 112–116.

Meuwissen, M. P. M., Feindt, P. H., Slijper, T. et al. (2021) 'Impact of Covid-19 on farming systems in Europe through the lens of resilience thinking', *Agricultural Systems*, 191, 103152.

Miele, M., Veissier, I., Evans, A. and Botreau, R. (2011) 'Animal welfare: Establishing a dialogue between science and society', *Animal Welfare*, 20, pp. 103–117.

Ministère de l'Agriculture et de l'Alimentation (2010) 'Recensement agricole' (2010) [WWW Document], available at https://agreste.agriculture.gouv.fr/agreste-web/methodon/S-RA%202010/methodon/ (accessed 23 March 2021).

(1988–2018) 'Réseau d'information comptable agricole: 1988–2018 (France métropolitaine)' [WWW Document], Agreste, la statistique agricole, available at https://agreste.agriculture.gouv.fr/agreste-web/disaron/RICA_METRO/detail/ (accessed 23 March 2021).

(2020) 'Viande bovine : stop à la baisse injustifiée de la rémunération de la production, la filière doit réagir et répondre à la détresse des éleveurs', available at https://agriculture.gouv.fr/viande-bovine-stop-la-baisse-injustifiee-de-la-remuneration-de-la-production (accessed 3 March 2021)

Montgomery, I., Caruso, T. and Reid, N. (2020) 'Hedgerows and ecosystems: Service delivery, management, and restoration', *Annual Review of Ecology, Evolution, and Systematics*, 51, pp. 81–102.

Mosquera-Losada, M. R., Santiago-Freijanes, J. J., Rois-Díaz, M., et al. (2018) 'Agroforestry in Europe: A land management policy tool to combat climate change', *Land Use Policy*, 78, pp. 603–613.

Reidsma, P., Spiegel, A., Paas, W., et al. (2019) 'D5.3 Resilience assessment of current farming systems across the European Union', Sustainable and resilient EU farming systems (SURE-Farm) project report, EU Horizon 2020 Grant Agreement No 727570.

Reidsma, P., Meuwissen, M. P. M., Accatino, F., et al. (2020) 'How do stakeholders perceive the sustainability and resilience of EU farming systems?' *EuroChoices*, 19, pp. 18–27.

Ryschawy, J., Disenhaus, C., Bertrand, S., et al. (2017) 'Assessing multiple goods and services derived from livestock farming on a nation-wide gradient', *animal*, 11, pp. 1861–1872.

11 The Resilience of a Farming System at Crossroads between Intensification and Environmental Sustainability

The Hazelnut Case in Viterbo (Italy)

SIMONE SEVERINI, SAVERIO SENNI, ALESSANDRO SORRENTINO, CINZIA ZINNANTI, AND FEDERICO ANTONIOLI

11.1 Introduction

Italy is the second-largest producer of European hazelnut in the world after Turkey. The farming system (FS) is in the province of Viterbo (Latium region), the largest production area in central Italy. According to the National Statistics Institute (ISTAT), 46,200 tons of in-shell hazelnuts were produced in 2018 within the FS.

Hazelnut cultivation is historically and culturally rooted in the area, covering around 23,000 ha and embracing more than 6,000 farms nowadays. Most hazelnut farms are family farms managed on a part-time basis, with around two-thirds having a size between 2 and 10 ha. The volcanic area of Cimini Mountains, surrounding the Vico lake, is regarded as the most traditional territory, characterised by highly fertile soil and a unique microclimate. The primary cultivar locally grown is the round-shaped nut 'Tonda Gentile Romana', registered under the Protected Denomination of Origin (PDO) scheme (Silvestri et al., 2021). The average nut and kernel quality is relatively high and suitable for further processing by the downstream processing industry (Figure 11.1).

The revenues generated by hazelnut cultivation represent a major economic resource in the province since any other type of farming does not offer similar profitability. Hence, this perennial crop provides satisfactory levels of income to farmers. Traditionally, hazelnuts coexisted with other woody species (e.g., olive or chestnut trees) in the southeast territory, particularly around the Vico Lake. However, the

Figure 11.1 Typical landscape in the Viterbo farming system.
Photo by personal archive of Saverio Senni.

last decade featured a soaring market demand for hazelnuts, while other crops' profitability levels plunged, leading to a significant spreading of the perennial cultivation in the surrounding areas, historically excluded (Nera et al., 2020). Furthermore, substantial modernisation led to growing specialisation and mechanisation levels in the hazelnut sector, with the confectionery industry asking for higher quality standards, fomenting irrigation systems, and chemical treatments. Simultaneously, irrigation ensures larger kernels, and agro-chemicals allow for higher quality levels and lower defects caused by insects (both on taste and appearance). The importance of chemical products for ensuring profitable campaigns hampers the development of organic farming, which represents less than 10 per cent of the whole production.

The irrigation system is pivotal for new plantations especially for those more affected by droughts and heatwaves in the less suitable areas. However, the paucity of groundwater sources is a severe concern. In contrast, farmers settled in traditional areas do not require to irrigate as the impact of heatwaves and droughts is limited.

Environmental organisations started raising their voice, concerned by the massive expansion and intensification of hazelnut farming and its effects on the landscape, biodiversity, soil pollution, and water resources. This fuelled a fierce local debate between farmers and their organisations, environmental groups, and public administrations, which reached the national level and affected the downstream confectionery industry, whose role is questioned (Liberti, 2019).

The supply chain is quite articulated since the very first steps: raw unshelled hazelnuts are channelled through a complex network of intermediaries, with six producer organisations (POs) handling most of the harvest; their role is relevant in terms of supply concentration and storage, albeit very few engage in further processing besides collecting and storing the harvest. Therefore, unshelling, processing to obtain semi-finished products (e.g., hazelnut flour and past), and marketing to retailers are usually performed by large companies such as Ferrero and Loacker. These were not located within the area until now, and even though they have recently acquired local factories in Viterbo province, they continue to operate on the international market of raw hazelnuts, where Turkey is the largest and most important player. Indeed, Turkey's production levels and policy decisions are relevant in determining the world market's hazelnut price. Other countries, such as Chile, Georgia, and Azerbaijan, are witnessing an essential rise in hazelnut cultivations, heavily stimulated by confectionery firms to enlarge their production basin and reduce dependency on one or two regions of origin.

The FS comprises farms and agricultural households engaged in the hazelnut production and local POs and further local downstream operators and wholesalers. The enabling environment consists of local public authorities – including those managing the Common Agricultural Policy (CAP) at the regional level – machinery providers, small confectionery industries, research institutions, professional associations, and input providers. As mentioned before, environmental activism and related organisations are increasingly influencing the FS, exerting political pressure to restrain the expansion and intensification of hazelnuts. The CAP also plays a role in developing the FS, particularly through the Common Market Organisation (CMO) and Pillar 2, i.e., the Rural Development Program (RDP). POs are entitled to channel the CMO's support, playing a crucial role for farm investments, technical advice, supply concentration, and environment-friendly

practices. At least 10 per cent of the PO's expenditure under operational programmes shall cover environmental actions or, alterna-
tively, two or more environmental actions with specific constraints in
terms of surface and duration. On the other hand, RDP supports farms
engaging in environment-friendly practices and supports Leader programs operated by Local Action Groups. However, RDP policies suffer
from heavy bureaucracy, limiting their uptake and potential impact.
Finally, direct payments provided via Pillar 1 of the CAP represent a
negligible share of hazelnut farms' total revenue.

This chapter offers an overview of the results obtained for this FS via
applying different approaches outlined in Chapter 1.

11.2 Exploring the Current State of the Resilience of the FS

FoPIA SURE-Farm workshops provide useful and relevant insights
into the current state of resilience. Investigating how the FS can be
described according to resilience capacities revealed a robust system,
nevertheless characterised by weak adaptability and transformability
capacities. Due to the perennial character of the hazelnut cultivation,
robustness, adaptability, and transformability are defined according to
the extent of changes and the time frame within which such changes
occur. Robustness relates to short-term changes, whereas adaptability
refers to changes occurring on a medium time horizon, and transformation requires relevant changes to occur over more extended periods
(Anderies et al., 2013; Severini et al., 2019). The system's robustness is
strongly and positively affected by the current significant mechanisation
of farming practices reducing labor costs by ameliorating labor productivity. Likewise, adaptability is somewhat enhanced by this strategy
(Severini et al., 2019). Concerning the functions the FS is able to ensure,
private functions embrace (i) offering healthy and affordable food products; (ii) securing the economic viability of farms, contributing to territorial development; and (iii) improving the local economy, hence life
quality, by providing employment and offering decent work conditions.
On the public side, the FS contributes to (i) maintaining local natural
resources in good condition, (ii) protecting the biodiversity of habitats
and different species, and (iii) ameliorating landscape quality. During
recent years, the FS performed well in profitability, generating a gross
margin between 5,000 and 8,000 €/ha, with a farm-gate price of
average-quality shelled hazelnuts of approximately 7.20 €/kg (2019).

The price level is strongly influenced by technical characteristics such as kernel size and shape, pellicle removal after kernel blanching or roasting, the mould incidence in the kernel, or other defects caused by insects (mainly different bug species). This probably incentivises the application of irrigation systems (Cristofori et al., 2014) and chemical products; instruments apt for increasing the product's quality. The crop's relatively good economic performance (i.e., gross margin) contributes to ensuring farming as a viable activity, supporting the local economy, which is mainly based on the agricultural sector. This has a positive effect on resilience attributes supporting rural life and on the social self-organisation of the system (concepts explained earlier in this book) that, in turn, support the whole farming system.

The capacity of being resilient in the future depends on the evolution of current FS challenges. Indeed, stakeholders are expecting significant changes to the FS, particularly due to the following: (i) on the environmental side: the increasing climate change; (ii) regarding the organisation of the hazelnut supply chain: the increasing bargaining power exerted by the confectionery industry; and (iii) regarding social and political changes: the possible introduction of more binding eco-friendly requirements, lately pushed by the rise in environment-related concerns.

Climate change – especially the random variation in temperatures and rainfall poorly distributed throughout the year – leads to more frequent and severe droughts and heatwaves, with negative impacts on production levels and, although to a lower extent, the whole FS viability. In certain years extended droughts and frosts are lowering both hazelnut quality and yields (Zinnanti et al., 2019), with the former further increasing the pressure on water resources as larger volumes and longer periods of irrigation are necessary. Besides, phytopathology and other biotic factors represent a critical challenge for growers, damaging the harvested product, affecting farms' profitability. Remarkably, there is growing concern about the infestations of *Halyomorpha halys*, a new bug species that may spread in the area as already happened in northern Italy, where hazelnut trees are also farmed (Bosco et al., 2018). This would result in heavier use of chemicals to preserve high quality standards and yield levels.

The concentration of the downstream confectionery industry and its purchase strategy became a challenge for the FS. Processing companies commonly influence protocols affecting production practices and costs.

In particular, prices are maintained low whenever hazelnut quality level is not consistent with the industrial production strategy. Thus, the FS seems strongly affected by the confectionery industry's decisions, hindering its adaptability and transformation strategies: high-quality standards required by the industrial processors contrast with the social request to maintain high environmental standards. This also constrains the growth of organic farming.

Reducing hazelnuts' ecological footprint and taking into account the impact of agricultural practices on public health and natural resources would undoubtedly produce public goods, but at the detriment of private interests – especially for the farmer, who will receive a lower price for a lower-quality product and a lower income from a lower volume of production. Some municipalities already introduced more stringent regulations on farming practices to limit the environmental impacts and curb the expansion of hazelnut cultivations. The trend is expected to endure and even to reinforce.

11.3 Exploring the Future State of Resilience

In recent years, stakeholders do not trust the FS's ability to adapt to challenging conditions envisaged in the next ten years. At the same time, they cannot imagine the FS without hazelnuts, dismissing any opportunity for a relevant change in production patterns (e.g., crop substitution), mainly because of its perennial nature and its historical and traditional character. Two FoPIA-SURE farm workshops involving FS stakeholders allowed for thresholds' identification regarding resilience indicators (e.g., gross margin), attributes (e.g., support rural life) and challenges (e.g., droughts) (for more details, see Accatino et al., 2020). For each indicator, attribute, and challenge, thresholds define a band of inaction within which the FS maintains the current state. Whenever thresholds (maximum or minimum) are exceeded, the FS performs differently, a situation depicted via the Causal Loop Diagram[1] in Figure 11.2, illustrating the cascading scale effects.[2]

---

[1] Described earlier in this book.

[2] Cascading effects refer to the impacts of an initiating event where: (i) System dependencies lead to impacts propagating to other systems; (ii) the combined impacts of the propagated event are of greater consequences than the root impacts; and (iii) multiple stakeholders and/or responders are involved.

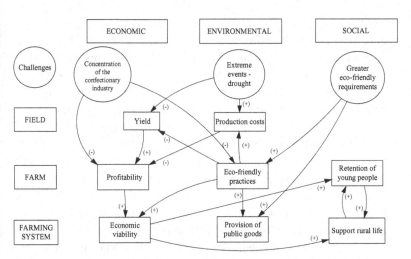

Figure 11.2 Impacts of challenges on key aspects of the hazelnut farming system in Viterbo.

Arrows between boxes indicate the existing positive (+) or negative (−) correlations among resilience indicators, attributes (squared boxes), and challenges (circle boxes). Interestingly, it shows several interactions across domains (economic, environmental, and social) and levels (field, farm, farming system) written in capital letters in horizontal and vertical axes, respectively (Accatino et al., 2020).

Concerning the unbalanced bargaining power, favouring industrial processors, some stakeholders perceive that the growing quality standards are pushing down prices, affecting farm profitability and the system's economic viability. Furthermore, the latter is utterly hampered by the lack of local product valorisation: all the transformation processing occurs outside the FS, excluding potential value-adding activities. This seems a significant missed opportunity, besides being a strategy to weaken the bargaining power of big industrial players. Finally, higher quality standards prevent environment-friendly practices, including organic production, threatening the provision of environment-related public goods.

Climate change is perceived as severe, particularly for non-traditional areas of production. This entails a decline in farm profitability, driving the general decline of FS's economic viability because of the lack of similarly profitable crop alternatives to the hazelnut cultivation. In this sense, a resilience attribute such as crop diversification is likely to reduce the FS's average profitability, eventually pushing out young people from farming.

Introducing more binding environmental constraints could limit yields and increase production costs (Coppola et al., 2020), lowering the FS's economic viability. However, shifting to an eco-friendly production process and promoting precision agriculture applications could be beneficial only if the system will be able to exploit the potential willingness of consumers to pay a premium price for organic products. Under these circumstances, this could permit to increase both the economic viability of the system and the provision of public goods. However, the confectionery industry is not pursuing any strategy in this direction, and most hazelnuts are not processed locally but sold to retailers by companies operating outside the FS. Hence, this valorisation strategy could be implemented only with the confectionery industry's active participation or with the FS's ability to develop a successful marketing strategy and create the ideal conditions for a small-scale local processing industry.

The previously mentioned challenges are putting the system under pressure, moving towards an alternative configuration of the FS when the thresholds of indicators, resilience attributes and challenges are exceeded. The following alternative configurations of the system have been identified during the second FoPIA workshop. Furthermore, some boundary conditions (i.e., conditions that need to be fulfilled before the alternative system can flourish) were identified.

i. A system oriented to satisfy the growing demand of raw hazelnut exerted by the big confectionery industries: increasing demand would generate, ceteris paribus, positive repercussions on the farms' profitability (Table 11.1). The promotion of hazelnut-based products in markets where demand is growing, such as China, could stimulate such a system. In turn, this may generate positive effects on the system's organisation, the infrastructure for innovation, and ultimately the private viability of the FS. Removal of trade barriers is among the boundary conditions which could make the alternative system happen.

ii. Local valorisation: a complex process involving a plurality of actors who have specific interests and potentially pursuing different – and sometimes conflicting – objectives and strategies. Product

Table 11.1. *Perceived performance expectations of the main functions and the presence of resilience attributes in future configurations of the FS*

Indicator	Current level	Future systems				
		Status quo	Sustained demand (high and stable prices)	Product valorisation	Technological innovation	Eco-friendly agriculture
Gross saleable production	High	↗	↗	↗	↗	↘|↗
Gross margin	High	→↗	↗	↗	↗	↘|↗
Organic farming (Ha)	Low	↗	↗	↑	↗	↑
Retention of young people	Moderate	↗	↗	↗	↗	↗
Socially self-organised	Moderate	→↗	↗	↗	↗	↑
Coupled with local and natural capital	Low	↗	↑	↗	↑	↑
Supports rural life	Moderate	↗	↗	↗	↗	↗
Infrastructure for innovation	Moderate	↗	↗	↗	↑	↗
Diverse policies	Low	↑	↑	↗	↗	↑

Table 11.1. (*cont.*)

Boundary conditions	Dimension				
Growing demand	Economic	V			V
Prices linked to the real cost	Economic	V		V	
Concentration of the confectionery industry	Economic	V			V
New markets	Economic	V	V		
Short supply chain	Economic		V		V
Brands with high local value	Environmental		V		V
Extreme weather events (droughts)	Environmental	V			V
Greater eco-friendly requirements	Environmental	V			V
Cultural changes	Social	V	V		V
Research	Social			V	V
More young people in the system	Social	V		V	
Information flow	Social			V	
CAP support	Institutional	V		V	V
Duty-free markets	Institutional	V			V

→ implies no change, ↑ implies moderate positive change, ↗ implies strong positive change, ↘ implies moderate negative change, ↓ implies strong negative change, V implies that a boundary condition is relevant for a future system.

194

valorisation could be pursued by developing locally processed and differentiated products exploiting the opportunities offered by the current and alternative geographical indications. This is expected to bypass large downstream processing firms or at least weaken their bargaining power. In this alternative system, there is a general improvement of the economic indicators, ameliorating the FS's competitiveness (Table 11.1). In this regard, boundary conditions are represented by developing local high-value brands allowing the valorisation of both the intrinsic and extrinsic quality of local production. CAP support for investments of local processors can play a crucial role in pursuing this strategy.

iii. Technological innovation is considered a driving strategy for the future of the FS because of its potential to reduce production costs and increase production value. Stakeholders mentioned, among others, precision agriculture and the digitalisation of the farm processes. CAP support does not play a relevant role in this process: policies, such as RDP, do not promptly adapt to the system needs because of their slow and complicated bureaucratic procedures. This future configuration of the FS requires increasing research activities at the field level, the presence of more young people in the FS, ensuring information flow among stakeholders along the value chain, increasing CAP support for technological investments, and reducing the red tape.

iv. Shifting to more eco-friendly agriculture: this would foster the conservation of natural resources. The performance of economic indicators may decline at the beginning due to lower yields and product quality. It should be considered that farmers in the area have limited knowledge of eco-friendly farming practices. Providing widespread training activities in this direction may facilitate such transition. Moreover, if consumers are willing to pay higher prices for the final product, this could offset lower production levels and higher production costs.

11.4 Strategies towards the Future

The alternative configurations of the system are not independent: technological innovations could facilitate the shift towards more eco-friendly practices, and, simultaneously, a system based on eco-friendly activities which could add value to the product if this is properly communicated to final consumers.

While some strategies are vital to maintaining the status quo, others are essential to trigger future alternative systems. Therefore, while mechanisation, consortia for technical advisory and more substantial cooperation among stakeholders are useful to maintain the status quo, more binding agro-environmental policies and requirements are essential for transitioning towards more environment-preserving agriculture. In contrast, the opening of international markets is needed, especially for a demand-oriented system.

On the other hand, to envisage alternative configurations, consortia for technical advice mixed with increasing CAP support may encourage environment-friendly agriculture and technological innovation; in addition, promotional activities could be useful for the alternative system based on local product valorisation to communicate with consumers. Participants at the workshops argued that the interaction among stakeholders in the supply chain and training activities are expected to generate positive effects on each alternative configuration system mentioned earlier. Nowadays, the FS requires trained stakeholders, able to collaborate vertically within the value chain. Indeed, cooperation among FS actors seems to be a fundamental resilience attribute for guaranteeing the system's efficient organisation. Finally, the EU public support could enhance the system's resilience when facing external changes/shocks: current RDPs and CMO instruments foster the robustness and adaptability of the local FS. However, the effectiveness of these measures depends on adjusting them according to the FS configuration to be pursued and to external shocks.

11.5 Conclusions

The relevant growth of hazelnut production in the last decades, both in terms of quantity and quality, brought the FS near to a crucial point: whether to embrace a path of intensification following the increasing demand of the confectionery industry or to move towards a system based on the local valorisation of the product adopting technological innovations and environment-friendly approaches.

Results suggest the current situation of the hazelnut FS relies mostly on robustness capacities to cope with challenges, although, to a lower extent, adaptability capacities are also detected. On the contrary, the ability to pursue radical transformations is minimal. Due to positive economic performances, the FS performs well in terms of food production and economic viability, but its performances concerning the quality of life, natural resources, biodiversity and habitat, and area attractiveness are questionable. Thus, the system looks resilient for specific short-term disturbances, tackled by a good organisation, redundancy, and significant financial resources availability. However, the hazelnut's perennial nature, the lack of alternative (profitable) crops, and the strong dominance of the downstream industrial process hinder its transformability capacities.

Nevertheless, the analysis has revealed that alternative configurations in response to climate change, increasing societal concerns over environmental quality and public health, and the increasing concentration of the confectionery industry would need relatively greater changes to occur. In this regard, four alternative systems have been identified.

The first alternative system aims at meeting the needs of the confectionery industry: the growing international demand for manufactured products would increase both robustness and adaptability capacities, mainly reinforcing the private functions provided. However, it would also exacerbate some critical environmental issues, negatively affecting the system's resilience through reducing its connection with natural and local capital. Furthermore, the increasing dependence on global markets may drive the system to be even less resilient.

On the contrary, local product valorisation may enhance resilience, reducing exposure to international markets, and strengthening ties with local resources. This would also generate attractive job opportunities for young people in the (new) local downstream enterprises, opening up new market channels, and improving the reputation and the attractiveness of the area, beneficial to non-agricultural activities too, such as local tourism. However, this strategy rests on enhancing vertical coordination led by the local production system: producers, when properly organised and supported by targeted policy measures, should manage the supply chain. Clearly, this requires identifying the market shares available to absorb valorised products and involves producer organisations.

A reconfiguration of the system based on technological innovation could positively affect farmers' income with a potentially positive impact on system resilience. However, while this is not necessarily the solution for the problems previously described, technological innovation offers opportunities for reconciliation, at least to some extent, between hazelnut production and the environment due to better use of chemical inputs and irrigation.

Finally, the system could shift to eco-friendly farming practices ensuring a higher level of environmental sustainability. This will require relevant changes along with all components of the FS, especially the marketing strategies of the dominant industrial processors: final industrial products based on organic hazelnut production would increase the likelihood of this alternative configuration to happen.

In conclusion, discussions with stakeholders have shown that there is room for improvement for the FS's resilience, primarily through an adequate mix of strategies to increase the connection with the local and natural capital. In this regard, a higher level of eco-compatibility and technological innovation may generate synergies if the Agricultural Knowledge and Innovation Systems (AKIS) orient research and technological innovation in this direction.

EU policies could have a crucial role in fostering the adoption of a local valorisation strategy. The current CAP, focused on providing financial support to operational programs (planned and implemented by POs), is factually oriented to promote a strategy based on local valorisation, innovation and environmental sustainability. The current European Commission orientation is to increase the share dedicated to environmental actions within the CMO policies up to 20 per cent. Indeed, the recent Green Deal and the Farm to Fork strategy are expected to strengthen such an orientation. However, its implementation in the investigated FS is constrained by the dominant position of confectionery companies not located in the area. Indeed, a strategy based on local valorisation, innovation and environmental sustainability requires strong cohesion between producers to be effective. This calls for a collective action involving different actors of the FS, the reduction of the fragmentation of the POs and the reinforcement of the local value chain. Nevertheless, as already mentioned, these conditions are still far from being satisfied.

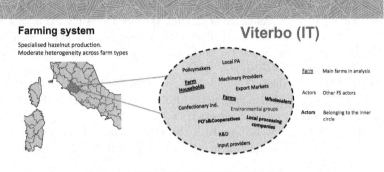

Farming system

Specialised hazelnut production.
Moderate heterogeneity across farm types

Viterbo (IT)

Farm — Main farms in analysis

Actors — Other FS actors

Actors — Belonging to the inner circle

Challenges

Institutional:
- Delay in RDP policies;
- Introduction of stringent environmental local regulations;

Environmental:
- Water scarcity;
- Climate change (drought);
- New bugs;

Economic:
- High down-stream market power;
- Prices' volatility;

Social:
- Societal conflicts (environment, health and landscape).

Adaptive cycle

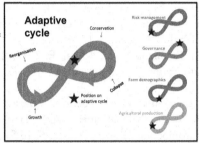

Essential functions

Private goods:
- Economic viability (sufficient income): *high performance*
- Food production (high quality product): *high performance*

Public goods:
- Negative environmental impact: *low performance*

Resilience capacities

Overall low to moderate resilience capacities

Mainly Robust (high profitability and self-organisation), medium Adaptability and low Transformability.

Current policy configuration enhance Adaptability while raising concern for Robustness in the short-run.

Future strategies

Risk management	Governance	Farm demographics	Agricultural production
• Non-agricultural activities and product diversification • *Ad-hoc* insurance instruments	• Increase upstream bargaining power (coops&POs) • Strenghtening demarcation of functions and policy goals between CMO and RDP	• Cementing the relationship with research centres	• New technologies&techniques • Local processing and valorization of local production

This project has received funds from the European Union's Horizon 2020 research and innovation programme under Grant Agreement No 727520

Annex 11.1 Factsheet synthesising resilience of the current farming system in Viterbo (Italy).

References

Accatino, F., Paas, W., Herrera, H., et al. 2020. 'D5.5 Impacts of future scenarios on the resilience of farming systems across the EU assessed with quantitative and qualitative methods'. Sustainable and resilient EU farming systems (SURE-Farm) project report, EU Horizon 2020 Grant Agreement No. 727520.

Anderies, J. M., Folke, C., Walker, B., Ostrom, E. 2013. 'Aligning key concepts for global change policy: Robustness, resilience, and sustainability', *Ecology and Society* 18(2): 8.

Bosco, L., Moraglio, S. T., Tavella, L. 2018. '*Halyomorpha halys*, a serious threat for hazelnut in newly invaded areas', *Journal of Pest Science* 91(2): 661–670.

Coppola, G., Costantini, M., Orsi, L., et al. 2020. 'A comparative cost-benefit analysis of conventional and organic hazelnuts production systems in center Italy', *Agriculture* 10: 409.

Cristofori, V., Muleo, R., Bignami, C., Rugini, E. 2014. 'Long term evaluation of hazelnut response to drip irrigation', *Acta Horticulturae* 1052: 179–185.

Liberti, S. 2019. 'Il gusto amaro delle nocciole', *Internazionale* 1312: 38. Available at www.internazionale.it/reportage/stefanoliberti/2019/06/21/nutella-gusto-amaro-nocciole-ferrero (accessed on 15 September 2019).

Nera, E., Paas, W., Reidsma, P., Paolini, G., Antonioli, F., Severini, S. 2020. 'Assessing the resilience and sustainability of a hazelnut farming system in central Italy with a participatory approach', *Sustainability* 12(1): 343.

Reidsma, P., Paas, W., Accatino, F., et al. 2020. 'D5.6 Impacts of improved strategies and policy options on the resilience of farming systems across the EU'. Sustainable and resilient EU farming systems (SURE-Farm) project report, EU Horizon 2020 Grant Agreement No. 727520.

Severini, S., Paolini, G., Nera, E., Antonioli, F., Senni, S. 2019. 'FoPIA-Surefarm case-study report Italy'. In: Paas, W., Accatino, F., Antonioli, F., et al., 'D5.2 Participatory impact assessment of sustainability and resilience of EU farming systems'. Sustainable and resilient EU farming systems. (SURE-Farm) project report. EU Horizon 2020 Grant Agreement No. 727520.

Silvestri, C., Bacchetta, L., Bellincontro, A., Cristofori, V. 2021. 'Advances in cultivar choice, hazelnut orchard management and nuts storage for enhancing product quality and safety: An overview', *Journal of the Science of Food and Agriculture* 101(1): 27–43.

Zinnanti, C., Schimmenti, E., Borsellino, V., Paolini, G., Severini, S. 2019. 'Economic performance and risk of farming systems specialised in perennial crops: An analysis of Italian hazelnut production', *Agricultural Systems* 176: 102645.

12 | Realising Transformation in Response to Future Challenges

The Case of an Intensive Arable Farming System in the Veenkoloniën, the Netherlands

ALISA SPIEGEL, PYTRIK REIDSMA,
YANNICK BUITENHUIS, THOMAS
SLIJPER, WIM PAAS, YANN DE MEY,
PETER H. FEINDT, JEROEN CANDEL,
P. MARIJN POORTVLIET
AND MIRANDA P. M. MEUWISSEN

12.1 Introduction

The Veenkoloniën (Figure 12.1) is located in two Northern provinces of the Netherlands – Drenthe and Groningen – and can literally be translated as peat (Dutch: *veen*) colonies (Dutch: *koloniën*). The prevalence of peat soils in the region has strongly affected its historical development. While small-scale peat extraction was common in the area in the Middle Ages, demand for peat exploded in the seventeenth century during the 'Dutch Golden Age' and expanded even further throughout the eighteenth and nineteenth centuries due to the development of the shipping sector that facilitated transport. Around the first half of the twentieth century, most peat was extracted in the region, resulting in sandy soils with relatively high organic matter content (Dutch: *dalgrond*) that characterise the region nowadays. Organic matter levels highly vary with a large share of inactive organic matter, which leads to low water-holding capacity, high vulnerability to wind erosion, and varying subsidence levels. The soil is unsuitable for cultivation of many crops and vegetables for two main reasons. Firstly, the relatively high organic matter content acts like a blanket, meaning that little energy can move from the soil to the air directly, making crops vulnerable to frost damage. Secondly, the potatoes and vegetables look dirty as a consequence of the brown peat-rich soil, which adheres to the products, making the product less aesthetically pleasing for consumers

Figure 12.1 Typical landscape in the Veenkoloniën.
Photo by Yannick Buitenhuis.

(Smit and Jager 2018). Consequently, the region largely relies on starch potato production in a 1:2–1:3 rotation,[1] with starch potato being rotated every second or third year with mainly sugar beet and wheat. Although starch potato has been the most profitable crop in the region,[2] such a tight crop rotation increases the risk of plant parasitic nematodes. Yet, extending crop rotation to control for nematodes risk is challenging, as current price margins are already low. With an estimated net present value per hectare of arable land of 2,541 €/ha (Diogo et al. 2017), the region ranks amongst the least profitable in the Netherlands. Most farms are specialised either on arable crops or livestock; we focus on the former. There are a number of cooperatives operating in the region – Avebe (starch potato), Cosun Beet Company (sugar beet), Agrifirm (wheat processor and feed supplier) – yet we only consider Avebe as a part of the farming system, since Avebe depends on farmers in the Veenkoloniën for the supply of food

---

[1] The narrowest rotation is a four-year rotation of starch potato, sugar beet, starch potato, and wheat, resulting in a 1:2 rotation for starch potato, where the other crop is alternating every two years.

[2] At the farm level, most of the revenue comes indeed from starch potato production. On a hectare base, sugar beet is more profitable, but farmers are restricted to a 1:4 rotation of sugar beet and also due to the LLBs from the sugar industry. LLBs are 'Leden Leverings Bewijzen', which have replaced the sugar quota system in 2017. Sugar beet cooperative Cosun Beet Company has introduced the LLBs to be able to match demand and supply of sugar beets and decides each year on the amount of sugar beets that can be delivered by farmers to the Company. Besides, in the past the gross margin of sugar beet was higher than of starch potato, but since 2018 it is the other way around, due to decreasing sugar beet prices and increasing starch potato prices.

products much more than other cooperatives. The Annex 12.1 provides a graphical illustration of the farming system as considered in the analysis.

Until recently, the general expectation was that the arable farming system in the Veenkoloniën would eventually collapse due to two main challenges: a low level of agricultural diversification, and changes in the Common Agricultural Policy (CAP)'s financial support. Increased frequencies of extreme weather events, such as wind erosion, drought, extreme heat, or excess precipitation (Schaap et al. 2013), were expected to particularly affect starch potato production (Diogo et al. 2017), while soil limitations did not allow diversifying crop portfolios to reduce risk. Gradual abolishment of CAP coupled support for starch potato production in 2013 was estimated to result in an average decrease of direct payments from 450–750 €/ha (coupled) to eventually 350–400 €/ha (decoupled, incl. greening) by 2019, putting pressure on farm incomes (Immenga et al. 2012). A general response to all stresses and opportunities in Europe is enlargement of farms, also in the Veenkoloniën, as the number of farms has steadily declined by 39 per cent from 4,377 to 2,651 farms between 2000 and 2017 (CBS 2020). While this means that some farmers quitted, the region has shown remarkable resilience in the last two decades at the farming system level.

As for the future, the results of our farm survey in the region (see Chapter 1 for details) reveal that institutional challenges are still perceived as highly relevant in the next twenty years, but that farmers currently mainly worry about tightening the environmental policy requirements. At the same time, many arable farmers perceive environmental challenges, particularly nematodes and more frequent extreme weather events, as even greater long-term threats. Both institutional and environmental challenges are aggravated by low farm income, societal pressure to improve sustainability, and significant soil limitations.

Against this background, we first explore how actors in the farming system have dealt with its challenges in the past by identifying the farming system's sources of three resilience capacities – robustness, adaptability and transformability (Section 12.2). Next, we explain that resilience in the past is no guarantee for the future (Section 12.3) and present our vision on the resilience of the farming system in the future by reflecting on challenges and opportunities in the medium- to long-term (Section 12.4). Section 12.5 concludes the chapter. While this chapter mainly focuses on challenges, resilience capacities, and attributes, as well as future strategies to improve resilience, the Annex 12.1 provides a summary of the complete analysis of the farming system following the resilience framework (Chapter 1), i.e., also summarising the importance and performance of private and public goods provision, as well as the current state of adaptive cycles.

12.2 Sources of Resilience in the Past

According to CBS (2020), arable farming in the Veenkoloniën is characterised by its strong specialisation in cultivating starch potato, sugar beet, and wheat, mainly maintained through a strong collaborative network between farmers and other stakeholders in the farming system, such as the starch potato processing cooperative Avebe. The strong specialisation led to a farming system that performs very well regarding (food) production and could survive severe shocks in its current form (i.e., stay robust) or via adaptation, yet it limits the transformative capacity of the farming system (for details on the three resilience capacities see Chapter 1 and Meuwissen et al. 2019). Based on the farm survey, we found that the infrastructure for innovation and social self-organisation have mostly contributed to resilience in the past and helped the farming system dealing with these challenges, although during a participatory sustainability and resilience workshop stakeholders agreed that the levels of these resilience attributes can be improved (Paas et al. 2019).

Farming system actors, in particular Avebe, aimed to maintain starch potato production and responded to any challenge in the past with innovations, while also quickly involving other actors in the farming system in the innovation process. For instance, the abolishment of coupled support of the CAP for starch potato production in 2013 was overcome due to Avebe quickly adapting its business model and developing new products, including potato protein for human consumption, which led to higher prices for farmers. Similarly, Avebe has actively supported development of more productive cultivars with a higher starch content and higher resistance to nematodes. Other stakeholders have played an important role in facilitating innovation among farmers, including an agricultural innovation platform Innovatie Veenkoloniën that brings together key stakeholders in the farming system and facilitates knowledge exchange in the stakeholder network. Additionally, an experimental farm of Wageningen University & Research located in the region has spread examples of good practices. Indeed, many farmers in the region were found to be open to innovative starch potato varieties, green manures, and even new crops (e.g., onion), in order to extend crop rotation and reduce environmental risks. Another important stakeholder contributing to minimising the impact of extreme weather events and to improving soil quality is the local water board (Dutch: *Waterschap Hunze en Aa's*). The water board runs multiple projects aiming, among other things, to ensure enough water supply in case of drought and to increase resistance of farming to floods (Hunze en Aa's 2020). Innovations in the past allowed adaptation in response to challenges; they, however, never triggered a more radical transformation, e.g., away from specialisation in starch potato production. Innovations have always been introduced in time, often completely removing effects of a challenge, while at the same time pushing down incentives for transformation.

Collaboration between the farming system's stakeholders has con-tributed to resilience in the past even in the absence of innovation, e.g., in the case of financial support against extreme weather events. Since Avebe depends on starch production by its members (i.e., the farmers) and needs to ensure their profitability, they have paid a higher price to farmers to compensate for losses due to extreme weather events at a cost to Avebe's financial savings. In addition, farmers have increased financial savings in good years with high yields and prices that, for instance, helped to financially overcome the severe drought of 2018. Likewise, collaboration between arable and dairy farmers via exchan-ging their land allows extending crop rotations. The currently imple-mented two-year-rotation system allows devoting more land resources to starch potato but increases the risk of nematodes due to the intensive character of the production system. In order to extend crop rotation and reduce the risk of nematodes, arable farmers cooperate with livestock farmers by putting their land in one pool. In this larger pool of land, starch potatoes can be better rotated with arable and feed crops (Paas et al. 2020). By pooling land, arable farmers are able to devote half or more of their initial land resources to starch potato, while more easily controlling for the risk of nematodes. Livestock farmers also benefit from this system in terms of manure disposal, feed crops production, and grassland renewal, while Avebe also benefits from lower yield risks and an increased starch potato supply.

12.3 Resilience in the Past Is No Guarantee for the Future

Although the farming system managed to cope with several challenges in the past, there is no guarantee for survival in the future due to two main reasons: (i) the farming system is approaching its limits and (ii) current challenges may undermine resilience in the long run (Paas et al. 2020). Avebe requires enough starch potato supply to continue operation and hence aims to make the business viable for farmers by covering their costs (Meuwissen et al. 2020). By paying higher prices to farmers in bad years, the financial reserves of Avebe diminish, and hence there is a limit to the extent and duration of shocks that Avebe can cope with. The strategy is not sustainable in the long run, since in worse scenarios Avebe might not be able to pay farmers high-enough prices to remain viable, and farmers might abolish the cultivation of starch potatoes, leading to a drastic system decline, possibly leading to collapse. System dynamics modelling and participatory workshops confirmed that even marginal intensification of a challenge (e.g., decreasing yields due to nematode pressure and extreme weather events) can cause the farming system to collapse (Accatino et al. 2020; Paas et al. 2020; Schütz 2020). If droughts like those experienced in 2018, which decreased yields by 21 per cent, occur in two subsequent years, the system is expected to collapse in the long run if no additional strategies are implemented to cope with the challenges (Accatino et al. 2020; Paas et al. 2020; Schütz 2020). Also, cooperation between arable and livestock farmers to reduce nematode risk has always been uncertain due to the limited number of livestock farmers in the Veenkoloniën (Paas et al. 2020). Innovative starch potato varieties were recently found not to be resistant to new nematodes, and stakeholders are concerned that a 1:2 rotation may be impossible to maintain in the future (Paas et al. 2020). These evidences highlight the crucial importance of continuous innovation to remain within a safe operating space. Moreover, while strong specialisation on starch potatoes was beneficial for resilience in the past, it is perceived as rather constraining the transformative capacity in the future. For instance, demographic interviews and the risk management focus group revealed that there are concerns that prices for starch potatoes increased by Avebe did not encourage farmers to implement changes to their businesses; thus, enhancing the status quo within the farming systems. Although the status-quo is not necessarily disadvantageous, it is not seen as sustainable in the longer term for this particular farming system. The innovations implemented in the latest years, e.g., crop protection, soil quality improvement, and protective measures against wind erosion, are examples of adaptation, but no transformation, and lead to a more fundamental issue of lock-in, making it more and more difficult for all farming system stakeholders to deviate from the path (see Chapter 5 for further examples on lock-ins in other farming systems).

To this end, the farming system might approach critical thresholds soon if solutions based on current strategies are not realised in time (e.g., new cultivars, new crop protection products). This is aggravated by the fact that current agricultural practices are focused too much on production, while being partly decoupled from local and natural production capital. Based on system dynamics modelling for most of the envisioned future scenarios for European agriculture (Mitter et al. 2020), continuous investment solely aiming to maintain starch potato production is likely to limit radical transformation (Paas et al. 2019). Indeed, several future challenges, especially long-term stresses, require resilience capacities beyond robustness or even adaptability. For instance, maintaining and improving soil quality is undermined by current strong dependency on the intensification of arable farming and requires the farming system to introduce structural changes. Yet, some minimum level of robustness in the short term is essential for building up resources that allow adaptation or transformation in the long run. An additional challenge for the farming system in the Veenkoloniën is therefore to find a proper balance between the three resilience capacities in the future.

12.4 Opportunities and Strategies for a More Resilient System in the Future

12.4.1 Focus on Long-Term Challenges and Risk Management

As explained earlier, major challenges in the Veenkoloniën have shifted from operational and short-term shocks towards more structural stresses with long-term impacts on farms and farming systems, such as constantly changing environmental regulations and more frequent extreme weather events linked to climate change. In this regard, strategies and alternative systems also need to become long-term oriented, addressing multiple challenges and involving all the actors in the farming system. In particular, risk management should be understood in the broader context of resilience, compared to the traditional interpretation of risk management as targeting mainly economic functions (see also Chapter 2). We suggest defining risk management as the portfolio of instruments adopted by farmers in order to minimise the impact of challenges on the economic, environmental, and social functions (Slijper et al. 2020). Furthermore, risk management should not only ensure short-term robustness, but also enhance adaptive and transformative capacities in the long run (Spiegel et al. 2020). The diversity of strategies adopted in the risk management portfolio reflects a farmers' anticipation, coping, and response diversity to risk and uncertainty, preparing farmers for the unknown future. While current risk management portfolios in the Veenkoloniën are already fairly diverse, according to the farm survey, risk management instruments rather cope with short-term shocks and enhance robustness, for instance financial savings (currently implemented by ca. 57 per cent of surveyed farmers), agricultural insurance (40 per cent), and work harder in bad times (20 per cent). Instead, diversification in production and protecting the environment are examples of risk management instruments that target long-term stresses. Accordingly, all stakeholders involved in risk management in the farming system should reconsider their roles and perspectives in the future. For instance, financial institutions managing savings and providing insurance could focus more on financing innovations, in particular environment-friendly ones.

12.4.2 *Exploit Existing Social Self-Organisation and Infrastructure for Innovation*

As explained earlier, successful examples of resilience in the past can be linked to social self-organisation and infrastructure for innovation. We suggest capitalising on these existing resilience attributes in the future through interrelated strategies of cooperation and learning, not only among farmers and their cooperatives but also with banks and insurance agencies. This would maintain the current level of robustness, while stimulating adaptive and transformative capacity as well.

Cooperation might facilitate adoption of new technologies by sharing data and good experience among actors; examples here are precision agriculture and new methods of promoting soil life that in the future may enable targeting specific parasitic soil communities. Yet, more importantly, networks are essential for many strategies, such as a new type of water management, redesigning nature areas, and circular agriculture, that require tight collaboration of multiple actors (Paas et al. 2020). As explained earlier, extending crop rotation is currently done via cooperation between arable and livestock farmers. This cooperation does not rely on any formal regulations and hence requires very tight interactions and trust among farmers. In this regard, cooperation between actors might potentially enhance adaptability as it improves connectedness of the farming system via developing and tightening relationships (Cabell and Oelofse 2012).

Learning is one of the most popular risk management instruments in the Veenkoloniën (currently implemented by ca. 52 per cent of surveyed farmers) aiming to accumulate knowledge from past experiences, to experiment, and to anticipate changes (Darnhofer et al. 2010). Currently, several cooperatives in the Veenkoloniën (e.g., Avebe, Cosun, Agrifirm) organise local study events and clubs that have great potential to facilitate learning. However, these learning opportunities are often visited by the same farmers, as the results of risk management focus group and policy workshops suggest. Although there are different types of farmers also in terms of their willingness to learn, cooperatives are recommended to actively recruit new farmers and other farming system actors to the study clubs and facilitate discussion about both successful and unsuccessful practices. Also, learning can be beneficial for establishing and securing niche markets for newly introduced or rarely cultivated crops with cooperatives playing a key role. Recent examples showed that although some farmers adopted blueberry production, they were reluctant to share data with other farmers worrying that additional supply might ultimately lower market prices. Here, cooperatives might explore the demand and ensure that newly introduced crops can be successfully marketed.

12.4.3 Opt for Transformative Strategies, while Keeping Specialisation on Starch Potato

There are opportunities in the Veenkoloniën to employ the current level of adaptability in order to prepare for needed transformations without abandoning starch potato production in the region. One example is a more nature-inclusive production system that includes introduction, processing, and trading of new crops (onions, valerian, barley, blueberries), as well as sustainable soil management, maintaining and improving landscape, and innovative agricultural production techniques, such as precision agriculture. Transforming the system while keeping specialisation on starch potato production should aim to reduce production risks and shift the focus towards other functions, such as maintenance of natural resources and attractiveness of the rural area. Another promising option relates to strategies aiming to improve profitability in the farming system accompanied with adaptive strategies that release the pressure of starch potato production on the performance of the farming system (and vice versa). For instance, some arable farmers have already opted for innovative strategies that are not directly beneficial for the cooperatives, such as introduction of new crops. The aim of improving profitability is clearly visible in all proposed alternative systems where developing a good business model is identified as an important strategy.

12.4.4 Exploit Opportunities of a More Radical Transformation beyond Starch Potato

Relaxing the already intensive crop rotation is another, probably more sustainable, option for the future. A 1:3 rotation would be more appropriate according to multiple experts within and outside the farming system (Paas et al. 2020). Yet, it would imply a substantial reduction of starch potato production and eventually reduces the strong specialisation on starch potato. Instead, farmers could gradually start introducing other protein-rich crops in their crop rotation, which is in line with the current political emphasis on a protein transition (Verstand et al. 2020). An alternative mentioned by Verstand et al. (2020) would be a transformation towards sustainable energy production by introducing solar panels. Non-farm activities, such as care farming and renewable energy production, could compensate for declines in farm income due to lower starch potato production. Any option, however, requires a certain level of support by stakeholders, whereas our stakeholder activities reveal their reluctance to move away from starch potato. In general, such a feeling of being stuck within a certain farming system is natural for every single stakeholder, especially when transformation would require joint actions of all stakeholders. In this case, a radical change is not likely to enter via the front door of joint vision and action, but rather via the back door of small-scale experimenting and learning between the farming system's actors and actors from other sectors, as well as citizens. Agricultural policy could support this process, by clarifying long-term regulatory boundaries, supporting innovation and providing compensation for the production of public goods (see, e.g., Buitenhuis et al. 2020; SURE-Farm 2020). This implies that agricultural policies should move away from generic measures that are in favour of the status quo within the Veenkoloniën, but instead offer tailored support for unconventional farming practices or alternative business models that help to reach desired outcomes.

12.5 Conclusion

The arable farming system in the Veenkoloniën showed that strategies successfully maintaining the status quo in the past are perceived by some actors as inefficient and even restrictive due to changes in the nature of major challenges and approaching critical thresholds, such that a transformation might be needed. The farming system needs to maintain robustness, while increasing adaptive and especially transformative capacities. Research on interdependencies between resilience capacities is extremely limited; literature suggesting specific strategies that maintain one resilience capacity, while improving the other two is lacking. Recommended future paths aiming to enhance resilience include an orientation towards long-term transformative strategies, as well as exploitation of existing strengths – enhancing social self-organisation, and fostering an infrastructure for innovation.

We have presented multiple strategies for a more resilient system without ranking them or highlighting any. It is important to note though that these strategies are not necessarily mutually exclusive. For instance, introducing precision agriculture might be an opportunity to develop an innovative and good business model. In fact, most of the alternatives rely on having a sustainable business model, tight collaboration between actors, active learning, and a developed infrastructure for innovation. These four elements might be addressed in different ways, depending on the specified pathways and goals that should be defined jointly by all actors. Furthermore, actors outside the farming system might contribute by bringing additional resources into the system and creating an enabling environment.

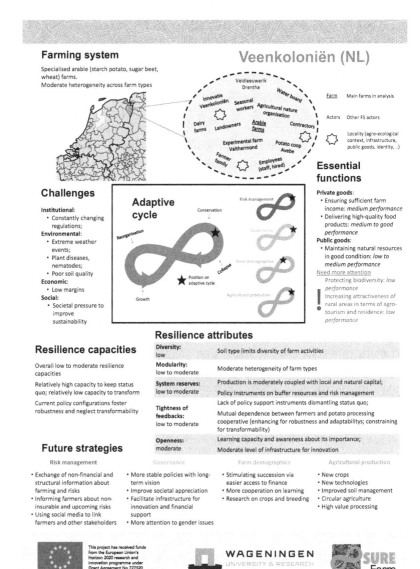

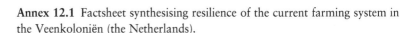

Annex 12.1 Factsheet synthesising resilience of the current farming system in the Veenkoloniën (the Netherlands).

References

Accatino, F., Paas, W. H., Herrera, H., et al. 2020. D5. 5 Impacts of future scenarios on the resilience of farming systems across the EU assessed with quantitative and qualitative methods. SURE-Farm. Available at www .surefarmproject.eu/wordpress/wp-content/uploads/2020/06/D5.5.-Future-scenarios-on-the-FS-resilience.pdf. Accessed 11 November 2021.

Buitenhuis, Y., Candel, J., Feindt, P. H. et al. 2020. Improving the resilience-enabling capacity of the Common Agricultural Policy: Policy recommendations for more resilient EU farming systems. *EuroChoices* 19(2), 63–71. https://doi-org.ezproxy.library.wur.nl/10.1111/1746-692X.12286

Cabell, J. F. and Oelofse, M. 2012. An indicator framework for assessing agroecosystem resilience. *Ecology and Society* 17(1), 18. http://dx.doi .org/10.5751/es-04666-170118

CBS. 2020. Website of the Dutch Bureau of Statistics. Available at www.cbs .nl/. Accessed 22 October 2020.

Darnhofer, I., Fairweather, J. and Moller, H. 2010. Assessing a farm's sustainability: Insights from resilience thinking. *International Journal of Agricultural Sustainability* 8(3), 186–198. http://dx.doi.org/10.3763/ ijas.2010.0480

Diogo, V., Reidsma, P., Schaap, B., Andree, B. P. J. and Koomen, E. 2017. Assessing local and regional economic impacts of climatic extremes and feasibility of adaptation measures in Dutch arable farming systems. *Agricultural Systems* 157, 216–229.

Hunze en Aa's. 2020. Website of the water board Hunze en Aa's. Available at www.hunzeenaas.nl. Accessed 22 October 2020.

Immenga, D. J., Munneke, K. and Lamain, M. 2012. Bouwstenen voor het advies van de Commissie Landbouw Veenkoloniën. Projectbureau Agenda voor de Veenkoloniën, Stadskanaal.

Meuwissen, M. P. M., Feindt, P., Spiegel, A., et al. 2019. A framework to assess the resilience of farming systems. *Agricultural Systems* 176, 102656. https://doi.org/10.1016/j.agsy.2019.102656

Meuwissen, M. P. M., Feindt, P. H., Midmore, M., et al. 2020. The struggle of farming systems in Europe: Looking for explanations through the lens of resilience. *EuroChoices* 19(2), 4–11.

Mitter, H., Techen, A. K., Sinabell, F., et al. 2020. Shared socio-economic pathways for European agriculture and food systems: The Eur-Agri-SSPs. *Global Environmental Change* 65, 102159.

Paas, W., Meuwissen, M. and Reidsma, P. 2019. FoPIA-SURE-FARM case-study report The Netherlands. In: Paas, W., Accatino, F., Antonioli, F., et al. D5.2 Participatory impact assessment of sustainability and resilience of EU farming systems. Sustainable and resilient EU farming

systems (SURE-Farm) project report. Available at www.surefarmproject
.eu/wordpress/wp-content/uploads/2019/06/D5.2-FoPIA-SURE-Farm-
Case-study-Report-The-Netherlands.pdf. Accessed 11 November 2021.

Paas, W., Meuwissen, M., van der Wiel, I. and Reidsma, P. 2020. FoPIA-
SURE-Farm 2 case study report The Netherlands. In: Accatino, F., Paas,
W., Herrera, H., et al. D5.5 Impacts of future scenarios on the resilience
of farming systems across the EU assessed with quantitative and qualitative methods. Sustainable and resilient EU farming systems (SURE-Farm)
project report. Available at www.surefarmproject.eu/wordpress/wp-con
tent/uploads/2020/06/D5.5.FoPIA-SURE-Farm_2_The_Netherlands.pdf.
Accessed 11 November 2021.

Schaap, B. F., Reidsma, P., Verhagen, J., Wolf, J. and van Ittersum, M. K.
2013. Participatory design of farm level adaptation to climate risks in an
arable region in The Netherlands. *European Journal of Agronomy* 48,
30–42.

Schütz, L. 2020. Analysing the resilience of an arable farming system in the
Veenkoloniën, NL, using system dynamics modelling. MSc thesis,
Wageningen University. Available at https://edepot.wur.nl/518846.
Accessed 11 November 2021.

Slijper, T., de Mey, Y., Poortvliet, P. M. and Meuwissen, M. P. M. 2020.
From risk behavior to perceived farm resilience: A Dutch case study.
Ecology and Society 25(4), 10.

Smit, B. and Jager, J. 2018. Schets van de akkerbouw in Nederland: Structuur-
, landschaps- en milieukenmerken die een relatie hebben tot biodiversiteit.
Wageningen Economic Research, Wageningen (NL). Available at https://
edepot.wur.nl/463816. Accessed 11 November 2021.

Spiegel, A., Soriano, B., de Mey, Y., et al. 2020. Risk management and its
role in enhancing perceived resilience capacities of farms and farming
systems in Europe. *EuroChoices* 19(2), 45–53.

SURE-Farm. 2020. Policy brief with a critical analysis of how current
policies constrain/enable resilient European agriculture and suggestions
for improvements, including recommendations for the CAP post-2020
reform (August 2020). Available at www.surefarmproject.eu/word
press/wp-content/uploads/2020/08/D4.6_Policy-Brief-on-the-CAP-post-
2020.pdf. Accessed 11 November 2021.

Verstand, D., Bulten, E. and Vijn, M. 2020. Naar klimaatbestendige agrar-
ische bedrijven op veen en moerige gronden in de Veenkoloniën.
Rapport / Stichting Wageningen Research, Wageningen Plant
Research (WPR), Business unit Open Teelten; No. WPR 825. Stichting
Wageningen Research, Wageningen Plant Research (WPR), Business
Unit Open Teelten. https://doi.org/10.18174/515384

13 | Accelerated Adaptability in Pursuit of Future Alternative Systems

The Case of Family, Fruit and Vegetable Farming System in Central-Eastern Poland

KATARZYNA ZAWALIŃSKA
AND PIOTR GRADZIUK

13.1 Introduction

Horticulture is one of the most important branches of agricultural production in Poland. Although it occupies an area of only 635,000 ha, i.e. 4.4 per cent of agricultural land in good condition (GUS 2020), the value of horticultural production accounted for more than 40 per cent of total plant production in 2019 (EC 2020). Poland is the largest producer of apples in the EU and the fourth in the world, as well as a leading producer of cherries, raspberries, currants and gooseberries (Wójcik and Traczyk 2020). Poland's revenues from the export of fruit and fruit preserves reaches EUR 2.04 billion and the export value of fresh vegetables and their preserves amounts to EUR 971 million (IERiGŻ 2020).

There are twenty times more horticultural farms in Poland than in much larger countries, such as Germany. The main horticultural production is carried out in small (less than 10 ha) private farms located in Central-Eastern Poland. Therefore, our case study analyses resilience of family, fruit and vegetable farming in two regions: Mazowieckie and Lubelskie (see Annex 13.1). The area is traditionally dominated by horticulture carried out on family farms and that is what distinguishes Poland from other horticultural systems in the Central East Europe (especially from Hungarian, Slovak and Czech farms). In these other countries, horticultural production is located, due to historical reasons, in corporate farms, which have proved less effective than family farms, so those countries are net importers of horticultural production from Poland (Kudová and Chládková 2008; Német and Masár 2014). According to Kraciński (2017), the revealed comparative advantage

Figure 13.1 Apple orchard in the Mazovian region.
Source: Jakub Kudach

Figure 13.2 Cauliflower from the Mazovian region.
Source: Jakub Kudach

(RCA) indicators of the ex post competitive position indicate that Polish apples were competitive in the world market in the years 2004–2015. Their position was increasing until the period 2013–2015, during which this position started decreasing. The key hard fruits cultivated are: apples, pears, plums, cherries, sweet cherries and, to a lesser extent, peaches and apricots; among soft fruits: strawberries, raspberries, currants (black and red) and gooseberries. Most popular vegetables cultivated are onions, carrots, cabbages, cucumbers, tomatoes and sugar beets. However, the system has its weaknesses. First, a minority of farmers within this farming system (FS) belongs to producer groups (e.g. for joint investments in storage facilities), as currently the network of horizontal integration connections in agriculture is poorly developed, with the exception of some fruit production (e.g. apples). The soft fruit market is also poorly organized, due to the lack of horizontal and particularly vertical integration links. There are very frequent distortions in this market, manifested by drops in purchase prices, at some points reaching levels below costs (e.g. apples, blackcurrants). Farms are also confronted with a lack of seasonal workers. Fruit and vegetable production as well as growing of industrial plants (tobacco, hops, herbs, sugar beets) requires high labour inputs, yet in recent years the demand for seasonal workers significantly exceeds supply, which influences the development of production – see the list of challenges in Annex 13.1.

From a historical perspective, the year 1989 was a ground-breaking moment for Poland and its agriculture, as that was when the country won its total independence from the USSR and started the process of transformation from a centrally planned to a market economy. By that time the state farms provided employment and housing for about 435,000 workers. However, taking into account their families, the state farms provided subsistence for about 2 million people (Milczarek 2002). These farms were inefficient, employing more people than necessary, as such employment was nearly the only source of income in rural areas. Ten years later, after privatization only 122,500 people remained employed there, 28 per cent of what was in 1989. At that time, the system had lots of buffer resources (in terms of labour, land, environmental amenities, etc.) and there were no alternative jobs for farmers outside of agriculture (as they had low education and there was high unemployment in the economy). However, there was a good demography in rural areas (e.g. due to high fertility).

However, the situation has changed very much since then and many processes that the system faces even reversed. For example, the situation at the labour market has reversed – there is almost no unemployment and yet a high shortage of the workers in off-agricultural sectors. Besides, over time, the farmers invested a lot in education of their children also thanks to CAP, as part of the direct payments were spent on education according to a survey carried out by Polish Ministry of Agriculture (MRiRW 2020). So the young generation has much better opportunities to choose good jobs, both in Poland and abroad. The introduction of the CAP also helped reverse the falling trend of support for agriculture and resulted in a significant increase in income for the agricultural households.

The horticulture FS in the case study area consists not only of the horticultural family farms but also: (i) other types of farms (especially medium arable, milk and poultry farms) providing manure supply or doing common crop rotation for those farms; (ii) producer groups and cooperatives; (iii) farm organizations (e.g. Agricultural Chambers, agricultural NGOs); (iv) local financial institutions (e.g. banks); (v) insurance companies; (vi) local retailers; and (vii) local wholesalers, seasonal workers (especially from Ukraine) and other entities and actors who affect the farms and the farms also have impact on them (see Chapter 1 for the definition of FS, and Annex 13.1).

According to Krupin et al. (2019), the key functions delivered by the FS are mainly focused on the provision of private goods – maintaining economic viability and carrying out food production – as well as public goods – delivering bio-based resources for the processing sector and protecting biodiversity of habitats, genes and species. The functions which are assessed by the stakeholders in the SURE-Farm project as the least performing are economic viability and maintaining natural resources (water, soil, air). More details on the evaluation of provision of the essential functions can be found in Annex 13.1.

The FS faces challenges, among which five are particularly hindering the resilience of the current and possibly future FS (see the summary in Annex 13.1), which are discussed next.

Succession problem (social challenge, classified as a long-term trend, see Annex 13.1). There is an uncertainty on the continuity of the farms although most of the interviewed farms in our FS had three or more children. There are push and pull factors behind it. As for the former, the parent-farmers changed their attitude and stopped pressing their children to stay at the farm, as they realized their children have better job opportunities outside of agriculture. So they paid for higher education for their children and in that way they increased their chances for better positions on the job market. As for the pull factors, the spouses of the young farmers usually looked for good quality of life and often did not want to live on a farm, far from urban facilities. Besides, what makes the real succession unattractive is a retirement law because the parents start retirement at age 55/60, when the children are in their thirties and already working in other industries. Succession to non-family members, as an alternative, still seems less typical. So far, the most probable reason for taking over the farm is in the case of emotional attachment, otherwise the demographic and economic conditions are rather discouraging.

Economic viability struggle (economic challenge, classified as a long-term trend, see Annex 13.1). Most of the surveyed farmers have run their farms for more than twenty years and all of them experienced a significant decline in the profitability of their production. Despite the undertaken investments (CAP support), such as increasing the scale, changes in the production structure, they are still not able to maintain profitability at the previous level. This is in line with research by Czyżewski (2017), showing the presence of a treadmill in European agriculture. The observed indicator is a much faster increase in production costs (fuel, pesticides, fertilizers, labour costs) than in the revenues of farmers. Average prices associated with the current means of production increased in the last fifteen years by at least 100 per cent, while sales prices, apart from a few years and during this period, remained unchanged. A very important factor determining profitability was the decrease in supply, mainly due to the Russian embargo, the difficult situation in Ukraine and the inflow of some products from China. Farmers also pointed out that even if the embargo with Russia eventually ends, it would be difficult to enter these markets, because in both countries there was a significant development of horticultural production. However, from the point of view of the entire FS and the enabling environment, the Russian embargo was an example of a successful resilient response. The actors who have helped facilitate adapting to the situation were the exporters (wholesalers, retailers) who found a way to export the products to old markets and establish relationships with new markets. Intermediaries (producer groups) invested in cold-storage facilities. Government initiated the intervention purchases of perishable horticulture products and compensation payments.

Extreme weather events (environmental challenge, classified as a noise, see Annex 13.1): Occurrence of extreme weather events (e.g. late frosts in May, hailstorms, droughts, violent rainfalls) are especially harmful in the case of horticulture. These events have a much greater impact on the volume of horticultural production than on traditional agricultural production (especially on the harvest of apples). For example, the same unfavourable weather conditions in the years 2016/2017 impacted the harvest of apples by about 32 per cent (a decline from 3,604.3 million tons to 2,444.4 million tons), while in the case of cereals the decline was about 16 per cent (from 31,925.0 million tons to 26,779.8 million tons). The countermeasures are very costly and sometimes difficult (e.g. investment in irrigation systems is a good example since difficulty stems from the fragmentation of farms into many non-neighbouring agricultural plots. Other related environmental problems are reduction of the pollinator population (due to the reduction of biodiversity), use of pesticides (not always in accordance with the Code of Good Agricultural Practice), increase in the occurrence of pests (with the simultaneous lack of effective pesticides to control them) and increasing deficit of organic matter (a decline in manure availability over the past twenty years due to a significant decrease in the number of livestock animals such as cattle, pigs, horses and sheep).

Shortage of workforce (economic challenge, classified as a noise, see Annex 13.1): The lack of seasonal workers is a gradually growing problem that affects Polish agriculture. The processes of industrialization in the twentieth century followed by post-industrial changes have decreased the rural population employed in agricultural activities, as well as causing major migration either to urban areas or abroad (about 2 million people emigrated abroad). Remuneration in agriculture is relatively low compared to other sectors of the Polish economy, which is decreasing the attractiveness of agricultural employment, especially on a seasonal basis.

Insufficient and overregulated policies (institutional challenge, classified as a cycle, see Annex 13.1): The ad hoc public intervention in this market is perceived by farmers as ineffective (mainly in the fruit market), as it only mitigates the occurrence of price fluctuations to a small extent. Processors benefited the most from CAP due to funding for investments, and to a small extent, producers. There is also an ineffective policy of agricultural production insurance. Despite the subsidies, the insurance premiums are very high, farmers have many complains about the liquidation of damages, and having had bad experiences, many of them no longer insure their production. There is also a common view that the system of direct payments inhibits structural changes at the agricultural land market. The respondents give examples of land owners who take subsidies and lease the land. The other difficulty is more and more restrictive pro-environmental and food safety policies which require certification and cumbersome documentation.

Based on the data collected by the SURE-Farm project (from in-depth interviews, mini-cases, surveys, learning interviews) and the applied SURE-Farm methodology, this chapter presents the lessons learnt on current and future resilience capacities of this FS – robustness, adaptability and transformability – as well as the possible future strategies for current and alternative FSs.

13.2 From Past to Current Resilience

13.2.1 Four Adaptive Cycles

The described challenges faced by the FS are difficult to address because they are embedded within a long-term dynamic setting depicted by four adaptive cycles, consisting of four stages: growth, conservation, collapse and reorganization. Those cycles identified in SURE-Farm adaptive cycles, explained in detail in Chapter 1, are: (1) "risk management" – related to environmental challenges; (2) "governance" related to policy instruments, work regulations, succession law, environmental deficiencies; (3) "farm demographics" with succession and workforce availability; (4) "agricultural production" with economic viability, changes in consumer tastes and policy instruments – see the middle part of Annex 13.1.

Concerning the risk management adaptive cycle, it is in the advanced growth phase but still far from the point of conservation as depicted by a star in Annex 13.1. The system has developed new management strategies but farmers are still hesitant about adapting them. For example, insurance for extreme weather events is still not common among farmers although the offer of private and public insurance tools increases. Some strategies are being implemented to mitigate the negative consequences of droughts and to promote good water management. However, many risk management practices are still not developed, e.g. towards environmental risks, price change risks and alike.

Concerning the governance adaptive cycle, it seems to be at the reorganization phase, as depicted by a star in Annex 13.1. The ResAT analysis (describe in Chapter 4) reveals that the policies seem to have more ambitious goals than the instruments available to support adaptability and transformability. The advancement in reorganization of the policy is visible but the learning and demographic interviews reveal that the farmers perceive the changes as not enough and some-times too constraining for their activities. They complained about overregulation and bureaucracy as well as the lack of long-term vision. However, from the policy-makers point of view it seems logical to introduce high demands (to avoid abuse of the funds) and if they realize they are too tight (the uptake from beneficiaries is low) then they release the conditions. That is why this governance adaptive cycle is classed as under reorganization as a result of learning processes from both sides – policy-makers and beneficiaries.

The farm demographic cycle has just passed the conservation phase and moves towards the collapse phase. This means that, from a statis-tical point of view, the demographic situation in this system is relatively good (in the Polish agriculture sector there is the highest percentage of young farmers in the EU), but that is likely to change quickly over the next few years. The signals from the learning and demographic inter-views are very clear, that there is already a problem with farm succes-sors, due to high emigration of young people abroad or moving into other occupations and at the same time low availability of foreign qualified workers for the system in Poland. The important factor influ-encing deteriorating demographics in rural areas is that the system fails to provide one of its main functions, i.e. attractiveness of rural areas in term of residence. The living conditions and a hard and risky occupation discourages young people and new entrants into the FS.

Concerning the agricultural production cycle, it is at a fast growth phase and it still has potential for further development if it manages to improve its overall resilience. The statistics show development of the horticulture sector and especially apple producers are very competitive and expanding further at the EU markets. However, it is important to mention that apart from small family farms (our case study system) there are also large corporate farms, which contribute to the overall success for that sector.

All in all, the stakeholders in our study assessed that taking the above into account, the resilience capacities of the current FS in the case study area is low to moderate. That is due to its relatively high robustness, i.e. the ability to maintain the basic functions of the system without major changes despite the presence of external disturbances (Urruty et al. 2016). At the same time the FS has a medium capacity of adaptability, i.e. the ability of the system to adapt internal elements and processes in response to changing external circumstances and thus continue to develop along the previous trajectory while maintaining all vital functions (Folke et al. 2010). The current FS shows very low capacity to transform, i.e. the ability to develop or incorporate new elements and processes to an extent that alters operational logic to maintain important functions when structural changes make the existing system unsustainable or dysfunctional (Walker et al. 2004). Since the current FS does not properly address two essential functions, i.e. ensuring economic viability and maintaining natural resources in good condition (see Annex 13.1), the strategies for alternative future FSs were explored in the study, as presented next.

13.3 Resilience Strategies for the Future

13.3.1 Alternative Farming Systems

The stakeholders proposed three alternative FSs in the case study area which would more effectively fulfil the private and public functions. Those FSs are: (1) higher specialization in fruit and vegetables of the area (horticulture production FS); (2) more focus on soft fruit production (shelter farming FS – farming under cover, e.g., greenhouses); and (3) specialization in organic products (local organic production FS). The alternative systems, firstly, improve delivery of private good functions by: (a) creating new opportunities for higher purchase prices of agricultural products, (b) providing sources of higher income and (c) enabling alternatives for high labour costs. Secondly, those systems also support public good functions, such as: natural resources, biodiversity and habitat, as well as increasing the attractiveness of the areas. In order to understand the mechanisms determining the current and future resilience, the so-called causal loop diagram (CLD – see Herrera 2017) was depicted (see Figure 13.3) showing the relationship between challenges (C), main resilience indicators (I), resilience attributes (A) and strategies relevant for alternative FSs, i.e. better serving the private and public functions in the areas (depicted by letter S). The loop shows five distinctive parts depicting five interrelating mechanisms determining resilience in a dynamic setting.

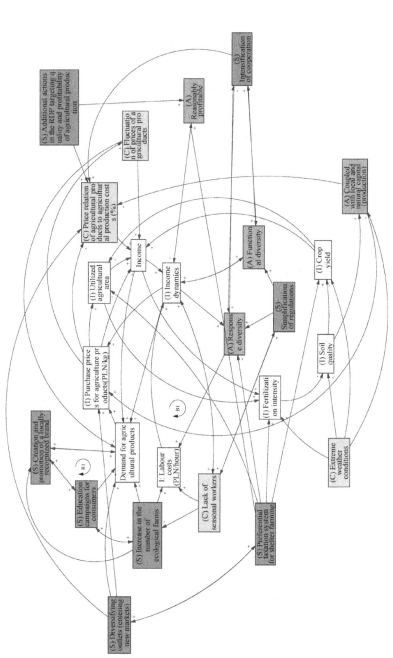

Figure 13.3 Causal loop diagram depicting the relations between indicators, challenges, resilience attributes and possible strategies in the horticulture FS in Poland. Where C – relates to challenges to resilience, I – resilience indicators, A – resilience attributes, S – strategies.

Source: Based on Kim and Andersen (2012) applied to CS report on Poland from Krupin et al. (2019)

Part 1 of the causal loop shows that lack of seasonal workers influences the labour costs thus impacting the income dynamics. Income dynamics has influence upon the uptake of additional employment by potential seasonal workers. The availability of the labour force can be one of the factors influencing the decision-making by farmers to convert to organic farming (possible alternative FS in the region), thus leading to increase in the number of ecological farms. Increasing the number of organic farms could have an impact on the increase in labour costs, as it generates additional demand for labour. It also has an impact on the demand for agricultural products, as well as consumer awareness (shifts in their behaviour – it is a two-way loop as by shifts in consumer behaviour it is also possible to increase the number of ecological farms). Increasing the number of ecological farms could intensify creation of new locally recognized brands. Consumer awareness influences the demand for agricultural products, just as emergence of a new brand on the market could shift the structure of demand. Changes in demand influence the shifts in prices for agricultural products, which in turn influence the farm income and income dynamics in the country. The level of farm income influences its financial abilities concerning the costs of inputs, including fertilization intensity. The latter feeds soil fertility (quality) and influences the quality and volume of outputs (crop yields). Achieved crop yields influence the farm income, but also the utilisation of agricultural land. Land use structure determines farming practices, e.g. crop rotation techniques affect the level of fertilization, that in turn influences the soil quality, the fertilization intensity thus affecting the local and natural capital. Local and natural capital (production) affects the price relationship between agricultural products and agricultural production costs. Demand for agricultural products influences the emergence of new locally recognized brands, while education campaigns for consumers further strengthens these relations (this is represented by reinforcing feedback loop; R1 in Figure 13.3).

Part 2 of the causal loop shows that actions in the RDP influence the price relation of agricultural products to agricultural production costs, as well as on the attribute 'reasonable profitability', which in turn affects the level of farm income and income dynamics in the country. Diversification of markets (outlets) affects the demand for agricultural products, simultaneously influencing the prices for agricultural products, thus also affecting the price relation of agricultural products to agricultural production costs. Diversification of markets (outlets) also influences the eventual focus on greenhouse and other types of farming under cover ('shelter farming'), which is supported by preferential taxation. This is a two-way relation.

Part 3 of the causal loop explains that extreme weather events are a variable impacting fertilization intensity (as it can lead to severe losses of organic matter in the soil and washing-out of nutrients in the soil), the severe weather conditions also affect the yields (e.g. hail or frosts can cause loss of crops, droughts decrease yields, while excessive rainfall leads to increased plant disease). The frequency of extreme weather conditions in the region impacts its local and natural capital. The natural capital (in other words local conditions) is most likely to influence the level of prices in local trade (e.g. in areas with frequent hail, producers quit cultivating soft fruit and the local price for these products would be most likely higher compared to other regions).

Part 4 of the causal loop indicates how simplification of regulations influences response diversity and functional diversity. It is important to emphasize that there is a two-way relationship between the procedures' simplification and lack of seasonal workers. Such simplification can impact labour supply, at the same time current availability of the labour force can lead to pressure upon policy-makers to simplify procedures regarding employment and labour markets (e.g. employee registration or unemployment support). Of course, indirectly such simplification could further lead to costs of employment. Overall, primarily the income dynamics in the economy influences the lack of seasonal workers, which in turn affects the availability of the labour force (being a balancing feedback loop; B1 in Figure 13.3).

Part 5 of the causal loop reveals the weakness of Polish farms, as it was mentioned by the stakeholders, relating to cooperation. Development of both horizontal and vertical cooperation influences functional diversity and response diversity – there will also be reciprocal relations; while searching for various solutions, the entities of the agricultural system would be interested in either intensifying or minimizing cooperation depending on what would be their mutual interests. Intensification of cooperation also impacts the price relation of agricultural products to agricultural production costs, as united they can achieve additional benefits from the scale of production and negotiate the wholesale prices for production inputs.

13.3.2 Future Strategies for Current and Alternative FSs

Alternative FSs are perceived as beneficial for rural areas in general and farmers in particular, as they potentially lead to improvement in incomes and are more efficient and environmentally safe farming approaches. Maintaining adequate profit margins and increasing cooperation (both horizontal and vertical) were often mentioned as crucial boundary conditions, which would have a positive effect upon the FS's development. According to stakeholders, the alternative system defined as 'horticulture production' requires implementation of the following strategies: entering new foreign markets, simplification of regulations (e.g. quicker processing of applications submitted in the framework of CAP financing programmes) and education campaigns for consumers (e.g. supporting consumption of domestic products, increasing the share of fruits and vegetables in the daily diet).

The alternative system 'shelter farming' defines several strategies important for implementation in order to achieve this alternative state: additional dedicated action in the Rural Development Programme framework targeting quality and profitability of agricultural production, preferential taxation system for shelter farming and creation and promotion of a locally recognized brand 'Sheltered strawberry'. The 'local organic production' was defined to require the following strategies: (1) increase the number of farms adopting ecological approaches and gradually (yet steadily) switching to organic farming, increase the use of mechanization in organic farming, target and support organic farming by the state policies and funds; (2) intensification of vertical cooperation ('farmers–wholesalers' relationship); (3) diversifying outlets: direct sales to consumers supported by promotion and educational campaigns (see Table 13.1).

In most cases the resilience attributes would benefit from the introduction and development of alternative systems. 'Coupled with local and natural capital (production)' was rather beneficial for all systems, with the highest positive return relationship in the case of 'local organic production'. 'Response diversity' is the most unpredictable, and dependent on the economic situation and investment conditions in the case of 'shelter farming', while the 'reasonably profitable' is hard to predict for 'local organic production' due to numerous possibilities in terms of prices and consumer behaviour.

According to the participants of our study, the current situation is close to the tipping point, especially in the case of profitability (derived

Table 13.1. *Current and future strategies for different FSs in the case study area*

Strategy	Domain	Current system	Future systems		
			Horticulture production	Shelter farming	Local organic production
Simplification of regulations	Institutional		**V**		
Awareness-raising campaigns for consumers	Economic/social		v		
Additional actions in the RDP targeting quality and profitability of agricultural production	Institutional			v	
Preferential taxation system for shelter farming	Institutional/economic			v	
Creation and promotion of a locally recognized brand	Institutional/economic			v	
Increase in the number of ecological farms	Social				v
Intensification of vertical cooperation	Social/economic	V	v		v
Diversifying outlets (entering new markets)	Economic				v
State support	Institutional	V			
Horizontal cooperation	Social/economic	V	v	v	v
Marketing	Economic	V	v	v	v
Insurance	Economic	V			
Enduring	Economic	v			
Diversification	Economic	v			

Note: "V" implies that a boundary condition is relevant for both current and future systems, while "v" indicates that only for a future system; Bold font indicates that these strategies were mentioned during the workshop for a specific system. Normal font indicates that, based on the discussions during the workshop, it seems likely that strategies will be applied in certain systems.

Source: Based on Krupin et al. (2019)

228

from fluctuating prices – confirmed, among others, by Świetlik 2019), weather conditions (extreme events as hail, droughts, frosts – analysed by Hamulczuk et al. 2016) and bureaucracy and administration (number and frequency of controls, complexity application for CAP payments – confirmed by studies of Drygas et al. 2019). Many of them express the feeling that if the situation with some of these issues worsens, they wouldn't be able to continue their business as usual. But they have quite clear understanding of their resilience capacities, mostly regarding adaptation.

13.4 Conclusion: Lessons Learnt

The lessons learnt from the past are summarized in Annex 13.1 and they are relevant for the future in the following ways.

First, the overall current resilience is between low and moderate, taking into account the stakeholder's assessment of resilience capacities and attributes as well as the policy assessment based on the ResAT wheel (Buitenhuis et al. 2020). Future resilience depends on the ability of the FS to strengthen its weak resilience attributes, such as reasonable profitability and response diversity. For both attributes the future resilience-enabling actors would be advisors (with the strategy of enhancing the transfer of knowledge) and government (facilitating and providing funding with proper incentives behind it).

Second, the current FS has a relatively high capacity for buffer resources (robustness) and medium for adaptability and very low for transformability. It is expected in the future that the buffer resources will deplete, especially in terms of human resources and financial ones due to demographic and economic challenges which are in the form of long-term negative trends. So adaptability is a must for future resilience, while transformability is a complementing option.

Third, the adaptation of the current FS leads to alternative future FSs (more focused on horticulture than now, oriented more towards shelter production and specializing in ecological production and sale). In order to achieve that, the most desirable adaptability strategies would be: increasing vertical and horizontal cooperation, enhancing knowledge (for instance, carrying out educational campaigns to improve consumers' dietary habits to include more fruit and vegetable consumption) and expanding horticulture and ecological sales into new foreign markets.

Fourth, in relation to policy, the current configuration mostly fosters robustness and neglects transformability, while adaptability is in the middle – supported by funds for investments. The resilience-oriented policy would need to overcome the main challenges identified, such as overregulation and bureaucracy, insufficient aid instruments (e.g. for insurance, income stability, knowledge transfer) and lack of long-term vision for resilience support.

All in all, achieving future resilience requires more emphasis on speeding up adaptability, which will trigger the evolution of the current system into more resilient alternative systems in the future. That means, in particular, enhancing the resilience attributes (indicated in red in Annex 13.1) by applying the resilience strategies towards (see the bottom part of Annex 13.1) the following:

(a) increasing policy diversity towards instruments supporting adaptability rather than buffer resources – i.e. with more flexible policies, oriented towards risk management tools, learning capacities, increased involvement of stakeholders in the policy-making, increasing effectiveness of agricultural insurance – see Chapters 2 and 4 for more details;

(b) adapting farmers to the shortage of labour – by replacing human labour with new machines; switching to less labour-intensive vegetable farming, e.g. beans and pumpkin instead of cauliflowers and broccoli;

(c) adapting the farms to the demographic situation – by stimulating succession via easier access to land, improving quality of life in rural areas, easing earlier retirement in agriculture, increasing work mobility for farmers' spouses;

(d) adapting farmers to the economic situation – by providing economic training for farmers, introduction of direct information exchange platforms on consumers' preferences, diversification of production, publishing a black list of unethical suppliers, teaching new technologies;

(e) increase cooperation – currently, the value share of the horticultural production sold by producer organizations in the total value of fruit and vegetables production and in the value of export of these products does not exceed 20 per cent in Poland (5 per cent for vegetables), compared to more than 50 per cent on average in the EU and above 80 per cent in Belgium and the Netherlands. That can happen by working on enhancing the trust and application of user-friendly legal solutions for cooperation.

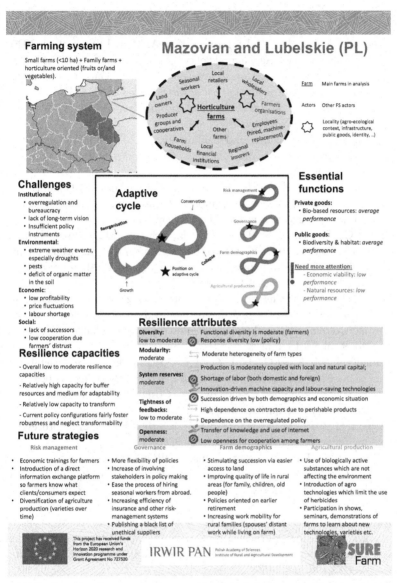

Annex 13.1 Factsheet synthesizing resilience of the current FS in Mazovian and Lubelskie (Poland).

References

Buitenhuis, Y., Candel, J. J. L., Termeer, K. J. A. M. and Feindt, P. H. 2020. Does the Common Agricultural Policy enhance farming systems' resilience? Applying the Resilience Assessment Tool (ResAT) to a farming system case study in the Netherlands. *Journal of Rural Studies* 80, 314–327.

Czyżewski, B. 2017. *Kierat rynkowy w Europejskim Rolnictwie*. Warsaw: Wydawnictwo Naukowe PWN S.A.

Drygas, M., Nurzyńska, I. and Bańkowska, K. 2019. *Charakterystyka i uwarunkowania rozwoju rolnictwa ekologicznego w Polsce*. Warsaw: WN Scholar.

EC. 2020. *Statistical Factsheet, Poland*. Brussels: European Commission. https://ec.europa.eu/info/sites/info/files/food-farming-fisheries/farming/documents/agri-statistical-factsheet-eu_en.pdf

Folke, C., Carpenter, S. R., Walker, B., Scheffer, M., Chapin, T. and Rockström, J. 2010. Resilience thinking: Integrating resilience, adaptability and transformability. *Ecology and Society* 15(4), 20. https://doi.org/10.5751/ES-03610-150420

GUS. 2020. Użytkowanie gruntów i powierzchnia zasiewów w 2019 roku. GUS Warszawa. https://stat.gov.pl/obszary-tematyczne/rolnictwo-lesnictwo/rolnictwo/uzytkowanie-gruntow-i-powierzchnia-zasiewow-w-2019-roku,8,15.html

Hamulczuk, M., Kufel-Gajda, J., Stańko, S., Szafrański, G. and Świetlik, K. 2016. *Ceny żywności w Polsce i ich determinanty*. Warsaw: IERiGŻ, Instytut Ekonomiki Rolnictwa i Gospodarki Żywnościowej – Państwowy Instytut Badawczy.

Herrera, H. 2017. Resilience for whom? The problem structuring process of the resilience analysis. *Sustainability* 9(7), 1196.

IERiGŻ. 2020. Fruit and vegetable market (Rynek owoców i warzyw), Nr 57 / 2020. Warsaw: IERiGŻ PIB. www.ierigz.waw.pl/publikacje/analizy-rynkowe/rynek-owocow-i-warzyw/24272,5,3,0,nr-57-2020-rynek-owocow-i-warzyw.html

Kim, H. and Andersen, D. F. 2012. Building confidence in causal maps generated from purposive text data: Mapping transcripts of the Federal Reserve. *System Dynamics Review* 28(4), 311–328. https://doi.org/10.1002/sdr.1480

Kraciński, P. J. 2017. The competitiveness of polish apples on international markets. *International Journal of Food and Beverage Manufacturing and Business Models* 2(1), 31–43. https://doi.org/10.4018/ijfbmbm.2017010103

Krupin, V., Zawalińska, K., Bańkowska, K. and Gradziuk, P. 2019. FoPIA-SURE-Farm case-study report Poland. SURE-Farm project deliverable

D5.3 "Current resilience – Case study report Poland", H2020 SURE-Farm Project No. 727520 (Internal report).

Kudová, D. and Chládková, H. 2008. Barriers to the entry into the fruit producing industry in the Czech Republic. *Agricultural Economics 9*, 413–418. https://doi.org/10.17221/2700-AGRICECON.

Meuwissen, M. P. M., Feindt, P. H., Spiegel, A., et al. 2019. A framework to assess the resilience of farming systems. *Agricultural Systems 176*, 102656. https://doi.org/10.1016/J.AGSY.2019.102656

Milczarek, D. 2002. *Privatization as a Process of Institutional Change. The Case of State Farms in Poland*. Aachen: Shaker Verlag.

MRiRW. 2020. Polska wieś i rolnictwo 2020 [Polish Village and Agriculture 2020]. Report by Grupa BST and EU-Consult, Warsaw. www.gov.pl/attachment/1b8b386b-f998-4314-aaa1-fbde8ed3c105

Német, S. and Masár, I. 2014. Fruit production and trade comparison in Hungary and Slovakia. *Ekonomika Poľnohospodárstva* 14(4), 4–15.

Świetlik, K. 2019. Zmienność światowych cen żywności w latach 2000–2018 [Changeability of World Food Prices during 2000–2018]. *Problemy Rolnictwa Światowego* 19(XXXIV), 196–209. https://doi.org/10.22630/PRS.2019.19.2.35

Urruty, N., Tailliez-Lefebvre, D. and Huyghe, C. 2016. Stability, robustness, vulnerability and resilience of agricultural systems. A review. *Agronomy for Sustainable Development* 36, 15. https://doi.org/10.1007/s13593-015-0347-5

Walker, B., Holling, C. S., Carpenter, S. R. and Kinzig, A. 2004. Resilience, adaptability and transformability in social-ecological systems. *Ecology and Society 9*. https://doi.org/10.5751/ES-00650-090205

Wójcik, M. and Traczyk, A. 2020. The development of orchard fruit-growing in Poland in the period of impact of the Common Agricultural Policy. Production-related and spatial issues. *Bulletin of Geography. Socio-Economic Series 49*. https://content.sciendo.com/view/journals/bog/49/49/article-p19.xml

14 | Towards a Better Understanding of Small Farming System Resilience in Romania

CAMELIA GAVRILESCU
AND MONICA-MIHAELA TUDOR

14.1 Introduction

14.1.1 Description of the Region

In the Nord-Est region more than half of the population (58.4 per cent) lives in rural areas. The regional landscape is highly diversified, including mountains, hills and plains, and climate conditions vary along altitude and landscape, from mountain to temperate-continental climate. The low hills and plains are favourable for a very diversified range of agricultural activities, being also exposed to extreme weather events, mostly frequent droughts. The agricultural area of the region totals 2.12 million ha and includes 65 per cent arable land, 32.6 per cent grassland, 1.5 per cent vineyards and 0.9 per cent orchards. The main crops are maize, wheat, sunflower and vegetables; important quantities of fruits and wine are also produced in the region. Livestock is composed mainly of cattle and sheep, pigs and poultry. In the last two decades, bee farming developed as well. Forests also cover 1.23 million ha. Agriculture, forestry and fishery produce 7.4 per cent of the GVA of the region. The case study concerns small, mixed, family farms (under 20 ha, with field crops and livestock), which represent 99 per cent of the total number of farms in the region. These operate 54 per cent of the utilized agricultural area (UAA) and own 89 per cent of livestock units in the region. Agritourism also developed in the region, based on local traditions, rich historical and cultural heritage and wonderful landscapes (Figure 14.1).

14.1.2 Historical Context and Background of the Farming System

In the period of the centrally planned economy (1949–1989), there were three main ownership forms of agricultural land in Romania:

Figure 14.1 Landscape in the Nord-Est region in Romania.
Photo by Codrin Anton.

state ownership (state-owned farms) which operated 30 per cent of the agricultural area (AA), collective ownership (collective farms) (61 per cent of AA) and private households (9 per cent of AA, located in high hills and mountain areas). The collective farms were established between 1949 and 1962 by forcing farmers to join their land and assets.

In the 1950s and 1960s, this structure of Romanian agriculture allowed its modernization compared to the pre-war development level. The large size of the agricultural units, the funding and investments coordinated through the centralized plans showed the advantages of economies of scale (new technologies, irrigations, use of tractors, agricultural machinery, fertilizers and pesticides). Since the 1970s, the centrally planned economic model with its main characteristics (almost complete elimination of private property, lack of decisional and financial autonomy of agricultural units, lack of demand and supply mechanisms as signals for production and resource allocation), began to show its limits. Centralized price fixing of agricultural commodities at low levels, which did not cover costs, aimed at transferring economic value from agriculture to industry, and pushed the agricultural sector into chronic inefficiency. Exports of agricultural products for the payment of external debt led to food shortages in urban areas. The overall deterioration of the economic and social environment eventually led to the major political and economic changes that started in December 1989, which represent an essential milestone in the Romanian history.

After the collapse of Communism in 1989, deep transformations occurred in the agricultural sector in terms of land ownership and farming systems. The former collective farms were dismantled, and land and assets were restituted to former owners or their heirs, resulting in a huge number of small farms, i.e. in the Nord-Est region there were 880,000 farms with an average size of 2.39 ha UAA (General Agricultural Census 2002). The former state farms were dismantled a decade later (year 2000), resulting in the emergence of large farms (over 100 ha) and agricultural companies. In the last fifteen years, land concentration occurred mostly in the small and medium-sized group, resulting in the diminution of the total farm number by 18 per cent, while the average area per farm increased to 2.65 ha (Farm Structure Survey 2016).

The food industry of the centrally planned economy period was concentrated in very large processing units that collected agricultural raw products from the large agricultural units. In the 1990s, all food industry enterprises were privatized, divided or went bankrupt and disappeared. Small private units emerged, but the former supply chains (adequate for large enterprises) disappeared as well.

The Romanian farming system is facing important challenges – economic, environmental, social and institutional. The rural population is heavily dependent on agriculture in economic terms (93 per cent of farms use more than half of the production for on-farm consumption). At the same time, when investment is needed for business development, small farms rely on private (family) funds and income from alternative off-farm jobs rather than on credit.

The rural population is characterized by an accelerated aging process, by low levels of education and by redundant skills in a labour market where the pace of adoption of technological innovation is very fast (Tudor 2017, p. 112). Statistically, there is an abundance of labour force in rural areas and agriculture in particular (agriculture takes 19.1 per cent of total employment), but in reality this results in under-employment of the rural population, hence a low level of income. Together with the lack of job opportunities in non-farming activities in rural areas, it became the main driver for a significant migration of people included in the active working age groups to either urban areas or abroad. As a consequence, in fact there is a chronic shortage of seasonal workers on farms.

There is a debate among different authors about the importance of subsistence and semi-subsistence farms in rural Romania. Some authors (Bohateret et al. 2018) consider that they have a social function as the main priority and an economic function as the subsidiary priority. For the last decades, the small farms acted as a social safety net and ensured food self-sufficiency for farmer families and their urban relatives. There are also other roles that small farms appear to play in the wider rural economy, e.g. as providers of environmental public goods, supplying specialty foods and ensuring the continuation of local and cultural traditions (Hubbard et al. 2014). Other authors (Steriu and Otiman 2013) argue that small farms are a loss of economic potential for agriculture, representing an inefficient form of land resource allocation and contributing to land fragmentation and low productivity.

In terms of environmental characteristics, water availability is a problem: frequent droughts affect the production and income levels, especially on the small and medium-sized farms located in areas with no irrigation systems. Other extreme weather events (flooding, hail, late spring frost) mostly affect the small- and medium-sized farms due to limited access to insurance instruments, prohibitive prices or unfavourable contract terms. Moreover, the intensive farming on medium- and large-sized commercial farms create water pollution problems due to the widespread use of fertilizers and pesticides.

Small farms have a limited access to financial resources from CAP for direct payments and rural development programmes, therefore they are less vulnerable to uncertainties related to the future of CAP. On the institutional side, in terms of the embedding in the value chain, the main problem is the lack of cooperation among small farmers, which results in lack of sales organization and poor development of local chains. It also results in poor bargaining power with more concentrated upstream input providers and downstream actors in the value chain (processors and retailers).

14.2 Current State of Resilience

14.2.1 Main Functions of the System and Their Performance

In the FoPIA-1 SURE-Farm Workshop, the participants appreciated that the private functions of the farming system in the Nord-Est region are more important than the public ones. In their opinion, food production is the main target of the whole agricultural system, and the focus should be on it, since their general perception is that at present Romania has not yet achieved its full production capacity and ability to ensure the population's food security. The functions considered as most important were the 'delivery of healthy and affordable food products' and 'ensuring economic viability' (see Annex 14.1). Crop, vegetable and animal production – indicators of the 'food production' function – was perceived to perform well, as it is seen as essential in the farming system. With regard to the 'economic viability' function, the highest score was for the 'subsidies' indicator, because subsidies were evaluated as very important for bringing incomes for small farms at a reasonable level. Availability of financial resources from CAP for direct payments is essential for small and medium-sized farms, since it may cover up to 30 per cent of production costs. 'Sales of crop and vegetable products' (indicator for 'bio-based resources for the processing sector' function) was ranked as the second important (Gavrilescu et al. 2019).

On the other hand, 'ensuring animal welfare' was seen as the key function in the delivery of public goods, since the activity in the farming system is mixed (crops and livestock). The diversification of farm activities and income sources (through local/on-farm processing, selling farm products on local markets, agri-tourism, etc.) also contributes to the sustainable development of the rural area in the region.

14.2.2 Past and Present Challenges

An important economic challenge identified for the farming system in the case study region is the *poor integration of small farms in domestic agri-food chains* (long-term pressure) (see Annex 14.1). Only part of the farm production is sold; the remaining production is consumed on-farm. There is reluctance in association (due to the bad memories of the 1950s and early 1960s when farmers were forced to join collective farms and were depleted of their land and assets). The lack of associative forms (or cooperatives) prevents the concentration of supply, hence wholesalers and retailers are not interested in buying products from small farmers, due to high transaction costs. Despite important efforts from public authorities that provided an enabling legislation and from advisory bodies, which are carrying out intense information campaigns, the number of associations/cooperatives is still low. Nevertheless, small producer associations started to emerge where small farmers found common interests, such as being eligible for grassland subsidies or being part of a group of farmers selling to supermarkets. There are several alternative selling channels for the small farmers: local and urban peasant (wet) markets, local selling networks and sales to direct customers (using 'customer lists'). Wet markets are very popular in urban areas, as they are perceived by consumers as supplying more diversified, cleaner, fresher and better-quality vegetables and fruit, at lower prices, as opposed to longer preserved and more processed products in the super- and hypermarkets. Prices are strongly influenced by competition from other small farmers. The farmers are influenced by the volatility of the demand and by the changes in the consumers' requirements concerning the origin of products: there is an increasing demand for local products (as opposed to imported products).

Another important challenge is the *lack of integration in EU markets and competition of imported products*. Due to the lack of supply concentration, processors and exporters are not willing to buy products from small farms. The large milk- and meat-processing units prefer to use imported agricultural raw products (milk from Hungary, meat from Poland, etc.), which are cheaper than the local products, because imported commodities come from specialized and more efficient farms in other member states. Supermarkets and hypermarkets prefer to import fruit and vegetables in large batches from other member states or from Turkey rather than buying them from local producers, which are not organized in associations and thus not able to concentrate supply so as to meet the retailers' requirements. There is an important debate regarding the low-quality 'counterfeit products' imported from other EU countries which also negatively influence local prices. A discussed example was honey; on the domestic market, imported low-quality 'counterfeit products' are much cheaper than the domestically produced products of good quality. Local producers therefore do not get the right prices. As a result, in this particular case, much of the production is exported.

Changing EU and national laws and regulations was perceived as a huge challenge – even as an obstacle. National regulations are changing too often and farmers can barely keep up with the changes. This creates problems in filling in the applications and in receiving the subsidies, which are amplified due to a perceived excessive bureaucracy imposed by public authorities. The participants in both FoPIA-1 and FoPIA-2 workshops expressed a major discontent with the fact that the Romanian authorities do not protect their own farmers. The example concerned eco-conditionality rules: the CAP proposed eleven different criteria to choose from; Hungary chose only four of them, Poland chose quite a few, while the Romanian authorities chose to fulfil all of them, thus disadvantaging its own farmers.

Another challenge discussed in FoPIA workshops is *climate change, pests and diseases*. Drought frequency increased in the last two decades as a result of climate change; the hill and plain areas in the case study region are more exposed to severe droughts. At the same time, excessive rainfall in some years and early frost resulted in an increased frequency of years when farmers incurred production losses. Besides lower yields, drought significantly diminishes feed availability for livestock, pushing up the costs that are not covered by the price of meat and milk. The lack of primary irrigation infrastructure prevents the development of the secondary irrigation networks, to which even small farmers might connect without major investments. Furthermore, input costs increased in the last decade; the higher prices of pesticides resulted in a lower use, thus exposing the crops to increased phytosanitary risks. In addition, the African Swine Fever severely affected small farms growing pigs, although they received a compensation for the pigs killed in order to prevent the spread of the disease. There are no insurance instruments tailored to the needs of small farms. Overall, with losses incurred in almost half of the years, the small, mixed farming system is highly vulnerable to extreme weather events as well as to pests and diseases.

14.2.3 Past and Present Risk Management Strategies

At the time of its accession to the EU (1 January 2007), the Romanian farming system was significantly less developed compared to the old member states and even compared to some of the new member states. Romanian small farmers are increasingly aware that they need to develop and increase their presence on the markets. There are two major directions to achieve that: increasing the size of their farms (by purchasing and/or leasing land and investing in livestock) and implementing technological and managerial improvements in order to increase productivity, sales and income. The strategy of introducing more technology is also essential for agriculture development in the case study area. Increasing farm size in combination with more technology is assessed to positively contribute to all three resilience capacities – robustness, adaptability and transformability. In the context of the EU Green deal objectives, farm consolidation policies dedicated to small farms represent an opportunity for Romania where the small-farming system is 'greener' than other agricultural systems (being less intensive, there is a general less usage of fertilizers and pesticides).

Although cooperation is not a popular organization form among most farmers (especially those over forty years old), younger farmers and especially those who worked in farming abroad for some time are more open to the idea and benefits of joining various forms of associations or producer groups in order to better cope with the challenge of entering the domestic agri-food chains.

Increasing the sales of high-quality products is considered as an important past and present strategy. However, it may be expected to have a negative effect on robustness and adaptability. It diminishes the current turnover – the price difference between 'regular' and 'high quality' products is not very important. Given the fact that the regular consumers' main driver is low price and not quality of products, high-quality products are still seen as niche products. The demand for (more expensive) high-quality products is currently low due to consumers' modest purchasing power. Hence, the producers of high-quality products have lower income as compared to those who sell regular products. The strategy is assessed to have positive effects on transformability only – e.g. by completely re-orienting the farm activity to niche products. Consequently, for this strategy a trade-off was perceived between robustness and adaptability on the one hand and transformability on the other hand.

14.3 Future State of Resilience

14.3.1 Future Challenges

In a survey performed among 122 small mixed farms in the case study area, the main future challenges identified by the farmers as very likely to occur were: small size of the farm (business), technological shortage of the farm, sale of products (due to lack of markets and low prices), climate change (mainly increased drought frequency), policy changes (in terms of subsidy reduction), lack of access to funding, the need for activity diversification in the farm and the lack of labour (skilled and unskilled workforce).

14.3.2 Future Alternative Systems

The stakeholders participating in the FoPIA-2 workshop selected and discussed four alternative systems as most probable for the next decade in the case study region (Figure 14.2): commercial specialization of mixed family farms (B1,2), cooperation and multifunctionality (R3), organic farming (R2) and alternative crops and livestock (R1) (Gavrilescu et al. 2020).

The relationships between challenges (C), resilience indicators (I), resilience attributes (A) and strategies for achieving future alternative systems are shown in the Casual Loop Diagram (Figure 14.2). The discussions pointed out that in general, the alternative systems can moderately improve the functions and resilience attributes of the farming system, but also showed that, in some cases, the alternative systems can induce strong positive changes. The resilience attributes were generally perceived to be maintained or improved in the alternative systems.

There are many loops in the farming system, but some of them stand out. Access to the European single market, and workers' free movement in particular, has two negative implications for the system of small, mixed farms in the Nord-Est region: increasing the supply of agri-food products at low import prices and the external migration of younger workers looking for better paid work, respectively.

Balancing loop (B1,2): Imports of low-priced agri-food products force a downward alignment of prices on the domestic market, which makes small farms unprofitable. As a result, they diminish their

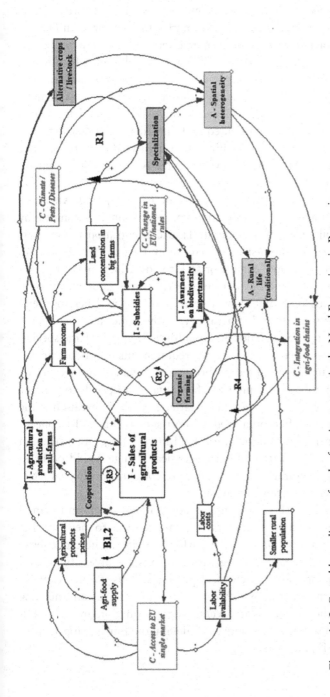

Figure 14.2 Causal loop diagram for the farming system in the Nord-Est region in Romania.

Notes: A '+' sign implies a positive cause–effect relationship and a '–' sign implies a negative cause–effect relationship. 'B' stands for a balancing feedback loop and 'R' stands for a reinforcing feedback loop. 'I' indicates an important system indicator related to the system's functions. 'C' indicates a system challenge. 'A' indicates an indicator related to a resilience attribute. Alternative systems are represented in orange boxes

243

production since the market no longer pays for their efforts. Hence, farm incomes decline, and small-scale agriculture becomes an increasingly less attractive activity in economic terms. A consequence is the migration of rural population to urban areas or abroad, which results in the lack of labour availability and hinders the generational renewal. Another important consequence is that some farmers exit the system by selling or renting their land to larger, more viable farms. Large farms are strongly commercially oriented and, in order to be efficient, they get specialized. Keeping that in mind, there are two different directions for the evolution of the farming system in the Nord-Est region that are expected to co-exist: (i) an intense concentration of land operations in very large farms (operating thousands of hectares) and which, in general, are practicing an industrial-type of farming, dominated by cereals and oilseeds; (ii) a moderate land concentration in commercially specialized medium-sized mixed family farms. These farms can either integrate in supply chains, or seek to cover local market niches by specializing in new crops and livestock, or in organic production. These directions of evolution will decrease the spatial heterogeneity specific to the small farms' system, but, at the same time, favour the integration in agri-food chains because: (i) the supply by large specialized holdings is better able to meet the requirements of product homogeneity and quantity required by processors, retailers and exporters, and, (ii) the supply of medium-sized family farms responds to the new preferences of local consumers. In the latter case, the integration in the agri-food chain is often organized in short supply chains. By concentrating the operation of agricultural land in very large, intensive and very narrowly specialized holdings, a radical change would occur in the specific agricultural landscape of the region, previously characterized by a mosaic of crops and livestock.

Reinforcing loop (R1): The introduction of new crops and animal species at the level of family farms, in response to new market niches, contributes to maintaining the local territorial heterogeneity, as well as to integration in agri-food chains by diversifying and increasing the sales of agricultural products. This would result in increasing farm income, which can allow for innovation and new products. Policies aimed at diversifying production in the small farms' system would contribute to achieving the European priorities of the Green Deal.

Reinforcing loop (R2): The strategy of orienting small farms towards organic farming is positively correlated with the level of awareness of biodiversity importance, since organic farms are more inclined towards nature conservation, thus contributing to the preservation of traditional rural life. Moreover, a higher awareness of biodiversity in organic farms leads to an increase in the level of subsidies (especially transfers for environmentally friendly agricultural practices), with a positive impact on farm income. This reinforces the orientation to organic farming and goes in the same direction as EU greening policy.

Reinforcing loop (R3): Small farms have mechanisms to keep themselves on the market. These farms can reunite in producer associations to be able to provide an aggregate response to the demand for agricultural products by the processing industry and retailing system. Functional producer associations facilitate increase in agricultural production and sales, while increasing the chances of integration of small farms into agri-food chains and improving their bargaining power with upstream and downstream actors in the chains. The integration of small farms in agri-food chains must become a priority of public policies so as to change the perception of agriculture in young people and make this activity more attractive for them.

The shortage of labour in rural areas as a result of migration results in increased farm operating costs and leads small farmers to change their production structure into less labour-intensive activities (e.g. by abandoning vegetable growing or animal husbandry and reorienting to field crops) or to simply exit farming. It results in a decrease in the number of small rural households, who are responsible for preserving the rural traditions and lifestyle.

14.4 Conclusions

As the literature shows, small farms are revealed to be the microeconomic systems with the highest resilience in the Romanian rural area. The lack of strict production specialization allows the small farms to quickly change their production orientation according to the market requirements – i.e. if they decide to sell (most of) the products obtained on the farm (yet, the on-farm consumption remains quite important). This change in the production structure is possible because small farms have the minimum knowledge (based on agricultural practice) as well as the technical means to produce (at a small scale) a wide range of crops, vegetables, fruit and/or animal products (both unprocessed and primarily processed). In contradiction with the general belief that specialization results in better economic performance, the argumentation made here show that the lack of strict production specialization in the particular case of small farms is a means of ensuring economic resilience in a market where agri-food preferences change continuously.

The current small, mixed farming system is very much adaptable and could satisfactorily become commercially specialized or multifunctional if it is included in real and effective association/cooperation forms. They could also adapt by better satisfying the local demand through short supply chains. Another form of adaptation would be to actively look for uncovered market niches.

Currently, there is a certain capacity for transformation: some small farms sell or lease out their land to large farms, highly specialized in cereals and oilseeds production (for processing or export). There is also capacity for a part of the small farms to transform by engaging in alternative crops or livestock. The orientation towards organic production is growing from year to year, mainly on small, mixed farms located in hilly and mountain areas, specialized in livestock raising. In the short and medium term, an important impediment to this is the low demand for organic products on the domestic market due to the high prices that only a small part of the population can afford, and the strong competition on international markets.

The cooperation alternative was perceived by stakeholders in the Nord-Est region as highly desirable, but its implementation, although very necessary for the integration of small farms in the agri-food chains, is hampered by negative historical memories and also by the lack of interpersonal trust between potential members and requires important changes of attitudes (towards increased cooperation), as well as changes (improvement and simplification) in the rules and regulations.

Future policies should be directed to stimulate investment for development and innovation in line with the European priorities and goals of the Green Deal and thus provide an enabling environment for the small, mixed farming system to become increasingly sustainable and resilient.

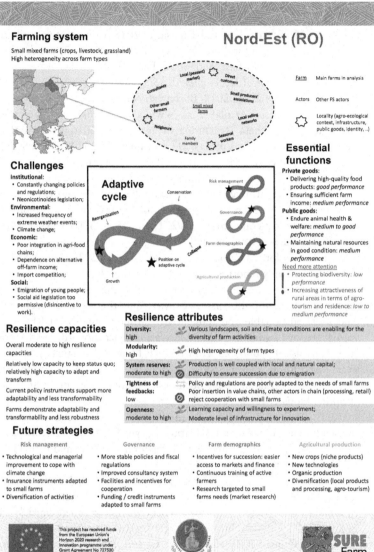

Annex 14.1 Factsheet synthesizing resilience of the current farming system in the Nord-Est region in Romania.

References

Bohatereţ, V. M., Brumă, I. S, and Tanasă, L. 2018. Comparative study on the profile of agricultural holdings without legal status in the development regions North-East and South-East of Romania. *Agricultural Economics and Rural Development*, 15(1), 93–113.

Farm Structure Survey 2016. 2018. Bucharest: National Institute of Statistics Publishing House. Available at www.insse.ro/cms/sites/default/files/field/publicatii/ancheta_structurala_in_agricultura_2016_vol2_1.pdf

Gavrilescu, C., Tudor, M., Voicilaş, D., and Luca, L. 2019. FoPIA-SURE-Farm case-study report Romania. In: Paas, W., Accatino, F., Antonioli, F., et al. D5.2 Participatory impact assessment of sustainability and resilience of EU farming systems. Sustainable and resilient EU farming systems (SURE-Farm) project report. Available at www.surefarmproject .eu/wordpress/wp-content/uploads/2019/06/D5.2-FoPIA-SURE-Farm-Case-study-Report-Romania.pdf

Gavrilescu, C., Tudor, M., Voicilaş, D., and Luca, L. 2020. FoPIA-SURE-Farm 2 case study report Romania. In: Accatino, F., Paas, W., Herrera, H., et al. D5.5 Impacts of future scenarios on the resilience of farming systems across the EU assessed with quantitative and qualitative methods. Sustainable and resilient EU farming systems (SURE-Farm) project report. Available at www.surefarmproject.eu/wordpress/wp-con tent/uploads/2020/06/D5.5_FoPIA-SURE-Farm_2_Romania_.pdf

General Agricultural Census 2002 Volume 5: North-East development region – general data. 2004. Bucharest: National Institute of Statistics Printing House.

Hubbard, C., Mishev, P., Ivanova, N., and Luca, L. 2014. 'Semi-subsistence agriculture in Romania and Bulgaria: a survival strategy?'. *Eurochoices*, 13(1): 46-51. Available at www.onlinelibrary.wiley.com/doi/10.1111/1746-692X.12052

Meuwissen, M. P. M., Feindt, P. H., Spiegel, A., et al. 2019. A framework to assess the resilience of farming systems. *Agricultural Systems*, 176(C). Available at www.sciencedirect.com/science/article/pii/S0308521X19300046. https://doi.org/10.1016/j.agsy.2019.102656

Steriu, V., and Otiman P. I. (eds.). 2013. *Cadrul naţional strategic pentru dezvoltarea durabilă a sectorului agroalimentar şi a spaţiului rural în perioada 2014–2020–2030*. Bucharest: Romanian Academy.

Tudor, M. M. 2017. *Factorii rezilienţei economico-sociale ai spaţiului rural românesc*. Bucharest: Romanian Academy.

15 | Adaptability of the High-Value Egg and Broiler Production in Sweden

GORDANA MANEVSKA-TASEVSKA,
JENS ROMMEL AND HELENA HANSSON

15.1 Introduction

Swedish egg and broiler farms produce high-value products. Production is located in the Southern part of Sweden, which is recognized for its fertile plain districts and agricultural activity which allows farms easy access to fodder and to grow their own fodder. The region covers approximately one third of the country's land surface, but the contribution to gross agricultural output is about 88 per cent, representing approximately 80 per cent of the regular labour employed in agriculture (Eurostat 2018). Family farms are very common, and they own and manage approximately 90 per cent of the total agricultural land (Jordbruksverket 2015).

In Sweden, intensive egg and broiler farming started in the late 1950s with the introduction of cage systems, based on new veterinary drugs and systematic disease control. This model soon become dominant due to its economic efficiency. Over the past decades, animal welfare concerns have been a main driver for changes in the production system. A ban on keeping laying hens in conventional cages was ratified in 1988 and became effective in 1999. Ever since, animal welfare concerns, high food quality standards, and consumer preferences have been a key driver of dynamic technology adoption and adaptation in the sector, causing continuous economic pressure.

Swedish egg and broiler farms produce mainly for the domestic market, especially eggs, breast meat, legs, and wings. The broiler meat market is growing fast and since 2010 has increased by 36 per cent in volume (Jordbruksverket 2020a). There is potential for further development of local markets, as in 2019, 71.6 per cent of consumed poultry meat was domestically produced. Self-sufficiency is high for eggs at 97.5 per cent (Jordbruksverket 2020b). Egg production has increased by approximately 34 per cent since 2010, and import regulation related to salmonella has contributed to this trend. Poultry meat and egg processing are rather concentrated. A few large companies contract several farmers, often for long term. While egg producers can sell eggs in on-farm shops, broiler producers must adhere to slaughter regulations.

In this chapter, we focus on the farming system and synthesize findings from five methods applied within the SURE-Farm project to assess the resilience capacity of the farming system. Following Meuwissen et al. (2019), we define resilience of farming systems as the ability to ensure the provision of the system functions in the face of economic, social, environmental, and institutional shocks and stresses, through the capacities of robustness, adaptability, and transformability (see Chapter 1).

The methods included: (i) the FoPIA participatory method (Paas et al. 2019), see Chapter 1; (ii) risk management focus groups (Soriano et al. 2020), see Chapters 1 and 2; (iii) learning interviews (Urquhart et al. 2019), see Chapters 1 and 2; (iv) farm demographic interviews (Coopmans et al. 2019), see Chapter 1; and (v) the policy assessment tool ReSAT (Termeer et al. 2018), see Chapters 1 and 4. The methods are fully described in Chapter 1, but the analysis is based on a multi-stakeholder approach, including farmers (intensive and organic producers) and representatives from farmer associations, the Swedish egg association, the poultry meat association, and value chain actors, such as processors, NGOs, government bodies, and researchers. The chapter is based on interaction with approximately 130 people (~100 surveys and/or interviews with farmers, ~30 stakeholders including farmers and other actors who contributed to workshops, focus groups, and the stakeholders' validation of the policy assessment). Data were collected during 2018–2020.

The main actors and the resilience characteristics were identified for the farming system, including: challenges, essential functions, resilience attributes, strategies, and the overall current resilience capacity. These are summarized in Annex 15.1. Whenever possible, we have included references in Annex 15.1 to guide the reader towards more detailed descriptions of the methods and results.

15.2 Synthesis of Results

15.2.1 *Economic Challenges Prevail: The Consequence of Regulation, Changing Market Needs, and Climate Change*

The high-value egg and broiler production in Sweden faces long- and short-term challenges, demanding continuous change from farming system actors. Table 15.1 summarizes the challenges identified in the farming system, across four sustainability dimensions (environmental, economic, social, and institutional). Wider analysis identifies other challenges, e.g., dependence on continuous deliveries and transports, but these challenges were not identified within the SURE-Farm project. Following SURE-Farm, the farming system is represented by farms, non-farm actors, and context actors, mutually (bilaterally or unilaterally) influencing each other, while delivering private and public goods (Meuwissen et al. 2019). Annex 15.1 shows the main actors representing, and the challenges faced by, the egg and broiler production in Sweden.

Economic challenges are scored highly by respondents as evident by the synthesis in Table 15.1. These challenges are interrelated and to a large extent a consequence of the institutional and environmental challenges. A major economic challenge is high input prices vs. low output prices, high production costs (often due to investments into new technology), and low bargaining power of producers, all of which lead to low profitability. Economic challenges put forward by stakeholders, often arise from strict animal welfare and environmental standards. Yet, stakeholders representing the farming system have not voiced concerns over strict regulation *per se*. Rather, in their perception, problems occur if standards are different and lower across the EU and other markets. Producers also perceive national regulation as poorly aligned with sector needs. It was stated that consultation with farms in the policy process is underdeveloped, leading to a legal framework that does not adequately account for its implications on the sector (Reidsma et al. 2019). It should be noted that we have not investigated the impact of animal welfare regulation on competitiveness, costs, or revenues.

The institutional challenges on high standards are generally supported by society, i.e., there is wide support for facilitating food safety, high animal welfare, health, and environmental standards (Reidsma et al. 2019). These general attitudes also result in a high demand for high-value products and organic eggs, but the demand is more erratic for broiler meat. In addition, there are often short-term demand fluctuations driven by media reports on animal welfare issues or the overall economic outlook. These challenges push the sector towards constant technological change in spite of continued low profitability, as well as price and other risks.

Table 15.1. *Summary of challenges identified with FoPIA, ReSAT, and risk management focus groups, across four sustainability dimensions: environmental (ENVM), economic (ECON), social (SOC), and institutional (INST) at the farming system level*

			Challenges			
		Method	ENVM	ECON	SOC	INST
Farming system	Shocks	FoPIA 1 and FoPIA 2		Scandals: social media and activists influencing the sale	Animal welfare activists	
		ReSAT (experts views)				High standards to prevent risks
	Long-term stresses	FoPIA 1 and FoPIA 2	Technology adaptation; Knowledge management;	Prices (inputs, output); High production costs; Changing technology; Changing consumer preferences; Different standards for Swedish and EU products; Knowledge;	Changing consumer preferences; Work load; Skilled labour; Succession; Gender issues; Social life;	Bureaucracy; High standards and strict regulation
		ReSAT (experts views)	Nutrient balance; Soil erosion; Climate change;	Different standards for Swedish and EU products; High production costs; Changing consumer preferences; Low value added at the farm level; Creditors do not support projects for high-value-added products;	Labour renewal; Gender structure; Skilled/educated labour; Social life; Changing consumer preferences	High standards and strict regulation

252

| Focus groups | Farm profitability;
Market power of processors;
Changing consumer preferences | High standards and strict regulation;.
Activists/media convey a negative image of the sector and shape long-term consumer preferences |

Source: Reidsma et al. (2019); Manevska-Tasevska (2018); Karlsson and Rommel (2019)

Environmental challenges highlighted by the respondents result from extreme weather events and disease outbreaks. The frequency of heat waves has increased, making ventilation and cooling of barns a major concern. Droughts, heavy rains, and storms can damage crops, affecting crop prices and leading to a shortage in fodder. Low precipitation has in some parts of the country led to low levels of ground water, which is a major production factor. Heat risks decrease animal welfare, as the hens and chickens suffer in hot barns; heat waves reduce the quality of eggs, as hotter barns lead to more hens laying their eggs on the floor, where it is cooler, instead of the warmer egg-laying compartments designed to keep eggs undamaged and clean; heat waves reduce the intake of food and water in animals; in a heat wave there is greater risk for the spread of pathogenic microbes (and other animal diseases).

Animal rights activists were identified by respondents as a risk. Activists can affect consumer demand, but they can also transmit diseases following illegal entry into barns. Last but not the least, poor attractiveness of job openings in agriculture can lead to difficulties in finding qualified labour and in the farm succession process.

15.2.2 Results from the FoPIA Participatory Assessment: The Farming System Focuses on Viable and High-Quality Production

The identity of a farming system is linked to the provision of functions, and workshop participants ranked the importance and the performance of essential functions with respective indicators (Paas et al. 2019). In SURE-Farm, functions relate to the question "resilience for what purpose?" and are subdivided towards the provision of private goods, including healthy and affordable food products, as well as other bio-based resources for the processing sector. Other functions are to ensure economic viability, to improve the quality of life in farming areas by providing employment and offering decent working conditions, and to provide public goods, such as, maintaining natural resources (water, soil, air) in good condition and protecting the biodiversity of habitats, genetic diversity, and species. Functions are also to ensure that rural areas are attractive places of residence and for tourism and to achieve high animal health and welfare (Meuwissen et al. 2019). The essential functions of the Swedish high-value egg and broiler production are presented in Annex 15.1.

The FoPIA workshop with stakeholders (Paas et al. 2019) revealed that 'viable income', 'animal health and welfare', 'protecting of natural resources' and 'maintaining food production' are among the most essential functions of the egg and broiler farming system in Sweden. Although highly important, the performance of 'viable income' and 'animal health and welfare' was assessed as medium. Indeed, challenges for the resilience of the farming system that relate to the economic performance and the need for fulfilling animal welfare requirements are emphasized by stakeholders (see Table 15.1 and Annex 15.1). The performance of protecting of natural resources and maintaining food production were assessed as medium to high (Reidsma et al. 2019).

Stakeholders also evaluated the importance and the performance of the indicators related to the respective functions. "Profit per m², product price, total production, nutrition loss, and "number of farms" fulfilling the criteria for animal welfare standards" were selected as the most important for delivering the main functions and thus the resilience of the farming system. The performance of the main indicators varies from low for the economic indicators, medium for the environmental indicator, to high for the production potential, and the fulfilment of criteria for animal health and welfare (Reidsma et al. 2019).

Following the specifications of the FoPIA model (Paas et al. 2019), the importance of the selected functions and indicators, and the assessed performance depends on stakeholders participating in the workshop. This subjective assessment relates to the resilience of the farming system, and how different stakeholders (producers, representatives from the Swedish egg association and the Swedish poultry meat association, NGO, value chain) perceive the importance of the functions and the indicators. For instance, the group of stakeholders did not include environmental activists, and the performance of the environmental indicators might be over-scored as a result.

15.2.3 Insights from Risk Management Focus Groups: Greater Cooperation to Address Power Imbalances in the Value Chain

Challenges, associated risks, and risk management strategies were discussed in focus groups (Soriano et al. 2020). Although risks from animal diseases were viewed as a major challenge in the farm survey (Spiegel et al. 2019), participants in the focus group agreed that risk management practices in this area are advanced and do not offer a lot of room for further improvement. The challenge herein lies mostly in the adoption of new technologies and related training of farm employees, as well as strict monitoring of fodder quality.

Low profitability and changing consumer preferences were viewed as challenges that offer more potential in terms of improved risk management. Broiler producers perceive upstream market power of slaughterhouses as problematic, and there were news reports on mergers and acquisitions among slaughterhouses at the time of the focus groups, creating worries among farmers about further market power imbalances. Consumer demand was perceived as erratic, especially for high-value organic broiler meat. Media reports and consumer perceptions – the increasing role of influencers and social media debates was explicitly mentioned – oscillating between a view of poultry meat and eggs as a healthy and climate-friendly alternative to pork and beef on the one hand. On the other hand, there are repeated episodes of negative news about animal welfare or food safety concerns. For both risks, an increased cooperation along the food value chain was viewed as critical. Consumer awareness and knowledge are one aspect; greater diversity and modularity in terms of product lines and marketing channels are another aspect mentioned as crucial to increasing the resilience of the system. It was mentioned that the collaboration of value chain actors should also be extended to banks who appear to have lost their sector-specific expertise over the past years, creating problems with loan allocation and financial risk management. Chapter 2 provides more details on the importance of risk management in European agriculture.

15.2.4 Adaptability as an Inevitable Process? Focus on Relevant Attributes, Strategies, and Policies

The farming system is adaptable, continuously implementing incremental change, in line with technological, legislative, and market developments. The great need for adaptability emerges from newly imposed regulation and changes in consumer preferences. Adaptability of the farming system is maintained via knowledge exchange and structural change.

Tightness of feedback, openness, functional diversity, and system reserves are among the main attributes characterizing the resilience of this farming system (see Annex 15.1). Tightness of feedback and openness are related to farmers' actively seeking out knowledge to support and build networks, and to the farmers' openness to learn from different knowledge sources. System reserves can be linked to strategies where knowledge is shared with family members and employees to ensure that the farm does not depend on a single person (Manevska-Tasevska and Rommel 2020; Reidsma et al. 2019).

Adaptation strategies imply structural adjustments in production, including: an increase in farm size, functional diversification (higher self-sufficiency of fodder or alternative businesses for income diversification to manage risks), and technological development for greater productivity and disease management (Manevska-Tasevska and Rommel 2020; Reidsma et al. 2019). Farms must often expand to benefit from economies of scale and to compete with foreign players via imports. Currently there is heterogeneity in the system, with most broiler farms having between 50,000 and 500,000 birds, whereas most farms specializing in egg production have between 10,000 and 100,000 birds. Larger farms often find it easier to integrate fodder production into the farm's activities. Larger farms can also adopt advanced technology more easily, allowing them to coordinate activities more efficiently.

Adaptation strategies also rely on knowledge management, access to skilled labour, as well as access to land and capital (Manevska-Tasevska and Rommel 2020; Reidsma et al. 2019). For the system to evolve, different kinds of knowledge and wide competences are required, including technical knowledge in daily operations, strategic planning of the different business activities, optimization of labour, knowledge on new trends, legislation, and regulation. Stakeholders cooperate along the value chain to make the soft components of these competencies and the knowledge widely available at the farm level. However, in some instances, new work routines or the implementation of new regulation demand more substantial and idiosyncratic change at the farm. The Swedish egg association and the Swedish poultry meat association take responsibility in addressing these demands by facilitating knowledge exchange. At the same time, the Swedish egg association and the poultry meat association act as interest groups to shield farms from stricter regulation and other external pressures.

Multiple policies impact the resilience of farming systems in Europe (Feindt et al. 2019). The results of the Swedish case study show that organic production support, investment support, knowledge development and support for cooperation and pilot projects, young farmers support, and support for re-structuring and modernizations of farms can strengthen the link between primary production and processors (Manevska-Tasevska 2018). The policy framework mostly supports the sector's adaptability. The main policy objectives are environment- and climate-friendly practices and technologies, a generational shift successors, and social learning. Policy support encourages high-quality products, which is highly appreciated by the consumers. The current policies and regulations are criticized for ignoring the extra costs they can cause for farms, while international competitors often operate under more liberal laws and regulations (Manevska-Tasevska 2018).

The robustness of the farming system mainly relates to processes at the farm level, including family support, family labour availability, labour division (including gender issues), off-farm employment, generational shift, and social networks (Reidsma et al. 2019). Functional diversification, i.e., not being dependent on a single income source of the farm enterprise, is among the most common solution for keeping the farm both robust and adaptable. For example, shaping the activities of the farm to fit the profile of the environment (fodder production, renting out holiday lets or making use of the wider consumer market found in towns and cities, forestry, etc.) were some of the mentioned strategies. Robustness has been associated with experience and learning by doing as well as learning from others (other farmers, consultants, and advisors in particular). In line with the Swedish CAP orientation towards "as long term as possible" objectives (Regeringskansliet 2014, p. 9), with a liberal, market-oriented, and competitive agricultural sector, taking into account the climate, environment, and rural development (Regeringskansliet 2014, p. 112), the policy support provided to enable the robustness of the poultry sector is very limited. As farms self-assess their robustness as relatively high (Spiegel et al. 2019), the policy focus on adaptability might be warranted.

Transformability remains a major challenge to be addressed across all actors in the farming system. There was no clear indication of transformative change in the farming system. Changes applied at different levels across the system are continuous and incremental, and the transformation of the farming system is gradual. Rapid transformation of the farming system was not identified as an option due to the large investments needed. Farmers have also made substantial livestock-sector-specific human capital investments, and it would be unrealistic to expect a shift to other activities without a major support system in place. Farmers exhibit entrepreneurial spirit, and they test and experiment, for instance with alternative energy sources. However, such small-scale experimentation does not trigger a greater transformation of the system. In many instances, changing to organic farming was pointed out as transformability. However, the conversion from conventional to organic egg and broiler production takes less than five years, and these changes can also be interpreted as adaptability to changing consumer preferences. From a policy perspective, transformability is supported with non-productive investments, support for vocational training and advisory services, support for agri-environment-climate commitments, cooperation, and building innovation groups and innovation projects, all with a focus on long-term social benefits.

15.3 Concluding Remarks

In this chapter, we synthesize findings on the current resilience of the high-value egg and broiler production in Sweden. The focus in this chapter is on the farming system.

Swedish egg and broiler farms produce high-value livestock products predominantly for the domestic market. The farming system faces a number of challenges but also fulfils important functions. The economic performance, strict regulation, changing consumer demand, animal welfare concerns of civil society, and power imbalances in the value chain are among the main challenges as subjectively perceived by stakeholders in the egg and broiler farming system. These challenges require change in technology as well as cooperation and a reorganization of the value chain. Production cost and subsequent farm profitability are considered the key performance indicators for keeping the sector resilient.

Overall, the current resilience capacity of the farming system is moderate to high, with high levels of adaptability, based on the perceptions of the representatives of the system. The potential for transformability is low, primarily due to the necessary investments in technology and human capital. The Swedish egg association and the Swedish poultry meat association play a key role in catalysing resilience. Tight networks among processors and primary producers, facilitated by the egg and poultry meat associations, should ensure sufficient information flows and feedbacks. Greater modularity and diversity in terms of processing channels and production lines, as well as openness to new technology, knowledge, and networks (e.g., peers, advisors), are among the identified pathways towards future resilience.

Future research should make an effort to understand better the role of social media as a driver of short- and long-term changes in consumer demand. An in-depth industrial organization study of the sector could also yield important insights to address increasing concerns about power imbalances of different value chain actors especially for broiler production.

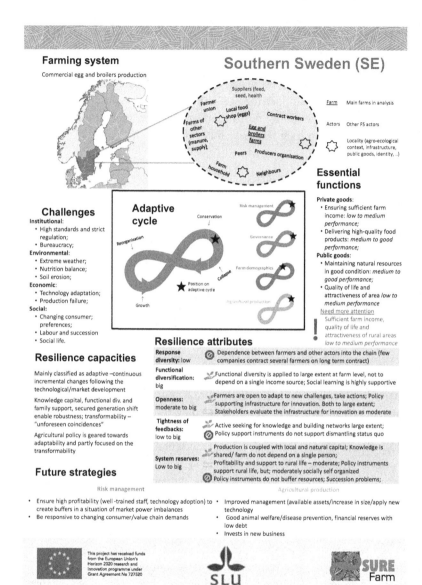

Annex 15.1 Factsheet synthesizing resilience of the current farming system in Southern Sweden.

Source: Reidsma et al. (2019)

References

Coopmans, I., Dessein, J., Bijttebier, J., et al. 2019. D3.2 Report on a qualitative analysis in 11 case-studies for understanding the process of farm demographic change across EU-farming systems and its influencing factors. Sustainable and Resilient EU Farming Systems (SURE-Farm) Project Report, EU Horizon 2020 Grant Agreement No. 727520.

Eurostat. 2018. Main farm land use by NUTS 2 regions. European Commission.

Feindt, P., Termeer, K., Candel, J., et al. 2019. D4.2. Assessing how policies enable or constrain the resilience of farming systems in the European Union: Case study results. Sustainable and Resilient EU Farming Systems (SURE-Farm) Project Report, EU Horizon 2020 Grant Agreement No. 727520.

Jordbruksverket. 2015. Jordbruksmarkens ägarstruktur i Sverige, Statistikrapport 2015:03. Sverige: Jordbruksverket.

2020a. *Marknaden för matfågel.* Sverige: Jordbruksverket.

2020b. *Marknaden för ägg.* Sverige: Jordbruksverket.

Karlsson, O. and Rommel, J. 2019. Focus group on risk management strategies – Sweden – High-value egg and broiler systems. Sustainable and Resilient EU Farming Systems (SURE-Farm) Project Report, EU Horizon 2020 Grant Agreement No. 727520.

Manevska-Tasevska, G. 2018. Assessing how policies enable or constrain the resilience of the egg and broiler system in Sweden. An application of the Resilience Assessment Tool (ReSAT). Sustainable and Resilient EU Farming Systems (SURE-Farm) Project Report, EU Horizon 2020 Grant Agreement No. 727520.

Manevska-Tasevska, G. and Rommel, J. 2020. FoPIA-SURE-Farm 2, case study report Sweden. Sustainable and Resilient EU Farming Systems (SURE-Farm) Project Report, EU Horizon 2020 Grant Agreement No. 727520.

Meuwissen, M., Feindt, P., Spiegel, A., et al. 2019. A framework to assess the resilience of farming systems. *Agricultural Systems* 176, 102656.

Paas, W., Accatino, F., Antonioli, F., et al. 2019. D5.2 Participatory impact assessment of sustainability and resilience of EU farming systems. Sustainable and Resilient EU Farming Systems (SURE-Farm) Project Report, EU Horizon 2020 Grant Agreement No. 727520.

Reidsma, P., Spiegel, A., Paas, W., et al. 2019. D5.3 Resilience assessment of current farming systems across the European Union. Sustainable and Resilient EU Farming Systems (SURE-Farm) Project Report, EU Horizon 2020 Grant Agreement No. 727520.

Regeringskansliet. 2014. Gårdsstödet 2015–2020 – förslag till svenskt genomförande, Ds 2014:6. Sverige: Regeringskansliet.

Soriano, B., Bardaji, I., Bertolozzi, D., et al. 2020. D2.6 Report on state and outlook for risk management in EU agriculture. Sustainable and Resilient EU Farming Systems (SURE-Farm) Project Report, EU Horizon 2020 Grant Agreement No. 727520.

Spiegel, A., Slijper, T., de Mey, Y., et al. 2019. D2.1. Report on farmers' perceptions of risk and resilience capacities – A comparison across EU farmers. Sustainable and Resilient EU Farming Systems (SURE-Farm) Project Report, EU Horizon 2020 Grant Agreement No. 727520.

Termeer, K., Candel, J., Feindt, P. H. and Buitenhuis, Y. 2018. D4.1. Assessing how policies enable or constrain the resilience of farming systems in the European Union: The Resilience Assessment Tool (ReSAT). Sustainable and Resilient EU Farming Systems (SURE-Farm) Project Report, EU Horizon 2020 Grant Agreement No. 727520.

Urquhart, J., Accatino, F., Appel, F., et al. (2019). D2.3. Report on farmers' learning capacity and networks of influence in 11 European case studies. Sustainable and Resilient EU Farming Systems (SURE-Farm) Project Report, EU Horizon 2020 Grant Agreement No. 727520.

16 | Managing Risks to Improve the Resilience of Arable Farming in the East of England

MAURO VIGANI, JULIE URQUHART,
DAMIAN MAYE, PHILLIPA
NICHOLAS-DAVIES, JASMIN E. BLACK,
AMR KHAFAGY, ROBERT BERRY
AND PAUL COURTNEY

16.1 Introduction

The East of England (EE) is considered the 'bread basket' of the UK thanks to its fertile flat lands producing a variety of high-yielding crops. Cereals, especially wheat and barley, are by far the most important crops covering almost half of the farmed area. Sugar beet is grown in rotation with cereals, with the region producing more than two thirds of England's total sugar beet crop. Other prominent crops include carrots, potatoes, oilseed rape, fruit, salad crops and pulses. The region is also important for pig and poultry production. With all these productive farming activities, the region contributes more to the UK's agricultural gross value added than any other in the UK, directly employing around 19,000 full-time equivalent farmers and workers (2013 farm structure data) and contributing £1.7 billion (about 1 per cent) to local Gross Value Added (GVA) in 2018. The contribution of the EE to domestic food security is therefore important. The majority of farms are capital intensive with an average size exceeding 100 ha and are mostly family or corporate driven. Farmers are mainly landowners and are highly market-oriented with high levels of specialization, investing heavily in seeds and chemicals.

The high-yielding and high-quality staple crops produced in EE are not only supplying the domestic food market but are also exported all over the world. In particular, the UK is a net exporter of wheat grains and flour to many countries in North Africa (e.g. Morocco, Algeria and Tunisia) and South Asia (e.g. Thailand and the Philippines), significantly contributing to global food security and safety, also thanks

263

to the strong integration of the EE farming system into global supply chains and the high-quality standards.

Despite its strengths and global importance, this farming system is under considerable pressure from trade and policy realignment and environmental challenges, with Brexit, market volatility, the Covid-19 pandemic and climate change impacting on its long-term viability. In order to assess and ensure the sustainable continuation of the EE's agricultural sector, it is important to understand its resilience to internal and external shocks and to investigate the coping strategies and responding capacity of its various operators, starting from the perspective of farmers as the primary producers on which the farming system is based.

This chapter provides a full description of the EE farming system in terms of its challenges, functions, resilience and future strategies, which were elaborated during the SURE-Farm project and are summarized in Annex 16.1. It uses results of a mixed-method research approach based on a quantitative survey, semi-structured interviews and narratives to analyse the challenges faced by the farming system

Figure 16.1 A crop of rape in the East of England
Source: Nicholas-Davies, P.

and the risk management and coping strategies adopted by farmers and other actors. In doing so, the chapter distinguishes between strategies that can lead to the robustness, adaptability or transformation of the farming system (see Chapter 1). In addition, the chapter investigates in detail the important role of knowledge networks and farmer learning for the development of resilience strategies. Key policy lessons derived from the SURE-Farm project are then summarized in the concluding section of the chapter.

16.2 Risks, Challenges and Their Management

In order to understand what challenges, coping strategies and type of resilience are prevalent in the EE farming sector, a large-scale survey was conducted in November–December 2018. Survey data were collected through telephone interviews for a sample of 200 arable farms located in the EE counties, namely: Bedfordshire, Hertfordshire, Essex, Cambridgeshire, Norfolk and Suffolk. The sample was stratified to ensure representativeness in terms of the geographical distribution of farms and farm size. In what follows, the results of the survey are analysed in combination with the results of semi-structured farmer interviews conducted to investigate the role of farmer learning for risk management and biographical narratives conducted to explore family farm histories (Coopmans et al., 2019; Urquhart et al., 2019; Nicholas et al., 2020).

Figure 16.2 shows the survey results in terms of the challenges projected to face EE agriculture over the next twenty years. Farmers answers were recorded on a Likert scale from 1 (not at all challenging) to 7 (very challenging), where a value of 4 indicated neutrality. As one can see, the most worrisome challenges for EE farmers are uncertainty about the future of agricultural policy in the UK, persistently low market prices and persistently high input prices (e.g. fertilizer, feed, seed).

Many of the higher-ranking challenges are related to regulations and to the UK's exit from the EU, the impacts of which are still largely unknown. The UK agricultural policy is currently being developed, with a new Environmental Land Management Scheme (ELMS) at its core based on the principle of 'public money for public goods'. Currently farmers are uncertain as to what this will mean in practice, but they are concerned about a reduction in direct payments (i.e. the

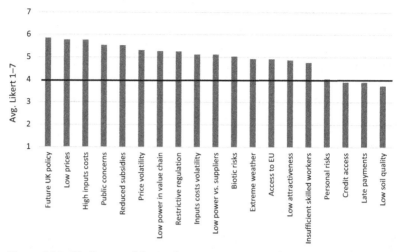

Figure 16.2 Challenges of the EE farming system over the next twenty years as perceived by farmers.

Source: Survey. The horizontal line identifies a value of 4 on the Likert scale, indicating farmers' neutrality with respect the challenge. All challenges above the line are statistically significant different from 4 (*t*-test mean >4) at 1% probability level (Pr(T > t) = 0.000)

Basic Farm Payment, BPS), access to EU markets, competition from new markets (such as the USA) and a reduction in skilled farm workers (many of which come from other EU countries). All of these elements have potentially critical impacts in terms of how the EE farming system will look in the next twenty years.

Farmers also shared concerns about policies and regulations beyond Brexit. A progressive reduction of direct subsidies is planned under the EU's Common Agricultural Policy, therefore EE farmers would have faced this challenge regardless of Brexit. According to interview results, the BPS is viewed as being crucial to making a profit most years and essential for paying interest due on the substantial bank loans secured against farmland. Moreover, farmers consider some regulations overly restrictive and inflexible. For example, the current crop protection regulations are perceived as a risk in terms of enabling or constraining what products a farmer can use, and thus what crops are viable to grow. The recent ban on neonicotinoids was seen by farmers as a barrier to growing oilseed rape and sugar beet, because of dramatically reducing yields.

A second key challenge is related to markets. On the one hand, some of the market challenges are linked to inputs and output prices and their volatility. This is not surprising given the intensive nature of the EE farming system that relies on inputs, with key products such as wheat globally traded. On the other hand, there are key challenges in the supply chain, especially in terms of imbalanced market power and the limited bargaining capacity farmers have with buyers and suppliers, that are often multinational holdings with large global market shares.

Weather was also cited as a major risk by the survey respondents. Although interview respondents feel that the climate is becoming slightly warmer, it is the extremes of cold (severe winters), heat (summer droughts) and severe storms and flooding that are difficult to manage. The EE is particularly prone to spells of dry weather during the summer months.

The lack of appeal of farming as a profession is an important challenge for the future of the EE farming system, as shown in Figure 16.2. Many farms' employees are approaching retirement age but working on a farm might not be an attractive career choice for many young people today, as they do not like the unsociable hours it requires. Therefore, there are concerns about succession of farms and how to replace the retiring and experienced farm workers.

Narratives collected from nine EE farmers at different career stages (three each of early, mid- and late career) explored the key turning points in their family farming histories, what drove those turning points and the response to them (Nicholas et al., 2020). Internal factors such as death, illness and intergenerational change were identified as being the greatest challenges to family farm business sustainability, with external factors (e.g. Figure 16.2) such as extreme weather events, price fluctuations and policy changes being viewed as something that they had to deal with in the day-to-day running of their businesses.

EE's farmers adopt a variety of strategies to cope with the aforementioned challenges and risks (see Chapter 2). These strategies are reported in Table 16.1. The most frequently adopted strategy consists in implementing measures to prevent pests or diseases. Arable farmers have to deal mainly with black rust (*Puccinia graminis*), blackgrass (*Alopecurus myosuroides*), the cabbage stem flea beetle (*Psylliodes chrysocephalus*), small mammals (rabbits) and birds (e.g. pigeons), which eat and damage crops.

Having updated market information is also a key strategy, especially with respect to wheat which is traded on the global market and subject to the volatility of global wheat prices. Therefore, farmers must manage these fluctuations and endeavour to sell their grain when prices are high and exchange rates favourable, keeping a check on global markets and events

Table 16.1. *Frequency of adoption of different types of risk management and coping strategies of EE farmers*

On-farm risk management strategies	% adoption
Measures to prevent pests or diseases	88
Market information to plan my farm activities for the next season	84
Worked harder to secure production in hard times	83
Flexibility in the timing of my production to deal with seasonality	73
Invested in technologies to control environmental risks	72
Diversified in other activities [e.g. agri-tourism, renewable energies]	72
Maintained financial savings for hard times	70
Low debts or no debts at all to prevent financial risks	70
Cost flexibility [e.g. temporal labour contracts instead of permanent contracts]	61
Diversified in production [e.g. mixed livestock and crop farming]	56
Had an off-farm job [either myself or a family member]	33
Opened up my farm to the public [e.g. open farm days]	16
Off-farm risk management strategies	
Learned about challenges [e.g. from a consultant or agricultural training]	70
Had access to a variety of input suppliers	68
Member of a producer organization, cooperative or credit union	65
Hedged production with futures contracts	58
Used production or marketing contracts	57
Cooperated with other farmers to secure inputs or production	55
Bought any type of agricultural insurance	39
Member of an organization [e.g. collaborate with processors, retailers]	36
Insurances	
Field crop insurance [e.g. hailstorms, flood, drought]	24
Grain in store insurance [e.g. fire, flood of storage]	18
Income/price insurance [e.g. volatile prices, drop in income]	8
Other type of insurance	7

Source: survey

that may impact on grain prices for the coming season (e.g. droughts in key grain growing areas of the world). Forward contracts are an important tool to manage global market risks. As emerged from the interviews, in EE 70 per cent of the grain is sold up to two years in advance, which helps with budgeting and cash flow. Against low prices, there is also the possibility to store the harvest to sell when prices are highest.

The interviewed farmers explain that the adoption of innovation and technological developments are opportunities for reducing labour costs and improving the efficiency of input use. Regarding climate change, having machinery capacity available (even via contractors) can help overcome climate variability to a certain extent. For example, operations such as harvesting that used to take a week can be done in a day or two now, reducing the negative effects of bad weather.

Regarding Brexit, farmers are adopting two main strategies: some are holding back on further investments in the farm until they have a clearer picture of what the future of British farming will look like, while others are investing in expensive machinery now while they still have the BPS.

With respect to intergenerational transfer, there is evidence (e.g. Zagata and Sutherland, 2015) that policies for installing young farmers and pensioning off others later on in their careers has only very weak impact on facilitating intergenerational transfer. The narratives work within the SURE-Farm project indicated that other factors, mostly taxation and welfare, have a more significant impact. Here is a need for greater advisory support for succession planning if the risks associated with this challenging period are to be reduced.

During the survey, farmers were also asked to provide a self-assessment of their farms' resilience, based on how much they agree with the statements in Table 16.2 on a Likert scale from 1 (strongly disagree) to 7 (strongly agree). On average, the survey's results suggest that EE farmers perceived themselves to be adaptable to challenges. This is mainly due to their personal capacity of being good at adapting and the possibility of adopting new practices and technologies in response to shocks. On the contrary, their perceived level of robustness is relatively lower mainly due to difficulties in bouncing back to a pre-shock state. In other words, EE farmers feel that they could adapt and eventually transform as a reaction to a shock, which implies certain degrees of change, but they would not be able to withstand a shock without taking measures that can lead to a change, suggesting a certain level of vulnerability of their current status. From interviews and

Table 16.2. *Farmers' perceived resilience of their farm (1 'strongly disagree' to 7 'strongly agree')*

Robustness	Average
After a shock, it is easy for my farm to bounce back to its current profitability	4.20
It is hard to manage my farm in such a way that it recovers quickly from shocks	4.18
I find it easy to get back to normal after a setback	4.28
A big shock will not heavily affect my farm, as I have enough options to deal with shocks	4.17
Robustness Avg.	**4.21**
Adaptability	
My farm can adopt new activities, varieties or technologies in response to shocks	4.61
As a farmer, I can easily adapt myself to challenging situations	4.94
I am good at adapting myself and facing up to agricultural challenges	5.01
My farm is not flexible and can hardly be adjusted to deal with a changing environment	3.28
Adaptability Avg.	**4.46**
Transformability	
For me, it is easy to make decisions that result in a transformation	4.52
It is hard to reorganize my farm if external circumstances drastically change	3.97
I still have the ability to radically reorganize my farm after a challenging period	4.43
I can easily make major changes that would transform my farm	4.17
Transformability Avg.	**4.27**

Source: survey. Average robustness, adaptability and transformability are statistically significant different from 4 (*t*-test mean >4) at 1% probability level (Pr(T > t) = 0.000).

narratives conducted with farmers, it emerged that, predominantly, it was shocks such as disease outbreak or fire which resulted in higher transformations of their farm businesses.

Finally, the current Covid-19 pandemic is an important challenge for the overall UK food system, and its impact on the resilience of the EE arable farming system was investigated through semi-structured interviews with different stakeholders in June–July 2020 (Meuwissen et al., 2021). From the resilience perspective, Covid-19 has highlighted a problem in that many farms are specialized into providing for either the food service industry or retail, making them less adaptable and resilient to external shocks. The farming system revealed its fragility with this pandemic, partly due to the dominance of too few food distributors with long food supply chains in the retail and food service sectors. Moreover, while supply contracts between farmers and buyers provide stability and robustness in normal times, they may limit the flexibility for farmers to find alternative markets for produce if the need arises, revealing a weak adaptability of the food supply chain.

Overall, the Covid-19 crisis is having a relatively small impact on the EE arable sector. However, some critical situations have been identified. For example, the potato supply chain was badly hit due to the closure of restaurants, pubs and fish and chip shops. Similarly, the closing of pubs and restaurants strongly reduced the demand for beer and, therefore, for malting barley, which raised issues for storing greater amounts of the cereal. The increased demand for flour in supermarkets resulted in temporary shortages because the supply chain needed to redirect the bulk flour to retailers in a packet format. Specialized horticulture farms suffered from labour shortages during the picking season as most pickers are migrant workers from Eastern Europe who were unable to travel to the UK. Moreover, the interruption of several business activities provoked slight delays with machinery parts.

Some actors of the farming system have been able to develop successful responses and coping strategies against the risks of the pandemic. For example, the businesses who maintained diversity in their markets were better able to adapt and the more entrepreneurial have been able to switch quickly and take advantage of the increased retail demand. Vegetable growers were the most rapid in redirecting from the food service sector to supermarkets and farm shops. Potato growers have shifted from chipping to bulk bags for consumers. However, such a shift was not always possible as not all potato varieties are suitable for retail, and stored potatoes treated with two applications of chlorpropham cannot be sold as fresh potatoes. Longer-term impacts include changes in potato contracts for the next year as a surplus from this year's harvest is expected, prompting growers to change to growing supermarket varieties.

16.3 Knowledge Networks and Learning

Within the EE arable farming system, the various operators do not act in isolation; on the contrary the farming system is composed of networks enhancing the sharing of resources, knowledge and experience, leading to mutual learning processes between actors. As a result, the farming system can effectively take advantage of collaborations and knowledge sharing in dealing with challenges and risks in a more efficient way than dealing with these issues individually.

While the farmer, or the farm manager, can be considered the central decision-maker of the business, the strategies to be resilient against shocks involve a number of actors participating in the wider farming system. First of all, the decision of adopting certain strategies and the intensity of changes needed to ensure that the farming business can overcome shocks depends on several factors, such as the farmer's/manager's perception and attitude towards risks, managerial skills and farm tenure (whether the farmer owns or rents land can affect attitudes and decision-making). Secondly, bankers, lenders, funders and business advisors can influence farmers strategies providing the financial means for investments and advising considering the farms' history and characteristics (Soriano et al., 2020). Moreover, traders provide market information and data sharing services which are critical for timely decision-making; cooperatives can contribute through collaboration, resource sharing and group-buying; collaboration with neighbours can involve machinery and land sharing, more land to farm, greater labour flexibility and reduced machinery costs; agronomists can provide advice and information on new crop varieties, crop trials, disease monitoring, biosecurity and crop rotation; research institutes can provide training, education and skills to support farming and diversification activities and may also be able to facilitate funding or collaborate on grant applications.

Our analysis revealed that, in most cases, the farms are family farms with several family members having a role in the farm management, so decision-making is shared. Hence, the most important influencers for the farmers interviewed were family members, who help develop confidence and provide support and joint decision-making. Agronomists were also influential, and their role has evolved from advice on plant protection products to broader knowledge of the agri-environmental scheme landscape. Financial advisors were also considered important, as was learning from other farmers. Other individual influencers iden-tified were business partners, employees, landowners and contractors.

Different types of organizations can also significantly influence the managerial behaviour of farmers. For instance, public research organ-izations were considered influential, although respondents felt that there was a lack of government-funded research. Seed companies and brokers were moderately influential, and government departments were either perceived as highly influential (as they provide the bound-aries within which farmers operate) or moderately influential. Some respondents indicated that supermarkets, environmental non-governmental organizations (NGOs), the National Farmers' Union (NFU), buying groups, the Agriculture and Horticulture Development Board (AHDB), the farming press and social media are somewhat influential.

Networks and learning were also investigated through the survey and Table 16.3 reports results about the farmers' self-assessment about their networking and learning capacity, measured on a Likert scale from 1 (strongly disagree) to 7 (strongly agree). As one can see, on average EE farmers have a relatively high level of networking (values >5), in particular between each other by developing farmer-to-farmer networks, but also with agricultural experts and value chain operators. Farmers feel a relatively high level of support from these networks, especially from neighbouring farmers.

The great importance of networks and collaboration across the farming system emerged during the current Covid-19 pandemic. As illustrated by farmer interviews, during the pandemic farms faced labour shortages and have advertised picking jobs. A big recruitment campaign started in EE, driven by individual companies but also by the NFU, the Country Land and Business Association (CLA) and the Department for Environment, Food and Rural Affairs (Defra). Initiatives such as 'Pick for Britain' by the government and 'Student Land Army' also started and social media has been used heavily for recruitment. As a result, those farms located nearer to urban centres had a good response, although those in more remote rural locations did not benefit as much because of difficulties in travelling to the farm and potential issues of accommodation.

Learning from peers and others in their network is a key strategy for EE farmers. Table 16.3 indicates that learning involves talking to farming neighbours, engaging in discussion groups, observing what

Table 16.3. *Farmers' self-assessment of networking and learning (1 'strongly disagree' to 7 'strongly agree')*

Networking	Average
I know a lot of other farmers in my region	5.55
I know a lot of agricultural professionals, experts or value chain actors	5.39
I feel I can receive support from agricultural network	5.34
Farmers in my region tend to support each other when there is a problem	5.30
Concerning farming, I often interact with neighbouring farmers	5.29
When I attend agricultural events and meetings, I interact a lot with participants	5.16
Learning	
Before making a change on my farm I seek out as much information as possible	5.86
I get a lot of information and ideas from talking to others in the sector	5.40
I learn a lot from observing what other farmers do on their farms	5.10
Over the years, my beliefs about how I should farm have changed	5.02
My most important source of information is my own past experience of farming	4.42
I am wary of new ideas and technologies in farming	3.89
I am too busy to find out about how I might improve my farm	3.28
I don't reflect much on whether I can improve the way I manage my farm	3.22
I learn a lot from other farmers via social media	2.84

Source: survey. All statements are statistically significant different from 4 (*t*-test mean >4) at 1% probability level ($Pr(T > t) = 0.000$) with the exception of 'I am wary of new ideas and technologies in farming' which is not significant.

other farmers are doing and seeking out advice from other farmers. This is particularly useful when farmers want to try out something new and engage in trials. Overall, farmers in the EE are more likely to seek as much information as possible before making changes on the farm. However, it is worth noting that social media does not seem to have a significant role in farmer learning, although a number of farmers explained that they find it useful for networking with farmers from other countries in terms of finding out about agricultural practices and innovations elsewhere that may have potential benefits to their own operations.

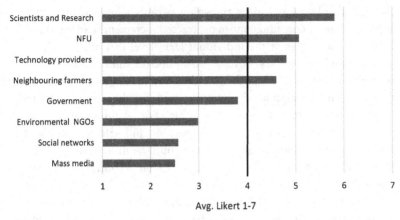

Avg. Likert 1-7

Figure 16.3 Farmers perception of trust in different sources of information.
Source: Survey. The vertical line identifies a value of 4 on the Likert scale, indicating farmers' neutrality with respect to trust. All sources are statistically significant different from 4 (*t*-test mean >4) at 1% ($Pr(T > t) = 0.000$) or 10% probability level ($Pr(T > t) = 0.093$) with the exception of 'I am wary of new ideas and technologies in farming' which is not significant

Finally, an important aspect driving learning is the degree to which farmers trust their sources. This is depicted in Figure 16.3, showing the average response of the farmers to the question 'What sources of information can be trusted?' during the survey (from 1 'do not trust at all' to 7 'strongly trust'). Scientists, the NFU, technology providers and neighbouring farmers tend to be trusted more than politicians, environmental NGOs and the social and mass media.

16.4 Conclusions and Lessons Learnt

From the analysis reported in this chapter, a number of important lessons have been learnt that can be useful for policymakers and stakeholders and that can inform future research. Firstly, the importance of policy and political changes as a source of uncertainty for farmers and actors of the farming system emerged. One could think that these challenges should be less worrisome than market and climate risks as they are under the responsibility of political institutions working for the benefit and not the disruption of economic activities. But our data showed a different picture, as Brexit, for example, became a long-term shock provoking uncertainty for the last four years which farmers have struggled to cope with. On top of this, the trade agreement to exit the EU market arrived with only a few days of notice but such critical policy changes should allow longer transition periods in which institutional support systems encourage more protracted incremental adaptation.

Second, strategies at the individual farm level can indicate the survival of single businesses, but the most effective solutions for both the resilience of the individual farm and of the farming sector are those that rely on the support of networks and collaborations, especially between farms that share similar goals. For example, peer-to-peer learning strategies proved to be important and effective in the EE arable sector, therefore these strategies could be more intensively promoted at the institutional level. Acting as a system inclusive of a variety of operators, the farming sector has more chances of long-term viability, therefore policy-makers could design solutions considering the relationships and power dynamics between actors instead of the interests of single groups. The role of farm advisors in this could be pivotal as they might have a wider perspective of the farming system.

From a broader perspective, the research conducted under the SURE-Farm project demonstrated how difficult it is to study the resilience of farming systems, in particular because of the difficulty in operationalizing the concept of resilience, which is inherently multidimensional, spanning the characteristics of farmers and associated actors, the sources and causality of shocks and the heterogeneity of effects. It is even more difficult to operationalize the resilience capacities of robustness, adaptability and transformability as their boundaries overlap – for example, there is a spectrum of successively stronger responses to drivers of change from robustness to transformation, and their application is relative to specific contexts. The narratives work also identified frequent small-scale changes, more significant than robustness but not enough to be characterized as adaptation of the farming system, but that cumulate eventually in a much broader overall change. This is an unexplored part of the resilience spectrum, and could be described as incremental change or 'creeping change'.

The SURE-Farm project demonstrated the value of a resilience framework, and the mixed methods approach taken in the project allowed assessing the EE's overall resilience. The case study showed low to moderate resilience capacities, with higher adaptability at the farm level and higher robustness at the system level. The Covid-19 pandemic highlighted how much resilience thinking is needed in order to react to crises, which points to a need to look beyond the farm and position the farm in a wider system perspective, such as the farming or the food system.

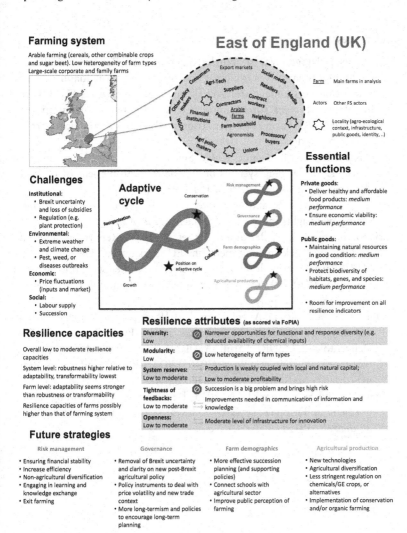

Annex 16.1 Factsheet synthesizing resilience of the current farming system in the EE (UK).

References

Coopmans, I., Draganova, M., Fowler, S., et al. 2019. Report on analysis of biographical narratives exploring short- and long-term adaptive behaviour of farmers under various challenges. Deliverable 2.2 SURE-Farm. Available at www.surefarmproject.eu/wordpress/wp-content/uploads/2019/05/SURE-Farm-D2.2-Report-on-analysis-of-biographical-narratives-report.pdf

Meuwissen, M. P. M., Feindt, P. H., Spiegel, A., et al. 2021. Impact of Covid-19 on farming systems in Europe through the lens of resilience thinking. *Agricultural Systems*, 191, 103152.

Nicholas, P., Fowler, S. and Midmore, P. 2020. Telling stories – Farmers offer new insights into farming resilience. *EuroChoices* 19, 12–17.

Soriano, B., Bardají, I., Bertolozzi, D., et al. 2020. Report on state and outlook for risk management in EU agriculture. Deliverable 2.6 SURE-Farm. Available at www.surefarmproject.eu/wordpress/wp-content/uploads/2020/02/D2-6-Report-on-state-and-outlook-on-risk-magagment-in-EU.pdfy

Urquhart, J., Accatino, F., Appel, F., et al. 2019. Report on farmers' learning capacity and networks of influence in 11 European case studies. Deliverable 2.3 SURE-Farm. Available at www.surefarmproject.eu/wordpress/wp-content/uploads/2019/07/D2.3-Report-on-farmers-learning-capacity-and-networks-of-influence.pdf

Zagata, L. and Sutherland, L. A. 2015. Deconstructing the 'young farmer problem in Europe': Towards a research agenda. *Journal of Rural Studies* 38, 39–51.

17 | Integrated Assessment of the Sustainability and Resilience of Farming Systems

Lessons from the Past and Ways Forward for the Future

FRANCESCO ACCATINO, WIM PAAS,
HUGO HERRERA, CORENTIN PINSARD,
SIMONE SEVERINI, FRANZISKA APPEL,
BIRGIT KOPAINSKY, KATARZYNA
BAŃKOWSKA, JO BIJTTEBIER, CAMELIA
GAVRILESCU, AMR KHAFAGY, VITALIY
KRUPIN, GORDANA MANEVSKA-
TASEVSKA, FRÅNZISKA OLLENDORF,
MARIYA PENEVA, CAROLINA SAN
MARTÍN, CINZIA ZINNANTI AND PYTRIK
REIDSMA

17.1 Introduction

European agriculture is coping with economic, environmental, social and institutional challenges that are expected to further accumulate in the future. Identifying strategies to cope with these challenges requires understanding of the mechanisms that make farming systems resilient. Following the definition adopted in SURE-Farm, a resilient farming system continuously provides economic (e.g., assuring economic viability), environmental (e.g., maintenance of natural resources), and social (e.g., ensuring a good quality of life) functions, even in the face of multiple challenges. These functions include ecosystem services, i.e., the goods and services that ecosystems provide to humans (Daily, 1997). The integration of economic, environmental, and social functions resonates with the concept of sustainability (Schader et al., 2016). We hypothesized a reinforcing interaction between sustainability and resilience. We argue that when dimensions of food production, environment, economy, and society are well and equally addressed, a farming system strengthens its ability to cope with challenges (Walker and Salt, 2012).

We first studied the levels of sustainability and resilience of current European farming systems in the past and present, and used insights derived from this to imagine the future. This has methodological difficulties. First, farming systems consist of multiple technical, ecological, economic, and social elements interacting in a non-linear way (Fischer et al., 2015). We took into account the multi-dimensional aspects of farming systems with an integrated system approach (van Ittersum et al., 2008). We further used the resilience framework of Meuwissen et al. (2019), presented in Chapter 1, to navigate the complex issue of farming systems' sustainability and resilience in five steps: identification of (1) the system, (2) the main challenges, (3) the main functions, (4) the resilience capacities and (5) the main resilience attributes. For operationalizing these steps, we used an Integrated Assessment (IA) (see Rotmans and van Asselt, 1996), consisting of an interdisciplinary mix of qualitative and quantitative methods, involving participatory approaches with stakeholders, models, and data analysis.

Second, Europe presents a wide heterogeneity of farming systems: from extensive ruminant systems in less favoured areas to intensive systems relying on feed imports; from integrated crop-livestock systems to monocultures. We selected eleven case studies with different characteristics in terms of geographic location, typology (arable, livestock, permanent crops, mixed crop-livestock), social, economic and historical context. Although not completely representative of Europe's farming system heterogeneity, the selection of eleven different farming systems supported the generalization of results and the formulation of policy recommendations. In the chapter, these case studies are referred to with abbreviations: arable system in Bulgaria (BG-Arable), mixed and arable system in Germany (DE-Mixed&Arable), arable system in the United Kingdom (UK-Arable), dairy system Belgium (BE-Dairy), extensive beef cattle system in France (FR-Beef), extensive sheep system in Spain (ES-Sheep), horticulture system in Poland (PL-Horticulture), hazelnut system in Italy (IT-Hazelnut), starch potato system in the Netherlands (NL-Arable), mixed smallholder farms system in Romania (RO-Mixed) and poultry system in Sweden (SE-Poultry).

In this chapter, we present an assessment of the eleven SURE-Farm case studies aimed at exploring linkages between sustainability and resilience. The narrative is primarily based on a selection of methods that allow for comparisons across case studies. Generalizable findings are given priority over farming-system-specific details. These details can be found in the case study chapters (Chapters 6–16) and in SURE-Farm deliverables (Paas et al., 2019; Reidsma et al., 2019; Accatino et al., 2020).

17.2 Contribution of Qualitative and Quantitative Methods to Resilience Assessment

In this section, we present how the three steps of the resilience assessment framework presented in Chapter 1 were operationalized: (i) identifying the key challenges that could impede the ability of the farming systems to deliver the desired functions, (ii) assessing the importance and performance of the functions provided by the farming systems, (iii) investigating the resilience-enhancing attributes, i.e., the characteristics of the systems that are likely to enhance resilience.

17.2.1 A Toolbox for Resilience Assessment

In SURE-Farm we assembled an IA toolbox with complementary qualitative and quantitative methods (see Herrera et al., 2018). The qualitative methods consisted of two participatory workshops with representatives of different stakeholder groups (e.g., farmers, food chain actors, NGOs, government) and were conducted in each farming system. The first workshop (FoPIA-SURE-Farm 1; Paas et al., 2019, 2021a) was focused on the resilience of current systems: we assessed the main challenges, the perceived importance and performance of functions, the strategies adopted to cope with past challenges, and the resilience attributes. The second workshop (FoPIA-SURE-Farm 2; Accatino et al., 2020; Paas et al., 2021b; 2021c) was focused on the resilience of future, hypothetical, systems. The quantitative methods included the assessment of current and future ecosystem services based on data and models and the simulation of farming system behavior based on system dynamics modelling.

17.2.2 Assessing Challenges (Resilience to What)

During the activities of the SURE-Farm projects (participatory workshops, focus groups, interviews), we identified and discussed key challenges in interaction with stakeholders in the case studies. For future resilience we assessed in interaction with stakeholders the closeness of the most important challenges to critical thresholds, whose exceedance would have a drastic impact on farming system functioning. This assessment was done in all case studies except two (BE-Dairy and FR-Beef, due to the COVID-19 crisis). Closeness of challenges to critical threshold was classified into 'not close', 'somewhat close', 'close', and 'at or beyond'.

17.2.3 Assessing Functions (Resilience for Which Purpose)

Eight farming system functions were identified and categorized as providing private or public goods. The provision of private goods includes (1) producing food, (2) producing other bio-based resources, (3) ensuring economic viability and (4) providing quality of life for people involved in farming. The provision of public goods includes (1) maintaining natural resources (2) maintaining biodiversity in good condition, (3) ensuring animal welfare and (4) ensuring that rural areas are attractive places for residence and tourism. In participatory workshops, stakeholders were asked to individually assess the importance and performance of the eight functions. Importance was assessed by letting stakeholders divide 100 points over the functions. Assessing performance was based on stakeholders' scores on a scale: (1) very low, (2) low, (3) moderate, (4) good and (5) very good performance.

The participatory assessment of functions was complemented with an ecosystem services assessment based on quantitative data, mostly related to the biophysical components of the system. For ecosystem services, the considered private goods were food crop production, fodder crop production, energy crop production, grazing livestock density, and timber removal. The considered public goods were carbon storage, habitat quality, atmospheric pollutant deposition, topsoil organic matter concentration, relative pollination potential, recreation potential, soil erosion control, and water retention. The assessment was based on gridded ecosystem service maps at the European scale made publicly available by the Joint Research Centre of the European Commission (see Maes et al., 2015). We calculated the average grid value of the ecosystem services in the farming systems as well as in the sub-national regions surrounding them (Nomenclature of Territorial Units for Statistics 3; NUTS 3). This allowed for comparing each farming system with the surrounding region in terms of ecosystem service provision.

In order to explore future sustainability and resilience, stakeholders were asked to determine critical thresholds for main challenges, functions, and resilience attributes, and, next, assess system performance in case critical thresholds would be exceeded (Accatino et al., 2020; Paas et al., 2021b; 2021c). Impacts on performance were classified as strongly negative (−2), moderately negative (−1), no trend (0), moderately positive (+1), and strongly positive developments (+2). As a baseline reference, researchers also assessed the development of farming system performance based on current levels and trends of functions and resilience attributes. Subsequently, stakeholders identified possible alternative configurations of the farming systems. Alternative systems were generated based on individual input and elaborated in small group discussions of three to eight stakeholders moderated by a researcher. In these discussions, stakeholders were invited to elaborate how an alternative system would perform regarding system functions and resilience attributes.

The assessment of future systems was completed with system dynamics modelling, which is based on a causal-loop diagram able to represent the cause–effect relationship present in the farming systems (Richardson, 2011). The advantage of this approach is that cause-effect relationships can be mapped coherently, which is otherwise challenging during a participatory assessment due to the limits of mental capabilities of researchers and stakeholders (e.g., bounded reality). Therefore, in a sense, the modelling approach can extend the reach of our mind (Sterman, 2000).

17.2.4 Assessing Resilience Attributes (What Enhances Resilience)

Resilience attributes are characteristics of the farming system or its surrounding environment which enhance resilience (Cabell and Oelofse, 2012; Paas et al. 2021a; see a complete list in Chapter 1). An example of a resilience attribute is 'ecologically self-regulated' which promotes resilience because it is argued that a system relying on natural regulation processes is more likely to withstand shocks due to input shortage. Based on input from FoPIA-SURE-Farm workshops, we assessed the presence of resilience attributes in the farming systems by looking at the strategies that farming system actors have already adopted and the strategies that are proposed to realize potential future systems. Strategies are linked to resilience attributes (see Reidsma et al., 2020a) as we argue that a strategy can be seen as a concrete example of supporting a certain resilience attribute. For example, if farmers aim to diversify their production, they are supporting the attribute 'functional diversity'. In this chapter we specifically reflect on those resilience attributes that were supported in the past and those that are likely to be supported in potential future systems. In addition to this, we used system dynamics to explore the relationships between functions and resilience attributes. Based on the results of the participatory workshops we built causal-loop diagrams, describing cause–effect relationships among system components, including system functions and resilience attributes. More details are available in Reidsma et al. (2020a).

17.3 Challenges of Farming Systems

The studied farming systems face a wide array of challenges in the environmental, economic, social and institutional domain (Table 17.1). Some challenges were common to a large number of farming systems, while other challenges were context dependent. Stakeholders perceived that some challenges were close to or have even already exceeded critical thresholds. It should be noted, however, that the actual position of critical thresholds may be different from the perceived position. In any case, a challenge whose intensity is perceived to be beyond a critical threshold needs to be regarded as of particular concern.

Low profitability and price volatility were identified as an economic challenge for all the farming systems. In addition, in some farming systems, low profitability was marked as close to or beyond critical thresholds. It was linked to context-specific factors: low margins (DE-Arable&Mixed), high production and labour costs (ES-Sheep), competition with foreign markets (FR-Beef, IT-Hazelnut, RO-Mixed), and possible production failures (SE-Poultry). In BE-Dairy low profitability was caused by a combination of increasing costs and high price volatility due to market liberalization. Specific economic challenges regarded the Russian embargo in PL-Horticulture and BG-Arable, and the weak position of the farmers in the value chain (IT-Hazelnut, FR-Beef, RO-Mixed).

Climate change was the environmental challenge mentioned in all case studies, and manifested itself in different ways: increasing drought frequency and changing rainfall patterns, harming grassland and crop

Table 17.1. *Overview of the main challenges in the SURE-Farm case studies and their closeness to critical thresholds according to stakeholders' perception*

Type	Challenge	BG-Arable	DE-Mixed&Arable	UK-Arable	BE-Dairy	FR-Beef	ES-Sheep	PL-Horticulture	IT-Hazelnuts	NL-Arable	RO-Mixed	SE-Poultry
Economic	Low prices and price fluctuation	C	A	C	P	P	P	S	S	P	N	P
	High production costs			C			A			C		
	Unbalanced value chain		P	P	P	P		P	P		P	P
	Competition with foreign markets		P	P	P	P		P	P		P	
	Technology adaptation			P								P
	Limited use of insurance	P		P				P				
	Dependency on alternative off-farm income			P				P			P	
	Import competition			P				P			P	
	Production failure											P
Environmental	Climate change (extreme weather events)	C	C	P	P	P	P	S	N	S	A	V
	Plant or cattle diseases			P		P		P			V	
	Conflicts with wild fauna						N		S	C		
	Low soil fertility quality		P	P	P							
	Water scarcity		P		P			P	P			
	Excess of nutrients	P								P	P	P
	Soil erosion							P				P

285

Table 17.1. (*cont.*)

Type	Challenge	BG-Arable	DE-Mixed&Arable	UK-Arable	BE-Dairy	FR-Beef	ES-Sheep	PL-Horticulture	IT-Hazelnuts	NL-Arable	RO-Mixed	SE-Poultry
Social	Depopulation/lack of labour	C	P	P			A	S			P	P
	Changing consumer preferences	P	P	P			A	P				P
	Low attractiveness		A									
	Poor infrastructure		A									
	Change in technology											C
	Lack of successors	P	P	P		P	P	P			P	P
	High societal expectations	P	P		P	P		P			P	P
	Poor quality of life		P				P					
Institutional	Continuous change of laws and regulations	S	S	P	P	P	P	C	S	C	P	
	Economic laws and regulations			A					S		S	A
	Environmental and animal welfare regulations			S				P	C		P	A
	Complicated administrative procedures		P			P		P				P
	Lack of long-term vision in policy	P		P	P			P				
	High land prices		P		P		P					

Agricultural trade and regulation	P				P	
Delay in rural development policies						P
Brexit (uncertainty and loss of subsidies)		P				
Unequal aids distribution				P		

Empty cells indicate that the challenge is not perceived a major in the farming system. A "P" indicates the Presence of the challenge as major in the farming system, but its proximity to the threshold was not assessed by the stakeholders. Other letters indicate the level of proximity to thresholds as indicated by stakeholders, namely: Not close to critical threshold ("N"); Somewhat close to critical threshold ("S"); Close to critical threshold ("C"); At or beyond critical threshold ("A"). For BE-Dairy the relationships of challenges with critical thresholds were not assessed, for FR-Beef they were assessed with a desk study (i.e., without stakeholder involvement).

Source: Reidsma et al. (2019); Accatino et al. (2020); Paas et al. (2021c) and elaboration from chapter authors.

productivity in extensive livestock, permanent, mixed, and arable systems; heat waves, harming chicken health and egg quality (SE-Poultry); and out-of-season frosts (PL-Horticulture). Stakeholders mentioned diseases as a major concern in both arable (especially NL-Arable and BG-Arable) and livestock systems (especially FR-Beef and DE-Arable&Mixed). Specific environmental challenges regarded, for example, conflicts with wild faunas (attack by wolves in ES-Sheep, although not close to critical threshold), excess of nutrients, soil erosion, low soil fertility, and water scarcity.

Social challenges regarded both internal (e.g., ageing of the farmers and difficulty to find successors) and external processes (high societal expectation about practices, social distrust, and changing of consumer preferences). The lack of successors was linked to the lack of attractiveness of farming (FR-Beef, ES-Sheep), because of high workload, unfavourable work-life balance, low attractiveness of the area, poor infrastructure (BG-Arable, ES-Sheep), poor cultural and social opportunities (DE-Arable&Mixed, even deemed at or beyond critical threshold). In BG-Arable, stakeholders pointed out the difficulty to transfer knowledge and technology: workers, due to ageing, might be reluctant to learn about new technologies. In RO-Mixed, young people often go abroad to work in the agricultural sector of western European countries. Some farming systems were subject to increasing public distrust regarding farming practices (FR-Beef), with a special attention to animal welfare (SE-Poultry). In DE-Arable&Mixed some farmers showed their discomfort about the very high societal expectations. Changes in consumer preferences consisted, e.g., in the lowering of lamb meat consumption (ES-Sheep). For SE-Poultry, change in technology was mentioned as a challenge of concern (close to critical threshold).

Institutional challenges regarded strict regulations, the administrative and bureaucratic burden, and the frequent changes in the rules. Frequent changes in regulations were widely mentioned and considered at least somewhat close to critical threshold in four case studies (BG-Arable, DE-Mixed&Arable, PL-Horticulture, IT-Hazelnut, NL-Arable). Strict regulations were mentioned, e.g., in SE-Poultry especially in relation to animal welfare standards. Administrative and bureaucratic burden was perceived as a cost by farmers in terms of money and time. In IT-Hazelnut the inefficiencies in the regional system were mentioned to cause delays in the CAP payments; in PL-Horticulture, bureaucracy added complication in regard to the many workers coming from Ukraine and agricultural land trade. For UK-Arable, the main institutional challenge was BREXIT, an over-arching challenge bringing other issues such as uncertainty about the future regulations and loss of the EU subsidies.

17.4 Functions of Farming Systems

In this section we present the assessment of functions in current systems, the identification of alternative systems, and the performance of functions in alternative systems. Regarding these assessments we present the higher-level principles emerging from a comparison across all farming systems, occasionally discussing particularities of specific farming systems.

17.4.1 Functions in Current Systems

Beyond the marked differences among case studies (Figure 17.1), we observed some common elements. First, in all case studies functions were perceived to have different performances and were assigned different importance. Second, stakeholders perceived food production to perform moderate to high in all case studies, while functions related to the social domain ('Quality of life' and 'Attractiveness of the area') performed consistently low to moderate. Two exceptions were observed in which policy changes led to lower economic viability and finally to lower food production: for ES-Sheep the decoupling of payments from production pushed non-land-owning farmers to rent hectares for maintaining payment rights; for PL-Horticulture the access to the EU provoked a lowering of product prices. Third, stakeholders tended to assign a higher importance to economic viability but, at the same time, they considered this function to perform poor to moder-ately. Exceptions were IT-Hazelnut and RO-Mixed: for IT-Hazelnut the reason was found in the high profitability of hazelnuts, produced in high quantities in the region. For RO-Mixed the reason was found in the subsidies, which covered an important share of costs in small farms.

Different relative performances were observed, across farming systems, among 'Food production'; 'Economic viability' and environment-related functions ('Natural resources' and 'Biodiversity and habitat'). In the arable systems the perceived performance of

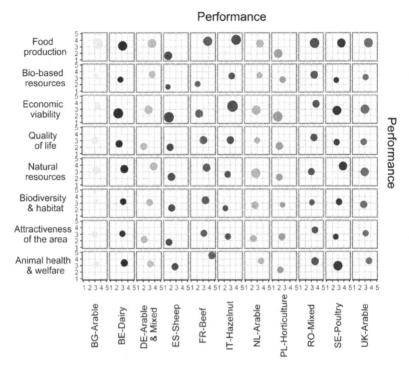

Figure 17.1 Perceived performance and importance of functions as assessed by stakeholders in the SURE-Farm case studies. Perceived performance is indicated on both the x- and y-axis to allow comparability among functions within a case study (vertically), and among case studies for a function (horizontally). The radius of the circles is proportional to the importance assigned. *Source*: Elaborated from Reidsma et al. (2020b).

'Food production' and 'Economic viability' was on average higher than in other systems, while environment-related functions were perceived to perform lower. The studied arable systems of western Europe (NL-Arable, UK-Arable, DE-Arable&Mixed) have historically invested more in the improvement of food production and economic viability, than in the improvement of public functions. In BG-Arable, stakeholders stated that food production was generally perceived not compatible with the conservation of natural resources in general, and nature conservation was considered more under the responsibility of policy-making rather than being a farmers' goal. In other cases, both 'Food production' and environment-related functions performed relatively well. In RO-Mixed this was favoured by the access of Romania to the EU in synergy with local policies and awareness about the importance of public goods. For FR-Beef the farming system is built upon a synergy between extensive beef production and maintenance of the landscape. In the ES-Sheep, the low performance of private functions, especially 'Food production', linked to the reduction of the number of sheep in the region, has decreased the contribution of the sector to nature conservation.

In our ecosystem service data assessment, we compared the multifunctionality of farming systems with the multifunctionality of their surrounding regions. We identified two groups: (i) farming systems that enriched the multifunctionality of the region providing a relatively rich array of ecosystem services and (ii) farming systems that were mostly focused on food production and reduced the diversity of ecosystem services provided in the region. Within group (i), IT-Hazelnut brought ecosystem services intrinsically connected to the presence of permanent crops (e.g., carbon storage, recreation potential); extensive livestock systems (ES-Sheep and FR-Beef) provided ecosystem services related with recreation potential and, in the case of FR-Beef, also erosion control. Within group (ii), BG-Arable was formed by monocultures poor in habitat quality and decreasing organic matter in soils; RO-Mixed decreased most of the public goods of the surrounding region (especially carbon storage, pollutant removal, habitat quality); NL-Arable, PL-Horticulture, DE-Arable&Mixed removed public goods to the surrounding region already poorly multifunctional; and SE-Poultry was clearly disconnected from the surrounding region which was mostly occupied by forests; UK-Arable was classified into group (ii) according to data analysis, but in participatory workshops stakeholders reported practices aimed at increasing some ecosystem services, such as carbon sequestration (e.g., practices of no-tillage, cover crops).

Participatory workshops and the ecosystem service assessment provide complementary information. For FR-Beef and RO-Mixed the multifunctionality of ecosystem services is confirmed by stakeholder perception, while this is not the case for ES-Sheep. For SE-Poultry, stakeholders perceive good performance of 'Natural resources'; however, elaboration of data suggests a separation between the broiler system and the surrounding forest. In DE-Arable&Mixed, data indicate poor performance of ecosystem services, but from a local stakeholder perspective, the presence of mixed crop–livestock systems are argued to ensure the maintenance of natural resources. For IT-Hazelnuts the system performs well with ecosystem services, but the intensive character of the system causes concerns among system actors. Results from the two methods align for PL-Horticulture and the arable systems. Overall, the participatory workshops provided information that is missing in satellite data about ecosystem services such as management practices that might contribute to ecosystem services provision.

17.4.2 Alternative Systems

For each farming system, three particular cases were considered in interaction with stakeholders: maintenance of the *status quo*, system decline when critical thresholds would be exceeded, and alternative systems for the future that could enhance sustainability and resilience. For each case study, at least one type of proposed alternative system was characterized by an increased use of technology. Examples are the investment in precision agriculture for NL-Arable, shelter farming in PL-Horticulture, technological innovation in IT-Hazelnut, use of robots in SE-Poultry, precision farming in BG-Arable, and advanced practices of pasture management in ES-Sheep. In many cases, the proposed alternative systems were related to organic and/or nature-inclusive agriculture (NL-Arable, UK-Arable, DE-Arable&Mixed, RO-Mixed, PL-Horticulture, IT-Hazelnut) and enhancement of diversification such as diversification of crops in BG-Arable, development of alternative crops in NL-Arable and RO-Mixed, and the achievement of fodder self-sufficiency in SE-Poultry. Other alternative systems were mostly specific to case studies, such as different forms of collaborations within the farming system (BG-Arable, NL-Arable, RO-Mixed), the valorization of products (BG-Arable, IT-Hazelnut), improvement of the attractiveness of the region (DE-Arable&Mixed), and valorization of the products locally processed and transformed (IT-Hazelnut).

17.4.3 Functions in Future Systems

In case the *status quo* is maintained in the future, no significant improvements were expected in functions' performances and some function indicators were perceived to likely decrease, such as 'Quality of life' (UK-Arable) and 'Economic viability' (BE-Dairy, ES-Sheep). However, in some case studies (IT-Hazelnut, SE-Poultry, NL-Arable), a moderate improvement was expected for the functions that are already performing moderately to well (especially 'Food production').

Stakeholders indicated that when critical thresholds are exceeded, most of the functions might worsen their performance. The most critical function was 'Economic viability': it was seen as the most urgent to improve, as in the longer term it may cause lower 'Attractiveness of the area' and therefore decrease the availability of labor to realize 'Food production'. In regard to 'Natural resources', UK-Arable and NL-Arable were perceived close to thresholds concerning soil quality, which directly affects the production of food.

Function performances were perceived to be different depending on the alternative systems. Still, some commonalities were observed: (i) Stakeholders were aware of the existence of trade-offs, i.e., not all functions could be improved at the same time. (ii) In many alternative systems, food production was expected not to change or only moderately improve, meaning that this function was not targeted as a priority to improve. (iii) 'Economic viability' and, when discussed, also 'Other bio-based resources', 'Attractiveness of the area', 'Animal health & welfare' were often expected to improve from moderately to strongly; 'Natural resources' and 'Biodiversity & habitat' were often expected not to change or moderately improve.

17.5 Generic Resilience in Farming Systems

17.5.1 Resilience Attributes and Capacities in Current Systems

When linking the strategies implemented in the current systems to resilience attributes, we observed that 38% of the strategies positively contributed to the resilience attribute "Reasonably profitable" (Figure 17.2). Many strategies also contributed to "Building human capital", "Socially self-organized", "Infrastructure for innovation", "Response diversity", "Functional diversity" and "Coupled with local and natural capital (production)". There seems to have been a lack of attention for improving "Optimal redundancy of crops, nutrients, and water", and for the "Spatial heterogeneity at landscape level".

17.5.2 Resilience Attributes and Capacities in Future Systems

The strategies identified by stakeholders to reach alternative systems were relatively more focused on strengthening "coupled with local and natural capital", both regarding production and legislation. Strategies to improve these resilience attributes include improving soil quality, improving circularity, reducing inputs, using varieties adapted to local

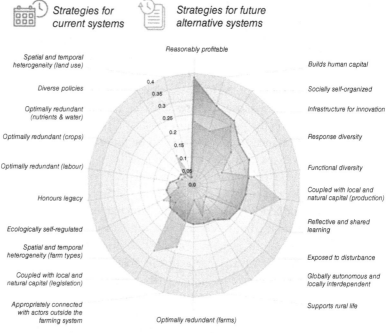

Figure 17.2 The contribution to resilience attributes of the identified strategies implemented and proposed in farming systems. The darker line shows the ratio of (past) strategies implemented for current systems contributing to an attribute, and the lighted line the ratio of future strategies for alternative systems contributing to an attribute. Attributes are ordered, starting with the attribute to which most past strategies contributed (based on Reidsma et al., 2020a).

climatic conditions, local branding, and policies that support this. The following attributes were more often strengthened when compared to strategies already implemented: "diverse policies" (although on average not mentioned often), "coupled with local and natural capital (legislation)", "appropriately connected with actors outside of the farming system", "coupled with local and natural capital (production)", "functional diversity", and "ecologically self-regulated".

17.6 Link among Functions and Resilience Attributes with System Dynamics

Causal-loop diagrams confirmed an alignment among functions and resilience attributes with the same goals. For instance, an improvement

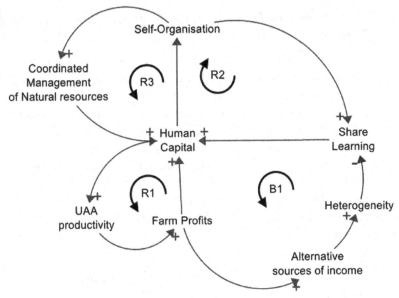

Figure 17.3 A causal loop diagram showing how economic, social, and environmental functions and attributes are related. An R refers to reinforcing and a B to balancing feedback loop. *Source*: Reidsma et al. (2020a).

of economic functions mainly enhanced "reasonably profitable", and social functions enhanced "supports rural life". Some cross-dimension relationships were observed. For example, "reasonably profitable" would benefit not only economic functions but also social and environmental functions (R1 in Figure 17.3). Similarly, "building human capital" would benefit not only social functions but also economic and environmental functions (R2 and R3 in Figure 17.3). However, economic functions could harm "Supports rural life" and "Spatially and temporally heterogeneity" (B1 in Figure 17.3).

17.7 Insights from the Integrated Resilience Assessment of Current and Future Systems

We explored the linkage between resilience and sustainability. Insights from our analysis showed that current systems are on average characterized by poor to moderate resilience and poor to moderate sustainability, whereas visions for future systems enhance the role of sustainability as a condition for achieving resilience.

17.7.1 Sustainability Dimensions Are Currently Not Addressed in a Balanced Way

Our assessment revealed that the main focus of our case studies was on food production, whereas other environmental, economic, and social functions were often overlooked. Strategies implemented in the past revealed that much attention was given to the attribute "reasonably profitable": while this led to an increase in food production, it did not improve economic viability for the farmers. The strategies ensured a certain robustness in the past, but economic viability remained close to perceived critical thresholds in many farming systems. The need to ensure economic viability induces myopia among farming system actors, as long as performance in the environmental and social domain is considered to be acceptable.

17.7.2 Lack of Sustainability Corresponds to a Lack of Resilience

Insights from our assessment suggested that the unbalanced attention to sustainability dimensions corresponds to poor resilience. First, according to stakeholders' input, the *status quo* is not resilient: if it is maintained for the future, most functions would likely not improve or deteriorate; in the case of exceeding critical thresholds, most functions are expected to strongly worsen. Second, in a current situation where sustainability dimensions are not equally addressed, challenges are currently present and most of them are close to critical thresholds (Table 17.1). The existence of common challenges raises concern about the resilience of European agriculture: current farming systems are under stress. Above all, economic issues are perceived as extremely critical by stakeholders. In addition, some of the challenges are internally generated (e.g., lack of successors and workforce), meaning that the current configurations generate problems. Third, the system dynamics analysis assessed that focusing on production and economic functions would erode resilience attributes.

17.7.3 Sustainability and Resilience for the Future

The view of stakeholders for future systems was clearly characterized by a joint improvement of sustainability and resilience, especially in regard to environmental and social aspects. The analysis performed with system dynamics showed that functions promote resilience attributes and *vice versa*. This suggests that there are pathways towards the joint improvement of sustainability and resilience. In the literature some studies highlighted the linkage among environmental and social functions and resilience. According to Altieri et al. (2015), resilience to extreme climate events is higher for systems that integrate ecological processes in their configuration and practices via, e.g., diversification, polycultures, crop-livestock systems, and organic soil management. Concerning the social component, studies highlight the importance of, e.g., creating a learning environment, enhancing the capacity of community self-organization (Berkes, 2007), and ensuring a good quality of life (Darnhofer, 2010) to promote resilience.

17.8 Improving the Sustainability and Resilience of European Farming Systems

We cannot consider farming systems as places for food production only. This is recognized in the literature (see Darnhofer et al., 2010), in our SURE-Farm approach, and also by the stakeholders involved in our study. Local stakeholders showed awareness about the importance of all the aspects of sustainability for promoting resilience. The functions enhanced in future systems were first of all economic viability, but also attractiveness of the region, natural resources and biodiversity, habitat quality, and animal welfare. The enhancement of resilience attributes such as "coupled with the local and natural capital" and "ecologically self-regulated" in future systems showed the importance of integrating ecosystem services into farm management.

Our assessment suggested that economic problems hinder the promotion of sustainability and resilience (Reidsma et al., 2020b). Although farmers are exposed to both economic and social challenges, they assigned a high importance to the function "Economic viability" and a low importance to social functions ("Attractiveness of the area" and "Quality of life"), revealing that economic issues are perceived as most urgent. Helping farmers with economic problems is therefore surely recommendable, but in the light of our findings also very challenging. The analysis of the challenges points out that all farming systems experience economic problems, but these have different context-specific origins and are ruled by different mechanisms. It is important to design diagnosis tools that monitor specific farming systems and study value chains, effects of subsidies, and other elements that might be important factors that help explain the low profitability of farming. When the burden of low profitability is removed, farmers are expected to be able to change their view from short-term to long-term and promote local solutions aimed at improving environmental and social aspects (Darnhofer, 2010).

Climate change was highlighted as a serious challenge, assuming different forms in the different case studies. Insurance schemes mostly provide only a temporary solution, without really transforming the system. Resilience-thinking and a number of resilience attributes enhanced in the alternative systems proposed by stakeholders suggest that promoting ecosystem services and nature-based solutions can make farming systems more robust to climate change (see also Altieri et al., 2015). For all of this, research needs to be supported and accelerated, as well as the spread of innovation practices (Herrero et al., 2020).

To cope with societal issues, it is of course of primary importance to promote practices among farmers that meet the consumer expectations, are environment-friendly and good for society. In this regard, we especially mention the continuous improvement of animal welfare, which is at the core of both consumer and producer values, even if our analysis denoted different perceptions about the performance of this function. Initiatives should promote communication and dialogue with the civil society. Moreover, some action should be taken to improve the attractiveness of the areas and of farming. Last but not least, the institutional context was often seen as a source of stress for farmers. Strict regulations, frequently changing regulations, excessive administrative burden are all things that can be directly addressed by governments and policy-makers.

17.9 Conclusion

We aimed at identifying factors that promote resilience and sustainability of farming systems, focusing on the link between the two. Our results show that sustainability and resilience are related and strengthening their link improves both. In the current systems, strategies were mainly focused on increasing economic functions, leading to trade-offs in the environmental and social domain. For the future of European farming, systems resilience can be improved when synergies are searched, identified, and enhanced, so that environmental, economic, and social aspects can sustain one another.

References

Accatino, F., Paas, W., Herrero, H., et al. 2020. D5.5 Impacts of future scenarios on the resilience of farming systems across the EU assessed with quantitative and qualitative methods. Sustainable and resilient EU farming systems (SURE-Farm) project report, EU Horizon 2020 Grant Agreement No. 727570.

Altieri, M. A., Nicholls, C. I., Henao, A. and Lana, M. A. 2015. Agroecology and the design of climate change-resilient farming systems. *Agronomy for Sustainable Development* 35, 869–890.

Berkes, C. 2007. Understanding uncertainty and reducing vulnerability: Lessons from resilience thinking. *Natural Hazards* 41, 283–295.

Cabell, J. F. and Oelofse, M. 2012. An indicator framework for assessing agroecosystem resilience. *Ecology and Society* 17, 18.

Daily, G. C. (ed.). 1997. *Nature's Services*, vol. 3. Washington, DC: Island Press.

Darnhofer, I. 2010. Strategies of family farms to strengthen their resilience. *Environmental Policy and Governance* 20, 212–222.

Darnhofer, I., Fairweather, J. and Moller, H. 2010. Assessing a farm's sustainability: Insights from resilience thinking. *International Journal of Agricultural Sustainability* 8, 186–198.

Fischer, J., Gardner, T. A., Bennett, E. M., et al. 2015. Advancing sustainability through mainstreaming a social-ecological systems perspective. *Current Opinion in Environmental Sustainability* 14, 144–149.

Herrera, H., Kopainsky, B., Appel, F., et al. 2018. D5.1 Impact assessment tool to assess the resilience of farming systems and their delivery of private and public goods Sustainable and resilient EU farming systems (SURE-Farm) project report, EU Horizon 2020 Grant Agreement No. 727570.

Herrero, M., Thornton, P. K., Mason-P'Croz, D., et al. 2020. Innovation can accelerate the transition towards a sustainable food system. *Nature Food* 1, 266–272.

Kinzig, A. P., Ryan, P., Etienne, M., et al. 2006. Resilience and regime shifts: Assessing cascading effects. *Ecology and Society* 11, 20.

Lebacq, T., Baret, P. V. and Stilmant, D. 2013. Sustainability indicators for livestock farming. A review. *Agronomy for Sustainable Development* 33, 311–327.

Maes, J., Fabrega, N., Zulian, G., et al. 2015. Mapping and assessment of ecosystems and their services: Trends in ecosystems and ecosystem services in the European Union between 2000 and 2010. Luxembourg: Publications Office.

Meuwissen, M. P. M., Feindt, P. H., Spiegel, A., et al. 2019. A framework to assess the resilience of farming systems. *Agricultural Systems* 176, 102656.

Paas, W., Accatino, F., Antonioli, F., et al. 2019. D5.2 Participatory impact assessment of sustainability and resilience of EU farming systems. Sustainable and resilient EU farming systems (SURE-Farm) project report. EU Horizon 2020 Grant Agreement No. 727570.

Paas, W., Coopmans, I., Severini, S., van Ittersum, M., Meuwissen, M. and Reidsma, P. 2021a. Participatory assessment of sustainability and resilience of three specialized farming systems. *Ecology and Society* 26, 2.

Paas, W., San Martín, C., Soriano, B., van Ittersum, M. K., Meuwissen, M. P. M. and Reidsma, P. 2021b. Assessing future sustainability and resilience of farming systems with a participatory method: A case study on extensive sheep farming in Huesca, Spain. *Ecological Indicators* 132, 108236.

Paas, W., Accatino, F., Bijttebier, J., et al. 2021c. Participatory assessment of critical threshold for resilient and sustainable European farming systems. *Journal of Rural Studies* 88, 214–226. https://doi.org/10.1016/j.jrurstud.2021.10.016

Reidsma, P., Spiegel, A., Paas, W., et al. 2019. D5.3 Resilience assessment of current farming systems across the European Union. Sustainable and resilient EU farming systems (SURE-Farm) project report, EU Horizon 2020 Grant Agreement No. 727570.

Reidsma, P., Paas, W., Accatino, F., et al. 2020a. D5.6 Impacts of improved strategies and policy options on the resilience of farming systems across the EU Sustainable and resilient EU farming systems (SURE-Farm) project report, EU Horizon 2020 Grant Agreement No. 727570.

Reidsma, P., Meuwissen, M. P. M., Accatino, F., et al. 2020b. How do stakeholders perceive sustainability and resilience of EU farming systems? *EuroChoices* 19, 18–27.

Richardson, G. P. 2011. Reflections on the foundations of system dynamics. *System Dynamics Review* 27, 219–243.

Rotmans, J. and van Asselt, M. 1996. Integrated assessment: A growing child on its way to maturity. *Climatic Change* 34, 327–336.

Schader, C., Baumgart, L., Landert, J., et al. 2016. Using sustainability monitoring routine (smart) for the systematic analysis of trade-offs and synergies between sustainability dimensions and themes at the farm level. *Sustainability* 8, 274.

Sterman, J. (ed.). 2000. *Business Dynamics: Systems Thinking and Modeling for a Complex World*. Boston: Irwin/McGraw-Hill.

van Ittersum, M. K., Ewert, F., Heckelei, T., et al. 2008. Integrated assessment of agricultural systems – A component-based framework for the European Union (SEAMLESS). *Agricultural Systems* 96, 150–165.

Walker, B. and Salt, D. (eds.). 2012. *Resilience Practice: Building Capacity to Absorb Disturbance and Maintain Function*. Washington, DC: Island Press.

18 | A Resilience-Enabling Environment for Farming Systems

Patterns and Principles

ERIK MATHIJS, JO BIJTTEBIER,
FRANCESCO ACCATINO, PETER H.
FEINDT, CAMELIA GAVRILESCU,
GORDANA MANEVSKA-TASEVSKA,
MIRANDA P. M. MEUWISSEN,
FRANZISKA OLLENDORF, MARIYA
PENEVA, CAROLINA SAN MARTÍN,
SIMONE SEVERINI, ALISA SPIEGEL,
MAURO VIGANI, KATARZYNA
ZAWALIŃSKA AND ERWIN WAUTERS

18.1 Introduction

Farming systems (FSs) operate in biophysical, political, social, economic and cultural environments, which are often far from stable. Frequently or unfavourably changing conditions can affect FS performance, i.e., the delivery of FS functions (such as food production or ecosystem services). The dimension and direction of the changes of the environment are often uncertain and there are many unknown unknowns, i.e., events that cannot be imagined currently nor their likelihood. This also means that it is not always clear how FSs have to evolve to perform well in the future, since we do not know how that future will look like. Hence, the institutional and socio-economic environment in which FSs are embedded should at the same time provide some direction to FSs, but also help FS actors keep their options open and facilitate their flexible and smooth responses (Mathijs and Wauters, 2020). An important policy implication is that to address the resilience issues of FSs, it is not enough to transfer a constant stream of transfer payments to compensate for the lack of resilience of these systems, as is the approach taken in the Common Agricultural Policy (CAP) where most resources are devoted to income support through direct payments. Rather, policy but also private agrifood actors should assist FS actors to build resilience capacities, starting with coping capacity (robustness) (see Chapter 1) – which can, amongst others, be enhanced through some kind of safety net but could be done through other approaches as well – but extending to responsive capacities (adaptability and transformability) through creating an enabling environment that supports adaptations and transformations (Buitenhuis et al., 2020).

A FS is a system hierarchy level above the farm at which properties emerge resulting from formal and informal interactions and interrelations among farms and non-farm actors to the extent that these mutually influence each other (Meuwissen et al., 2019). The environment can then be defined as the context of a FS on which FS actors have no or little influence. Hence, actors belonging to the environment may be food processors, retailers, financial institutions, technology providers, consumers, policy makers, implementation agencies, the judicial system, etc. This concept corresponds to the institutional environment, as defined by Lynggaard (2001), who has distinguished three domains of farmers' institutional environment: (1) the farmer/market domain that is preoccupied with exchange between economic actors, (2) the farmer/policy domain that entails public intervention into the farming sector and (3) the farmer/farming community domain that encompasses professional aspects of farming, such as associations, schools, advisory bodies and research institutions. The aim of this chapter is to formulate principles for an enabling environment that fosters the resilience of FSs in Europe based on a retrospective analysis of concrete challenges and responses to them. The chapter also seeks to translate these principles into recommendations on how public and private actors and institutions in the enabling environment can support the resilience of FSs.

18.2 Methodology

To investigate how the institutional environment enables or hinders FS resilience, we expanded the original SURE-farm resilience framework to analyse how resources and institutions were mobilised in both the FS and environment and how they affected resilience capacities in the past, i.e., following a set of challenges and adverse events in the past ten years. For this, a five-step methodology was followed. The analysis was performed for eleven case studies: large-scale arable farming in Northeast Bulgaria, intensive arable farming in Veenkoloniën, the

Netherlands, arable farming in the East of England, large-scale corporate arable farming with additional livestock activities in the Altmark in East Germany, small-scale mixed farming in Northeast Romania, intensive dairy farming in Flanders, extensive beef cattle systems in the French Massif Central, extensive sheep farming in Northeast Spain, high-value egg and broiler systems in Southern Sweden, small-scale hazelnut production in Lazio (central Italy) and fruit and vegetable farming in the Mazovian region, Poland.

Step 1: Identification of the FS and enabling environment actors and institutions

This step details the first step of the SURE-farm resilience framework (i.e., the identification of FSs in their own locality, see Chapter 1), by identifying all relevant actors and institutions in the enabling environment. In order to ensure that all relevant actors and institutions are included in the analysis, both formal and informal institutions on the one hand and public and private institutions on the other were considered. Formal institutions include legally codified rules and regulations (e.g., fiscal policy, private standards, CAP, nitrate directive); informal institutions equally guide actors' practices and interactions between them but not formally codified (e.g., local customs with regards to cooperation, level of representation in policy design, common visions on the ideal farm). Public (including all government levels and domains) as well as private (including business actors such as processors, retail, farmers) institutions and civil society organisations in both the FS and the enabling environment were considered.

Step 2: Identification of challenges and adverse events in the last ten years

This step coincides with step 2 of the SURE-farm resilience framework, but details broaden the characterisation of stresses following Maxwell (1986) to obtain better insight into the dynamics of challenges:

• A shock: sudden changes that are usually difficult to predict, such as the COVID-19 crisis or the Russian embargo.
• A trend (or stress): gradual changes that are usually easier to predict than shocks but not necessarily less important. Examples are increasing societal pressure to produce more sustainably, declining

real farm gate prices, and increasing pressure on land from non-agricultural stakeholders.

- Noise (normal variation): the kind of variation that occurs regularly, unlike a shock, and usually less challenging than stress (trends). Examples are typical weather variability, moderate price volatility and typical rainfall variability.
- Cycles. This is a type of change which does not often occur (any-more) in socio-ecological systems such as FSs, but some challenges could be in this category. Commodity price cycles are an example. Hence, this category is mentioned here for the sake of completeness.

Between 5 and 10 challenges or adverse events that the FS had faced in the last decade were described in each case study. The type of challenge may matter as the dynamics of reactions in the FSs and the enabling environment may be different for different types of challenges.

Step 3: Analysis of reactions

This step replaces steps 3, 4 and 5 of the SURE-Farm resilience framework by taking a more dynamic perspective. More specifically, for all or a sub-set of identified challenges, a number of analytical steps were taken. The following questions were used for orientation:

- How were challenges perceived to influence the delivery of FS functions and did this threat materialise, i.e., what has been the actual impact?
- To what extent were challenges anticipated by actors in the FS and in the enabling environment?
- How did the FS cope with challenges (referring to robustness)? Here, for the ease of analysis and interpretation (as data are often only available at farm level) the FS is narrowly defined as the set of farmers in the FS, classifying the other actors as part of the enabling environment. A further question was, what role the enabling environment played in these coping reactions?
- How did the FS (so mainly the farmers) respond (referring to adaptation and/or transformation) to the challenges, and again were they assisted (or hindered) by the enabling environment?

Step 4: Pattern analysis

In order to explore the resilience-enabling or constraining effect of the environment (and more specifically its impact on resilience capacities), the identified actions were interpreted using systems archetypes. Kim (2000: 2) defines systems archetypes as a 'class of tools that captures the "common stories" in systems thinking – dynamic phenomena that occur repeatedly in diverse settings. They are powerful tools for diagnosing problems and identifying high-leverage interventions that will create fundamental change'. Archetypes capture the vicious circles in acting and thinking that are usually depicted as causal loop diagrams, and explain how these vicious circles lead to undesirable outcomes. For instance, Brzezina et al. (2017) have used systems archetypes to analyse the development of organic farming in Europe. Oberlack et al. (2019) carried out a systematic review of archetype analysis in sustainability research, including the main motivations for and limitations to carrying out this type of analysis. The reader is referred to Kim (2000) for an overview of systems archetypes used in this analysis.

Step 5: Cross-case analysis

Cross-case analysis was carried out using all eleven cases to investigate whether the same patterns or systems archetypes were found, but also to match these patterns to the type of challenge. In other words, do patterns of acting and thinking differ when reacting to shocks or trends. This allowed us to identify leverage points or principles for the enabling environment to change from hindering to fostering FS resilience, for each archetypical problem has a set of archetypical solutions that break the vicious circle. These principles were illustrated by examples of an enabling environment identified in the various case studies.

18.3 Patterns in the Enabling Environment

In this section, we discuss the archetypes that occurred most often in the case studies. We refer to Mathijs et al. (2021) for an analysis by case study. Four archetypes were found across a number of case studies: (1) a pattern in which mitigating symptoms prevail over finding structural solutions (fixes that fail/shifting the burden), (2) a pattern in which actions are taken to downplay the challenge itself (eroding goals), (3) a pattern in which the enabling environment inhibits FS action (limits to success) and (4) a pattern in which too much attention is given to particular solutions (success to the successful). We illustrate each of these patterns with examples from the various FS case studies.

Archetype 1: Fixes That Fail / Shifting the Burden

In this pattern, a challenge triggers a coping reaction in which the enabling environment provides external interventions to mitigate the symptoms generated by the challenge rather than providing a structural solution to the challenge (fixes that fail). Moreover, such interventions may produce a side effect that undermines the structural solution in the long run (shifting the burden).

This pattern occurs when the following conditions prevail:

- The challenge cannot be sufficiently absorbed by the FS or business actors in the enabling environment without substantial loss of income (insufficient coping capacity), triggering a request to the enabling environment to mobilise resources or change rules.
- The financial losses are large enough, and the interests of those hurt are represented well enough to trigger action by government (a form of connectedness).
- Responsive capacity is insufficient, which can have several reasons: solutions are not known, adjustment costs are too high, vested interests in the status quo, etc.

Actions are primarily taken by government, based on the financial reserves it can mobilise or the amount of leeway that exists to temporarily change certain regulations. This may be enough when the challenge is temporary and/or the impact is relatively small, but when the challenge persists, reappears or spreads, the problem also reappears (e.g., extreme weather events, price drops, lack of labour). Also some private actors may lobby to put resources into fighting the symptoms rather than into structural solutions, due to the vested interests they have in maintaining production at current levels.

Moreover, in this pattern, mobilising resources or changing rules to cope with the challenge undermines the development and implementation of structural solutions. Strictly speaking this is always the case, as resources mobilised for developing symptomatic solutions cannot be devoted for developing structural solutions. However, we could argue that as long as effects are not irreversible, such resource allocation only results in a delay, not in the impossibility of a structural solution.

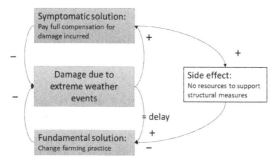

Figure 18.1 Causal loop diagram of the shifting-the-burden archetype.

Hence, an important condition for a shifting-the-burden pattern to occur is that the coping strategy involve actions with implications that are relatively difficult to revert (for instance, the destruction of certain resources or the creation of technical, economic or institutional lock-ins). This pattern has been observed in all case studies, following different types of challenges, both as a reaction to shocks and to trends.

Reactions to shocks such as extreme weather events fit this pattern well. The enabling environment – primarily government – frees up reserves to pay out farmers for income losses. When the government keeps doing this unconditionally, farmers have no incentive to invest in solutions in which they adapt towards a system that is less exposed to these types of events (see Figure 18.1). This was found in the British, Polish, French, Spanish, Dutch and Belgian case studies. For instance, in the French beef FS, droughts induced farmers to change land use and cropping for feed, i.e., they reacted to the decreased grassland productivity by reducing permanent grassland while increasing cereal production and temporary grassland. In addition, farmers increased feed purchases from providers external to the FS. Structural solutions, in contrast, would imply adapting the system towards more drought tolerance through improved practices and technologies and even different cattle breeds.

In the Dutch starch potato FS, the processing cooperative increased prices paid to farmers following a decrease in EU subsidies, so that farmers did not need to adapt their production plan. However, this reduced the incentive for farmers to reduce their specialisation in starch potatoes, which had made them vulnerable in the first place. A similar pattern could be observed in response to nematode pressure: rather than applying a more extended crop rotation, farmers intensified potato production, using seemingly more resistant varieties. The innovative varieties, however, were later found not to be resistant to new strands of nematodes.

The pattern was also observed in the Spanish lamb FS, where income support was identified as a fix that failed. The FS has been under economic pressure due to decreasing national lamb consumption, but this trend was not picked up by the FS and its enabling environment. One reason was that FS actors were too occupied with short-term challenges to notice emerging trends (low anticipatory capacity). At the same time, the enabling environment fostered primarily solutions aimed at increasing robustness, such as marketing campaigns to promote lamb consumption, which failed to compensate the strong counter trend.

Reactions to price volatility also seem to fit this pattern well. For instance, the 2009 milk price drop was regarded as a shock by most actors in the Belgian dairy FS, even though it was part of a long-term trend: dairy farmers in most of the EU were becoming more increasingly exposed to price volatility as a result of market liberalisation and reduced border protection after the CAP reforms since 1992. Farmers exhibited some coping capacity by using buffer capacity (financial reserves, off-farm income), networks and relationships (negotiating solutions with suppliers and banks, possibly including transfer of property), savings on costs, early culling and delayed investments. The enabling environment acted swiftly to increase coping capacity, mainly through the mobilisation of public resources, i.e., market measures intervention and income support measures (EU), bridging loans (Flanders) and a temporary bonus on milk prices paid to farmers (which retailers passed on to consumers). At the same time, limited signs of responsive capacity were observed: the FS did not really adapt or transform.

Another observed example of the fixes-that-fail archetype is when FSs insufficiently deliver public functions, such as keeping natural resources in good condition, e.g., through too many harmful emissions. Technical fixes that reduce the amount of emissions per unit of production are a frequent response, even if their implementation typically requires mandatory regulation. However, over time these kinds of fixes often fail and the challenge remains or even grows more severe. The root cause may be the density of intensive farming practices, e.g., high spatial concentration of livestock in a certain area, which would require more fundamental solutions than reducing emissions per animal.

A final example are the problems related to land ownership in North-East Bulgaria, where the privatization of state-owned land resulted in land fragmentation and unclear property rights. During the last three decades many solutions have been searched for, but the radical changes which are needed to force land owners to be interested in long-term decisions are still only discussed, e.g., property taxes, to take responsibility in land management and to be accounted for damaging soil quality.

All these examples involve actions by the FS and the enabling environment that aim to strengthen robustness and coping capacity in the short run, but that neither address the challenge itself nor support an adaptation of the FS that would reduce exposure to the challenge. As a result, FS actors may become dependent on external support that reduces the symptoms of an ongoing or exacerbating root problem.

Archetype 2: Eroding Goals

A challenge creates a gap between a goal and the actual condition. In this pattern, rather than taking actions to improve conditions, actors adjust the goals by, e.g., downplaying the challenge or redefining or reinterpreting the problem, in order to justify inaction.

This pattern occurs when the following conditions prevail:

- The challenge is a trend of which the impact has not yet fully materialised, e.g., as a loss of income or public goods, because the effect is delayed or absorbed by the FS.
- The impact is erroneously perceived as small, because, for example, the cause–effect relationship between trend and damage might be ambiguous due to other conflating factors, or the trend itself is being underestimated, or resources are invested in shielding the FS from the challenge.

This pattern not only involves a lack of anticipatory capacity so that the challenge is not adequately identified, but also deliberate action to deflect attention from the challenge. A typical example is the shifting of a deadline for reaching a goal in order to delay action or in the hope that the problem will 'go away'. This pattern can result in a situation

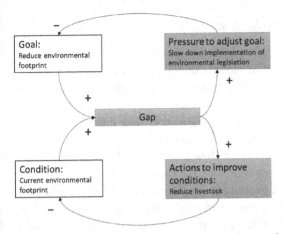

Figure 18.2 Causal loop diagram of the eroding-goals archetype.

that ultimately cannot be solved anymore (which is why it is often referred to as the 'boiling frog' archetype).

The pattern was observed in several of the SURE-Farm case studies, often in response to societal concerns. For instance, the Belgian dairy FS is exposed to growing civil society opposition against intensive livestock farming, based on environmental, animal welfare and health concerns. This trend has been present for quite a long time. Whereas initially meat production was the main target, recent years have seen a large increase in opposition and now also milk producers have become a target. Efforts of the FS actors and the enabling environment mainly focused on removing or slowing down the trend. Examples include public relations campaigns to off-set negative images – from communicating about progress being made to attempts to discredit civil society organisations and individuals – and lobbying to delay new environmental or animal welfare regulation, or to lower proposed standards (Figure 18.2).

A similar pattern could be observed in the Spanish lamb FS where neglect of the seriousness of several simultaneously occurring challenges (decreasing consumption, access to land, etc.) led to insufficient response by both FS actors and the enabling environment. One observed reaction – marketing campaigns to increase consumer demand – had the intention to slow down or even reverse the trend.

Archetype 3: Limits to Success

In this pattern, actions taken by the FS actors, for instance to address challenges, are inhibited or slowed down by actions in the enabling environment. FS actors are willing to take coping or responsive actions, but they are constrained by the enabling environment, for instance because of too much bureaucracy ('red tape'), insufficient resources devoted to the proposed solutions, etc.

An example of this pattern was found in the Polish horticulture case. High levels of bureaucracy following the request for more precise data, monitoring and control procedures and variability of regulations have provided an important impediment to developing solutions. The low attractiveness of working in the agricultural sector which leads to a lack of farm successors, can also be explained with the limits to growth archetype, in cases where the enabling environment has a negative impact on the attractiveness of the sector. In several cases, the weak bargaining power of farmers in the value chain was identified as a constraining factor (Figure 18.3).

Archetype 4: Success to the Successful

In this pattern, all resources are allocated to a limited number of apparently successful actions (or actors) while neglecting other, necessary activities (and/or institutions). Here, the FS and the enabling environment allocate resources unequally to different solutions or actors. For instance, allocation of resources may be conditional on the ability to demonstrate earlier success. As a result, underinvestment in other solutions and actors is likely, which may backfire if the supported solution turns out to be insufficient or even detrimental.

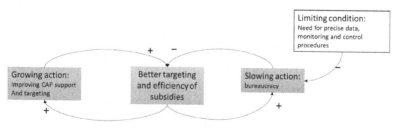

Figure 18.3 Causal loop diagram of the limits to growth archetype.

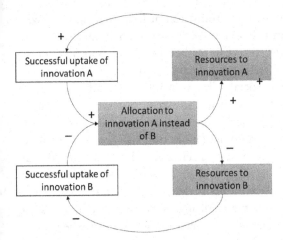

Figure 18.4 Causal loop diagram of the success-to-the-successful archetype.

This archetype can also create path dependencies where it becomes difficult to change the course of action (Figure 18.4).

An example of this pattern could be observed in the German case study. The Altmark region has been allocated relatively few resources for infrastructure and public services by the enabling environment due to its spatial remoteness and low population density, which further exacerbates the marginalisation of the region. Lack of infrastructure, such as fast internet, reduces opportunities (e.g., internet-based sales, precision farming).

18.4 Guiding Principles to Create a Resilience-Enabling Environment for Farming Systems

To derive guiding principles underpinning an enabling environment that fosters (rather than hinders) FS resilience, we identified interventions in the four archetypes that lead to more FS resilience (addressing robustness, adaptability and transformability). On this basis, we derived six principles for a resilience-fostering enabling environment.

Principle 1: When a FS cannot cope with a challenge to avoid loss of FS functions, the enabling environment – and particularly government – should provide temporary resources to cope with the adverse consequences of the shock, but only to buy time while working on a remedy that addresses the causes of the vulnerability.

Before a system can adapt or transform, it first needs to cope with the challenges at hand to survive. When a system cannot cope with challenges in the short run, it can neither adapt nor transform in the long run, as adaptation requires sufficient resources of all types, i.e., financial, legal, human, social. This principle is already very much being applied in most FSs, often to the extent, however, that it gives rise to the 'shifting-the-burden' archetype, whereby all resources are allocated to solving the symptoms. This in turn reduces the pressure to implement more adequate solutions. Hence, in line with the subsidiarity principle, it is important to note that resources from the enabling environment should only be mobilised when a FS cannot cope with itself, for instance because the challenge is too systemic and has too large impacts. Ideally, rules should determine when and when not to intervene. Furthermore, the temporary nature of the compensation is crucial, albeit depending on the type of damage. If the compensation pervades, the incentive to adapt decreases. Hence, these temporary resources should only be used to buy time while working on long-term solutions. An example is an extreme weather event, such as drought. When the drought hits, only coping is possible which justifies the mobilization of resources. However, resources should also be invested into structural solutions that reduce the impacts of droughts, such as the development of drought-tolerant varieties or implementing risk-transferring insurance. To the degree that droughts are related to climate change, mitigation of greenhouse gases should also be part of the solution.

Principle 2: Before shocks occur, resources should be shifted towards building anticipatory capacity as well as responsive capacity, to prevent dependence on external solutions and to increase the future coping capacity of the FS. This should be done jointly by all types of actors in the FS and the enabling environment.

Often, unusual or new types of shocks are regarded as a very exceptional event that does not require systemic changes. However, the occurrence of a severe shock should be used to put the development of anticipatory capacities on the agenda. Too often, actors limit their agenda to alleviating the immediate consequences – if they are too severe to be coped with by the FS (Principle 1) – and to discuss whether the same type of event might occur again. Typical failures are that actors in both the FS and the enabling environment underestimate the likelihood that a severe event occurs again (e.g., the 'one-in-thousand-years' flood event) or that they focus on responses to a narrow range of possible shocks from well-known types of events. Instead, actors should increase resilience to a range of possible and accumulating shocks through enhancing adaptability and transformability. Besides anticipatory capacities, responsive capacities should be built.

Examples from the case studies include responses to extreme weather events and price drops. Experiences from previous shocks can be used to better cope with the challenge next time (also by better anticipating the challenge) and to prepare adaptation strategies. Such a pattern can be observed in the EU dairy sector: the first price drop in 2007 was largely unexpected, but the next price drops were better anticipated and more coping strategies (e.g., financial futures instruments) and adaptation or transformation strategies (e.g., shift to organic farming) were applied. However, this only occurred after the third price drop, and, in between, time and resources were lost. Private sector involvement (e.g., the development of distribution channels for organic produce) is important to ensure that these strategies are economically feasible.

Principle 3: The enabling environment should assist the FS to detect, assess and address long-term trends that challenge the future resilience of the FS in a way that increases future robustness, including through adaptation or transformation to that trend in the long run.

To avoid an eroding-goals pattern, trends should not only be detected, but their potential impact on the future resilience of the FS should also be forecasted in order to raise awareness and create a sense of urgency to invest resources in adaptation rather than in the status quo. This can help to enhance robustness vis-à-vis identified challenges, which often requires the implementation of adaptations or transformations. If FS actors have insufficient resources to invest in such anticipatory capacity, public-private investment is needed. However, private actors should be convinced of the importance of foresight activities. Communication should be improved not only regarding identified challenges but also regarding the potential of possible solutions. An example of this principle has been the consistent approach of the Swedish government towards raising environmental standards in the poultry sector.

Principle 4: The enabling environment should foster a potential diversity of responses, rather than focusing too much on a limited set of actions.

It is important to keep options open and set up learning experiments related to a wide set of structural solutions for several reasons. First, resilience tends to thrive with diversity. Second, focusing on one particular strategy may backfire if the strategy turns out to have negative consequences. Keeping options open and fostering a diversity of potential options does not inherently mean that the actual response should be diverse, as sometimes coordinated action might be preferred. However, the diverse potential of possible solutions should be regarded, instead of focusing only on a limited set. This also refers to Principle 6, which considers a more systemic in-depth analysis of the root causes of challenges on the one hand, and the vulnerability of the FS to these challenges on the other hand. A too superficial analysis of the problem (or even a deliberate redefining of the problem) can cause blindness for possible solutions. For instance, government agencies may request advisory services to analyse multiple strategic options in the framework of the CAP's support for advice.

Principle 5: The ensemble of the FS and its enabling environment should develop a sufficient degree of ambidexterity, i.e., find a balance in putting resources in immediate versus future challenges.

Since structural solutions require time, there is a danger of under-investment in such solutions. Therefore, a good balance should be achieved between investing resources in strategies enhancing coping capacity of FS on the one hand and in strategies enhancing responsive (and thus future coping) capacities on the other. Unhealthy patterns are situations in which resources are invested in coping strategies only or when decisions are made without having sufficiently invested in adaptation strategies, such as in the neonics and Brexit case in the UK, because this situation can lead to shifting-the-burden problem, whereby the problem returns, possibly even more severe. A healthier pattern occurs when the enabling environment provides the right incentives for adaptation, while spending enough resources to overcome temporary income losses following, for instance, stronger regulation. Examples include the Swedish poultry FS and the French beef FS, where supply chain actors assist the FS by developing quality labels leading to price premiums.

Principle 6: A more systemic, data-driven and in-depth analysis of the root causes of challenges on the one hand and of the drivers of FS vulnerability to these challenges on the other hand needs to be carried out, to avoid a redefinition of the problem and the implementation of solutions that do not fix the real problem.

Often, the identification of solutions to deal with challenges is already largely determined by how the challenge itself and the reasons for vulnerability to the challenge are defined. Such redefinitions (or too superficial definitions) of the challenge lead to fixes that do not solve the real problem, or do only temporarily, and hence lead to archetypes like fixes that fail or to the problems associated with the success to the successful archetype. The advice would be to detect the root causes of the symptoms, which can lead to real solutions that increase FS resilience.

18.5 From Principles to Recommendations

The systems analysis has led to six principles to guide FSs and enabling environment actors on how to stimulate resilience. Translating these principles into concrete recommendations needs to be done through a regional and/or FS-specific approach. Recommendations will mainly relate to actors, resources and institutions. Actors are those within the FS and within the environment of the FS. These actors make decisions on how to use resources (e.g., financial resources, human capital, social capital) and several principles refer to these decisions. Principle 1, for instance, suggests that resources should be used less for symptom-oriented solutions and more for causal solutions. Institutions include formal (e.g., regulation, policy instruments, directives) and informal institutions, which are socially shared rules, usually unwritten and created and enforced beyond formal channels. They can refer to attitudes, routines, ideologies and habits, especially regarding how actors interact with each other. These institutions influence either directly or indirectly which decisions actors are making, amongst others with respect to the use of resources. Hence, concrete recommendations for implementing the principles in practice will also include recommended changes to formal and informal institutions.

The approach for moving from principles to recommendations should be on co-creation with the variety of actors that are relevant for a specific FS, and its approach has to be based on the guidelines of a policy dialogue (see Wauters et al., 2021). A policy dialogue is part of the policy- and decision-making process and intends to develop and/or implement a change following a round of evidence-based discussions/ workshops/consultations on a particular subject. Policy dialogues bring diverse interest groups to the table, focus on a regulatory, policy, or planning issue that is of common interest, and seek to formulate practical solutions to complex problems. Policy dialogues, often called roundtables or task forces, are not entirely new, and are in some countries even common practice. We advocate to set up a resilience-enhancing policy dialogue gathering all relevant actors from a FS and its environment.

Several success factors for an effective policy dialogue have been described in the literature (e.g., Dovlo et al., 2016). First, they should have a collectively agreed-upon purpose, in this case, improving the resilience of FSs. It is further important that the issue be 'ripe', meaning that all stakeholders around the table have experienced or at least observed the problem sufficiently and have become frustrated by repeated manifestations of the issue. This means that a policy dialogue to improve the resilience of FSs – hence to improve its anticipating capacities, coping capacities (robustness) and responsive capacities (adaptability and transformability) – should not be confused with a policy dialogue to stimulate adaptations and/or transformations to improve its sustainability. Convincing stakeholders that supporting resilience is more than supporting robustness and protecting the status quo, through evidence and data, will be crucial, otherwise the policy dialogue will not be based on a common understanding of the problem and a shared goal. This aspect will likely be the most critical part of a policy dialogue, since some of the identified system archetypes and the proposed principles suggest that actors will find it difficult to agree on what the issues are and hence what the proposed solutions need to be. Principle 6, for instance, suggests that often too superficial an analysis or even a deliberate reframing of the problem is being done, leading to fixes that fail. The identification of the widespread existence of the system archetype 'eroding goals', whereby actors devote resources to downplaying societal pressure and political restrictions, suggests that not all actors agree that the fundamental issue that challenges their resilience is that the FS does not comply with societal expectations, but rather the societal expectations themselves.

Second, it is imperative that the preparation of the policy dialogue include the gathering of information and data. The presentation of these data can give rise to the co-creation of evidence through a reflection process in which the data is interpreted in a collaborative manner. As such, the co-produced evidence will help justify the implementation of change, referring to the point earlier, and will help in identifying possible directions of change. The evidence for a policy dialogue to improve the resilience of FSs should be based on a systemic assessment of resilience in its many forms, as described in the framework for analysing resilience by Meuwissen et al. (2019), of which many examples can be found in this book. Specific attention should be given to enhancing trust in data and evidence through improving its quality, internal and external validity and reliability, to avoid different stakeholders using certain evidence to support their own position and disregard or even discredit evidence that is not in favour of their position.

Third, the policy dialogue should be formalised and have a commonly agreed time frame. It should be formalised in order to stimulate subsequent implementation of the changes so that it does not remain a voluntary exercise. An a priori agreed time frame will help in setting priorities, devoting resources and keeping stakeholders engaged. There can (and should) be room for informal dialogues and working groups outside the formal channels and meetings but they should all feed into the formal processes. It should avoid taking decisions outside the official platform.

Fourth, a monitoring and evaluation framework should be agreed upon in order for stakeholders to be able to monitor progress, receive early feedback and observe results of the implemented changes (Bijttebier et al., 2021). The policy dialogue should be used to agree on desired changes and key performance indicators as measures of success. The monitoring and evaluation framework should pay attention not to privilege interests that can easily be linked to clearly measurable – and often pre-existing – indicators, such as profits or production volumes, but also consider aspects such as social well-being, biodiversity and mental health.

References

Bijttebier, J., Mathijs, E., Wauters, E. (2021). D6.5 From principles for enabling resilience to implementation: Implementation and monitoring protocol. Sustainable and resilient EU farming systems (SURE-Farm) project report, EU Horizon 2020 Grant Agreement No. 727520.

Brzezina, N., Biely, K., Helfgott, A., Kopainsky, B., Vervoort, J., Mathijs, E. (2017). Development of organic farming in Europe at the Crossroads: Looking for the way forward through system archetypes lenses. *Sustainability*, 9(5), Art.No. 821.

Buitenhuis, Y., Candel, J., Feindt, P., et al. (2020). Improving the resilience-enabling capacity of the common agricultural policy: Policy recommendations for more resilient EU farming systems. *EuroChoices*, 19(2), 63–71.

Dovlo, D., Nabyonga-Orem, J., Estrelli, Y., Mwisongo, A. (2016). Policy dialogues – The "bolts and joints" of policy-making: Experiences from Cabo Verde, Chad and Mali. *BMC Health Services Research*, 16(4), 327–335.

Kim, D. H. (2000). *Systems Archetypes I: Diagnosing Systemic Issues and Designing High-Leverage Interventions*. Waltham, MA: Pegasus.

Lynggaard, K. (2001). The farmer within an institutional environment: Comparing Danish and Belgian organic farming. *Sociologia Ruralis*, 41(1), 85–111.

Mathijs, E., Bijttebier, J., Accatino, F., et al. (2021). D6.2 Report on combinations of conditions for successful and unsuccessful fostering of resilience in agricultural sectors. Sustainable and resilient EU farming systems (SURE-Farm) project report, EU Horizon 2020 Grant Agreement No. 727520.

Mathijs, E., Wauters, E. (2020). Making farming systems truly resilient. *EuroChoices*, 19(2), 72–76.

Maxwell, S. (1986). Farming systems research: Hitting a moving target. *World Development*, 14(1), 65–77.

Meuwissen, M. P. M., Feindt, P. H., Spiegel, A., et al. (2019). A framework to assess the resilience of farming systems. *Agricultural Systems*, 176, Art. No. 102656.

Oberlack, C., Sietz, D., Bürgi Bonanomi, E., et al. (2019). Archetype analysis in sustainability research: Meanings, motivations, and evidence-based policy making. *Ecology and Society*, 24(2), 26.

Wauters, E., Mathijs, E., Coopmans, I., et al. (2021). D6.4 Roadmaps for the implementation of principles for a resilience enabling environment. Sustainable and resilient EU farming systems (SURE-Farm) project report, EU Horizon 2020 Grant Agreement No. 727520.

19 | Lessons Learned on Resilience from a Multi-scale Co-creation Methodology
From Regional to European Scale

BÁRBARA SORIANO, ISABEL BARDAJÍ,
YANNICK BUITENHUIS, DANIELE
BERTOLOZZI-CAREDIO, JEROEN
CANDEL, PETER H. FEINDT, MIRANDA
P. M. MEUWISSEN, WIM PAAS, PYTRIK
REIDSMA, CAROLINA SAN MARTÍN,
THOMAS SLIJPER, ALISA SPIEGEL
AND ALBERTO GARRIDO

19.1 Introduction

The farming systems (FSs) in Europe faces a broad array of challenges. The ability of FSs to deal with challenges can be assessed with the concept of resilience (Chapter 1). Assessing FSs' resilience is a complex issue (Folke, 2016; Meuwissen et al., 2020) and can benefit from the stakeholders involvement to move towards a better understanding of the dynamics and interactions that should be addressed. Co-creation is gaining interest as a method to involve stakeholders in reaching the applied research goals (Füller et al., 2011; Prahalad and Ramaswamy, 2004; Romero and Molina, 2009). Due to its interactive nature, co-creation facilitates innovation processes (Frow et al., 2011; Jaakkola et al., 2015) and leads to strong stakeholder engagement and awareness (Byrd, 2007; Carmin et al., 2003).

Co-creation activities can be conducted in physical and virtual modes. Focus groups and workshops are traditional physical meetings (Kamberelis and Dimitriadis, 2011; Nanz and Steffek, 2004; Wilkinson, 2004). Digital platforms (also called virtual communities) are rapidly gaining ground, providing stakeholders a new space for interaction and information and opinion sharing. There are several reasons explaining the importance of the digital platforms over the physical modes. First, the digital platforms overcome the physical barriers of the face-to-face activities, favouring the participation of stakeholders from different countries and the assessment of issues at multiple regional scales of integration. Second, the digital platforms offer the participants the option to run the online activities over a longer period of time, leading to closer relationships and sense of community (Füller et al., 2009; Gebauer et al., 2013). Third, digital platforms allow time flexibility for participants, meaning that they can select and participate in the online activities at any time (Füller et al., 2009; Sawhney et al., 2005; Stanke, 2016).

The aim of this chapter is to address how European FSs' resilience assessment can benefit from involving stakeholders using a multi-scale co-creation methodology. The co-creation activities were organized at two different spatial scales – regional and European scales – and combined physical and online stakeholder deliberations. According to Reed (2008), replication of participatory processes at multiple scales increases validity through comparison/triangulation and effectiveness as more relevant stakeholders can be involved.

The remainder of this chapter is structured as follows. First, the multi-scale co-creation methodology is explained. Second, the results are presented into two sub-sections: current resilience assessment and resilience in the future. Third, conclusions are drawn.

19.2 Multi-scale Co-creation Methodology

The multi-scale co-creation methodology consisted of conducting in parallel the same co-creation activities on the same resilience assessment topics at two different scales: the regional and European. To this end, two different co-creation modes were designed: physical meetings to co-create with stakeholders, who are knowledgeable and experienced in the farming system they belong to (FS stakeholders), and a digital co-creation platform to co-create with stakeholders, knowledgeable and experienced in the European FSs as a whole (European stakeholders). In total 360 stakeholders participated in the co-creation process: 233 FS stakeholders participated in physical meetings and 27 European stakeholders participated in the digital co-creation platform (Table 19.1). The stakeholders who participated in the physical meetings did not participate in the digital co-creation platform, and vice versa.

As Table 19.1 shows, the stakeholders were participating in co-creation activities related to current resilience assessment topics

Table 19.1. Topics in the current resilience and resilience in the future assessed by stakeholders in the physical meetings and the digital co-creation platform

Resilience assessment topics		Physical meetings			Digital co-creation platform
		Risk Management focus groups	SURE-Farm FOPIA-workshops	Co-design policy workshops	
		11 FS-78 FS stakeholders	11 FS-184 FS stakeholders	6 FS-71 FS stakeholders	27 European stakeholders
Current resilience	Challenges	■	■		■
	Functions	■	■		■
	Resilience attributes		■		■
	Resilience capacities		■	■	■
Resilience in the future	Improved strategies	■		■	■
	Resilience-enabling policies			■	■

Source: Own elaboration. Grey colour indicates that the resilience assessment topic was assessed in the corresponding co-creation mode

(Chapter 1): (i) Identify the challenges threatening the European FSs.[1] The perceived challenges are classified according to the duration of the impact of the challenge (shocks and long-term pressures) and its nature (economic, environmental, institutional and social) (Meuwissen et al., 2019). (ii) Identify and assess the performance of European FSs functions. Functions of the FSs are classified into two groups: the provision of public goods and private goods (Chapter 1). (iii) Assess the presence of resilience attributes in the European FSs. Stakeholders also participated in the assessment of topics related to resilience in the future: (i) Co-create improved strategies to deal with challenges. Strategies are classified in risk-sharing strategies and on-farm strategies. (ii) Co-design policies that enable resilience.

Co-creation activities provided quantitative and qualitative information regarding the stakeholders' perceptions on resilience topics at two different scales. Quantitative information was assessed by applying frequency analysis and analysing descriptive statistics. Qualitative information was assessed by following a qualitative analysis that entailed the elaboration and coding of collected information (Maxwell, 2005). As a result, convergent and divergent perceptions between FSs and European stakeholders were identified.

19.2.1 *The Physical Meetings*

A diverse set of physical meetings were organized through the whole project to involve the stakeholders in FS resilience assessment (Chapter 1). The activities conducted in three physical workshops were replicated on the digital co-creation platform.

Participatory sustainability and resilience assessment workshops (SURE-Farm FoPIA workshops) were held between November 2018 and March 2019 in eleven FSs.[2] The activities revolved around

---

[1] The activities defined to assess the challenges threatening FSs were different in the co-creation approaches. Participants in the focus groups agreed with the challenges previously identified in 1,890 farmer's surveys on risk perception and risk management decision making. In the digital co-creation platform, participants selected the ten most important challenges from a list of forty-five challenges threating European farming systems.

[2] FSs covered different sectors, farm types, products and challenges. They included large-scale arable farming in Northeast Bulgaria; intensive arable farming in Veenkoloniën, the Netherlands; arable farming in the East of England (United Kingdom); large-scale corporate arable farming with additional livestock

the assessment of the relevance and perceived performance of the FS functions, the strategies implemented to reduce the impact of the challenges on the FS functions, and the perceived presence of the resilience attributes and their perceived potential contribution to the FS resilience capacities (Reidsma et al., 2019).

Between April 2019 and September 2019, risk management focus groups were conducted in the eleven FSs. The aim of the focus group was to identify the challenges threatening the FSs and the strategies to deal with them as the basis to co-create improved resilience-enabling strategies. Stakeholders also assessed the contribution of risk management to FS resilience (Soriano et al., 2020). The focus groups built on results from a survey of 1,890 farmers on risk perception and risk management decision making (Spiegel et al., 2019).

Finally, between November 2019 and January 2020 co-design policy workshops were conducted in six FS.[3] The stakeholders were involved in identifying promising policy options for the CAP and its national implementations for maximizing its support to more resilient EU farming systems. In addition, a final workshop was organized in Brussels with fourteen Brussels-based experts from different backgrounds, to discuss and validate the national workshop and digital co-creation platform findings and share reflections on the proposed policy options (Buitenhuis et al., 2020; Candel et al., 2020).

The leaders of the SURE-Farm FoPIA workshops, risk management focus groups and co-designed policy workshops provided guidelines to conduct the activities in the same manner in every case study. The guidelines also described the selection criteria to invite participating stakeholders. The leaders of the workshops encouraged the participation of a wide variety of the stakeholders representing the FS actors, i.e. farmers and farmers' organizations, cooperatives, value chain actors,

---

activities in the Altmark in East Germany; small-scale mixed farming in Northeast Romania; intensive dairy farming in Flanders; extensive beef cattle systems in the Massif Central; extensive sheep farming in Northeast Spain; high-value egg and broiler systems in Southern Sweden; small-scale hazelnut production in Lazio, central Italy; and fruit and vegetable farming in the Mazovian region, Poland.

[3] They included intensive arable farming in Veenkoloniën, the Netherlands; arable farming in the East of England; intensive dairy farming in Flanders; extensive sheep farming in Northeast Spain; small-scale hazelnut production in Lazio, central Italy; and fruit and vegetable farming in the Mazovian region, Poland.

financial institutions, environmental and consumers' organizations, university and research centres and policymakers among others.

19.2.2 *The Digital Co-creation Platform*

The SURE-Farm digital co-creation platform operated from July 2018 to December 2019 aiming to assess and improve the resilience of FSs in Europe. The existing digital co-creation platforms are classified according to the degree of openness. In the "Crowd of people" digital platform participation is free, while access is limited in the "Group of experts" digital platform in which selected experts who meet certain specific criteria are invited to co-create innovations and breakthrough ideas (Orcik et al., 2013). The SURE-Farm co-creation platform is a group of expert digital platforms in which the following selection criteria were defined: (i) proven experience and background in the agricultural sector at national/European level; (ii) having knowledge about or surrounding risk management, policy, farm demographics and/or agricultural production; (iii) working in public or private organisations in any of the following activity areas: farmers organizations, policy-makers, insurance companies, banks, research centres and universities, value chain actors, environmental NGOs, consumer associations; and (iv) pertaining to one of the next staff category: experts, managers or directors.

The general goal of the digital co-creation platform was to assess the resilience of the European FSs. The online activities on the digital co-creation platform were organized under specific goals (challenges) (Figure 19.1) that correspond to key topics in resilience assessment.

The activities in the digital co-creation platform were carefully designed to attract the interest of the stakeholders. To this end, the activities were intuitive and demanded little time, were accompanied by a detailed explanation about the aim and how to conduct them and were organized under flexible schedules to facilitate participants to fulfil the activity. Furthermore the participation was intensely moderated to keep the participants engaged in the digital platform by: (i) sending weekly/biweekly newsletters with new activities on the platform, articles and videos of interest; (ii) running a repository of reports, scientific papers and videos; (iii) sending alerts on new entrants in the digital platform to encourage networks; (iv) sharing results of previous activities to foster two-way feedback; (v) defining and publishing

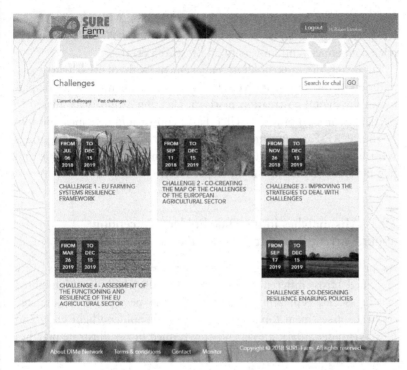

Figure 19.1 Interface of the challenges defined in the digital co-creation platform.
Source: SURE-Farm co-creation platform

rankings based on the participation in the activities; and (vi) awarding economic prizes to those topping the participation rankings. Two 500€ awards were granted to the top participants in challenges 1–4 (Figure 19.1) in May 2019 and two 250€ awards were granted to the top participants in challenge 5 (Figure 19.1) in December 2019.

Ninety-seven European stakeholders were contacted by e-mail, of which sixty logged-in the digital co-creation platform and twenty-seven actively participated in nineteen online activities. Stakeholders from eight European countries participated in the activities, where Spain and the Netherlands contributed the largest numbers of participants.[4]

---

[4] Participants per country: Spain (11), the Netherlands (6), United Kingdom (3), Germany (2), Switzerland (2), Belgium (1), France (1), Italy (1). Participants by activity sector: university/research center (9), financial institutions (7), farmers' organizations (6), policymakers (2), value chain actors (2), environmental NGOs (1).

Six sectors are were represented by participants, with a greater presence of farmers' organizations, financial institutions (banks and insurance companies) and university and research centres.

To foster the stakeholders' engagement with SURE-Farm goals, additionally, a representative selection of the stakeholders participating in the digital co-creation platform (steering group) was invited to participate in two physical SURE-Farm consortium meetings and join in the SURE-Farm partners' reflections on resilience. The meetings were held on 19 April 2018 and 25 September 2019, and nine and five EU stakeholders attended, respectively.

19.3 (Mis)matches in the Stakeholders' Perception about Current Resilience and Resilience in the Future

As presented in Figure 19.2, both matches and mismatches were identified across different co-creation methods. The boxes highlighted in grey scales represent mismatches in the perception on the key resilience assessment topics between EU stakeholders (light grey) and FS stakeholders (dark grey). The grey-framed boxes illustrate matches

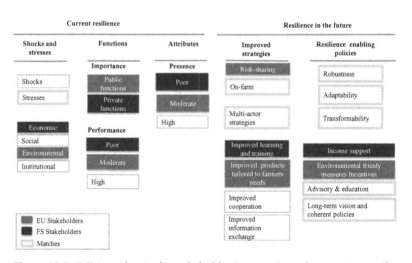

Figure 19.2 (Mis)matches in the stakeholders' perceptions about current resilience and resilience in the future.

Source: Own elaboration

between EU and FS stakeholders. When presenting the major results for perceived current resilience, we focus on the three elements of the resilience framework: shocks and stresses (Section 3.1.1), FS functions (Section 3.1.2) and resilience attributes (Section 3.1.3). As the major results for the assessment of resilience in the future, we distinguish between improved future risk management strategies to enhance resilience (Section 3.2.1) and policy recommendations aiming to enhance the resilience-enabling capacity of the CAP (Section 3.2.2).

19.3.1 Current Resilience

19.3.1.1 The Challenges of the EU Farming Systems
The findings in Figure 19.3 indicate that both European and FS stakeholders were more concerned about long-term pressures than shocks. However, different perceptions between stakeholders are identified regarding the nature of the perceived long-term pressures. European stakeholders perceived environmental long-term challenges, such as global warming, water scarcity and pollution, change in precipitation patterns and decline of pollinators, to be the main challenges to deal

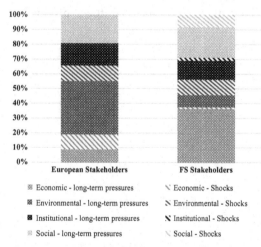

Figure 19.3 The stakeholders' perception of the challenges of the European farming systems. The percentage show the number of times the challenge has been mentioned by stakeholders in relation to the total number of mentions.
Source: Own elaboration

with in the future. In contrast, FS stakeholders were mostly concerned by economic long-term challenges, such as decline in profitability forced by constantly increasing production costs and decreasing food prices. This is in line with Assefa et al. (2017), who found that farmers, wholesalers, processors and retailers were more concerned about long-term price changes than with short-term price volatility. Social and institutional long-term pressures also concerned the stakeholders. For example, European stakeholders highlighted the lack of generational renewal and FS stakeholders noted farmers' quality of life.

19.3.1.2 The Functions of the EU Farming Systems

European stakeholders perceived a more balanced importance of functions at the European level than FS stakeholders at the regional level. As a result, greater importance is allocated to social and environmental functions by EU stakeholders, while FS stakeholders highlighted the importance of economic functions. FS stakeholders named provision of private goods, such as food production and economic viability, as the most important functions of the FS explaining that these functions could influence other FS functions. In contrast, European stakeholders nearly unanimously stressed on maintaining of natural resources and biodiversity and habitat – both public goods. Both European and FS stakeholders highlighted the importance of food production (Figure 19.4).

Figure 19.4 Perceived importance (size of circles) and performance (y-axis) of FS functions. Scale from 1 to 5; where 1: very poor, 2: poor, 3: moderate, 4: good, 5: perfect performance.
Source: Own elaboration

Regarding the performance of the functions, there was a consensus among European and FS stakeholders that the functions of the European FSs show a low performance. Performance of private functions was assessed higher by European stakeholders than by FS stakeholders. As for public functions, European and FS stakeholders reported similar low performance levels. Lower performance of food production perceived by FS stakeholders might be due to a link they perceived between food production and economic viability, i.e. stakeholders might perceive higher production to be necessary to maintain economic viability. For the EU stakeholders, rather a trade-off between food production and environmental and social functions might be more obvious. Indeed, trade-offs between economic or production functions on the one hand and environmental functions on the other hand are well studied at different levels. For instance, Teillard et al. (2017) show for France that selective optimization of either food production or ecosystem services at the regional level can provide a win-win solution at the national level. Similarly, Schulte et al. (2019) show that prioritization of a few out of multiple soil functions per member state of the EU can help to achieve goals at the EU level. Trade-offs at lower levels may indeed lead to better results at higher levels. Unfortunately, studies presenting a trade-off between social and environmental functions are not common. Low social performance can be related to multiple causes, including a bad public image, low profitability, lack of political willingness and lack of facilities in rural areas. These causes are hard to quantify and model, making participatory multi-level co-creation activities more suitable to perform multi-level trade-off and synergy analyses.

19.3.1.3 The Resilience Attributes of the EU Farming Systems
Having identified challenges and FS functions, stakeholders were asked to assess pre-defined resilience attributes – characteristics of the European FSs that are supposed to convey resilience to a system (Cabell and Oelofse, 2012). Both European and FS stakeholders agreed on the key resilience-enhancing attributes, namely: (i) "Reasonably profitable";[5] (ii) "Production being coupled with local and natural

---

[5] Individuals involved in agriculture are able to make a livelihood from the work they do without relying too heavily on subsidies (Cabell and Oelofse, 2012).

capital";[6] (iii) "Heterogeneity of farm types";[7] (iv) "Social self-organization";[8] and (v) "Infrastructure for innovation"[9] (Paas et al., 2019).

Stakeholders also agreed on the low presence of these attributes in the FS when explaining low performance of FS functions. Yet, European stakeholders were generally more positive about the presence of these resilience attributes at the European level, than FS stakeholders at the FS level. *Reasonably profitable* was perceived to have a low presence, but was expected by local and European stakeholders to perform as a buffer for many shocks. European stakeholders perceived a higher presence of *functional and response diversity* for the EU FSs, e.g. through insurance. *Heterogeneity of farm types* was also perceived to have a higher presence for the European FSs, which could be seen as the result of the aggregation of the diverse FSs each with their own degree of specialization. *Social self-organization* of the European FSs and its connections with actors outside FS boundaries was also perceived higher and probably relates to the fact that at the European level, policy development is included within the system boundaries. Regarding legislation, European stakeholders perceived that *legislations are moderately coupled with local and natural resources*. On the contrary, FS stakeholders perceived that policy goals and instruments do not meet the FS needs. *Reasonably profitable* is perceived to have a low presence currently, but is expected by European and FS stakeholders to perform as a buffer for many shocks. *Optimal redundancy* of farms was the only resilience attribute whose presence was perceived lower by European stakeholders than FS stakeholders. This attribute relates to generational renewal and lack of successors and may currently be seen as an opportunity for some FS actors to expand, while being a challenge for many policymakers at the national and European levels.

The more positive perception of the presence of resilience attributes of the European stakeholders compared to the FS stakeholders might

---

[6] The systems function as much as possible within the means of the bioregionally available natural resource base and ecosystem services (Cabell and Oelofse, 2012).

[7] Patchiness across the landscape (Cabell and Oelofse, 2012).

[8] The social components of the system are able to form their own configuration based on their needs and desires (Cabell and Oelofse, 2012).

[9] Existing infrastructure facilitates knowledge and adoption of cutting-edge technologies (e.g. digital) (Reidsma et al., 2019).

be related to several aspects: (i) at the EU level, the diversity in farming and the enabling environment is richer than the diversity within the FSs panel; (ii) European stakeholders may be better informed than FS stakeholders regarding response diversity, infrastructure for innovation, legislation and policies, e.g. new ways of insurance or innovative environmental management practices, including supporting policies at the EU level; and (iii) at the same time, European stakeholders might be less informed on how the effects of resilience attributes can trickle down to specific FSs, taking into account local conditions.

19.3.2 Resilience in the Future

19.3.2.1 Improved Strategies

Although both European and FS stakeholders mainly mentioned on-farm strategies (Figure 19.5), there are interesting differences between the stakeholder's perceptions with respect to on-farm strategies. The European stakeholders primarily mentioned strategies towards sustainable and efficient management of natural resources and adaptation to/mitigation of climate change: (i) improve chemical inputs (pesticides,

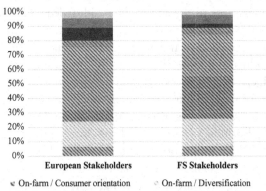

Figure 19.5 Strategies to deal with future challenges proposed by the stakeholders. The percentages show the number of times the strategy has been mentioned by stakeholders in relation to the total number of mentions. *Source*: Own elaboration

fertilizers) management, (ii) implement water and soil optimization strategies, (iii) transition to organic farming; (iv) adapt plant varieties and (v) design climate emergency response plans. The FS stakeholders clearly prioritized the strategies targeting economic measures, such as increasing profitability (reducing cost, increasing prices), dispose of financial buffers, gaining scale economy by increasing farm size (new building, lands acquisition), improving labour and workers management and adapting to new regulations. Reidsma et al. (2000) also found a mixed of technological and ecological strategies to deal with future challenges.

As for risk-sharing strategies, European stakeholders perceived insurance contracts to be the most interesting strategy to share risks with financial institutions. These results are in line with previous studies where insurance schemes are perceived as efficient tools to manage risk and uncertainty (Heyder et al., 2010; Meuwissen et al., 2001).

Stakeholders were also asked to design improved risk management strategies towards more resilient FSs. For this purpose, stakeholders identified actors involved in the risk management strategies, analysed their roles and generated ideas on how actors' performance could be improved for better risk management. Stakeholders provided more than 500 ideas. The assessment of the stakeholders' ideas led to four main pillars to improve risk management: (i) fostering learning and training, (ii) reinforcing knowledge and information exchange, (iii) promoting FS stakeholders' cooperation and (iv) adapting and developing new products and services tailored to farmers' needs. These pathways are interlinked, as information exchange is important to adapt insurance services to farmers' needs (Lunt et al., 2016), and cooperation enhances learning, training and advisory processes (Hermans et al., 2015). Yet, the European and FS stakeholders did not prioritize these improvements in the same manner. While FS stakeholders highlighted fostering learning and training, European stakeholders prioritized adaptation or definition of new products better suited to farmers' needs. As agriculture is constantly shifting and changing, farmers and other actors in the FSs were aware that they need to be up-to-date and participate in continuous learning and training programs on farm management, new technologies and financial planning. Although European stakeholders also perceived learning as a way to improve risk management, their ideas were mostly centred on the need for defining new income, contracts with suppliers and consumers, and insurance products. To this end, all four pathways are in line with the literature (Heyder et al., 2010; Meuwissen et al., 2001; Šūmane et al., 2018).

There was a general consensus between FS and European stakeholders that improving risk management requires joint actions, i.e. every actor involved in the strategies' implementation has the opportunity to improve risk management in FSs. It is not surprising that farmers and farmers' organizations were identified as the key actors to improve risk management in FSs being able to: (i) improve information exchange by keeping up-to date online information about prices, technologies, policies, new challenges, good practices in financial/management planning; (ii) foster joint training programs with other actors in the FSs regarding challenges, long-term management planning and cooperation; and (iii) enhance cooperation by collecting good practices in terms of cooperation in agriculture, creating networks at different regional levels and creating a joint job exchange for actors in FSs. According to the literature, local and regional learning communities are indeed important channels to share good practices, information and knowledge between farmers (Laforge and McLachlan, 2018; Thomas et al., 2020). Value chain actors, such as input providers and distributors, were also relevant to improve risk management. More specifically, value chain actors may (i) improve the provision of updated information about new technologies/products and joint initiatives and good practices in the value chain (also confirmed by Cholez et al., 2020), (ii) boost the training programs on sustainable practices and input/machinery usability options and look for new joint training programs with other actors in the FS, (iii) lease machinery for experimenting and (iv) develop a comprehensive contract along the supply chain. Finally, opportunities for financial institutions to improve risk management were proposed, namely (i) improve the information exchange by increasing the number of consultants in the rural areas with deep knowledge in the specificities of the FS; (ii) reinforce cooperation to exploit potential synergies between financing and insurances products; (iii) ensure less complex, automatic and digital access to financial services (apps); and (iv) adapt or develop new products to better fit farmer's needs. Examples of the latter include adapted debt payments to the farm cash flow, definition of beneficial conditions for high innovative and/or environmentally friendly projects, broadening guarantees and providing insurances to cover new environmental- and climate-change-related emerging risks based on satellite data.

19.3.2.2 Resilience-Enabling Policies

Comparison of the policy recommendations that followed from the workshops and the digital co-creation platform mainly revealed similarities in stakeholders' views on how policies can strengthen robustness, adaptability and transformability of European FSs.

More specifically, increasing incentives for adopting agri-environmental and climate measures were clearly recommended by European and FS stakeholders, such as converting the basic payments into more result-based payments related to agri-environmental and climate outcomes (though differences can be depicted in the FS). A much-preferred policy intervention, at both the FS and European levels was to increasingly encourage social learning processes for exchanging knowledge and promoting cooperation, e.g. through advisory services, training services, education programs and public-private collaborations. The CAP was regarded as having an important function of communicating about developmental directions for the future of European FSs. Such a long-term vision should be based on norms and priorities and a clear sense of the vulnerabilities of European FSs. Moreover, the CAP could include clear and coherent policy objectives and instruments that reinforce rather than undermine each other.

The results are in line with other project's deliverables. Feindt et al. (2019) found that the CAP and its national implementations support the robustness of different FSs to varying degrees, provide less support for adaptability and often even constrain transformability by incentivizing the status quo. In addition, Buitenhuis et al. (2019, 2020, chapter 4) concluded that the ways in which multilevel policy configurations enable or constrain the resilience capacities are experienced very differently across European FSs depending on the systems' context (regional context, challenges and national policy framework). These studies imply that developing policies for improving the resilience of FSs requires a comprehensive understanding of FSs' characteristics and contexts.

19.4 Conclusions

Three lessons are drawn from the application of the multi-scale co-creation approach on resilience assessment in SURE-Farm.

First, co-creation is an advisable method to engage stakeholders in research projects. The SURE-Farm experience shows that co-creation allowed the stakeholders to actively follow almost the whole lifetime of the project. Co-creation has been defined as a cross-sectional methodology in the project and hence its results fed into and enriched other research activities conducted to address the risk and challenge perception, the strategies to deal with challenges, the resilience impact assessment and the definition of enabling resilience policies.

Second, we learnt about the key advantages and shortcomings to overcome in future co-creation processes. Physical meetings allowed capturing the great diversity across FSs in Europe. This is a valuable insight to foster strategies and policies that respond to farming system characteristics and needs. Regarding the digital co-creation platform, one of the main challenges was to keep stakeholders engaged in the platform activities during the project lifetime. Learning from experience, digital co-creation platforms targeting complex issues require a solid multidisciplinary team of (i) researchers to set clear goals and formulate questions, (ii) co-creation experts to translate the goals and questions into simple and attractive digital activities, (iii) technical experts to develop the platform functionalities for performing designed activities and (iv) communication experts to keep stakeholders engaged. All these ingredients are essential for a successful digital co-creation process. Furthermore, flexible selection criteria are needed to adapt the potential participants to the participation needs to reach the co-creation goals.

Third, the multi-scale approach is one of the major contributions of the SURE-Farm co-creation process in resilience assessment. Working in parallel with stakeholders knowledgeable and experienced at the regional and European scales broadens the knowledge about resilience by identifying convergent and divergent perceptions on different resilience assessment topics. While we identified several matches in the perceptions, we observed some striking mismatches as well. On the one hand, European stakeholders prioritized environmental long-term stresses, public functions and risk management strategies targeting environmental challenges. On the other hand, we observed that FS stakeholders perceived economic challenges, private functions and economic risk management strategies as most important. The European stakeholders seem to be more optimistic when assessing resilience at the European FSs level.

The perceptions' divergence may have policy implications. Mismatches in the stakeholder's perceptions may explain the existing gap between the European policies, influenced and designed by European stakeholders', and the FSs' diverse needs illustrated by the FS stakeholders. The latter are mainly farmers and other mutual dependence actors who are close to business and remain primarily worried about the unsolved economic issues while European policies move forward to foster the greater balance between environmental and economic issues.

Finding the way to reduce this gap seems crucial to make the European FSs more resilient. Within the scope of agricultural policy, the CAP 2020, as it is defined in the proposal, succeeds in adding the eco-schemes defined by each Member State in the system of farm support mechanisms. Eco-schemes will be based on quite specific climate, geographical and socio-structural parameters. We thus conclude that the discrepancy might be solved within a common framework of support but flexible enough to stimulate the broad range of farmers' responses with the potential to success in their own context.

References

Assefa, T. T., Meuwissen, M. P. M. and Oude Lansink, A. G. J. M. (2017) Price risk perceptions and management strategies in selected European food supply chains: An exploratory approach. *NJAS – Wageningen Journal of Life Sciences*. Royal Netherlands Society for Agriculture Sciences, 80, 15–26. doi: 10.1016/j.njas.2016.11.002.

Buitenhuis, Y., Candel, J., Termeer, K., et al. (2019) D4.3. Policy bottom-up analysis – All case study report. SURE-Farm Deliverable (7527520). doi: 10.5281/zenodo.4349208

Buitenhuis, Y., Candel, J., Feindt, P. H., et al. (2020). Improving the resilience-enabling capacity of the Common Agricultural Policy: Policy recommendations for more resilient EU farming systems. *EuroChoices* 19(2), 63–71. https://doi-org.ezproxy.library.wur.nl/10.1111/1746-692X.12286.

Byrd, E. T. (2007) Stakeholders in sustainable tourism development and their roles: Applying stakeholder theory to sustainable tourism development. *Tourism Review* 62(2), 8. doi: 10.1108/16605370780000309.

Cabell, J. F. and Oelofse, M. (2012) An indicator framework for assessing agroecosystem resilience. *Ecology and Society* 17(1), art no. 18. doi: 10.5751/ES-04666-170118.

Candel, J., Feindt, P.H., Termeer, K., et al. (2020) D4.5: Policy recommendations for strengthening the Common Agricultural Policy's resilience impacts. SURE-Farm Deliverable (727520). doi: 10.5281/zenodo.4349506

Carmin, J. A., Darnall, N. and Mil-Homens, J. (2003) Stakeholder involvement in the design of U.S. voluntary environmental programs: Does sponsorship matter?. *Policy Studies Journal* 31(4), 527–544. doi: 10.1111/1541-0072.00041.

Cholez, C., Magrini, M. B. and Galliano, D. (2020) Exploring inter-firm knowledge through contractual governance: A case study of production contracts for faba-bean procurement in France. *Journal of Rural Studies* 73(July 2019), 135–146. doi: 10.1016/j.jrurstud.2019.10.040.

Feindt, P. H., Termeer, K., Candel, J., et al. (2019) D 4.2: Assessing how policies enable or constrain the resilience of farming systems in the European Union: Case study results. SURE-Farm Deliverable (7527520). doi: 10.5281/zenodo.4349078

Folke, C. (2016). Resilience (republished). *Ecology and Society, 21*(4).

Frow, P., Payne, A. and Storbacka, K. (2011) Co-creation: A typology and conceptual framework. Australian . & New Zealand Marketing Academy conference ANZMAC 2011, Australia.

Füller, J., Mühlbacher, H., Matzler, K. and Jawecki, G. (2009) Consumer empowerment through internet-based co-creation. *Journal of Management Information Systems* 26(3), 71–102. doi: 10.2753/mis0742-1222260303.

Füller, J., Hutter, K. and Faullant, R. (2011) Why co-creation experience matters? Creative experience and its impact on the quantity and quality of creative contributions. *R and D Management* 41(3), 259–273. doi: 10.1111/j.1467-9310.2011.00640.x.

Gebauer, J., Füller, J. and Pezzei, R. (2013) The dark and the bright side of co-creation: Triggers of member behavior in online innovation communities. *Journal of Business Research* 66(9), 1516–1527. doi: 10.1016/j.jbusres.2012.09.013.

Hermans, F., Klerkx, L. and Roep, D. (2015) Structural conditions for collaboration and learning in innovation networks: Using an innovation system performance lens to analyse agricultural knowledge systems. *Journal of Agricultural Education and Extension* 21(1), 35–54. doi: 10.1080/1389224X.2014.991113.

Heyder, M., Theuvsen, L. and Davier, Z. V. (2010) Strategies for coping with uncertainty: The adaptation of food chains to volatile markets. *Journal on Chain and Network Science* 10(1), 17–25.

Jaakkola, E., Helkkula, A. and Aarikka-Stenroos, L. (2015) Service experience cocreation: Conceptualization, implications, and future research directions. *Journal of Service Management* 26(2), 182–205.

Kamberelis, G. and Dimitriadis, G. (2011) Focus groups: Contingent articulations of pedagogy, politics and inquiry. *The Sage Handbook of Qualitative Research*, 4(March), 545–562.

Laforge, J. M. L. and McLachlan, S. M. (2018) Learning communities and new farmer knowledge in Canada. *Geoforum* 96(September), 256–267. doi: 10.1016/j.geoforum.2018.07.022.

Lunt, T., Jones, A. W., Mulhern, W. S., Lezaks, D. P. and Jahn, M. M. (2016) Vulnerabilities to agricultural production shocks: An extreme, plausible scenario for assessment of risk for the insurance sector. *Climate Risk Management* 13, 1–9. doi: 10.1016/j.crm.2016.05.001.

Maxwell, J. A. (2005) *Qualitative Research Design: An Interactive Approach*, 2nd ed. Newbury Park, CA: Sage.

Meuwissen, M. P. M., Huirne, R. B. M. and Hardaker, J. B. (2001) Risk and risk management: An empirical analysis of Dutch livestock farmers. *Livestock Production Science* 69(1), 43–53. doi: 10.1016/S0301-6226 (00)00247-5.

Meuwissen, M. P. M., et al. (2019) A framework to assess the resilience of farming systems. *Agricultural Systems* 176(June), 102656. doi: 10.1016/j.agsy.2019.102656.

Meuwissen, M. P. M., Feindt, P. H., Midmore, M., et al. (2020) The struggle of farming systems in Europe: Looking for explanations through the lens of resilience. *EuroChoices*. Forthcoming.

Nanz, P. and Steffek, J. (2004) Global governance, participation and the public sphere. *Government and Opposition* 39(2), 314–335. doi: 10.1111/j.1477-7053.2004.00125.x.

Orcik, A., Stojanova, T. and Freund, R. (2013) Co-creation: Examples and lessons learned from South-East Europe. *Proceedings of International Conference for Entrepreneurship, Innovation and Regional Development ICEIRD 2013*, (August 2014), pp. 36–44. doi: 10.13140/2.1.3035.4561.

Paas, W., et al. (2019) D5.2 Participatory impact assessment of sustainability and resilience of EU farming systems. Sustainable and resilient EU farming systems (Sure-Farm) project report, EU Horizon 2020 Grant Agreement No. 727520. doi: 10.13140/RG.2.2.25104.25601.

Prahalad, C. K. and Ramaswamy, V. (2004) Co-creating unique value with customers. *Strategy & Leadership* 32(3), 4–9. doi: 10.1108/10878570410699249.

Reed, M. S. (2008) Stakeholder participation for environmental management: A literature review. *Biological Conservation* 141(10), 2417–2431. doi: 10.1016/j.biocon.2008.07.014.

Reidsma, P., Meuwissen, M. P. M., Accatino, F., et al. (2020) How do stakeholders perceive the sustainability and resilience of EU farming systems? *EuroChoices* 19(2), 8–27.

Reidsma, P., Spiegel, A., Paas, W., et al. (2019) D5.3. Resilience assessment of current farming systems across the European Union. SURE-Farm Deliverable (727520).doi: 10.5281/zenodo.4351106

Romero, D. and Molina, A. (2009) Value co-creation and co-innovation: Linking networked organisations and customer communities. *Working Conference on Virtual Enterprises*, 307, 401–412. doi: 10.1007/978-3-642-04568-4_42.

Sawhney, M., Verona, G. and Prandelli, E. (2005) Collaborating to create: The Internet as a platform for customer engagement in product innovation. *Journal of Interactive Marketing* 19(4), 4–17. doi: 10.1002/dir.20046.

Schulte, R. P., O'Sullivan, L., Vrebos, D., Bampa, F., Jones, A., and Staes, J. (2019) Demands on land: Mapping competing societal expectations for the functionality of agricultural soils in Europe. *Environmental Science & Policy* 100, 113–125. doi: 10.1016/j.envsci.2019.06.011.

Soriano, B., Bardají, I., Bertolozzi-Caredio, D., et al. (2020) D2.6. Report on state and outlook for risk management in EU agriculture. SURE-Farm Deliverable (727520). doi: 10.5281/zenodo.4338357

Spiegel, A., Slijper, T., de Mey, Y., et al. (2019) D2.1. Report on farmers' perceptions of risk and resilience capacities – a comparison across EU farmers. SURE-Farm Project. doi: 10.5281/zenodo.4335942

Stanke, T. (2016) Co-creation with online communities: What are the benefits and risks for companies? Part 1: Co-creation and online co-creation communities, Brandba.

Šūmane, S., Kunda, I., Knickel, K., Strauss, A., et al. (2018) Local and farmers' knowledge matters! How integrating informal and formal knowledge enhances sustainable and resilient agriculture. *Journal of Rural Studies* 59(December 2017), 232–241. doi: 10.1016/j.jrurstud.2017.01.020.

Teillard, F., Doyen, L., Dross, C., Jiguet, F. and Tichit, M. (2017) Optimal allocations of agricultural intensity reveal win-no loss solutions for food production and biodiversity. *Regional Environmental Change* 17(5), 1397–1408. doi: 10.1007/s10113-016-0947-x.

Thomas, E., Riley, M. and Spees, J. (2020) Knowledge flows: Farmers' social relations and knowledge sharing practices in 'Catchment Sensitive Farming'. *Land Use Policy* 90(May 2019), 104254. doi: 10.1016/j.landusepol.2019.104254.

Wilkinson, S. (2004) Focus group research. *Qualitative Research: Theory, Method, and Practice* 2, 177–199.

20 Understanding and Addressing the Resilience Crisis of Europe's Farming Systems

A Synthesis of the Findings from the SURE-Farm Project

PETER H. FEINDT, MIRANDA P. M.
MEUWISSEN, ALFONS BALMANN,
ROBERT FINGER, ERIK MATHIJS,
WIM PAAS, BÁRBARA SORIANO,
ALISA SPIEGEL, JULIE URQUHART
AND PYTRIK REIDSMA

20.1 Introduction

The SURE-Farm project started with the assumption that Europe's farming systems are exposed to a variety of stresses and shocks which could culminate in a significant threat to the delivery of the private and public goods on which Europe's food security, rural livelihoods and many value chains depend. The notion of resilience had been adopted by the European Commission in response to concerns about increasing vulnerabilities of Europe's food systems. However, a comprehensive analysis of the factors that threaten or enhance the resilience of Europe's food systems was lacking. Within this broader context, the SURE-farm project focused on farming systems (see Chapter 1), thereby centring on the production element of Europe's food systems.

The composition of the SURE-Farm consortium emphasized three basic assumptions about what is required to understand and enhance the resilience of farming systems:

- first, a systemic approach that integrates a broad range of disciplines, from agricultural economics and rural sociology to agronomy, agroecology and political science;
- second, a context-sensitive approach that takes into consideration that the characteristics and social and biophysical environments of farming systems differ widely, and hence also their resilience challenges and needs;

- third, the systematic inclusion of the perspectives and experiences of actors within the farming system and its relevant environment.

To structure the enormous complexity of the topic, the SURE-Farm consortium developed an integrative framework to assess the resilience of farming systems (Meuwissen et al., 2019), which provides guidance to determine the composition and limits of differing farming systems, their main functions, challenges, resilience capacities and resilience-enhancing attributes (Chapter 1). The framework facilitates the identification of the resilience needs of a farming system. On this basis, resilience-enhancing strategies can be developed. These include risk management strategies (Chapter 2), strategies to address adverse demographic developments which lead to a lack of skilled labour and farm successors (Chapter 3), resilience-enhancing public policies (Chapter 4) and resilience-oriented agricultural practices (Chapter 5). The case studies (Chapters 6–16) demonstrate the diversity of resilience challenges, needs and strategies of Europe's farming systems. However, despite the differences, the integrated assessment across the case studies (Chapter 17) and the assessment of stakeholders in the co-creation platform (Chapter 19) clearly show that Europe's farming systems face a resilience crisis and that new approaches are necessary to create a resilience-enabling environment (Chapter 18).

This chapter aims to synthesize key findings from the SURE-Farm project. We first discuss key lessons about the resilience concept as a framework to understand the current resilience of Europe's farming systems and as a tool to develop strategies for improvement. We then establish why Europe's farming systems face a formidable and structural resilience crisis that is unlikely to improve without appropriate resilience-enabling strategies; this section also emphasizes the implications of the diversity of Europe's farming systems in terms of their resilience challenges, capacities and different resilience-enabling or constraining environments. On this basis, we formulate cornerstones for possible resilience-enhancing strategies. The chapter concludes with critical reflections and suggestions for further research.

20.2 Seven Lessons Learned on the Resilience Framework

The SURE-Farm framework to assess the resilience of farming systems builds on earlier work that has translated concepts from the analysis of social-ecological systems to bio-based production systems (Ge et al.,

2016), of which farming systems are one type. Inspired by the panarchy concept (Gunderson & Holling, 2002), the SURE-Farm framework emphasizes the temporal dimension and the interplay across different system levels for understanding the resilience of a farming system. With regard to time, the framework considers both the past and present of a farming system to understand its developmental dynamic (its pathway) as well as its possible future configurations to develop and assess alternative and desired pathways (Chapter 17). With regard to cross-level effects, the SURE-Farm framework emphasizes the interplay between agricultural practices, farm demographics, risk management and public policies for the resilience of a farming system, which are considered as four interwoven cycles (Chapter 1). The concept of the adaptive cycle is used as a sensitizing heuristic to create awareness that the resilience of a system depends on its developmental dynamic, which is symbolized through the four phases of the adaptive cycle: growth, conservation, collapse and reorganization (Holling et al., 2002). The adaptive cycle concept hypothesizes that a "foreloop" is marked by a period of slow, incremental growth, while a "back loop" entails a quick release of resources or loss of structure and creates an opening for reorganization (Gunderson & Holling, 2002).

The experiences and findings from the project lead us to draw the following seven lessons about the resilience concept with regard to farming systems.

Resilience capacities must include anticipation: The SURE-Farm framework distinguishes between three resilience capacities: robustness, adaptability and transformability (Meuwissen et al., 2019). However, in particular the analysis of the responses of the farming systems in the case studies to the Covid-19 crisis (Meuwissen et al., 2021) demonstrated the importance of anticipation as a capacity that enables preparedness (Mathijs & Wauters, 2020). Anticipatory capacities enhance the ability of a system or organization to cope with crises (robustness) and to respond (Duchek, 2019), where responses can pertain to adaptation or transformation. Improved anticipation was emphasized in work on risk management (Chapter 3) and public policies, where in particular a coordinated long-term vision was seen as essential to enhance the resilience of Europe's farm sector (Chapter 4).

While resilience is a latent characteristic of a system, resilience attributes and critical thresholds are good predictors of resilience: Resilience capacities are mobilized in response to shocks and stresses.

Whether a system has been able to cope with and to respond to perturbations can be determined only in hindsight. Moreover, resilience includes the ability to deal with "unknown unknowns". For logical reasons, the resilience of a system to cope with unforeseen events of novel types is difficult to predict. An important implication is that certain system attributes, which are generally associated with higher resilience, do not guarantee that a system can cope with any kind of shock or stress over time. A seemingly resilient system can collapse quickly if an unforeseen event pushes it beyond a critical threshold. Conversely, crises can mobilize unexpected capacities, as became particularly visible in the narrative interviews with farmers about the history of their farms (Chapter 2). Despite these limitations, the resilience attributes of the SURE-Farm framework – diversity, openness, adequate feedbacks, system reserves and modularity – were generally confirmed as relevant predictors of resilience, although the precise materialization of these attributes differs across time, place and scale. During the SURE-Farm project, these attributes were specified for farming systems, and the most important ones in the recent past were: reasonable profitability, social self-organization, infrastructure for innovation, production coupled with local and natural capital, and response diversity (Chapter 17; Paas et al., 2019; Reidsma, Meuwissen, et al., 2020). However, while these attributes are perceived to contribute to robustness and adaptability, the contribution to transformability was questioned by stakeholders, with the exception of infrastructure for innovation, if it is implemented with a vision. In assessing the resilience capacities, the identification of critical thresholds is essential, even if exact threshold values cannot always be determined (Chapter 17; Biggs et al., 2018; Paas, Accatino, et al., 2021). Many farming systems in the case studies seemed robust at first sight but on closer inspection appeared to be operating near critical thresholds. Farming system actors tended to focus on economic viability, as this function was often assessed as close to critical thresholds, and aimed to increase food- and bio-based production, while giving less attention to the maintenance of natural resources, biodiversity and social functions (Chapters 5, 17 and 19). The ensuing deterioration of the ecological and social conditions is likely to undermine productivity and economic viability in the long run. Hence, a strong profile across the range of resilience attributes is more suited than a plain focus on reasonable profitability to enable the system to cope with a larger variety of shocks and stresses (Reidsma, Paas, et al., 2020).

Vision, leadership, shared learning and experimentation, and agility are important resilience attributes: The analysis of demographic dynamics (Chapter 3), of the governance framework (Chapter 4) and several case studies suggests that farms, farming systems and enabling environments that lack a vision found it difficult to respond to shocks and stresses. Strong leadership from either within a farming system or from the enabling environment was found to enhance resilience. Shared learning and experimentation are specifically important for transformability (Paas, Coopmans, et al., 2021; Termeer et al., 2017; Urquhart et al., 2019). The analysis of responses to the Covid-19 crisis (Meuwissen et al., 2021) suggests that agility – i.e. the ability to change internal processes and arrangements quickly in response to a changing environment – constitutes a distinct resilience attribute that enhances robustness, adaptability and transformability. Agility is likely enhanced by shared learning, leadership and vision. Furthermore, agility is supported by anticipation. Overall, these additions lead to more emphasis on the future-oriented, pro-active dimension of resilience and resilience capacities.

General resilience in farming systems requires more than financial buffer resources: Dealing with unexpected shocks requires general rather than specified resilience. Consequently, the resilience attributes play a larger role, as illustrated by the resilience strategies of stakeholders and farmers which emphasized the availability of buffer resources, in particular financial means, but also "working harder" and mobilizing additional family labour (Chapter 2), or public income support (Chapter 4). Savings and subsidies can be exchanged for specific assets or services when needed. Family labour enhances general resilience to the degree that it comes with the necessary skills. Yet the findings indicate that the ability to learn, connectedness with others, innovativeness, creativity and agility are also characteristics of a farming system that increase its general resilience. They are more associated with adaptability and transformability and also facilitate a more creative and innovative use of buffer resources. The analysis also found that coupling production with local and natural capital enhances general resilience by reducing dependence on external inputs, substitutability of own products by competitors and ecological and climate change vulnerabilities.

Non-resilience is difficult to study: The farming systems in our case studies and the farms and other businesses that are part of them have been resilient, at least up to the point of research. Yet a full comprehension of farming system resilience includes an understanding of its opposite. Unfortunately, it is more difficult to study non-resilience – ceased farm operations, suspended value chains or obsolete farming systems can no longer be observed in operation and the processes that led to their demise must be reconstructed from written records, oral accounts, historical data, artefacts and geological or archaeological findings. The sequence of events is likely associated with failure and people who were involved might be difficult to find or hesitant to participate; records might have been discontinued, artefacts abandoned and land uses changed. Resilience studies must therefore be careful not to embrace a one-sided history of those who persevere and survive. The underlying interest is vulnerability.

Resilience is context specific, and so are resilience needs: The case studies (Chapters 6–16) clearly indicate that the resilience of farming systems depends strongly on their specific contexts. While many challenges to farming systems originate from the same macro-trends – climate change, liberalized markets, geo-political uncertainty, growing societal concerns about pesticides and animal welfare – these pressures are mediated in very different ways, depending on the specific biomaterial, institutional and economic context. The general resilience attributes – diversity, openness, tightness of feedbacks, system reserves and modularity – enable different actions and strategies, depending on the components of each farming system. Furthermore, the enabling environments differed widely across the case studies, with very different and often uneven effects on the different resilience capacities. The practical consequences are significant: the required capacities depend on the circumstances, in particular on the level of uncertainty (Darnhofer, 2014; Meuwissen et al., 2020), while the resilience effects of public policies are subject to specific farming system characteristics (Chapter 4; Buitenhuis et al., 2019; Feindt et al., 2019). Nevertheless, the importance of the general resilience attributes applies to all cases. In the long run, addressing all resilience attributes and keeping a balance between economic, environmental and social functions and attributes contributes to resilience, even if the concrete materialization of these attributes and functions differs across contexts.

Resilience capacities, needs and strategies differ across scales: The panarchy concept emphasizes effects across scales. Accordingly, the SURE-Farm framework distinguishes between the three levels of the farm, the farming system and the enabling environment. This facilitated the identification of cross-scale effects and misfits (Meuwissen et al., 2020). For example, in response to the Covid-19 crisis, the strategies and actions taken by the farming system often differed strongly from those of the enabling environment (Meuwissen et al., 2021). In another example, the Spanish case study, policies did not take into consideration that the needs of the farmers depend on the characteristics of the farming system (a cross-scale effect) – in this case, extensive sheep grazing farmers used public land and therefore did not receive direct payments, undermining the viability of the system (Chapter 9). The CAP and its national implementations, which are an essential part of the enabling environment, were found to be strongly robustness-oriented (Chapter 4), which fit the resilience needs of some but not all farming systems in the case studies. Moreover, public policies mostly addressed farms and not farming systems. Stakeholders, too, when identifying past strategies to cope with challenges, focused on the farm level, while farming systems encompass many different kinds of actors (Chapters 4 and 5). When stakeholders were asked to identify strategies needed to reach more resilient alternative systems, the focus shifted towards the enabling environment and the role of government (Reidsma, Paas, et al., 2020). Here the resilience framework helped to reveal conceptual shortcomings in the policy framework and to broaden the strategic thinking of stakeholders.

These seven lessons reflect that our conceptual understanding of the resilience of farming systems is not yet complete, and that any general theory of farming system resilience needs to take into account the importance of contextual factors. Still, some general observations about the resilience challenges facing Europe's farming systems can be derived very clearly from the case studies, as we will discuss in the next section.

20.3 The Crisis of Europe's Farming Systems from a Resilience Perspective

The resilience assessment in the eleven case studies found that Europe's farming systems face a broad range of economic, social, political, institutional, agronomic and ecological resilience challenges. While these challenges differ across farming systems and are mediated through different contexts and enabling or constraining environments, the general picture suggests that many farming systems in Europe face a looming resilience crisis.

First of all, based on the integrated assessment presented in Chapter 17, and confirmed by the stakeholders in the co-creation platform (Chapter 19), Europe's farming systems struggle to achieve the expected functions, apart from food production. The provision of public goods was generally evaluated as weak or deficient. The profitability of the farming systems was assessed as low in almost all case studies, too. Still, in particular in arable systems, the provision of private goods (production, income) scored significantly better than the provision of public goods (biodiversity, ecosystem services). Nevertheless, stakeholders most often considered economic viability as the most critical function and the one that most urgently required improvement. The dominant concern was that economically unviable farming systems would be unable to attract the necessary workforce and therefore undermine food production.

Across the case studies, an accumulation of challenges was assessed as pushing the farming system towards critical thresholds, i.e. as threatening the continuation of the status quo (Chapter 17; Paas, Accatino, et al., 2021):

- In seven case studies, stakeholders identified *economic challenges* that pushed their system into critical territory. Price fluctuations and low prices were a challenge in all cases, unbalanced value chains in eight and international competition in seven cases. In several case studies, these pressures were exacerbated by issues around technology adaptation, inadequate insurance and dependency on alternative off-farm income.
- All farming systems faced at least two *environmental challenges*, one of them always *climate change*. Other frequent environmental challenges were plant or animal diseases and low soil fertility, but several systems also struggled with water scarcity, excess of nutrients and soil erosion. In five case studies, stakeholders felt that climate change was pushing their farming system towards a critical threshold, and in two cases also diseases.
- In five case studies, stakeholders felt that *social challenges* pushed the system towards critical thresholds, in particular lack of successors, depopulation of rural areas and lack of suitable labour, but

also high societal expectations and changing consumer preferences, poor quality of life and insufficient infrastructure.

- In eight case studies, *public policies and institutional challenges* were seen as pushing the farming system towards a critical threshold. Constantly changing policy regulations were seen as a challenge in ten case studies, high standards and strict regulations in five, complicated administrative procedures and the lack of long-term vision in policy in four and high land prices in three cases. Land ownership and regulation was a challenge in the Polish and Bulgarian case.

The ability to translate these challenges into manageable risks has been limited so far. Exposure to risks is generally expected to intensify for European farm businesses and farming systems in the future, in particular due to climate change, more volatile markets, changing societal demand, policies and regulation, geo-political risks and biosecurity issues such as pandemics and diseases in a globalized world (Chapter 2). From the perspective of farmers, as evidenced by surveys conducted in the case studies, institutional risks (e.g. reduction of CAP direct payments and tighter regulations) and environmental risks (e.g. extreme weather and disease events) generally scored even higher than economic risks (e.g. persistently low market prices and high costs). However, in responses to an open question, long-term pressures on profitability were raised most frequently, and institutional, environmental and economic challenges were complemented by social challenges and difficulties in access to technology and innovations (Chapter 2). Risk management strategies were found to be highly variable across farms (Spiegel et al., 2020). Some farm-level strategies to increase financial robustness – like working harder and avoiding debt – can reduce the capacity to adapt and transform. While learning, cooperation and exchange were found to be essential for appropriate risk management, it were mostly farmers characterized as "proactive learners" who adopted risk management strategies in anticipation of expected challenges, explored new knowledge and engaged across social networks. In contrast, "reactive learners" were found to be risk averse, lacking self-efficacy, oriented towards business-as-usual models and hesitant to adopt new approaches or technologies (Chapter 2).

The case studies found relatively few examples where financial risk management was linked to adaptation or transformation. Discussions in the SURE-Farm stakeholder platform (Chapter 19) revealed examples of private insurance companies that made compensation for damage from extreme weather events conditional on adaptive measures on the farm; e.g., drought insurance would require suitable water retention management and irrigation systems. Risk management arrangements were generally focused on compensation for income loss from reduced ability to produce private goods. They were barely linked to the public goods which, among their many functions, support the long-term productivity of farming systems.

The ability to attract skilled, highly motivated and entrepreneurial people has become a major challenge for many farming systems in Europe (see Chapter 3). Several detrimental developments are accumulating: first, the general outmigration from the more remote rural areas, which is driven by comparative disadvantages in the general location attractiveness, low-level public infrastructures and social services, limited social opportunities, and barriers to professional and business development due to lack of other business and value chain partners, training opportunities and support structures; second, an increasing mismatch between farming as a long-hours profession with many lonely activities and the lifestyle ambitions of the younger generation; third, uncompetitive income opportunities for skilled labour; fourth, the widely shared reputation of farming as a sector that struggles with issues around environmental and climate protection, animal welfare and social standards (e.g., public debates on the working conditions of seasonal workers and slaughterhouse staff). However, simulations of two case study regions using the AgriPoliS model showed that a difference in farm succession rates had little impact on the amount of farmed land, on production or gross value added (Chapter 3). The simulation runs found differences in the distribution of land and the remuneration of the factors of production. Hence, the discontinuation of individual farms due to lack of successors, which can be seen as lack of resilience at the farm level, affects the developmental pathway of the farming system, but does not necessarily reduce the resilience of the farming system as long as the remaining farms have sufficient access to capital and labour or technology to take over and manage the abandoned land (Chapter 3). However, if farm growth translates mainly into intensification and specialization at ever larger scales, "limits to growth" might be reached at some point as yields are close to their potential and the land area available for farm size increase is limited (Chapters 5 and 17). Concentration of highly specialized farms could also undermine resilience attributes such as diversity and modularity (heterogeneity of farm types) or coupling of production to local and natural capital.

At the sector level, fewer farm successors and less supply of skilled labour necessitate adaptations which reduce the demand for labour, e.g. by changes to the farm organization and production programme or the deployment of labour-saving technologies such as robotics. This in return requires access to capital and might increase the exposure of farming system actors to financial risks which need to be addressed through appropriate risk management. In order to adapt to the demographic challenges, farming system actors need an enabling environment that provides access to technology and capital and to the skilled labour to implement and run new technologies. Such a technology-intensive scenario, however, might contradict public sympathies for smaller farms and more traditional farming methods.

Many European farming systems are locked in on developmental trajectories that combine a strong reliance on chemical and/or biological inputs with an orientation towards global commodity food systems, as the analysis of three case studies in Chapter 5 exemplifies, based on the typology of farming systems as "socio-technical regimes" by Therond et al. (2017). The exposure to global competition reduces profitability, and the response is intensification with reliance on external inputs and pathways. However, the intensive farming methods are generally not environmentally sustainable since the frequent use of pesticides, the ample addition of nitrogen and phosphorus, irrigation, tillage, landscape simplification and the emission of greenhouse gases have negative impacts on ecosystem functions and natural resources. In the long run, sustainability deficits are likely to undermine the resilience of the farming systems through, e.g., soil erosion, reduced water quality and quantity, and decline of ecosystem services such as pollination, water retention or buffer against extreme weather (e.g., wind breaks, shadow, flood protection). Changing the developmental trajectory of the farming systems, however, is difficult due to economic, institutional, cultural and social lock-in mechanisms (cf. Burton & Farstad, 2020). While participating stakeholders in the case studies identified pathways towards a more sustainable development of their farming systems, these require support from an enabling environment, in particular public awareness of the linkages between farming systems and ecosystem services, coherent government support for the provision of public goods, targeted advice and training, valorizing environmentally sustainable products, support for cooperation and for local and regional value chains. Stakeholders also called for supporting technologies, in particular better use of environmental and geo-spatial data, which could be developed inter alia through farmer-led innovation processes. Finally, they suggested to facilitate cooperation to foster knowledge exchange, trust and a sense of community.

The stakeholder evaluation of the public policy framework provided by the CAP and its national implementations was very critical (Chapter 4). An analysis of the CAP instruments and budget found that most of the financial resources were devoted to income support measures, in particular area-based payments. These were broadly perceived as a reliable financial buffer that enhances the robustness of farms. However, several negative side-effects on the robustness of farming systems were identified: area-based direct payments increased competition for eligible land and thereby contributed to rising land prices, which in turn constrained access to land for newcomers and reduced the profitability of farms that work on leased land. By enabling otherwise unprofitable and unviable farms to continue, stakeholders concluded, the payments restricted competition and change. At the same time, the area-based direct payments funnelled very few resources into farming systems that use little eligible land.

Attempts to link income support to the provision of public goods and thereby to stimulate adaptation have been mostly ineffective (Chapter 4). The Rural Development Programs (RDPs) contain a few adaptability-oriented measures that encourage environment-friendly farming practices, social learning, cooperation and innovations. However, complex and bureaucratic application procedures, significant up-front costs, slow programming and lack of flexibility limit the potential of RDP measures to enhance adaptability. Financial support for insurance schemes, another policy option in RDPs, could be expected to form a key element to enhance robustness, in particular to address losses from climate change and extreme weather. Yet, where offered (in the Dutch and Polish case), it was mostly met with reservation by stakeholders due to perceived high financial or transaction costs and lack of trust.

Most concerning was the finding that the CAP constrained the transformability of Europe's farming systems (Chapter 4). This assessment was consistent across methods. The top-down analysis of the policy instruments found that the CAP provided strong support for business-as-usual approaches – which should not be an option, given the objectives of the Green Deal, the Farm to Fork strategy and the EU's zero emission ambition, all of which require transformative change (Lóránt & Allen, 2019), and that many farming system actors also expressed the need for transformation (Meuwissen et al., 2020). The bottom-up analysis found that respondents in all farming systems felt that the CAP and other policies provided little long-term guidance. They cited too frequent policy changes without a clear sense of direction. Stronger regulations on animal welfare and the use of manure or pesticides without readily available alternatives were seen as threatening the viability of farms if international competitors were not subjected to similar demands.

It also became clear that networks and learning processes were mostly limited to farmers. This tendency was reinforced by the CAP and its national implementations which offered little support for cross-sectoral cooperation, in-depth learning or radical innovations. The relatively closed networks within the farming systems could in turn constrain the potential of policy interventions which aim to introduce new actors, knowledge or perspectives (Chapter 4).

The tendency to operate within relatively confined circles is probably one important reason why several problematic patterns were repeatedly found across case studies (Chapter 18). Shifting the burden to third parties who provide additional support and compensation, eroding goals rather than addressing problems, an enabling environment that constrains efforts to develop and implement novel solutions, or allocation of most of the resources to a limited number of well-established solutions are examples of unhealthy dynamics, which are systemically entrenched, difficult to recognize and hard to change. They all contribute to a misallocation of resources to reiterate the responses to problems of the past rather than addressing impending and future challenges.

Overall, the analyses in the SURE-Farm project suggest that many European farming systems face an accumulation of challenges that push them towards critical boundaries. While the systems still perform well with regard to food production, profitability is low and the provision of public goods is often not satisfactory. Lack of profitability and other social and economic opportunities in rural areas reduce the interest of potential farm successors and skilled labour to work in the sector. While scale enlargement and intensification have contributed to robustness in the past, there are limits to growth, and a more balanced attention is needed for economic, social and environmental dimensions. The CAP and other public policies are geared to compensate for a lack of robustness in order to maintain a status quo that is increasingly becoming untenable. While the EU is embracing ambitious long-term goals, e.g. in its Farm to Fork Strategy (European Commission, 2020b), the transformation pathways are unclear and not supported by the current policy instruments. This raises the question of what a coherent strategic approach to enhance the resilience capacities of Europe's framing systems could look like.

20.4 Resilience-Enabling Strategies

The need to develop encompassing strategies to enhance the resilience of Europe's food systems is now widely shared. The Farm to Fork Strategy, which the European Commission (2020b) proposed in May 2020, uses the terms "resilience" and "resilient" fourteen times. The experience of the pandemic has visibly generated a sense of urgency: "The COVID-19 pandemic has underlined the importance of a robust and resilient food system" (p. 3), and, with a view to the "interrelations between our health, ecosystems, supply chains, consumption patterns and planetary boundaries", the Commission concludes that "our food system is under threat and must become more sustainable and resilient" (p. 3). The Commission further calls to strengthen the resilience of Europe's food system (p. 5) and of food systems in general (p. 6). The Farm to Fork Strategy mentions several threats to resilience when it calls to increase climate resilience (p. 6) and to build up resilience to possible future diseases and pandemics (p. 18). The European Commission (2020b) also proposes several resilience-enhancing attributes of farming systems: "increasing the sustainability of food producers will ultimately increase their resilience" (p. 12), and "short supply chains which increase the resilience of local and regional food systems" (p. 13).

Given the diversity of Europe's farming systems, their resilience challenges and capacities, it is not possible to formulate one resilience-enhancing strategy that fits all. However, based on the findings from the SURE-Farm project, we can formulate lessons and principles that can help farming system actors and their enabling environment to develop strategies that enhance the necessary resilience capacities.

The resilience strategies articulated by stakeholders during the workshops often focused on reduced costs. This, however, is unlikely to enhance adaptability or transformability. Only when asked how their systems could move to an alternative constellation, stakeholders suggested a broader range of strategies that can be divided into four groups (Chapter 17):

- Economic viability: enhancing the profitability of the farming system and providing financial support;
- Social connectedness: better cooperation among the actors within the farming system, improving social self-organization, improving consumer-producer relationships, improving connectedness with actors outside the farming system, such as the Agricultural Knowledge and Innovation Systems (AKIS) and policymakers;
- Ecological connectedness: enhancing coupling with the local and natural capital, promoting circularity or crop–livestock integration, enhancing functional diversity;
- Supportive policies: diverse policies and simplification or relaxation of regulations, more support for public goods.

The overall consideration is that actors within and outside the farming systems need to collaborate to enable a transformation towards novel business models that address the long-term challenges of farming systems (Reidsma, Paas, et al., 2020). To address the range of resilience challenges, it is important to develop strategies that link up across the four domains of agricultural production, risk management, farm demographics and governance.

First, there is a need for a *joined-up vision on agricultural production and food systems in Europe.* On the bright side, food production was consistently seen as the most important and best-performing function of Europe's farming systems. But the emerging bioeconomy with its demand for biomass might demand changes to production programmes. The protein gap for animal feedstuffs persistently drives imports and leakage of environmental problems to other parts of the world. Under competitive pressure, many farming systems reduce resilience attributes such as diversity and modularity in the interest of specialization and economies of scale. Adaptation to climate change was a major concern in all case studies. And the relatively poor performance of public-goods-related functions requires more environmentally friendly forms of production. In order to meet the Sustainable Development Goals (and the objectives of the Farm to Fork Strategy), especially in north-western European countries, reductions in pesticide use, nitrogen surplus, greenhouse gas emission and share of protein supply of animal origin, along with an increase in nitrogen use efficiency, are needed (Gil et al., 2019). Furthermore, the EU's Biodiversity Strategy (European Commission, 2020a) calls for a reduction of farmed land, while the Farm to Fork Strategy's objectives of reduced use of pesticides and fertilizers along with 25 per cent organically farmed land imply lower productivity on the affected areas (although it can be argued that considering the overuse of inputs in many places, farm productivity can remain at similar levels when inputs are used more efficiently). Any shortfall must be made up of a combination of more intensive production on the remaining land, reduced food loss and waste, imports and reduced or less land-consuming consumption patterns (i.e., less meat consumption). A further yield increase has little leeway in Europe, especially in the north-western countries where yields have already reached 70 per cent or more of their potential (Schils et al., 2018; Silva et al., 2017). There is hence a need for an integrated assessment of food and non-food needs and priorities and a vision of what Europe wants to produce on its agricultural land and how.

This should include a *vision of resilience-enhancing agricultural landscapes* (i.e. rural landscapes shaped by agriculture) and how they can be maintained, restored or created. This should be guided by the functions of the farming system and landscape and resilience-enhancing attributes, such as diversity, modularity and system reserves. Such an approach would in particular recognize the functions of landscape elements and ecological services for agricultural production, in addition to social connectedness. Discussions should be guided by an analysis of critical thresholds. The compatibility of the overall European and the regional visions need to be ensured through a bidirectional, iterative process, enhancing reflexivity of visions across scales (Feindt & Weiland, 2018). In order to improve sustainability and resilience of farming systems, agricultural production needs to be better coupled with local and natural capital, which includes improving soil quality and circularity, reducing inputs, using varieties that are adapted to local climatic conditions, and local branding. Further potential for strengthening ecological processes lies in increasing functional diversity and creating ecologically self-regulated systems (Chapters 5 and 17).

A more integrated, resilience-oriented approach to agricultural production and resource management entails the need for *a skills-oriented vision of farm demographics*. Currently, farm demographics in Europe are characterized by mutually reinforcing structural restrictions. Intergenerational transfer of the farm within the family remains the main route of succession. The family farm model helps to overcome entry barriers like access to land and capital and also enables the mobilization of additional resources like (unpaid) family labour and private savings. The analyses in the SURE-Farm project also emphasize the importance of personal relations and networks for access to land, capital, business opportunities and knowledge. Such barriers would constitute less of a restriction for the development of farming systems if there was an ample pool of interested people. However, many rural areas are perceived as not very attractive and provide fewer opportunities for social life, education and public services. The lack of successors and skilled labour as well as the barriers for new entrants are likely to reduce the adaptability and transformability of farming systems since they constrain the influx of new ideas and fresh thinking. Since innovativeness and entrepreneurship are scarce skills, agricultural systems have to compete with other sectors.

Hence, from the perspective of the resilience of farming systems, the issue is less whether farms find a successor within their family rather than the *encouragement of successors and skilled people who embrace an integrated vision of farming that includes the sustainable provision of both public and private goods*. Chapter 3 elaborates a range of strategic measures to address these demographic issues. They range from enhanced attractiveness of rural areas to territory-based instruments, skills training that is consistently oriented towards strengthening sustainable agricultural practices, the opening up of networks, improved conditions for start-ups and new entrants to facilitate new business models, joined-up risk management along all stages of generational renewal, support with mental health issues and reinforcing the positive effects of cooperation, peer exchange and learning cycles.

An alternative strategy would be to substitute scarce labour with technology, such as ICT and robots, and to bring in new concepts and ideas through training and education, advisory services, service providers and knowledge included in "smart farming" products. But this raises important questions about the availability of capital to acquire technology and knowledge-based services, the speed of development of such new technologies, and their compatibility with incumbent farmers, their skills, practices and business models.

Finally, the discussion of farm demographics leads to the broader question of whether the current mechanisms that determine which farms are discontinued are conducive to the resilience of farming systems. From an evolutionary perspective, the take-over of unsuccessful and dysfunctional farms by more successful competitors can enhance system performance. However, a systemic and guiding vision of how farm demographics can be linked to improved functionality and resilience of farming systems is lacking – apart from supporting measures like education, training and start-up grants.

Risk management in the case studies of European farming systems was found to be generally status quo oriented. To address the resilience challenges, *more synergies are needed between financial risk management and support for other desired functions of farming systems.* Again, there is no one-size-fits-all solution. The diversity of farming systems and the variegated risk landscapes require a *diversity of risk management strategies.* Chapter 2 identified a number of strategy elements. These include a full mapping of risks facing each of Europe's agricultural systems and the available risk management tools to identify gaps and mismatches, the deployment of financial risk management (insurance schemes) to incentivize adaptation, the use of novel technologies to develop new risk management tools and innovative insurance mechanisms, and the encouragement of cooperation, learning and sharing of risks between all actors in the farming system, not least through differentiated strategies that address different needs (Vroege & Finger, 2020).

The strategies to improve agricultural practices, risk management and farm demographic require an enabling environment. The *principles to create a resilience-enabling environment for farming systems* presented in Chapter 18 provide some general guidance: emphasis on the development of anticipatory and responsive capacity; transfer of external resources to address shocks but not to compensate long-term stresses; adaptation or transformation to increase robustness to challenging long-term trends; fostering the capacity for response diversity; ambidexterity to respond to both current and future challenges; thorough analysis of the root causes of challenges.

The policy framework is the most important part of the enabling or constraining environment. The analyses in the SURE-Farm project found a clear *need for more tailored policy mixes that address the specific resilience needs of Europe's farming systems.* The CAP is the dominant policy for Europe's farming systems. It provides the overarching policy framework for most national and regional policy initiatives, equipped with a budget of more than 50 billion Euros per year, most of which is spent on income support through area-based direct payments. This is broadly understood to support the robustness of Europe's farming systems while support for adaptability is limited and transformability is rather constrained by the status quo orientation. However, strictly speaking, income support does not increase resilience, it rather compensates a lack of resilience. Hence, instead of stretching the resilience concept to justify policies that have been inherited from the past, it is necessary to *develop a proper resilience foundation and resilience orientation for the CAP.*

A revised CAP could enhance all resilience capacities of Europe's farming systems (Buitenhuis et al., 2020). To foster the *robustness* of Europe's farming systems, the CAP should enhance the ability and willingness of farming system actors to anticipate stresses and shocks and to develop their own coping and response strategies, and conduct foresight exercises linked into strategy development and outreach and engagement schemes. To enhance *adaptability*, the CAP should provide a coherent and sufficient remuneration of public goods; increase flexibility and variability through reducing red tape; provide more support for project-type funding, for AKIS that integrate production and provision of public goods, and for collaboration between agriculture and societal actors. To enhance *transformability*, the CAP should formulate a coordinated long-term vision; support deep learning; adopt reflexive modes of governing that influence people's assumptions about the future, their self-perceptions and identities; develop EIP-Agri and LEADER into cross-sectoral support for rural cooperation; and embrace cross-sectoral approaches in rural development programs.

Overall, the CAP needs a long-term vision for resilient and sustainable farming systems. The Farm to Fork Strategy is one important step into this direction.[1] The immediate SURE-Farm recommendations for

---

[1] The European Commission (2020b) clearly has doubts whether the historically grown CAP provides a resilience-enabling environment when it calls for an

the CAP were to *reduce direct payments* with a view to phasing them out by 2028 and to divert the budget into those CAP measures that specifically address resilience needs. The *eco-schemes* should be used to foster public goods (e.g. biodiversity, attractive landscapes) and adaptation to environmental and climate change. The member states' *national strategic plans* should primarily support adaptability to meet the ambitions of the Green Deal, the Farm to Fork Strategy and the Biodiversity Strategy. Member states should provide ample support for cooperation and cross-sectoral networking in rural development programmes and enable producer organizations to coordinate adaptation to shifting markets and changing environments. The AKIS should be strengthened through more project-type funding and more funding for advisory services to integrate advice for production and provision of public goods. The RDPs should enable transformative innovation, reflexivity and deep learning through more support for LEADER projects and European Innovations Partnerships (EIP-Agri).

The importance of cooperation, exchange and learning emphasized above is also essential to make a resilience-oriented policy approach effective. The case studies consistently found that active engagement in social learning processes was important to empower farming system actors to understand policies and make effective use of funding and support opportunities (Chapter 4). Resilience-enhancing policies require a dedicated support infrastructure, whereas direct payments can be administered through clerks and inspectors.

Several of the case studies found an important role of more hybrid governance arrangements that combine private and public elements. Vertical coordination along value chains or horizontal coordination by producer organizations was often instrumental in coordinating adaptation or even transformation of farming systems (e.g. Chapters 11 and 12). This resonates with the literature on hybrid food governance which has found numerous constellations where actors from the

evaluation "to establish the contribution of income support to improving the resilience and sustainability of farming" (p. 10, fn 24). It points to several elements of a resilience-enabling environment: a contingency plan in times of crisis (p. 12), prevention of fraud which "undermines the resilience of food markets" (p.15), investment support to improve the resilience and accelerate the green and digital transformation of farms (p. 17), cooperation to improve nutrition and to alleviate food insecurity by strengthening resilience of food systems and reducing food waste (p. 18), and "international cooperation to enhance resilience and risk preparednesss" (p. 18).

public, private and civil society sector collaborate to enable fairer or more sustainable value chains (Verbruggen & Havinga, 2017). These arrangements are often dominated by food processors or retailers, which raises questions about market power. It is also clear that these meso-level assemblages are not the original drivers of sustainability and resilience, but enable coordinated responses to changing framework conditions and challenging macro-trends that require sustainability-oriented and resilience-enhancing strategies.

A little-discussed element of the enabling or constraining environment concerns the *role of markets, or the political unleashing or harnessing of market mechanisms.* Stakeholders in all case studies insisted that enhancing the robustness of farms and farming systems requires to improve their profitability. The liberalization of Europe's agricultural markets since the MacSharry reform of the CAP and the EU's Eastern enlargement since 2005 have increased competition for most farmers. The shift in the provision of income support from managed markets to area-based direct payments reduced state-induced market failure – the old system of market interventions had suppressed price signals as a feedback mechanism between supply and demand, which had led to overproduction and generated ever new needs for government intervention. However, since the managed markets have been widely abandoned, other market failures have become more pertinent. Many externalities of farming have not been internalized in the price for marketable goods, e.g. greenhouse gas emissions, landscape amenities or habitat quality from structural elements in the agricultural landscape. Internalising these externalities would increase costs and further reduce competitiveness in open markets, unless border adjustments are put in place.

From the perspective of many farming system actors, the tension between price pressure on internationally competitive markets and increasing demands to cater for public goods has not been solved. On open markets, the use of less productive farming methods reduces international competitiveness and justifies – or even requires – compensation. Yet the instruments used to remunerate public goods are rather bureaucratic and inflexible and do not stimulate learning, flexible solutions or entrepreneurship. In the long run it would also be very expensive for Europe's tax payers to recompense the provision and maintenance of all public good components associated with Europe's farming systems. Hence, a resilience-enabling environment needs other market configurations, such as the inclusion of higher sustainability standards in transnational public or private regulations, border adjustment mechanisms, or the development of new markets that enable the internalization of externalities, such as carbon emission certificates. A comprehensive and long-term resilience strategy for Europe's farming systems needs to engage with these broader questions of the political economy of farming.

20.5 Reflections and Outlook

While the SURE-Farm framework and analyses have generated substantial results, a number of limitations need to be acknowledged.

First of all, the *scope of the SURE-Farm concept* is limited to farming systems. While the shift of attention from the farm level to the farming system level has already been challenging, an even broader approach is needed. The EU Farm to Fork Strategy emphasizes the resilience of entire food systems, and calls have been made for a more encompassing integrative food system approach. The exclusive focus on farming systems tends to reproduce the productivist, producer-oriented outlook of farm policy in general and the CAP in particular (Daugbjerg & Feindt, 2017), unless it is understood to include the resilience of the entire value chain, including specific vulnerabilities of different consumer groups. There is hence a need to put farming system resilience into the wider context of food system resilience and sustainability. For the successful transformation of food systems in order to meet climate change targets, Europe will need farming systems that are both sustainable and resilient. Without resilience it will be difficult for farming systems to be sustainable. But Europe also needs farming systems that enhance the resilience of Europe's public health. This implies, e.g., that the functions of farming systems should include their contribution to healthy dietary patterns or food-related illnesses, or that the use of antibiotics in animal breeding does not create life-threatening vulnerabilities in the health system.

Second, the framework could strengthen the *critical assessment of the functions provided by farming systems*. Currently, the SURE-Farm framework contains eight generic functions – production of food, production of other bio-based resources, economic viability, quality of life, maintenance of natural resources, protection of biodiversity and habitats, attractiveness of the area as well as animal health and welfare.

The perceived importance and level of performance of each function was assessed, complemented by a quantitative assessment for some ecosystem services indicators. This allows to identify unbalanced or low levels of performance of the system. However, one might also ask whether each function is addressed in the most desirable way – this would require a reflection on, e.g., the type of food and other resources produced, the distribution of economic gains, the underlying ideas about quality of life, the instrumental or intrinsic valuation of natural resources, biodiversity and habitats, productivist or post-productivist perceptions of landscape attractiveness, and differing concepts of animal health and animal welfare (Feindt & Weiland, 2018; Marsden, 2013). The social standards of valuation for each function are historically contingent and in pluralist societies they are usually contested. Hence, even if the eight categories provide a complete taxonomy of farming system functions, different distributions of importance given to them, or different ideas about the best manifestation of each of them, can lead to very different concepts of a good and desirable farming system. It is likely that future policies and governance arrangements will put more emphasis on public goods, animal welfare and climate friendliness. Since the resilience analysis starts with the challenges and since low performance of functions is one type of challenge, new understandings of each function or shifting weights between them likely affect the overall assessment. Including alternative manifestations of functions into the resilience framework would require a counter-factual analysis. To a certain degree, this was implied in the FoPIA-SURE-Farm 2 workshops (Chapter 5, 17 and 19) when participating stakeholders were asked to think about alternative systems. These exercises revealed a high degree of path dependence. The articulated imagination of stakeholders was strongly shaped by their understanding of the current system, and participating stakeholders came mostly from the current system. It would therefore be necessary to involve a broader range of perspectives, e.g. by inviting "critical friends". Another option would be to stimulate thinking out of the box, e.g. by confronting stakeholders with alternative scenarios. Yet, the experience in workshops was that stakeholders from the farming systems found it difficult to engage with scenarios that they felt were remote from their lifeworld experience, or to imagine alternative farming systems that would focus on different products.

Third, the SURE-Farm project did not develop a definitive set of a small number of *indicators to measure the resilience of farming systems*. One reason is that the SURE-Farm framework comprises a large number of incommensurable entities. Furthermore, the relationship between the resilience attributes and resilience capacities appears to be context-dependent. Nevertheless, it is conceivable to create a resilience scale from the various scales that have been deployed during the project, e.g. the Resilience Assessment Tool for policies (Termeer et al., 2018), the performance indicators for farming system functions (Chapter 17) or the assessment of resilience attributes (Paas, Coopmans, et al., 2021; Reidsma, Paas, et al., 2020). An important aspect is to measure resilience attributes – but these are difficult to operationalize, and determining a "good" level of, e.g., diversity or tightness of feedback is an intricate task. The operationalization into twenty-two more specific attributes (of which thirteen were assessed in stakeholder workshops) including explanatory statements, which could be assessed with a participatory approach, was one step towards such a measurement, but remains qualitative (Paas et al., 2019). An alternative approach is to measure system outputs, outcomes and the performance of system functions using representative indicators – the identification of problematic trends can serve as an early warning system for system decline (Chapter 17; Paas, Accatino, et al., 2021). Quantitative models can be used to assess specific indicators, but quantification is generally limited to a few specific indicators (Herrera, 2017).

Fourth, the *concept of the adaptive cycle*, an influential concept in resilience thinking (Gunderson & Holling, 2002), has been used as a heuristic to sensitize researchers to the processes of decomposition of a system and reorganization of its resources (Reidsma et al., 2019). However, attempts to determine at which stage of the adaptive cycle farming systems are found have met with difficulty (see case study Chapters 6–16). For example, should risk management be assessed as growing or reorganizing? Many farming systems seem to be in the conservation phase, but does that imply that collapse and reorganization are the next phases, or can deliberate transformation be achieved by smaller, shorter and more manageable cycles in the conservation phase? It also turned out that the concept was difficult to apply to a system marked by fragmented (polycentric) agency and resources.

Fifth, *the resilience concept requires further methodological integra-tion.* The SURE-Farm project deployed a range of qualitative (mostly participatory assessments) and quantitative methods (mostly based on data and models). These were united through an Integrated Assessment (IA) toolbox that consisted of the Framework of Participatory Impact Assessment for Sustainable and Resilient Farming Systems (FoPIA-SURE-Farm), an ecosystem services assessment and the AgriPoliS model, and a system dynamics approach using causal loop diagrams (see the overview in Chapter 1). Integrating the results from the differ-ent methods proved all but easy. Most of the academic outputs so far built on just one method. While a mixed-methods approach is benefi-cial or even necessary for understanding such a multi-faceted concept as resilience, its empirical application remains challenging. Chapter 17 provides an overview, but neglects most results from quantitative models, as these focused on one or a few challenges, indicators and/ or case studies, because of the complexity to quantitatively analyse a farming system. A particular barrier is the integration of multiple methods within one academic journal paper. Here, the dominant pub-lication culture constitutes a significant restraint. Proper mixed-methods approaches require more extensive formats to sufficiently explain and make each method transparent.

Sixth, there is a need to *reflect and address more systematically how actors understand resilience.* As explained by Giddens's concept of a "triple hermeneutics", resilience is an academic concept that has been taken up by societal groups and actors, in the process acquiring new meaning-in-practice, which in turn needs to be reconstructed by aca-demic researchers (Giddens, 1984). The resilience concept will always be interpreted and used in the context of dominant discourses and actors likely pick up elements of the resilience concept that resonate with their worldviews. The different resilience capacities emphasize either the need to defend or to change the status quo, thereby reverber-ating with different values. It is then to be expected that actors select-ively adopt or mix elements of the resilience concept. Even more, its different aspects make the resilience concept politically ambiguous, and this ambiguity can be rhetorically exploited to create a consensus frame (Candel et al., 2014) that conceals significant disagreements.

Seventh, there is a *need to develop more thorough foundations of resilience governance, at least with regard to farming systems.* The strategies identified to enhance the resilience capacities of farming systems require strong coordination of a broad range of actors with different interests, ideas and identities. This raises the question about the necessary coordination capacities. If the resilience of a farming system is a collective good, collective action (Ostrom, 1990) of the system members is required to retain it. If resilience is an emerging property of a farming system that results from the interactions of its elements, an enabling environment is needed to "supervise" the system's direction of development and create suitable context conditions, more akin to reflexive governance approaches (Feindt & Weiland, 2018). If the resilience challenges and needs differ across Europe's farming systems, what is the appropriate level of policy interventions to create an enabling environment? How do resilience strategies relate to established principles of good governance, such as the subsidiarity or the polluter-pays principle? What are principles of a resilience-oriented policy design (Feindt et al., 2020)? The context dependency of the effects of public policies on resilience suggests that a shift in programming capacities in the CAP from the European to the national and regional level, as implied in the "New Delivery Model", is preferable. But this requires strong coordinative capacities at the regional level and in the farming systems. At the same time, stronger coordination is not always better. The Dutch and Flemish case studies, e.g., pointed to disadvantages if coordination within the farming system is too strong and farmers stop thinking for themselves. There is a fine line between coordination and paternalism. In contrast, the Spanish case demonstrated the benefits if a strongly coordinated sector successfully lobbies the government.

Despite these shortcomings, the SURE-Farm analyses clearly indicate that the resilience capacities of many of Europe's farming systems are likely not sufficient to address the accumulating resilience challenges and to maintain the provision of private and public goods at desirable levels, when new encompassing strategies are not developed and implemented. The stakeholder involvement found widespread concern about long-term vulnerabilities, while at the same time a significant number of actors are currently successful and happy with the dynamics, indicating a mismatch between individual and collective rationales as well as between short-term and long-term interests.

In the long run, the development of the resilience attributes will be essential – and here many trends are going into the opposite direction: economies of scale rather than diversity, consolidation rather than modularity, separation of consumers and producers rather than tightness of feedbacks. Translating the academic findings into practical strategies would begin with a broad agreement on the need to reverse course, i.e. on the need for a transformation. The resilience assessment can help to identify problematic trends, even if the consequences of the long-term deterioration of environmental and social functions have not yet fully materialized. Here the SURE-Farm framework can be used to conduct a participatory assessment of the situation of a farming system and derive the resilience needs (Paas, Accatino, et al., 2021; Paas, Coopmans, et al., 2021). Hence, the framework can serve as heuristic and then be supported with relevant data.

Many farmers in the SURE-Farm case studies shared a sentiment that "the next generation must do it differently" and expected that they would do it differently. This perspective betrays at the same time a sense of crisis, a lack of self-efficacy and a delegated optimism. It also confirms that it is difficult to start the transition of farming systems, given the combined and mutually reinforcing lock-in mechanisms of vested interests, entrenched mental models, historically grown regulations, policy legacies and sunk investments.

Against this background, the weaknesses of the resilience approach need to be addressed – both for academic and for practical reasons. While the SURE-Farm project has been able to develop a systematic framework to assess the resilience of farming systems and generated a plethora of evidence from the case studies, many important questions remain. We suggest in particular *five avenues for future research*:

1. Resilience assessment: There is a need for systematic assessments of the vulnerabilities of farming systems and food systems more broadly. It would be worthwhile to develop a coherent methodology for conducting stress tests of farming systems that consider a broad range of accumulating stresses and shocks. This would include, inter alia, scenario development and a system to rank the severity and likeliness of a broad range of perturbations.

2. Resilience and sustainability: The relationship between resilience and sustainability of farming systems appears more problematic at the end of the SURE-Farm project. Unsustainable farming systems can be resilient as long as their lack of sustainability does not undermine their viability. Generally sustainable farming systems can lack resilience, such as the extensive grazing system in the

Spanish case study. The finding that public goods were not in a good condition in many farming systems in the case studies while resilience strategies mostly focused on robustness and the provision of private goods suggests the possibility that short-term and medium-term resilience could be enhanced at the expense of long-term resilience and sustainability. Clearly, the relationship between resilience strategies and sustainability requires more attention.

3. Transformative capacities: While the case studies generated a good understanding of robustness and adaptability capacities of farming systems, transformative capacities are much less understood. Stakeholders were not convinced of the contribution of the main resilience attributes to transformability, with the exception of "infrastructure for innovation" (Reidsma, Paas, et al., 2020). Transformative capacities are difficult to assess, as deliberate transformations of farming systems rarely take place, and if they do, they generally take a long time and can often only be analysed in hindsight. The SURE-Farm framework considers changes in the materialization or weight of functions delivered by a farming system as one possible transformation. Yet, this was rarely observed in the case studies. Farming system actors and also the enabling environment were mostly oriented towards maintaining and preserving current functionality. Production methods were intensified and food production increased, but the main functions and representative indicators (e.g. starch potato production in the Dutch Veenkoloniën, see Chapter 12) did not change. This limited the willingness and ability to consider alternative constellations that would include modified and possibly enhanced functions. One avenue for further research would be historical studies of farming system transformations, in particular transformations that involved modifications of system functions (e.g., Termeer et al., 2019).

4. Resilience attributes: The five core resilience attributes – diversity, openness, tightness of feedback, system reserves and modularity – deserve further analysis and possible revision. They are currently pitched at the level of structural characteristics. However, an analysis of the responses of the eleven farming systems in the SURE-Farm case studies to the Covid-19 crisis found that agility and leadership were essential for the resilience of the farming systems to the unexpected shock of the pandemic (Meuwissen et al., 2021). For participatory assessments, a list of twenty-two more specific attributes was

developed based on Cabell and Oelofse (2012), and reduced to thirteen to facilitate discussion (Paas, Coopmans, et al., 2021; Reidsma, Meuwissen, et al., 2020). It was clear that sustainable and resilient systems require a strengthening of attributes in the economic, social, ecological and institutional domain (Figure 17.2), but a quantitative assessment of the necessary minimum levels is still lacking.

5. Resilience strategies: The case studies revealed that it is not well understood how transformative capacities of farming systems can be stimulated. It is clear that anticipation and foresight, visioning, learning, open attitudes, connectedness and societal support play a role. However, these elements still need to be integrated into a clear framework that can guide experiments and comparative case studies of farming systems. In particular, we need to understand better how resilience strategies can simultaneously enhance public and private goods.

References

Biggs, R., Peterson, G. D., & Rocha, J. C. (2018). The Regime Shifts Database: A framework for analyzing regime shifts in social-ecological systems. *Ecology and Society*, *23*(3), Article 9. https://doi.org/10.5751/ES-10264-230309

Buitenhuis, Y., Candel, J., Feindt, P. H., et al. (2020). Improving the resilience-enabling capacity of the common agricultural policy: Policy recommendations for more resilient EU farming systems. *EuroChoices*, *19*(2), 63–71. https://doi.org/10.1111/1746-692X.12286

Buitenhuis, Y., Candel, J., Termeer, K., et al. (2019). Policy bottom-up Analysis – All case study reports. SURE-Farm project, Deliverable 4.3. Wageningen et al.: Sure-Farm Consortium. www.surefarmproject.eu/wordpress/wp-content/uploads/2020/12/D4.3-Bottom-up-policy-analysis.pdf

Burton, R. J. F., & Farstad, M. (2020). Cultural lock-in and mitigating greenhouse gas emissions: The case of dairy/beef farmers in Norway. *Sociologia Ruralis*, *60*(1), 20–39. https://doi.org/10.1111/soru.12277

Cabell, J. F., & Oelofse, M. (2012). An indicator framework for assessing agroecosystem resilience. *Ecology and Society*, *17*(1), Article 18. https://doi.org/10.5751/ES-04666-170118

Candel, J. J., Breeman, G. E., Stiller, S. J., & Termeer, C. J. (2014). Disentangling the consensus frame of food security: The case of the EU Common Agricultural Policy reform debate. *Food Policy*, *44*, 47–58.

Darnhofer, I. (2014). Resilience and why it matters for farm management. *European Review of Agricultural Economics, 41*(3), 461–484. https://doi.org/10.1093/erae/jbu012

Daugbjerg, C., & Feindt, P. H. (2017). Post-exceptionalism in Food and Agricultural Policy: Transforming public policies. *Journal of European Public Policy, 24*(11), 1565–1584.

Duchek, S. (2019). Organizational resilience: A capability-based conceptualization. *Business Research.* https://doi.org/10.1007/s40685-019-0085-7

European Commission. (2020a). *EU Biodiversity Strategy for 2030. Bringing Nature Back into Our Lives. Communication from the Commission to the European Parliament, the Council, the European Economic and Social Committee and the Committee of the Region. COM (2020)380 Final.* Brussels.

(2020b). *A Farm to Fork Strategy for a Fair, Healthy and Environmentally-Friendly Food System. Communication from the Commission to the European Parliament, the Council, the European Economic and Social Committee and the Committee of the Regions, COM(2020) 381 Final.* Brussels.

Feindt, P. H., Proestou, M., & Daedlow, K. (2020). Policy design for resilience in the emerging bioeconomy – The RPD framework and application to German bioenergy policy. *Journal of Environmental Policy and Planning, 21*(5). https://doi.org/10.1080/1523908X.2020.1814130

Feindt, P. H., Termeer, K., Candel, J., & Buitenhuis, Y. (2019). Assessing how policies enable or constrain the resilience of farming systems in the European Union: Case study results. SURE-Farm project, Deliverable 4.2. Wageningen et al.: SURE-Farm Consortium. www.https://surefarmproject.eu

Feindt, P. H., & Weiland, S. (2018). Reflexive governance: Exploring the concept and assessing its critical potential for sustainable development. Introduction to the Special Issue. *Journal of Environmental Policy & Planning, 20*(6), 1–20. https://doi.org/10.1080/1523908X.2018.1532562

Ge, L., Anten, N. P. R., van Dixhoorn, I., et al. (2016). Why we need resilience thinking to meet societal challenges in bio-based production systems. *Current Opinion in Environmental Sustainability, 23* (December 2016), 17–27. https://doi.org/10.1016/j.cosust.2016.11.009

Giddens, A. (1984). *The Constitution of Society: Outline of the Theory of Structuration.* Berkeley: Berkeley University Press.

Gil, J. D. B., Reidsma, P., Giller, K., Todman, L., Whitmore, A., & van Ittersum, M. (2019). Sustainable development goal 2: Improved targets and indicators for agriculture and food security. *AMBIO, 48*(7), 685–698. https://doi.org/10.1007/s13280-018-1101-4

Gunderson, L. H., & Holling, C. S. (Eds.). (2002). *Panarchy: Understanding Transformations in Human and Natural Systems.* Washington, DC: Island Press.

Herrera, H. (2017). From metaphor to practice: Operationalizing the analysis of resilience using system dynamics modelling. *Systems Research and Behavioral Science, 34,* 444–462. https://doi.org/10.1002/sres.2468

Holling, C. S., Gunderson, L. H., & Peterson, G. D. (2002). Sustainability and Panarchies. In L. H. Gunderson & C. S. Holling (Eds.), *Panarchy: Understanding Transformations in Human and Natural Systems,* pp. 63–102. Washington, DC: Island Press.

Lóránt, A., & Allen, B. (2019). *Net Zero Agriculture in 2050: How to Get There. Report by the Institute for European Environmental Policy.* Brussels & London: IEEP. https://europeanclimate.org/wp-content/uploads/2019/11/02-19-net-zero-agriculture-in-2050-how-to-get-there.pdf

Marsden, T. (2013). From post-productionism to reflexive governance: Contested transitions in securing more sustainable food futures. *Journal of Rural Studies, 29,* 123–134. https://doi.org/10.1016/j.jrurstud.2011.10.001

Mathijs, E., & Wauters, E. (2020). Making farming systems truly resilient. *EuroChoices, 19,* 72–76. https://doi.org/10.1111/1746-692X.12287

Meuwissen, M., Feindt, P. H., Midmore, P., et al. (2020). The struggle of farming systems in Europe: Looking for explanations through the lens of resilience. *EuroChoices, 19*(2), 4–11. https://doi.org/10.1111/1746-692X.12278

Meuwissen, M., Feindt, P. H., Slijper, T., et al. (2021). Impact of Covid-19 on farming systems in Europe through the lens of resilience thinking. *Agricultural Systems, 191,* 103152, https://doi.org/10.1016/j.agsy.2021.103152.

   (2019). A framework to assess the resilience of farming systems. *Agricultural Systems, 176,* 102656. https://doi.org/10.1016/j.agsy.2019.102656

Ostrom, E. (1990). *Governing the Commons. The Evolution of Institutions for Collective Action.* Cambridge: Cambridge University Press.

Paas, W., Accatino, F., Antonioli, F., et al. (2019). Participatory impact assessment of sustainability and resilience of EU farming systems. SURE-Farm Deliverable 5.2. Wageningen et al.: SURE-Farm consortium. www.surefarmproject.eu/wordpress/wp-content/uploads/2019/06/D5.2-FoPIA-SURE-Farm-Cross-country-report.pdf

Paas, W., Accatino, F., Bijttebier, J., et al. (2021). Participatory assessment of critical thresholds for resilient and sustainable European farming systems. *Journal of Rural Studies, 88,* 214–226, https://doi.org/10.1016/j.jrurstud.2021.10.016.

Paas, W., Coopmans, I., Severini, S., et al. (2021). Participatory assessment of sustainability and resilience of specialized EU farming systems. *Ecology & Society*, 26(2):2. https://doi.org/10.5751/ES-12200-260202.

Reidsma, P., Meuwissen, M., Accatino, F., et al. (2020). How do stakeholders perceive the sustainability and resilience of EU farming systems? *EuroChoices*, 19(2), 18–27. https://doi.org/10.1111/1746-692X.12280

Reidsma, P., Paas, W., Accatino, F., et al. (2020). Impacts of improved strategies and policy options on the resilience of farming systems across the EU. Deliverable 5.6 of the SURE-Farm project. Wageningen et al.: SURE-Farm Consortium. www.surefarmproject.eu/wordpress/wp-con tent/uploads/2020/10/D5.6-Impacts-of-improved-strategies-on-resili ence-final.pdf

Reidsma, P., Spiegel, A., Paas, W., et al. (2019). Resilience assessment of current farming systems across the European Union. SURE-Farm project, Deliverable 5.3. Wageningen et al.: SURE-Farm Consortium. https://surefarmproject.eu/wordpress/wp-content/uploads/2019/12/D5 .3-Resilience-assessment-of-current-farming-systems-across-the-European-Union.pdf

Schils, R., Olesen, J. E., Kersebaum, K.-C., et al. (2018). Cereal yield gaps across Europe. *European Journal of Agronomy*, 101, 109–120. https://doi.org/10.1016/j.eja.2018.09.003

Silva, J. V., Reidsma, P., & van Ittersum, M. K. (2017). Yield gaps in Dutch arable farming systems: Analysis at crop and crop rotation level. *Agricultural Systems*, 158, 78–92. https://doi.org/10.1016/j.agsy.2017 .06.005

Spiegel, A., Soriano, B., de Mey, Y., et al. (2020). Risk management and its role in enhancing perceived resilience capacities of farms and farming systems in Europe. *EuroChoices*, 19(2), 45–53. https://doi.org/10.1111/ 1746-692X.12284

Termeer, C. J. A. M., Dewulf, A., & Biesbroek, G. R. (2017). Transformational change: Governance interventions for climate change adaptation from a continuous change perspective. *Journal of Environmental Planning and Management*, 60(4), 558–576. https://doi .org/10.1080/09640568.2016.1168288

Termeer, K., Candel, J., Feindt, P. H., & Buitenhuis, Y. (2018). Assessing how Policies enable or constrain the Resilience of Farming Systems in the European Union: The Resilience Assessment Tool (ResAT). SURE-Farm project, Deliverable 4.1. Wageningen et al.: SURE-Farm Consortium. www.surefarmproject.eu

Termeer, K. J. A. M., Feindt, P. H., Karpouzoglou, T., et al. (2019). Institutions and the resilience of bio-based production systems: The historical case of livestock intensification in the Netherlands. *Ecology and Society*, *24*(4), Article 15. www.ecologyandsociety.org/vol24/iss4/art15/

Therond, O., Duru, M., Roger-Estrade, J., & Richard, G. (2017). A new analytical framework of farming system and agriculture model diversities. A review. *Agronomy for Sustainable Development*, *37*(3), 21. https://doi.org/10.1007/s13593-017-0429-7

Urquhart, J., Accatino, F., Appel, F., et al. (2019). Report on farmers' learning capacity and networks of influencein11 European case studies. SURE-Farm Deliverable 2.3. Wageningen et al.: SURE-Farm Consortium. www.surefarmproject.eu/

Verbruggen, P., & Havinga, T. (Eds.). (2017). *Hybridization of Food Governance*. Cheltenham: Edward Elgar.

Vroege, W., & Finger, R. (2020). Insuring weather risks in European agriculture. *EuroChoices*, *19*(2), 54–62. https://doi.org/10.1111/1746-692X.12285

Index

Printed in the United States
by Baker & Taylor Publisher Services